# Climate Adaptation and Resilience Across Scales

*Climate Adaptation and Resilience Across Scales* provides professionals with guidance on adapting the built environment to a changing climate. This edited volume brings together practitioners and researchers to discuss climate-related resilience from the building to the city scale. This book highlights North American cases that deal with issues such as climate projections, public health, adaptive capacity of vulnerable populations, and design interventions for floodplains, making the content applicable to many locations around the world. The contributors in this book discuss topics ranging from how built environment professionals respond to a changing climate, to how the building stock may need to adapt to climate change, to how resilience is currently being addressed in the design, construction, and operations communities. The purpose of this book is to provide a better understanding of climate change impacts, vulnerability, and resilience across scales of the built environment. Architects, urban designers, planners, landscape architects, and engineers will find this a useful resource for adapting buildings and cities to a changing climate.

**Nicholas B. Rajkovich**, PhD, AIA, is an Associate Professor in the Department of Architecture at the University at Buffalo. His research investigates the intersection among energy efficiency, renewable energy, and adaptation to climate change in buildings. Prior to earning a PhD in Urban and Regional Planning from the University of Michigan, he was a Senior Program Engineer at Pacific Gas & Electric Company (PG&E). At PG&E, he was responsible for developing their first zero net energy program. He has a Master of Architecture from the University of Oregon and a Bachelor of Architecture from Cornell University.

**Seth H. Holmes**, AIA, LEED AP BD+C, is an Associate Professor of Architecture in the Golisano Institute for Sustainability at the Rochester Institute of Technology. His research addresses climate adaptation and resilient design with focuses on the integration of climate change projections with building performance modeling and methods for predicting overheating in buildings. His publications include a chapter in *Planning for Community-based Disaster Resilience Worldwide* (edited by A. Awotona), and articles in *Building Research and Information* journal and *ASHRAE*, and he advised the LEED Resilient Design pilot credit update. He practices architecture with his firm Benefit Street Design. He holds a Master in Design Studies for Sustainable Design from the Harvard Graduate School of Design and a Bachelor of Architecture from Roger Williams University.

# Climate Adaptation and Resilience Across Scales

From Buildings to Cities

Edited by Nicholas B. Rajkovich and Seth H. Holmes

An electronic version of this book is freely available, thanks to the support of libraries working with Knowledge Unlatched (KU). KU is a collaborative initiative designed to make high quality books Open Access for the public good. The Open Access ISBN for this book is 9781003030720. More information about the initiative and links to the Open Access version can be found at www.knowledgeunlatched.org.

First published 2022
by Routledge
605 Third Avenue, New York, NY 10158

and by Routledge
2 Park Square, Milton Park, Abingdon, Oxon, OX14 4RN

*Routledge is an imprint of the Taylor & Francis Group, an informa business*

© 2022 Taylor & Francis

The right of Nicholas B. Rajkovich and Seth H. Holmes to be identified as the authors of the editorial material, and of the authors for their individual chapters, has been asserted in accordance with sections 77 and 78 of the Copyright, Designs and Patents Act 1988.

The Open Access version of this book, available at www.taylorfrancis.com, has been made available under a Creative Commons Attribution-Non Commercial-No Derivatives 4.0 license.

*Trademark notice*: Product or corporate names may be trademarks or registered trademarks, and are used only for identification and explanation without intent to infringe.

*Library of Congress Cataloging-in-Publication Data*
Names: Rajkovich, Nicholas, editor. | Holmes, Seth H., editor.
Title: Climate adaptation and resilience across scales: from buildings to cities / edited by Nicholas Rajkovich and Seth H. Holmes.
Description: New York, NY: Routledge, 2022. | Includes bibliographical references and index.
Identifiers: LCCN 2021022127 (print) | LCCN 2021022128 (ebook) | ISBN 9780367467340 (hardback) | ISBN 9780367467333 (paperback) | ISBN 9781003030720 (ebook)
Subjects: LCSH: Sustainable development. | Sustainable design. | Sustainable buildings—Design and construction.
Classification: LCC HC79.E5 C5928 2022 (print) | LCC HC79.E5 (ebook) | DDC 338.9/27—dc23
LC record available at https://lccn.loc.gov/2021022127
LC ebook record available at https://lccn.loc.gov/2021022128

ISBN: 9780367467340 (hbk)
ISBN: 9780367467333 (pbk)
ISBN: 9781003030720 (ebk)

DOI: 10.4324/9781003030720

Typeset in Corbel
by codeMantra

# Contents

List of Figures — vii
List of Tables — x
Contributor Biographies — xi
Foreword — xx
ANN KOSMAL

1. Introduction — 1
   NICHOLAS B. RAJKOVICH AND SETH H. HOLMES

2. Resilient Design Modeling: Where Are We and Where Can We Go? — 6
   SETH H. HOLMES

3. Planning for a Changing Climate without Accurate Predictions — 35
   PARAG RASTOGI AND MOHAMMAD EMTIYAZ KHAN

4. Tools for Community Energy Empowerment: A Co-Design Approach — 50
   BESS KRIETEMEYER

5. RHOnDA: An Online Tool to Help Homeowners and Tenants Increase Resilience — 68
   MICHELLE LABOY AND DAVID FANNON

6. Resilience Hubs: Shifting Power to Communities through Action — 89
   KRISTIN BAJA

7. Climate Change and Health: Connecting the Dots, Building a Resilient Future — 110
   KIM KNOWLTON AND YERINA MUGICA

8. Increasing Adaptive Capacity of Vulnerable
   Populations through Inclusive Design    125
   JORDANA L. MAISEL, BRITTANY PEREZ AND KRISTA MACY

9. Passive Survivability: Understanding and
   Quantifying the Thermal Habitability of Buildings
   during Power Outages    141
   ALEX WILSON

10. Designing Resilient Coastal Communities with
    Living Shorelines    153
    WENDY MEGURO AND KARL KIM

11. Adapting Inland Floodplain Housing to a
    Changing Climate: Disturbance, Risk, and
    Uncertainty as Drivers for Design    172
    JAMIE L. VANUCCHI

12. 4D! Resilient Design in Four Dimensions    189
    ILLYA AZAROFF

13. Understanding Sustainability and Resilience as
    Applied: Tracking the Discourse in City Policy    207
    MARTHA BOHM

14. Perspectives from Practice    223
    JASON SWIFT, BRADEN KAY, TERRY SCHWARZ, DANA
    KOCHNOWER, KEVIN BUSH, JODI SMITS ANDERSON,
    ALLISON ANDERSON, MATTHEW ELLEY, ERIN HATCHER,
    JANICE BARNES, AND RACHEL MINNERY

Index    257

# Figures

3.1 Precision vs accuracy, as illustrated by shooting at a virtual target. 37
3.2 Energy use for heating and cooling simulated with a composite typical year versus actual complete years from several decades, New York City, John F. Kennedy International Airport weather station. 42
3.3 Energy use for heating and cooling simulated with a composite typical year versus actual complete years from several decades, New York City, Central Park Observatory station. 43
3.4 Heating and cooling loads from measured weather from JFK Airport (top) and Central Park Observatory (bottom), plotted with typical files from three stations each – JFK Airport, Central Park Observatory, and La Guardia Airport. 44
3.5 A large sample of historical data showing good coverage of the 'future' climate (2001–2017) using nearby stations, to provide the best coverage. 44
4.1 Conceptual framework for generating co-designed climate adaptation strategies through the integration of datasets and user-driven visualizations. 55
4.2 Images of the interactive energy visualization platform installation at the Milton J. Rubenstein Museum of Science and Technology (MoST) in Syracuse, NY. 58
4.3 Diagram of the software workflow integrating a 3D digital model, simulated geospatial data visualizations, and 3D user pointcloud data into the vvvv live programming environment. 60
4.4 Screenshot of 3D depth pointcloud data of museum visitors gesturing to select data sets to view within the installation. 60
4.5 Diagram illustrating the translation of temporal climate data charts into spatiotemporal climate change visualizations. 61
4.6 Diagram illustrating layers of intersecting datasets, including climate data, strategies, and potential impacts. 63

| | | |
|---|---|---|
| 5.1 | Graphic adaptation of the MCEER TOSE model of resilience expanded to multiple hazards and mapped to scales of the built environment. | 77 |
| 5.2 | Representative diagrams of the five building types based on sampling the Boston residential building under five stories. | 82 |
| 6.1 | Resilience Hub. | 92 |
| 6.2 | Three modes. | 95 |
| 6.3 | Foundational areas. | 98 |
| 6.4 | Workshop facilitation. | 99 |
| 9.1 | Indoor drift temperatures for different types of buildings based on thermal modeling by Atelier Ten, assuming typical construction practices for existing buildings in New York City. | 145 |
| 9.2 | Indoor drift temperatures for different types of buildings based on thermal modeling by Atelier Ten, assuming energy-efficient construction practices for the buildings in New York City. | 145 |
| 10.1 | Waves and elevated water levels during King Tides temporarily flood developed areas in Waikiki. | 154 |
| 10.2 | Large winter waves at Rocky Point on the North Shore of O'ahu cause severe coastal erosion and sea level rise will accelerate beach loss. | 154 |
| 10.3 | Elements of living shoreline design as flood mitigation strategies. | 155 |
| 10.4 | Sunset Beach map shows the projected 3.2-foot SLR-XA area, including flooded stretches of the coastal road. | 160 |
| 10.5 | A scale model of Sunset Beach shows houses and a roadway threatened by erosion and potential dune restoration after relocation of buildings and road. | 161 |
| 10.6 | Map of Waikiki shows the projected 3.2-foot SLR-XA, flooded stretches of a major road, and existing coral reef. | 163 |
| 10.7 | Living shoreline strategies for Waikiki to mitigate flooding including coral restoration, vegetated shorelines, and beach nourishment. | 164 |
| 10.8 | Coral reef propagation presented alongside the Waikiki scale model; augmented reality sandbox presented alongside the Sunset Beach scale model. | 166 |
| 11.1 | Living in the floodplain. A levee acts as a gate to a floodplain neighborhood. | 173 |
| 11.2 | Study communities within the Susquehanna Basin, shown with projected precipitation change. | 174 |
| 12.1 | Rezoning Sendai City post-Tohoku disaster. | 194 |
| 12.2 | Section of new zoning and infrastructure Sendai City Japan. | 194 |
| 12.3 | New community housing Sendai City, Sendai Japan. | 195 |

| | | |
|---|---|---|
| 12.4 | Final displacement and resettlement using social cohesion strategies. | 195 |
| 12.5 | Sectional development to resilient Onagawa town, cut and fill coupled with rezoning residential and commercial districts. | 196 |
| 12.6 | Onagawa town model illustrating the spatial and sectional relationship to the waterfront from the town center and coastal highway. | 197 |
| 12.7 | Indicates extent of cut and fill. | 198 |
| 12.8 | Achieving resilience through layers of redundancy. | 201 |
| 12.9 | Layers of redundant measures for each category of infrastructure aligned with the most sustainable on the outermost layer or first layer of resilience. | 201 |
| 12.10 | Known population and facilities at risk to daily flooding and permanently underwater due to sea-level rise projections. | 203 |
| 12.11 | Resilient neighborhood initiative. | 204 |
| 12.12 | Loss of property values based on zip code. | 205 |
| 13.1 | Weak and strong sustainability models. | 209 |
| 13.2 | Adaptive cycle diagram. | 211 |
| 13.3 | Panarchy diagram showing interactions of adaptive cycles at various scales of space and time. | 213 |

# Tables

| | | |
|---|---|---|
| 2.1 | Comparison of Literature Review Papers for Weather File, Climate Change. Simulation Methodology, Case Study Building Types, and Analysis Metrics. | 20 |
| 2.2 | Comparison of Literature Review Papers for Energy Conservation or Resilient Design Measures. | 24 |
| 3.1 | Summary Statistics of Heating and Cooling Load Calculated from Typical and Historical Files for the JFK Airport Station. | 45 |
| 9.1 | The New Orleans Principles. | 142 |
| 10.1 | Legend for Elements of Living Shoreline Design and Additional Flood Mitigation Strategies. | 156 |
| 10.2 | Site Characteristics and Applicability of Living Shoreline Techniques, Sunset Beach and Waikiki. | 158 |
| 13.1 | Subjects of Sustainability Actions. | 214 |
| 13.2 | Objects of Sustainability Actions. | 214 |
| 13.3 | Mechanisms of Sustainability Actions. | 215 |
| 13.4 | Subjects of Resilience Actions. | 215 |
| 13.5 | Objects of Resilience Actions. | 216 |
| 13.6 | Mechanisms of Resilience Actions. | 217 |

# Contributor Biographies

**Allison Anderson**, FAIA, LEED AP BD+C, is the founding principal of unabridged architecture, a firm recognized for incorporating sustainability, adaptation, and resilience against climate challenges across a wide variety of project types. She has published peer-reviewed articles on resilience for the Oxford Research Encyclopedia, National Institute of Building Sciences, and other organizations. Allison was the first LEED Accredited Professional in Mississippi; is a Fellow of the American Institute of Architects; and has served on the AIA Resilience and Adaptation Advisory Group, Sustainability Leadership Group, and the Climate Action Plan Task Force prior to joining the Committee on Climate Action and Design Excellence.

**Jodi Smits Anderson**, AIA, LEED AP BD+C, is the Director of Sustainability Programs for the Dormitory Authority of the State of New York (DASNY) and an architect who is engaged in policy work including collaborative implementations supporting New York State (NYS) goal achievement. She has spoken at the International Living Futures Institute unconference in Seattle, and multiple times at the U.S. Green Building Council (USGBC) Greenbuild, the Northeast Sustainable Energy Association (NESEA) Building Energy, and the NYS Green Building Conferences. She is a NYS Energy Code trainer and has contributed in research for Project Drawdown. She served on national and local USGBC committees, is a NESEA Board Member, and received the 2018 Green Building Advocate award from the NYS Green Building Conference.

**Illya Azaroff**, FAIA, is an Associate Professor at New York City College of Technology (CUNY) and founder of +LAB Architect PLLC, whose mission is to build resilient capacity and advance goals for a sustainable, regenerative future. Recently, he was part of the Resilient Housing Task Force under the auspices of United States Department of Housing and Urban Development (HUD) creating new federal guidance for resilient housing. He worked with the International Code Council (ICC) and the Alliance for National & Community Resilience (ANCR) developing Community Resilience Benchmarks as well on the Hazard Mitigation Plans for U.S. Virgin Islands and New York City. He served as a Technical Advisor to the Assistant Secretary for Preparedness and Response informing the National Disaster Recovery Framework. His office is advancing culturally significant, community resilience hubs and regenerative cluster housing in communities across the world. He holds a Master of Architecture and a Bachelor of Architecture from Pratt Institute, and a Bachelor of Science in Architectural Studies and Bachelor of Arts from the University of Nebraska, Lincoln.

**Kristin Baja** is the Program Director for Climate Resilience at Urban Sustainability Directors Network (USDN). She is responsible for helping local governments identify strategic ways to operationalize equity in their climate resilience planning and implementation, and build capacity to take action. She supports local governments and partners in designing new and innovative projects while also advancing learning, collaboration, and momentum around climate resilience and racial equity. In 2016, she was recognized by the Obama Administration as a Champion of Change for her work in climate resilience, climate adaptation, and racial equity. She holds a Master of Urban Planning and a Master of Science from the University of Michigan and is a Certified Floodplain Manager (CFM).

**Janice Barnes**, PhD, AIA, LEED AP, RELI AP, is the founder of Climate Adaptation Partners (CAP), a mission-driven firm focused on resilience strategy, advocacy, and partnership-building. With the City of New York Mayor's Office of Resiliency and the Charleston Medical District, she is co-creating Climate Adaptation Roadmaps for near-term action/long-term strategy. She is a member of the New York City Panel on Climate Change and the NASEM Resilient America Roundtable, and lead author for "ARC 3.3: COVID-19, Cities, and Climate Change" by UCCRN. She holds a PhD and Master of Science from the University of Michigan, Master of Architecture from Tulane University, Bachelor of Arts from the University of Tennessee, and a certificate in Municipal Finance from Harris School of Public Policy at University of Chicago.

**Martha Bohm** is an Associate Professor and Associate Dean in the Department of Architecture at the University at Buffalo (SUNY). She teaches design, ecological practices, sustainability, resilience, and environmental systems. Her research seeks to find productive overlap between sustainable performance and ecological practice. She was the faculty lead on UB's GRoW Home, winning second prize at the 2015 U.S. Department of Energy Solar Decathlon. She was a Ginsberg Research Fellow at U.S. Green Building Council (USGBC) and authored the USGBC Research Committee's National Green Building Research Agenda. She earned a Bachelor of Arts in Earth and Planetary Sciences from Harvard and a Master of Architecture from the University of Oregon.

**Kevin Bush** is the Deputy Assistant Secretary for Grant Programs at the U.S. Department of Housing and Urban Development (HUD). At HUD, Kevin oversees affordable housing and community development programs, including the Community Development Block Grant Program (CDBG), the HOME Investment Partnerships program, the Housing Trust Fund, and CDBG Disaster Recovery funds, in addition to Department-wide energy and environmental policy. Previously, he served as Washington, DC's first Chief Resilience Officer, where he led efforts to prepare the nation's capital for climate change, technological disruption, and a changing economy. He also served as the Chief of Resilience and Emergency Preparedness at the District's Homeland Security and Emergency Management Agency during the District's response to the COVID-19 pandemic. He received a Master of Urban Planning from the University of Michigan and a Bachelor of Arts in Business from Michigan State University.

**Matthew Elley**, LEED GA, is the Vice President of Development with AMLI Residential in Seattle. He is involved in all aspects of AMLI's Seattle developments and is a member of the Urban Land Institute. Before joining AMLI in 2012, he worked for Alliance Residential and SRM Development in Seattle and spent four years developing condominiums in San Diego with DR Horton's Urban Development Division. He received a Bachelor of Science in Construction Management from the University of Washington and a Master in Design Studies for Real Estate Development & Finance from the Harvard Graduate School of Design.

**David Fannon**, AIA, Member ASHRAE, LEED AP BD+C, is an Associate Professor in both the School of Architecture and the Department of Civil and Environmental Engineering at Northeastern University. He is architect and building scientist whose work integrates research, analysis, and design to provide occupant comfort and well-being in long-lasting, low-resource consuming buildings. He holds a Bachelor of Architecture from Rensselaer Polytechnic Institute and a Master of Science from the University of California Berkeley.

**Hope Forgus** is an architectural associate currently working in residential planning and design. She received a Master of Architecture from the School of Architecture and Planning at the University at Buffalo. She has a Bachelor of Arts in Electronic Media and Advertising from Xavier University.

**Erin Hatcher**, LEED AP BD+C, CDT, is the Vice President of Sustainability at AMLI Residential. She oversees the sustainability initiatives at AMLI with a focus on building certifications and investor reporting. In supporting company-wide sustainability initiatives, her role is highly collaborative and works with internal development, construction, and operation teams. She was a Sustainability Consultant focused on new construction prior to her current position. In 2018, she was recognized as a Waste Fit Champion for her work. She holds a Bachelor of Fine Arts in Interior Design from the Illinois Institute of Art—Chicago.

**Seth H. Holmes**, AIA, LEED AP BD+C, is an Associate Professor of Architecture in the Golisano Institute for Sustainability at the Rochester Institute of Technology. His research addresses climate adaptation and resilient design with focuses on the integration of climate change projections with building performance modeling and methods for predicting overheating in buildings. His publications include a chapter in *Planning for Community-based Disaster Resilience Worldwide* (edited by A. Awotona), and articles in *Building Research and Information* journal and *ASHRAE*, and he advised the LEED Resilient Design pilot credit update. He practices architecture with his firm Benefit Street Design. He holds a Master in Design Studies for Sustainable Design from the Harvard Graduate School of Design and a Bachelor of Architecture from Roger Williams University.

**Braden Kay**, PhD, is the Director of Sustainability for the City of Tempe. His academic and professional experience and interests are in urban planning, sustainability assessment, and sustainability implementation. Previously, Braden managed community engagement, sustainability assessment, and strategy building for the City of Phoenix's Reinvent Phoenix grant. He was the sustainability project manager for the City of Orlando, where he led sustainability implementation in waste diversion, urban forestry, and urban agriculture programs. He received a PhD from Arizona State's School of Sustainability for his dissertation work on stakeholder engagement and strategy building within the City of Phoenix.

**Mohammad Emtiyaz Khan**, PhD, is a team leader at the RIKEN center for Advanced Intelligence Project (AIP) in Tokyo, where he leads the Approximate Bayesian Inference (ABI) Team. His research focuses on developing new machine-learning algorithms, as well as new principles of learning from data. His work spans many areas in machine learning, such as approximate inference, deep learning, reinforcement learning, active learning, and online learning. He holds a PhD from the University of British Columbia.

**Karl Kim**, PhD, is a Professor in the Department of Urban and Regional Planning and Executive Director of the National Disaster Preparedness Training Center (ndptc.hawaii.edu) at the University of Hawaii. He conducts research on risk, transportation, and disaster management. He is Editor-in-Chief of *Transportation Research Interdisciplinary Perspectives*; Section Editor (Disaster and Resilience) for *Transportation Research Part D: Transport and Environment*. He serves on several committees for the Transportation Research Board. He served as Chairman of National Domestic Preparedness Consortium and Chair of the Pacific Risk Management Ohana. He holds a bachelors from Brown University and a PhD in Urban Studies and Planning from MIT.

**Kim Knowlton**, DrPH, is a Senior Scientist at the Natural Resources Defense Council and Deputy Director of NRDC's Science Center.

She is an Assistant Professor of environmental health sciences at Columbia University's Mailman School of Public Health, and specializes in the public health impacts of climate change. She served as co-convening lead author for the human health chapter of the 2014 "U.S. Third National Climate Assessment" and as a member of the 2nd and 4th New York City Panel on Climate Change. She also participated in the Intergovernmental Panel on Climate Change's 2007 Fourth and 2013 Fifth Assessment Reports.

**Dana Kochnower** is a Vice President in the Social Change Group at Ogilvy. Supporting a Federal Emergency Management Agency (FEMA) contract, Dana manages engagement and risk communication to help communities across New York, New Jersey, Puerto Rico, and the U.S. Virgin Islands understand their flood risks and take action to build resilience. Previously, Dana served as the Assistant Director for Land Use and Buildings in the NYC Mayor's Office of Resiliency where she led the city's flood risk awareness, mitigation, and insurance portfolio. She also co-developed Flood Watch, a community science program documenting "sunny day" flooding events and the impacts of living with water. She holds a Master of Marine Biodiversity and Conservation from Scripps Institution of Oceanography.

**Ann Kosmal**, FAIA, LEED AP BD+C, CPHC, PDC, is a Climate Response Architect. She works to safeguard assets from the observed and expected changes in climate for prudent investment, risk management, and to augment life safety, public safety, health, and security for all. She seeks to prompt design innovation in the emerging sector of climate security which cannot be offshored or outsourced. She is the co-author of the "Fourth National Climate Assessment's Built Environment" chapter and works closely with multiple technical professional societies to adapt together and integrate climate information into standards and professional practice. She is a graduate of Harvard's Senior Executive Fellows, a Certified Passive House Consultant, and a Certified Permaculture Designer.

**Bess Krietemeyer**, PhD, is an Assistant Professor at the Syracuse University School of Architecture. Her research centers on developing design decision frameworks that merge techniques for energy modeling with visualization and interactive methods to integrate user input and energy feedback in the design process. She is a Faculty Research Fellow at the Syracuse Center of Excellence, where she leads the Interactive Design and Visualization Lab. Her research has been sponsored by the NSF Smart and Connected Communities Program and the NYSERDA Advanced Buildings Program, and she is the Principal Investigator on a project sponsored by the U.S. Department of Energy under the Advanced Building Construction Initiative. She received her PhD in Architectural Sciences from Rensselaer Polytechnic Institute.

**Michelle Laboy**, PE, is an Assistant Professor of Architecture at Northeastern University and co-founder of FieLDworkshop. Her teaching, research, and professional work advances socio-ecological thinking in the design of resilient buildings and urban communities. Her work on RHOnDA, a Resilient Home Online Design Tool, was awarded the 2015 AIA Upjohn Research Initiative Grant. She is a co-PI of "Future-Use Architecture: Design for Persistent Change", which was recognized with the 2017 Latrobe Prize by the AIA College of Fellows. She holds a Bachelor of Science in Civil Engineering from the University of Puerto Rico, and Master degrees in Architecture and Urban Planning from the University of Michigan.

**Krista Macy**, Assoc. AIA, is a Design Research Associate at the Center for Inclusive Design and Environmental Access with experience in design for accessibility, sustainability, and universal design. She is engaged in diverse research projects intended to meet the needs of an increasingly diverse population. Her recent activities include designing home modifications; conducting accessibility and universal design assessments for industry partners; drafting literature reviews; and investigating the current state of climate resilience, home modifications, and universal design in the U.S. She has co-authored several papers and publications including the design resources for the innovative solutions for Universal Design (isUD™).

**Jordana L. Maisel**, PhD, is the Director of Research at the Center for Inclusive Design and Environmental Access (IDEA) and an Assistant Professor in the Department of Urban and Regional Planning at the University at Buffalo (UB). She has led research in the areas of public transportation, street infrastructure, and accessible housing policy. She currently directs the Rehabilitation Engineering Research Centers (RERC) on Universal Design and the Built Environment (RERC-UD) and co-directs the RERC on Accessible Public Transportation (RERC-APT), both funded by the National Institute on Disability, Independent Living, and Rehabilitation Research (NIDILRR). She co-authored the *Goals of Universal Design* and *Universal Design: Creating Inclusive Environments* (Wiley & Sons). She earned her Bachelor of Science in Human Development from Cornell University, and her Master's degree in Urban Planning and her PhD in Industrial and Systems Engineering from UB.

**Wendy Meguro**, AIA, LEED AP BD+C, is an architect and Assistant Professor at the University of Hawaii at Manoa (UHM) School of Architecture focusing on high-performance architecture and adaptation to sea-level rise, and is the Director of its Environmental Research and Design Laboratory. She is also a member of Hawaii Sea Grant's coastal resilience and sustainability team and directs the Center for Smart Building and Community Design. Previously, at Atelier Ten, she collaborated on climate-responsive architecture informed by building performance analysis. Wendy holds a

Bachelor of Architecture from UHM, and a Master of Science in Architecture Studies in Building Technology from Massachusetts Institute of Technology, and is a LEED Accredited Professional.

**Rachel Minnery**, FAIA LEED AP, is an architect and Senior Director of Resilience, Adaptation and Disaster Assistance at the American Institute of Architects (AIA). She co-leads a coalition of over 50 signatories of the Building Industry Statement on Resilience, and she has been instrumental in the development of resilience rating systems for buildings and communities as well as the launch of the AIA's resilience online certificate program. Rachel's previous experience includes design and management in the non-profit and private sectors focusing on environmentally and socially responsible design. She is the co-founder of Architects Without Borders Seattle and has been recognized for leading groups of volunteer architects to disaster-stricken places.

**Yerina Mugica** is the Managing Director of Healthy People and Thriving Communities Program at Natural Resource Defense Council (NRDC). She leads multidisciplinary teams to advance strategies that support strong, just, and resilient communities—bringing together economic, social, and environmental solutions to help maintain health and prosperity in the face of climate disruption. Her program puts people at the center of environmental solutions by taking a holistic approach, fighting for the right to clean air and water, healthy homes and food, green space and infrastructure, and efficient buildings and transportation—fostering the development of vibrant, healthy, and sustainable communities. She holds a Master of Business Administration from the University of North Carolina at Chapel Hill with a concentration in sustainable enterprise and a Bachelor's in Business Administration from Northeastern University.

**Brittany Perez**, OTD, OTR/L, is a Program Officer for Local Initiatives Support Corporation (LISC) Western New York, a community development financial institution. At the time of authorship, she was the Director of Outreach and Engagement at the Center for Inclusive Design and Environmental Access (IDEA) where she led IDEA Center efforts in advocacy and community engagement as well as co-founded and co-directed the local advocacy network Age Friendly Erie County, an AARP/WHO Age Friendly Community. She was Co-Lead Investigator on a federally funded Field Initiated Research Project on wheelchair securement in public transportation, and coordinated research in the Rehabilitation Engineering Research Centers (RERC) for Universal Design and Accessible Public Transportation. She holds degrees in psychology and occupational therapy from Washington University in St. Louis.

**Nicholas Rajkovich**, PhD, AIA, is an Associate Professor in the Department of Architecture at the University at Buffalo. His research investigates the intersection among energy efficiency, renewable energy, and adaptation to climate change in buildings. Prior to earning a PhD in Urban and Regional Planning from the University of Michigan, he was a Senior Program Engineer at Pacific Gas & Electric Company (PG&E). At PG&E, he was responsible for developing their first zero net energy program. He has a Master of Architecture from the University of Oregon and a Bachelor of Architecture from Cornell University.

**Parag Rastogi**, PhD, CEng, MCIBSE, is a building scientist at arbnco, an innovative building performance optimization company based in Glasgow, UK. As manager of the company's health, well-being, and controls products, his work integrates building physics, data science, and climate science to use and understand measured and simulated outdoor and indoor environmental data for the built environment. He has led the creation of affordable and scalable tools and services for healthy, sustainable, and robust design and operation of buildings in a changing climate. He has been a visiting scientist at the University of Strathclyde, Glasgow, and RIKEN-AIP in Tokyo, Japan, and is a visiting instructor at CEPT University, Ahmedabad, India. The research presented in his co-authored chapter was funded by the Swiss National Science Foundation (Grant No. p2elp2_168519). He holds a PhD in Civil Engineering from the Federal Polytechnic of Lausanne (EPFL), Switzerland, and two degrees from Purdue University.

**Terry Schwarz**, FAICP, is the Director of Kent State University's Cleveland Urban Design Collaborative (CUDC) and teaches at KSU's College of Architecture and Environmental Design. Her work includes neighborhood and campus planning, commercial and residential design guidelines, and ecological strategies for vacant land reuse. She launched CUDC's Shrinking Cities Institute to understand and address the implications of population decline and large-scale urban vacancy in Northeast Ohio, and established Pop Up City, a temporary use initiative for vacant and underutilized sites in Cleveland. She received the Cleveland Arts Prize for Design. She holds a Master's in City and Regional Planning from Cornell University.

**Jason Swift**, AIA, LEED AP, is a Principal at ECI in Anchorage, Alaska. His work across Alaska is focused on creating designs that are responsive to the environment and reflect the unique communities they serve. His passion and drive in architecture centers around pre-development, high-performance envelope systems, building forensics, preservation, and remote construction. He holds a Master of Architecture degree from the University of Oregon and a Bachelor of Fine Arts from the University of Northern Iowa.

**Jamie Vanucchi** is an Assistant Professor in the Department of Landscape Architecture at Cornell University. She is interested in the potential of design research to complement and expand scientific research, especially for wicked problems. Jamie's research involves flood risk, floodplains, and landscapes for carbon removal, and the roles of disturbance, novelty, and uncertainty in generative and adaptive design. Her chapter in this volume includes findings from the federal capacity-funded research project titled *Increasing the Success of Community Adaptation to Climate Change: Assessing FEMA Buyouts of Flood-prone Housing*.

**Alex Wilson** is the President of the Resilient Design Institute, a non-profit organization in Vermont that seeks to advance the adoption of resilient design into buildings and communities. He is also founder, and for many years was the President of BuildingGreen, Inc., a highly respected publishing and consulting firm serving the green building industry. He is the author or co-author of several books and hundreds of articles on green building and resilience. He served on the national board of the U.S. Green Building Council from 2000 until 2005 and received the organization's Leadership Award for Education in 2008. He received the second annual Hanley Award for Vision and Leadership in Sustainability in 2010.

# Foreword

*Ann Kosmal*

You cannot unknow this.

Once upon a time, the names Harvey, Michael, Florence, Maria, Paradise were once names that would not be associated with racist polices, economic effects, death, and long-term health impact but,

now we have a new name—not a given name or a place name but still a name—COVID-19.

This experience is personal for everyone that is still alive right now.

I could have written this foreword with Nick and Seth in January 2020, but I did not. Many people could have done many things in January 2020, but did not. I was personally overtaken by events, and likely so were you.

We were all OverTaken By Events (OT.B.E.).

What you read in this collection cannot be unknown. Whether you are already convinced by the evidence or not just yet, this collection of cross and interdisciplinary approaches to address climate change has insights to the COVID-19 crisis we face right now and the need for leadership and innovation.

You have skin in the "climate destabilization game", knowingly.

Your individual action affects others. Right now and in the future.

This applies whether you are a licensed design professional protecting the public's health, safety, and welfare, or anyone connected to investment and decision-making from the scale of a private residence to public land use planning.

Kindly consider these advices and queries as you read this collection.

## COVID-19 as a jumping off point to climate change

Likely you have already read and heard multiple comparisons of COVID-19 and climate change: both are crises requiring preparedness and response informed by science. COVID-19 and climate change are both global and deadly to many, especially the vulnerable, and not readily visible. Given the preparedness and response, COVID-19 is an acute shock and is expected to "pass" eventually in the near term. Meanwhile, given the preparedness and response, climate change is not expected to "pass" either in the near term or eventually. Climate change is a chronic stress with intermittent acute shocks. Climate change is a multigenerational challenge, whereas COVID-19 is a prompt for intergenerational collaboration. The COVID-19 lockdown has shown that an urgent response made significant changes to mitigate greenhouse gases. Such an action seemed beyond possibility previously. Many things seemed beyond possibility previously. Today, it is abundantly clear that the advancement of antiracist polices is fundamental to address climate change. Without antiracist policies, the status quo will be maintained for some and the suffering of many that currently have limited rank, access, and privilege will advance, period.

Possibly and hopefully, this near-term experience will be a jumping off point for deeper imagination, meaningful storytelling, innovation, leadership, and timely action which are reflected in this collection. I share this as I observe that fundamental climate readiness and preparedness concepts regarding adaptive infrastructure are readily transferrable between COVID-19 and other large-scale societal disruptions/evolution as you will find in this collection and the world around you today. The "climate kindred" are keenly skilled in methods to stress testing systems to innovate coping measures, designing for flexibility in changing conditions, generating options, and working in relational complexity and entanglement with equity. They also viscerally know that while climate destabilization can prompt the deepest remorse, grief, and guilt, the "climate kindred" persist to develop a positive vision and to design the future we want.

Given what we are learning and observing regarding parallels between COVID-19 and climate change, it is not my intent to comment on how seriously (or not) that people use science to inform their decisions about personal health, safety, and welfare. Describing the likelihood could be stated as "not if, but when and how strong." Hopefully, we are all clear that the actions of a few threaten the health, safety, and welfare of all, hence it is vital for every citizen to reflect deeply on this collection. Likely those that could transform the most by reading this collection with their rank, access, and privilege combined with their accountability, authority, and responsibility to make meaningful change will not read this collection.

But you are.

This collection conveys the imagination, design thinking, innovation, and storytelling that can transform leadership. It reminds us that multiple disciplines, together, are taking action right now. Our built environment today reflects our values, expectations, and policies whether antiracist or racist, yet does our built environment reflect the future we all want and expect? Although I may personally, as an architect, know some aspects of the built environment, I am grateful to those who have knowingly and unknowingly helped me to discern this work. This includes those who are not yet convinced by the evidence. I am especially grateful for the tender guidance from many over time so that I could account for the state of the science in the Fourth National Climate Assessment chapter on Built Environment, Urban Systems, and Cities. I have been honored to work with multiple professional societies to deeply consider the implications to professional practice regarding the future of design and designing the future. In tandem and just as important, I am grateful for the tender mentoring and modeling by many to overcome my racist personal narratives and advance antiracist narratives to professional practice.

Show up for action.

The opportunity for reflection at this time of solitude and physical separation is profound. Yet, it must be understood that this opportunity is a privilege for some and not all. What we do right now with this time matters. What we do right now with this privilege matters. Carefully consider how restrictions placed upon a population without support make the stressor (virus/climate change) less visible to the privileged and push more of the impacts of the stressor (virus/climate change) to the most marginalized and vulnerable who do not have circumstances to physically distance or to readily move away from rising sea levels. Consider your initial response to the first time you heard about COVID-19. Perhaps you used the time to innovate and build capacity in your household or community? Perhaps you developed new skills or honed existing skills? Perhaps you considered your connections and found that the connections you choose to maintain and make right now matters especially to those that build unity not fear.

This experience is an opportunity for action.

Are you showing up for action?

Has this experience informed and prepared you to take action on your most important work?

Perhaps this pandemic experience will change you forever and prepare you. Perhaps not. Either way, your skin is in the game. We are learning real time that decisions that privilege the present can have irreversible and deadly consequences. Understanding decision and consequence is not about climate science, technical integration, or politics. This is about discernment and leadership. A leadership imbued with a coordinated, global, long-term strategic vision to adapt and manage the unavoidable whether it is the "grey rhino" of climate destabilization or a pandemic from a zoonotic virus.

Will we choose to continue growing systemic fragility, or develop robustness through discerning our choices, our values, in the way we live now and for the future we want?

Let us be tender with ourselves that when we fall short, we quickly return ready to persist and preserve to design the future we want as we are individually and collectively…

Adapting together.

# 1
# INTRODUCTION

*Nicholas B. Rajkovich and Seth H. Holmes*

This book began as two symposia hosted by the University at Buffalo and the New York State Energy Research and Development Authority (NYSERDA),: "From Sandy to Snowvember" in 2016 and "Adapting Buildings for a Changing Climate" in 2018. These symposia drew together academics and practitioners from the Northeast and Great Lakes regions to discuss the impacts climate change will have on our built environment, spanning across scales from buildings to cities.

After the conclusion of both events, and at the encouragement of our editor Kate Schell at Routledge, we expanded the circle of contributors to include researchers and designers from most of the climate zones in North America. Although the COVID-19 pandemic slowed the production and publication of the book, we are pleased with the outcome and hope that it encourages a vigorous debate on how we prepare our communities to address stressors in the future.

This book is a collection of a wide variety of perspectives and expertise on the topic of adaptation and resilience. Some of the contributors are academics, studying and developing new adaptive design methodologies; while others are practicing architects, planners, and developers working to execute new resilient strategies in the built environment.

This book is not a prescriptive approach of one discipline; the chapters that follow consider climate adaptation and resilience through lenses of architecture, landscape architecture, planning, and engineering. There is a mix of technical information, academic writing, and stories, highlighting personal and professional experience.

The content of the book begins with Chapters 2 through 5 examining some of the simulation and modeling tools that are being used to understand, interpret, predict, and visualize the effects of climate change. Resilient building design must include consideration of energy and human health constraints as they relate to emergency events and long-term climate change. Whole building energy simulation techniques are used to predict energy consumption and indoor environmental

DOI: 10.4324/9781003030720-1

conditions such as temperature, humidity, mean radiant temperature, and sometimes air movement, for new and existing buildings.

Chapter 2 provides a survey of building simulation studies from the past decade that (1) utilize climate change weather projections to assess building impacts, (2) assess resilient design measures that mitigate impacts, and (3) have clear metrics for evaluating climate change-related impacts. These insights help to quantify successful metrics and best practices within resilient building simulation research, and to determine remaining research gaps.

Simulation is an informative tool to plan the design and renovation of engineering systems, but its use requires accurate inputs from its users. Current simulation practices select a small set of "representative" future climates (typical weather) and use this small sample of outputs to make decisions. The research described in Chapter 3 explores alternative simulation methods that use imprecise, long-term predictions from climate models and simulations with diverse plausible operating conditions, to inform design. Simulating energy performance for a large sample of possible future climates can enable more robust building designs.

Chapter 4 considers who these simulation tools are designed for, and how they might be improved to better engage community stakeholders in a co-design approach. There is a growing need for visualization tools that enable interactive exploration of local conditions and adaptation measures. This research develops critical capabilities not yet integrated within existing climate and energy feedback tools, and makes them more accessible to the average person. This platform has the potential to empower communities through heightened communication, shared knowledge, and design decision-making, in relation to energy management and strategies for climate adaptation.

One new design tool, called the Resilient Homes Online Design Aid (or RHOnDA), seeks to broaden that audience even further. Rather than focusing on unique, high-value, exceptional projects and an expert audience, the work described in Chapter 5 targets populations living in the existing fabric of repetitive, residential buildings. This research seeks to provide decision-making tools for homeowners and tenants by identifying a broadly applicable set of generic, probabilistic trends based on sampling, modeling, and communicating findings to the widest possible audience.

Following the initial simulation section of the book, Chapters 6 through 13 address how simulation data might be integrated with social concerns at the scale of buildings, communities, and entire cities. These next series of chapters provide insight about which areas and populations are most vulnerable, and how designers and policy makers might prioritize the needs of communities facing the greatest hardships due to climate change.

Climate change will disproportionately impact Black, Indigenous, People of Color (BIPOC) and low-income individuals who are on the frontline of climate impacts. Community resilience must be rooted in neighborhoods, in respectful ways that shift power to communities, to increase self-determination and improve adaptive capacity. Chapter 6 discusses how Resilience Hubs provide an actionable project grounded in community needs and capacity, with the intention of helping residents thrive year-round, while enhancing quality of life and connectivity. These community spaces focus on (re)development in five foundational areas: services and programming, buildings and landscape, power systems, communications, and operations. They are designed to meet community needs in multiple operational modes, including everyday, disruption, and recovery.

Long-term, multidisciplinary planning that takes a holistic approach can lead to a more resilient social safety net, which reinforces equity and improves health outcomes. Chapter 7 addresses how design considerations, such as energy efficiency and materials, affect public health and equity. Adapting buildings to be more resilient to the effects of climate change includes planning for more frequent heat waves and associated greater demand for cooling, for more frequent extreme rains and flooding events, which can damage homes and businesses, and compromise indoor air quality and health. Resilience includes promotion of affordable housing, and infrastructure that is responsive to community needs.

Chapter 8 outlines the role of inclusive design in resiliency. Climate change also disproportionately affects older adults and people with disabilities, making them among the most vulnerable during both climate-related emergencies and slow-onset disasters. Functional limitations and reduced mobility are often compounded by other characteristics, such as lower incomes, race, and age. This is further complicated by their greater dependence on physical, social, and economic networks and support systems, which are often disrupted during weather-related events. There is an urgent need to identify, implement, and promote more inclusive design, communication, and policy strategies, in order to enhance climate change resiliency and build adaptive capacity for these populations.

A secondary impact of extreme weather conditions due to climate change is the growing risk of power outages. Buildings should be designed and built to ensure that they will passively maintain habitable temperatures in the event of lost power—this is the concept of "passive survivability." Such measures could eventually be incorporated into building codes as important life-safety measures. Chapter 9 explores new methodologies and metrics for quantifying and assessing the passive survivability of buildings, and provides recommendations for further research needed to advance this agenda.

Coastal cities face flood-related hazards exacerbated by climate change and sea level rise, including erosion, storm surge, high wave events, and increased flood frequencies. Nature-based infrastructure and living shorelines can provide habitat, dissipate wave energy, and maintain people's connection to the water, in order to minimize flood damage and prolong the use of coastal lands. Chapter 10 investigates the living shoreline approach in two case studies on the Island of Oʻahu, Hawaiʻi. The research highlights principles, tools, and techniques for planners, designers, and practitioners; interactive visualization methods for site-specific restoration; and future research needs.

In the northeastern US, many municipalities are reckoning with keeping residents of floodplain housing safe, while struggling with population loss and economic decline. At the same time, climate models predict increasing frequency of flooding, due to larger and more intense storms. The current National Flood Insurance Program (NFIP), created to dissuade floodplain development, leaves homeowners "blind to dangers," or trapped in flood-prone homes. Chapter 11 speculates that, just as disasters create policy windows, socio-economic and environmental disturbances, and uncertainty can be drivers for experimental and adaptive design of community floodplains.

Urban resilience will be defined by those cities whose populations will be displaced en masse, or by the cities that receive those displaced populations from around the globe. Forced migration, managed retreat, and strategic location are among the terms used to reference the current crisis. Chapter 12 examines current resilient design and risk management strategies in New York City and Japan.

Sustainability and resilience are two design paradigms that have attempted to frame relationships between the built environment and its ecological and social context. Both address complexity, design for the long-term, and suggest an ethical framework for action. However, the two suggest different emphases and modes of operation, which are at times compatible and at times in conflict, and usually conflated. Chapter 13 uses a subject-object-mechanism framework to assess the extent to which each of these terms is manifested through the primary sustainability and resilience planning document for New York City.

To round out this discussion of resilience and adaptation to climate change, this book concludes with interviews of professionals in Chapter 14. These perspectives from practice are from both the public and private sectors in architecture, planning, policy, and real estate development. The interviewees work in locations across North America, from Florida to Alaska, and New York to Arizona. These conversations provide a glimpse into the challenges and triumphs of working on climate and resilience issues, in the field, every day. What makes these resilience pioneers so passionate about their work? What are they working on and how did they get to where they are? What advice do they have for others? And what do they see as some of the most important challenges that lie ahead?

We hope that this book will kickstart interdisciplinary dialogue and collaborative action among policy, planning, design, and construction disciplines by introducing a range of adaptation and resilient design approaches. In this way, this book is a handheld symposium, and we hope that it will serve as the foundation for future discussions of adaptation and resilience in the built environment.

We would like to acknowledge a number of people for supporting us during the development of this book. First, we thank the contributors for both their scholarship and their patience as the publication of this book was delayed due to the COVID-19 pandemic. Second, we would like to recognize Tom Phillips, and Amanda Stevens of NYSERDA, for their ongoing support of our research. Third, a number of graduate students at the University of Hartford and the University at Buffalo assisted with research and editing include Fahed Baker, Ashley Chiffy, Hope Forgus, Elizabeth Gilman, Gwyneth Harris, Nathaniel Heckman, Yasmein Okour, Krista Macy, Thomas Mulligan, Brenna Reilly, Kelley Mosher St. John, Harlee Tanner, and Michael Tuzzo. Finally, we would like to show gratitude to our families for their unwavering support: Julie Chen, Hudson Holmes, Stacey Kartub, and Nikola (Cole) Rajkovich.

# 2
# RESILIENT DESIGN MODELING

## Where Are We and Where Can We Go?

*Seth H. Holmes*

### Introduction

Contemporary building increasingly rely on advancements in building performance simulations and their resulting estimations of building energy use, indoor environmental conditions, carbon emissions, etc. As the climate continues to change, building performance simulations allow architects, engineers, builders, and policy makers to better predict climatic vulnerability and risk to buildings and their occupants.

Building codes and standards worldwide more frequently include building performance requirements to help produce more energy-efficient buildings (Young, 2014). These codes often rely on building energy and thermal performance standards created by organizations such as the American Society of Heating, Refrigeration, and Air-conditioning Engineers (ASHRAE) in the US, the Chartered Institute of Building Service Engineers (CIBSE) and British Standards Institute (BSI) in the UK. Standards such as ASHRAE 55 and BS EN 15251 regulate performance criteria for adaptive comfort criteria in naturally ventilated buildings (ASHRAE 2013) (BSI 2007). To satisfy many of these codes and/or standards, designers conduct building performance simulations to estimate building energy and/or comfort performance.

Numerous building performance simulation tools exist including simple excel-based BIN calculation models, advanced hygrothermal envelope models, whole-building energy models, and complex urban energy models. Whole-building energy models include variables such as climate; site; building geometry; construction assemblies; heating, ventilation, and air conditioning (HVAC); electric lighting; and occupancy schedules. The simulations estimate annual energy use and internal environmental variables (air temperature, humidity, radiant temperature, and airflow). Frequently used whole-building energy model tools include Energy Plus, IES, eQuest (DOE2), TRNSYS, Trane TRACE, and ESP-r, among others (Sousa 2012). Though these simulation tools are typically used to increase energy efficiency in buildings, they are increasingly used for building resilience and climate adaptation research and design.

Climate change poses a risk to domestic, institutional, and commercial buildings in many ways. Steven Burroughs suggests that measuring a building's resilience requires assessment for six dimensions: Physical, Infrastructural, Environmental, Economic-Social, Political-Regulatory, and Organizational/building owner (Burroughs 2017). He describes the physical dimension as the design, configuration, materials, and engineering of a building's systems (architectural, structural, life-safety, mechanical, electrical, plumbing, communication, and contextual infrastructure). At the contextual and regional scale, city, state, and national governments are producing resiliency plans and measures to reduce climate impact risk and improve building resiliency. In 2013, New York City's developed building-focused plans to improve flood and wind resiliency, replace vulnerable housing stock, create passively habitable housing, reduce summertime solar heating, increase solar power and battery capacity, and ensure operable windows in housing (City of New York 2013). Similarly, a report by Enterprise Green Communities outlines five residential resilient design categories: Protection, Adaptation, Backup, Community, and Putting it all together (Enterprise Green Communities 2016). The first three categories address building design criteria including wet and dry-proofing, envelope efficiency, elevated living space and equipment, window shading, distributed heating and cooling, backup-power, and potable water access. Even though flood and wind impacts are critical resilient building design variables, many building resiliency simulation projects focus on building energy use and indoor environmental impacts, often related to overheating (Gupta and Gregg 2012).

Whole-building energy models simulate buildings using annual weather data files comprised of numerous inputs such as air temperature, humidity, wind speed, solar gain, etc. Weather data file types include Typical Meteorological Years (TMY), the Test Reference Year (TRY), and Design Reference Year (DRY), among others, each representing a "typical year" constructed with average months from the past 30 years. Furthermore, UK codes require overheating simulations using Design Summer Year (DSY), representing the third hottest summer over 30 years (Jentsch, Eames and Levermore 2015). To simulate a building for climate change impacts, simulators generate "future weather files" to reflect various climate scenarios. Two primary methods exist for creating future weather files: (1) generating synthetic weather files from a weather generator using historical averages and climate projections, or (2) "morphing" existing weather files using climate projections (Cellura, et al. 2018). The morphing method involves "shifting" and "stretching" the climate data from an existing weather file to include projected monthly statistical changes (Belcher, Hacker and Powell 2005). More recently, weather files have been generated using a probabilistic approach examining numerous years based on their probability of occurrence. The UKCP09 project used created TRY and DSY files from 30 years of historical weather data, based on the 10th, 50th, and 90th percentile of occurrence (Hacker, Belcher and White 2014). This data is either morphed or synthetically processed using future climate data from climate projections outputted from a Global Circulation Model (GCM) or Regional Climate Model (RCM). The GCM and RCM help produce the globally accepted climate change scenarios, including the 2000 Special Report on Emissions Scenarios (SRES) and the 2014 Representative Concentration Pathway (RCP) scenarios, which supersede the SRES scenarios (Stocker and Qin 2013).

Simulating with future weather files allows designers to see how climate change may impact a building's energy use and/or indoor environment, and clear simulation metrics are necessary to evaluate these impacts. Given their impact on indoor thermal comfort, many energy conservation measures (ECM) double as resilient design measures (RDM), including envelope conductivity, window-to-wall ratio (WWR), solar absorptance, natural ventilation design and operation, and shading systems (Gupta and Gregg 2012). With regard to indoor comfort, increased heatwave frequency and severity are a potential climate-related impact, which garners significant attention from building standards and researchers. An adaptive comfort model that includes seasonal operative temperature is typically used to evaluate overheating, as specified in ASHRAE 55 and BS EN 15251, as well as the CIBSE adaptive criteria and the Passivhaus criterion (Lomas and Porritt 2017). Other studies utilize the wet-bulb globe temperature (Holmes, Phillips and Wilson 2016) or the weighted cooling degree-hours and potential discomfort index (DI) (Hacker, Belcher and White 2014) to more directly assess indoor overheating.

Though climate resilient simulation is increasing in research agendas, a British industry survey found that design professionals still did not consider climate-related overheating a major factor in the design of residential structures, but were open to increased use of simulation tools (Gul and Menzies 2012). Another UK-based project focused on developing action steps to address adaptation in social housing stock for asset managers (Jones, et al. 2017). The study proposed an adaption-planning model that included building simulation for testing the adaptive capacity of the residential projects in relation to identified climate threats (flooring and overheating). Similar building performance simulation methodologies can have a critical role in helping designers assess the risks and vulnerabilities of existing and future buildings.

### Objective

This chapter's objective includes documenting building simulation studies from the past decade that demonstrate one or more of the following criteria:

1. Utilize climate change weather projections to assess climate change impacts on building simulations.

2. Assess resilient design measures that help mitigate impacts and/or reduce vulnerability to climate change impacts in some form.
3. Have clear metrics for evaluating climate change-related impacts (energy use, overheating, etc.).

With this information, this chapter aims to highlight and quantify successful metrics and best practices within resilient building simulation research, as well as identify research gaps related to estimating, measuring, and designing for climate change and occupant health.

## Methodology

A global literature search of key databases and energy modeling conference proceedings was conducted using a pre-defined list of keywords to retrieve peer-reviewed literature focused on resilient building simulation from the past ten years (2008–2018). Databases searched include: Scopus, ScienceDirect, ProQuest Science, and EbscoHost. Conference proceedings searched include International Building Performance Simulation Association (IBPSA) conferences; regional IBPSA conferences including SimBuild (USA), BSO (England), and eSIM (Canada); and the Symposium on Simulation for Architecture and Urban Design (SimAUD) conferences.

The following search terms were used in the database search:

*Simulation*: Building Simulation, Building Performance Simulation, Whole-building energy modeling, building energy model.
*Resilience*: Resilience, Resilient, Passive Survivability (PS), Passive Habitability, Adaptive, overheating, vulnerability.
*Climate Change and Overheating*: Climate Change, Climate Change Adaptation, overheating, vulnerability.

The retrieved literature was examined to pinpoint specific research projects that met one of the three criteria listed in the objective section of this chapter. These research papers are described in the literature review section and are divided into four categories of research and then directly compared for climate change-related resilience variables in the discussion section of this chapter to help determine successful trends and best practices as well as to identify gaps and future avenues of research. Resilience variables identified fall into four categories:

1. Climate change weather data;
2. Building typologies;
3. Resilience metrics; and
4. ECM and/or RDM.

## Literature Review: Climate Resilient Simulation

The literature review describes building simulation papers that include some form of future climate weather data in the research. The papers are divided into two categories based on the primary metrics examined in the research: Building Energy Resilience (20 papers) and Indoor Comfort/Overheating Resilience (19 papers). Projects are listed primarily by project similarity with most of the research focused on building design projects in the UK, Europe, North America with a few projects also in Asia, Australia, and South America.

## Building Energy Resilience

As the climate changes, building heating and cooling energy use will change in response to new weather patterns. This section illustrates projects focused on heating and/or cooling energy and costs in relation to natural ventilation, probabilistic assessment, the use of multiple GCMs, and large-scale continental or global energy use intensities. The first study focuses on heating demand impacts in residential building types for five climates around the world: Temperate-hot, Temperate-mild, Temperate-cold, Sub-polar, and Polar (Andrić, et al. 2017). The study used future weather files created from the HadCM3 GCM synthetic weather files and morphed for low-, medium-, and high-RCP emissions scenarios (2.6, 6.0, and 8.5) for ten-year intervals through 2050. Using heating Energy Use Intensity (EUI) and heating degree-days (HDD) as metrics, a six-story multi-family building was simulated using a MATLAB model. Envelope retrofit measures were applied in ten-year intervals to 50% of the building stock. Results show that all climates saw similar annual and peak heating load reductions of ~29% from 2010 to 2015. However, the reductions for extreme climates are higher than the temperate-hot climate seeing a 43% reduction while the polar climate had 0.8% reduction. Another study examined atriums and courtyards in Dutch multi-family buildings with respect to heating demand and thermal comfort (Taleghani, Tenpierik and van den Dobbelsteen 2014). This study used a typical weather file for De Bilt, NL, adjusted for four different climate change scenarios generated by the Royal Dutch Meteorological Institute using the IPCC SRES scenarios. A baseline rectangular multi-family building was compared to similar buildings with either a courtyard, an atrium, or an operable atrium. Results show that open transitional spaces can help reduce overheating in summer, but experience heating demand increases due to their larger building envelope. The optimized model shows an open courtyard to be most useful between May and August under all climate change scenarios.

For studies examining heating and cooling, a Montreal-based study examined the effects of roof insulation and reflectance on heating and cooling energy in a one-story commercial building (Hosseini, Tardy and Lee 2018). This study morphed the Montreal Canadian Weather Year for Energy Calculation (CWEC) weather file to create future climate files for 2020, 2050, 2080 using the A2 SRES scenario and examined 126 roof design options. The models with increased insulation and reflectance lowered annual heating and cooling energy use for each climate period. A similar study examines ECM in Brazilian social housing for a hot-humid climate (Salvador), and moderate-humid climate (Sao Paulo) (Triana, Lamberts and Sassi 2018). The study used synthetic weather files generated from the HadCMe GCM and morphed to create future climate files representing the A2 SRES scenario. The study analyzed a detached one-story home using the annual EUI and cooling degree-days (CDD)/HDD metrics under two operating modes: natural ventilation and HVAC. RDM included envelope insulation, albedo, shading, ventilation, and raised buildings. Key takeaways include: roofs with high albedo and insulation levels performed the best, shading performed better than natural ventilation, and high-mass walls performed better than framed walls for HVAC analyses. A similar study on one-story residential homes in Australia found that higher level of roof insulation produced the most energy-efficient buildings, assuming 100% mechanical heating and cooling (Karimpour, et al. 2015).

A US-based study examined projected energy consumption in office buildings for Miami, Phoenix, Los Angeles, Washington DC, and Colorado (Wang, Liu and Brown 2017). This project used both a morphed synthetic weather file from the HadCM3 GCM (SRES A2), and synthetic future weather files generated by CESM1 (RCP 2.6, 4.5, and 8.5). A 3-story, 15-zone office building was simulated using various ECMs (HVAC schedules, setpoints, Variable Air Volume (VAV) airflow, and mixed-mode cooling). All five locations saw increased energy use, but warmer climates saw a greater proportional increase. Mixed-mode cooling was the most effective ECM under all climate scenarios. Another study in four US climates (cold, mixed-humid, hot-humid, and hot-dry) uses downscaled synthetic weather data from the HadCM3 GCM and morphed future SRES A2 climate files (Shen 2017). This study evaluates EUI, heating/cooling load, HDD, and CDD while simulating a three-story multi-family building and a six-story office building. The results show increased cooling and decreased heating for both building typologies, increased total residential energy consumption, and minimal change in total energy for internal load-dominated buildings.

Similar climate change-related simulation research evaluates energy costs along with heating and cooling energy. One study evaluates the return on investment and payback period related to ECMs (Holmes and Reinhart 2013). The study examined a three-story office building for Boston and Phoenix using TMY and morphed future weather files for all four SRES scenarios. The analysis linked projected energy prices and projected temperature changes using associated radiative forcing projections. Using the metrics of EUI, return on investment, and payback period, the results show energy price projections due to greenhouse gas (GHG) mitigation policies increase life cycle operations, and energy-efficient buildings show less sensitivity to climate change when compared to generic building stock. A similar study expanded this process to include building envelope optimization using parametric energy model simulations and genetic algorithms (Glassman and Reinhart 2013). The study added Fairbanks, Alaska and utilized the same TMY3 and future weather files. The metrics of cost optimization and carbon optimization were studied to analyze changes to wall insulation, WWR, and external shading. Results indicate that a façade's optimized solution (energy use and installation cost) is not static and will change with the climate. Another study coupled Energy plus and MATLAB using a genetic algorithm to identify cost-optimal retrofit solutions for energy efficiency and future climate resilience (Ascione, et al. 2017). The study simulated a three-story residential building in Italy under four climate scenarios (baseline, low, medium, and high). To simulate a 2050 climate, the study uniformly increased the dry-bulb temperature of an existing weather file 0.6°C (low), 1.2°C (medium), and 1.8°C (high). Various envelopes and HVAC ECMs were evaluated using primary energy consumption and global cost metrics. The results recommend upgrading HVAC to a high-efficiency boiler and chiller, increasing roof and wall insulation and albedo, and adding low-e glazed windows.

The following four studies use the SRES scenarios while examining mechanical cooling and natural ventilation. The first study examined the climate resilience of an Italian childcare center (Pagliano, et al. 2016). The simulation assesses a singular retrofit proposal upgrading envelope insulation, solar shading, windows, air-tightness, and HVAC systems. Metrics examined include a Summer Climate Severity Index, HVAC energy, and the BS EN 15251 adaptive comfort model. The results indicate increased cooling needs and recommend the prioritization of passive cooling. The research suggests modifying the adaptive comfort model to include children, who are more active. Another study examined a one-story residential building for three Brazilian cities for the years 2020, 2050, 2080 (Invidiata and Ghisi 2016). The simulation added a low-albedo envelope, external shading, thermal insulation, and combinations of those three; analysis metrics included EUI and adaptive comfort. The results show an increase of EUI in 2080 over current conditions for each location, even with the combined ECM strategy. A third study examined two residential and seven commercial building types in seven US climate regions using a synthetic weather file generated from the HadCM3 model (Wang and Chen 2014). The results show that a net increase of heating and cooling source energy will occur under all scenarios for US climate zones 1–4; however, a decrease occurs in zone 6 and 7. The simulation also indicates that natural ventilation will be less effective, particularly in hotter locations. Finally, a study analyzed mixed-mode cooling in multi-family buildings in Taipei, Taiwan (Huang and Hwang 2016). This simulation used a synthetic weather file from the Micro3.2-MED and the A1B, A2, and B1 scenarios. The study evaluated the apartment retrofit measures using customized climatic stress indices, an adaptive comfort model, and cooling energy; RDM include envelope insulation, window Solar Heat Gain Coefficient (SHGC) and U-value, external shading. The results indicate a combination of roof and wall insulation, SHGC improvements, and external shading proved the most effective.

Other resilience simulation studies explore statistical analysis. A Swedish study uses synthesized weather files from the RCA3 RCM to calculate relative difference between retrofitted and non-retrofitted residential buildings (Nik, Mata and Sasic Kalagasidis 2015). This study measures the robustness of an ECM by quantifying variation of retrofit measures across different climate time scales and scenarios. A single-zone MATLAB model simulates upgrades to lighting and the building envelope. A custom "relative difference" metric and Standard Deviation identify the robustness of ECMs across the study's time scales. The paper concludes that assessing the robustness of an ECM is possible by studying one 20-year time, and that relative performance of ECM can change with each timescale studied; therefore, each timescale should be considered. Another study illustrates a methodology evaluating building robustness using multiple weather file inputs to produce probabilistic energy performance results from a range of future scenarios (Chinazzo, Rastogi and Andersen 2015). The study uses a Robustness Index (RI) indicating how robust a measure is to climate uncertainty, and an Energy Savings Index (ESI) reflecting the normalized energy savings across the range of simulations. A robust solution has the least sensitivity to all scenarios. The study focuses on 22 refurbishment strategies applied to a residence in Turin, IT, and produces morphed SRES future weather files. Four groups of ECMs were analyzed: Insulation, Shading, Thermal mass, and Airtightness. The simulation used 15 weather files from representing combinations of 3 time periods, 3 climate scenarios, and 2 weather stations. The results indicate cooling uncertainty is higher than heating; however, the paper primarily focused on developing the probabilistic methodology.

Other studies focus on selecting appropriate GCMs to generate synthetic weather files. One study examines energy impacts to a test one-story office building in Spain, France, Italy, Greece, and Turkey (Cellura, et al. 2018). The study utilized 24 different GCMs to create synthetic weather files for 15 cities. Each synthetic weather file was compared using error studies with historical weather data. The synthetic weather file with the lowest error result is selected for each city's simulations. The synthetic weather files were morphed to create future weather files at 2035, 2065, and 2090 for the four RCP climate scenarios. WWR and roof insulation options are simulated and evaluated using EUI and cooling/heating load metrics. For all climate scenarios and years, the study showed increases in cooling energy over the 2010 baseline. A similar study examines Swedish wood-framed building using multiple GCMs (Nik 2017). This study examines different methods of synthesizing weather based on dry-bulb temperature, relative humidity, and precipitation to perform hygrothermal simulations of a wall assembly. The study generated future weather files using the RCA3 RCM and two other GCMs for the RCP 4.5 and 8.5 emissions scenarios. Separate baseline weather files were synthesized using historical weather datasets: dry-bulb temperature, humidity, and precipitation. The test wall was analyzed using dry-bulb temperature, relative humidity, moisture content, and mold growth metrics. The study found that moisture content of the wall was best simulated using the synthetic weather file generated from typical and extreme dry-bulb temperature datasets, compared to humidity and precipitation datasets.

Finally, two studies examine national or global level energy use. The first paper quantifies climate-related energy consumption sensitivity across 925 US locations (Huang and Gurney 2016). The study uses TMY3 weather files for 15 US climate zones, and synthetic weather files generated for future SRES climates using the World Climate Research Programme's CMIP3 model. The study simulates 15 commercial building types, including 3 separate age classes, and 2 residential types reflecting new building stock. Evaluation metrics include two EUI-based metrics: Relative Difference and Intensity Difference. The results found an increase in energy consumption by 2090, with greater increases in commercial buildings, particularly in southern climates. Larger energy use variation appears between building types (i.e. 39% increase in schools vs. 22% decrease in warehouses). Another larger study evaluates the potential global increase in air conditioning usage and subsequent energy consumption based on three climate change scenarios (Santamouris 2016). This project calculates cooling energy costs using estimated CDD and projected development data from the SRES scenarios. The paper combines air conditioning usage and efficiency projections with projected global building square footages and CDD for three climate scenarios. The study examines 144 case studies in 40 different cities in Europe, Asia, America, and Australia. The results indicate that global combined cooling and heating energy may increase 67% by 2050 and 166% by 2100. The paper recommends three policy tracks: (1) actions aimed at mitigating climate change, (2) adapt buildings to improve energy performance, and (3) improve efficiency of mechanical and alternative cooling technology.

### Indoor Comfort and Overheating Resilience

In response to the likelihood of increased heatwave frequency and duration, increasing building simulation research focuses on indoor overheating, particularly for free-running, passively cooled buildings (i.e. no A/C). The studies in this section each evaluate indoor overheating RDM and is grouped by building type, metric type, RDM type, codes and standards focus, and probabilistic assessment.

The first study evaluates naturally ventilated cooling for a hospital under current and projected climate conditions (Lomas and Ji 2009). Four types of advanced stack ventilation are compared to traditional side ventilation design in UK-based free-running hospital rooms. The simulation weather files include the London TRY, DSY, and morphed future climate files for the SRES A2 climate scenario, and metrics include operative temperature, adaptive comfort, indoor $CO_2$, humidity, and dry-bulb temperature. The study analyzed the following RDMs to determine their effectiveness in maintaining occupant comfort: WWR, shading, operable area, low-e glazing, window orientation, and thermal mass. The results indicate (1) existing naturally ventilated hospitals have a risk of being non-functional in the future; (2) an adequate method for assessing overheating hours, particularly at night, is not available; and (3) stack-ventilated designs are more effective side ventilated strategies. Another study analyzes impacts on thermal and visual comfort in a typical Chicago office by introducing microclimate data and urban canyon morphology into the simulation process (Kalvelage, Dorneich and Passe 2015). This study assesses the impact of two site-level variables (urban canyon terrain and urban microclimate) and one ECM (improved window SHGC) on indoor comfort in a mechanically cooled building for current and future climates. Assessment metrics include predicted percentage dissatisfied (PPD), predicted mean vote (PMV), and mean radiant temperature (MRT) in relation to standard heating and cooling setpoints. The results indicate that the simulation of microclimate and urban canyon conditions decreased the PPD, PMV, and MRT over the baseline in summer for both current and projected years.

Many residential-focused studies examine how buildings maintain comfortable or habitable indoor conditions without mechanical cooling, a concept known as thermal autonomy (TA) or PS. One study examines TA in UK-based housing using historical conditions from the 2003 European heatwave (Porritt, et al. 2013). The study analyzed a generic single-family home, a duplex, a row-house, and an apartment using a TA metric measuring the number of hours indoor operative temperature was above 28°C. The following RDMs were evaluated: envelope and window conductance, shading, infiltration, natural ventilation, and night purge ventilation. The results indicate upper-floor apartments and single-family homes experience the most overheating, while external shades perform best at reducing overheating. Another study analyzes a single-zone apartment in Toronto, Canada, for summertime heatwaves and wintertime cold-snaps (O'Brien 2016). Using ten-day extreme hot and cold periods extracted from a TMY file, the study examines four RDMs: WWR, window type, balcony shading, and active occupants (lowering blinds and opening windows). Metrics used in the analysis include PPD for TA and operative temperature for PS (>30°C summer; <15°C winter). The results indicate that apartments without balconies or active occupants were the only variation to breach the summertime PS threshold. Another study examines TA and PS for a residential apartments using color-coded and time-based charts (Ozkan, et al. 2018). This simulation similarly uses extreme hot and cold weeks selected from weather files for Vancouver, Canada, and Adana, Turkey, and uses operative temperature as the primary metric with a TA range of 18°C–24°C and a PS threshold of <30°C. The RDMs analyzed include: WWR, shading, natural ventilation, fixed balcony, high-performance envelope, and window SHGC. The simulation output includes color-coded, time-based charts indicating TA and PS as either "too cold", "acceptable", or "too hot" for a 12-month period. The study found that as TA increases, EUI decreases exponentially.

A few studies evaluate indoor thermal mass in relation to overheating of residential buildings. A Dutch study of three housing types examines how thermal mass, among other RDMs, affects indoor overheating under passive conditions (Van Hooff, et al. 2015). This simulation uses a historically hot week to predict indoor conditions and estimate overheating for three housing types (detached, terraced, and apartment) of various ages. The study concludes that less mass was beneficial at night, provided the building could release heat to the outside. Older homes in the study (less massive/less insulation) benefit from increasing the building's external albedo, while all homes benefited from increased natural ventilation and vertical solar shading. A London-based study simulates a two-bedroom apartment using the TRY, DSY, and morphed SRES future climate files while assessing overheating using operative temperature metrics from the CIBSE TM 52 guide (Din and Brotas 2017). Along with thermal mass, other RDMs examined include shading, WWR, and indoor airspeed. The results show that thermal mass is most advantageous when evenly distributed throughout a building. Another UK-based residential overheating study simulates three types of thermally massive PassivHaus (PH) design types for probabilistic climates through 2080 (McLeod, Hopfe and Kwan 2013). The simulation uses the 50th TRY and 90th SRY percentile weather years for 1980–2080 generated from UKCOP09 Weather Generator. The study's overheating metric quantifies the percentage of hours indoor conditions exceed 25°C and 28°C. Other RDMs analyzed include south façade glazing percentage, external shading, airtightness, and non-occupant internal gains. The results show that overheating risk rises uniformly for future years; however, including more thermal mass, less south glazing, and restricted ventilation helped reduce the risk of overheating.

Some studies examine how building codes and/or standards address overheating of residential buildings with respect to climate change. One UK-based study evaluates how a generic three-bedroom, semi-detached home might overheat when designed for five different UK-based building standards (Mulville and Stravoravdis 2016). The standards analyzed include the UK Standard Assessment Procedure part L 2006 and 2010, Passive House, and Voluntary Standard for Sustainable Homes levels 4 & 5. The simulations used TRY and DSY weather data as well as the 50th percentile future weather for the UKCP09 SRES A1B scenario. Analysis metrics included adaptive comfort and operative temperature exceedance, and RDMs include envelope U-value, infiltration, SHGC, shading, ventilation, orientation, WWR, and thermal mass. The results indicate better performance with the PH and Sustainable Homes standards, and that increased thermal mass and ventilation reduce overheating risk, though less so in future years. A US-based study evaluates the ASHRAE 90.1 (2004 and 2013) and IECC (2006 and

2015) impact on overheating resiliency using a ten-story multi-family residential building case study in multiple locations (Baniassadi and Sailor 2018). The study simulates for the hottest three-day period from the TMY files of 15 US climate zones and measures indoor overheating as degree hours above 26°C DI. Based on code requirements, the only RDMs examined were insulation upgrades and airtightness. The results suggest that indoor conditions exceed critical thresholds and that codes are producing buildings that are more resilient and energy efficient in warmer climates, but less resilient in colder climates.

Other European and UK-based studies examine a larger scope to estimate the resiliency of a country's entire residential buildings stock. One study validates the use of a neural network metamodel to asses UK residential stock (Symonds, et al. 2016). The study simulates three UK locations using 2050 weather files generated from the UKCP09 model for the SRES A1F1 scenario, and uses a custom overheating threshold metric that combines indoor operative temperature and outdoor average maximum temperature. Eight housing types are examined along with numerous RDMs including: envelope U-value, infiltration, terrain, orientation, window opening temperature, shading, and occupancy types. The metamodel successfully simulates the variables and provides a 50% better performance when compared to a support vector regression model. Another study of Dutch housing stock quantifies overheating risk, ranks building types for overheating sensitivity, and assesses ventilate cooling strategies (Hamdy, et al. 2017). The study simulates eight housing types using future climate files from the Royal Dutch Meteorological Institute's climate and introduces three new operative temperature bases metrics: Indoor Overheating Degree, Ambient Warmness Degree, Overheating Escalation Rate. The RDMs evaluated include envelope construction and age, orientation, shading, comfort criteria, ventilation rate, and internal heat gain. The results indicate that 97% of the buildings simulated can suppress overheating impacts to some degree. Dutch dwellings with high solar heat gain and/or low heat transmission have the highest risk of overheating, while ventilated cooling and solar protection most effectively reduced overheating. A third study evaluates indoor overheating and air pollution (PM2.5) in UK dwelling stock (Taylor, et al. 2015). The simulation uses synthetic weather files from the UKCP09 project representing current (typical), current (hot), and 2050 high emissions (SRES A1F1) weather. The study uses the BSEN 15251 adaptive comfort overheating criteria to evaluate eight residential building types and examines the following RDMs: envelope U-value and envelope permeability. The results indicate that apartments had higher PM2.5 levels than houses under current conditions as well as higher future PM2.5 levels due to increased ventilated cooling. Retrofit measures may increase overheating risk, but pollutant levels could be reduced using filtered ventilation strategies.

Several UK-based projects utilize UK-based probabilistic future climate files generated by the UKCP09 project for low, medium, and high SRES scenarios. One study examines the thermal performance of four case study buildings in Birmingham UK (de Wilde and Tian 2012). Using the metrics of EUI, heating and cooling energy, degree-days, operative temperature, and carbon emissions, the study evaluates a house, office, school, and supermarket for the following ECMs and RDMs: envelope U-value, air infiltration, HVAC efficiency, and lighting efficiency. The study found that the current stock is more resilient than assumed due to redundant systems, large safety factors, and 15–20-year system replacement schedules. The study concluded that probabilistic evaluation of buildings is possible if clear long-term assumptions are necessary for building maintenance, renovation, and systems intervention. Another project examines natural ventilation viability in office buildings and compares the TRY morphing method from UKCP02 with the COPSE and PROMETHEUS weather data outputs from UKCP09 project (Barclay, et al. 2012). The study examines two Manchester-based office buildings and evaluates how external shading strategies and operable window percentages affect overheating using the CIBSE Guide A and BSEN 15251 adaptive comfort criteria and indoor air changes per hour (ACH) as metrics. The PROMETHEUS dataset simulation illustrates the highest ACH in both building models (between 0.1 and 0.9 ACH higher). Results also show that passive ventilation is not enough to counteract outdoor temperature increases over time.

A final group of studies use a regression tool, developed for the Low Carbon Futures project, designed to reduce the number of simulations required when using future weather files. The first project presents the regression tool, validates it, and uses it to analyze a building for one random climate out of 100 probable future climates (Jenkins, et al. 2014). Using the UKCP09 weather data for low, medium, and high emissions scenarios through 2049, the study simulates a three-bedroom residence and one-story school for two UK locations (London and Edinburgh) using the dynamic building simulator ESP-r. The study uses an overheating metric of indoor operative temperature >28°C to evaluate the following RDMs: natural ventilation, shading, and internal load shedding. The study compares probabilistic overheating curves for each simulation with results processed for 100 random future climates. The resulting probabilistic curve from the regression tool lands within 1°C of the 100-random year mean, proving that the tool can produce accurate results. A second study expands on three-bedroom residence simulation to compare 3,000 probabilistic years and present a method to visualize an overheating evaluation (Patidar, et al. 2014). Using the regression tool, the study calculates indoor conditions for the 2030s, 2050s, and 2080s under low, medium, and high emission scenarios and evaluates the buildings using operative temperature threshold (>28°C) and consecutive days of threshold breaches; ECM and RDMs are not considered. Results from the averaging of 3,000 probabilistic year's simulated data are that nighttime bedroom temperatures could reach 26°C–28°C by 2080, well above the current 24°C baseline. A third study also examines the residential building for the RDMs of WWR, shading, and internal loads, but provides another method of visualizing and quantifying the results (Banfill, et al. 2013). The study indicates that other simulation programs (IES, TRNSYS, etc.) can incorporate the regression tool for overheating analysis. Finally, a fourth study uses the regression tool to compare morphing vs. synthetic weather file generation (Gupta, et al. 2013). The study simulates four UK residential types using current, DSY, and future weather for 50% and 90% percentile years using SRES A1B for 2050 and 2080. Results indicate greater variation between downscaling methods (statistical or morphing) when producing future climate years, which could lead to varying design decisions for the same location if left unchecked. The study recommends future research to harmonize downscaling approaches.

## Analysis and Discussion

The range of projects presented in this chapter highlight trends and gaps in current building simulation research related to climate change and resilient design. In total, 39 papers are summarized, 20 of which predominately address energy resilience (heating and cooling), and 19 that primarily address indoor overheating. Tables 2.1 and 2.2 offer a visual comparison of all 39 papers, with the papers listed from top to bottom in the same order they are presented in the literature review section. Both tables indicate the author's name, year of publication, country name, and number of locations simulated. The columns in Table 2.1 represent weather file types, climate change simulation methodology (future weather), building types, and analysis metrics, while Table 2.2 continues to list ECM or RDM variables. Metrics or variables that did not appear frequently (three or more papers) are included in an "other" column. All the categories in columns are summed at the bottom of each table to indicate frequency.

The studies analyzed were published from 2012 to 2018 (median = 2016), with the exception of one 2009 paper. Regarding location, one study examined global cooling energy at a macro level across all populated continents (Santamouris 2016). Two-thirds (25/39) of the studies are European focused (UK 13, Italy 3, Netherlands 3, Italy 3, Sweden 2, and Turkey 1). North America represented 11/39 case studies (USA 8 and Canada 3), while South America had 2 case studies (Brazil), and Australia and Asia (Taiwan) each had one. The Euro-centric nature of the studies is likely a reflection of available data, such as the probabilistic weather files generated by the UKCP09 project, and the political will and research funding provided by European governments.

A visual inspection of the tables helps highlight noticeable trends in these simulation methodologies. Most of the studies (33/39) equally

Table 2.1 Comparison of Literature Review Papers for Weather File, Climate Change Simulation Methodology, Case Study Building Types, and Analysis Metrics.

| Paper | Year | Location (City Qty) | TMY, TRY, IWEC, or Sim (Weather) | DSY or Sim (Weather) | Synthetic Weather (Future Weather) | SRES Scenarios (Future Weather) | RCP Scenarios (Future Weather) | Custom Scenario (Future Weather) | Morphed (M) or Synthetic (S) | Multiple CC Scenarios | Probabilistic Future Climates |
|---|---|---|---|---|---|---|---|---|---|---|---|
| Andrić, et al. | 2017 | EU (3), CAN (2) | | | ● | | ● | | M | ● | |
| Taleghani, et al. | 2014 | Netherlands (1) | ● | | | ● | | ● | S | | ● |
| Hosseini, et al. | 2018 | Canada (1) | ● | | | | ● | | M | | |
| Triana, et al. | 2018 | Brazil (2) | ● | | | | ● | | M | | |
| Karimopour, et al. | 2015 | Australia (1) | ● | | | | ● | | M | ● | |
| Wang, et al. | 2017 | USA (5) | ● | | ● | ● | ● | | B | ● | |
| Shen | 2017 | USA (4) | | | ● | ● | | | M | ● | |
| Holmes and Reinhart | 2013 | USA (2) | ● | | | | ● | | M | ● | |
| Glassman and Reinhart | 2013 | USA (3) | ● | | | | ● | | M | | |
| Ascione, et al. | 2017 | Italy (1) | ● | | | | | ● | | ● | |
| Pagliano, et al. | 2016 | Italy (1) | ● | | | | ● | | M | | |
| Invidiata and Ghisi | 2016 | Brazil (3) | ● | | | | ● | | M | | |
| Wang and Chen | 2014 | USA (15) | | | | ● | ● | | M | ● | |
| Huang and Hwang | 2016 | Taiwan (1) | ● | | | | ● | | M | | |
| Nik, et al. | 2015 | Sweden (1) | | | | ● | ● | | S | | ● |
| Chinazzo, et al. | 2015 | Italy (1) | ● | | | | ● | | M | ● | ● |
| Cellura, et al. | 2018 | Europe (15) | | | ● | ● | ● | | M | ● | |
| Nik | 2017 | Sweden (1) | | | | ● | ● | | S | ● | ● |
| Huang and Gurney | 2016 | US (925) | ● | | | | ● | | S | ● | |
| Santamouris | 2016 | Global (12) | | | ● | ● | | ● | | ● | |

# RESILIENT DESIGN MODELING

| Residential | Commercial | Multiple Building Sub-Types | EUI or Similar | Heating & Cooling Energy | Energy Cost | Heating / Cooling Degree Days | Adaptive Confort Model | Indoor Operative Temp. | Fanger Comfort Model | Indoor Air Change Rate | Consec. Days/Hours Overheat | Custom Metric |
|---|---|---|---|---|---|---|---|---|---|---|---|---|
| Bldg. | | | Metrics | | | | | | | | | |
| ● | | | ● | | | ● | | | | | | |
| ● | | | ● | ● | | | ● | | | | | |
| | ● | | ● | ● | | | | | | | | |
| ● | | | ● | | | ● | | | | | | |
| ● | | | ● | ● | | | | | | | | |
| | ● | | | ● | | | | | | | | |
| ● | ● | | ● | ● | | ● | | | | | | |
| | ● | | ● | ● | ● | | | | | | | |
| | ● | | ● | | ● | | | | | | | |
| ● | | | ● | | ● | | | | | | | |
| | ● | | | ● | | ● | ● | ● | | | | |
| ● | | | ● | ● | | | ● | ● | | | | |
| ● | ● | ● | ● | ● | | ● | | ● | | | | |
| ● | | | ● | ● | | | ● | | | | ● | |
| ● | | | | ● | | | | | | | | |
| | | | ● | | | | | | | | ● | |
| | ● | | ● | ● | | | | | | | | |
| ● | ● | ● | ● | | | ● | | | | | | |
| ● | ● | | ● | | | ● | | | | | | |

(Continued)

Table 2.1 Continued Comparison of Literature Review Papers for Weather File, Climate Change Simulation Methodology, Case Study Building Types, and Analysis Metrics.

| Paper | Year | Location (City Qty) | TMY, TRY, IWEC, or Sim | DSY or Sim | Synthetic Weather | SRES Scenarios | RCP Scenarios | Custom Scenario | Morphed (M) or Synthetic (S) | Multiple CC Scenarios | Probabilistic Future Climates |
|---|---|---|---|---|---|---|---|---|---|---|---|
| | | | Weather | | | Future Weather | | | | | |
| Lomas and Ji | 2009 | UK (2) | ● | ● | | ● | | | M | | |
| Kalvelage, et al. | 2015 | US (1) | ● | | | | | ● | | | |
| Ozkan, et al. | 2018 | CAN (2), TUR (1) | ● | | | | | ● | | | |
| O'Brien | 2016 | Canada (1) | ● | ● | | | | ● | | | |
| Porritt, et al. | 2013 | UK (1) | ● | ● | | | | ● | | | |
| Van Hoof, et al. | 2015 | Netherlands (1) | | ● | | | | ● | | | |
| Din and Brotas | 2017 | UK (1) | ● | ● | | ● | | | M | | |
| McLeod, et al. | 2013 | UK (1) | ● | ● | ● | ● | | ● | S | | ● |
| Mulville, et al. | 2016 | UK (2) | ● | ● | ● | ● | | | S | | ● |
| Baniassadi, et al. | 2018 | USA (15) | ● | | | | | | | | |
| Symonds, et al. | 2016 | UK (3) | ● | ● | ● | ● | | | S | | |
| Hamdy, et al. | 2017 | Netherlands (1) | ● | ● | ● | | ● | | S | ● | |
| Taylor, et al. | 2015 | UK (1) | | | | ● | ● | | S | | |
| de Wilde and Tian | 2012 | UK (1) | ● | | | ● | ● | | S | ● | ● |
| Barclay, et al. | 2012 | UK (1) | ● | ● | | ● | ● | | MS | ● | ● |
| Jenkins, et al. | 2014 | UK (2) | ● | | | ● | ● | | S | ● | ● |
| Patidar, et al. | 2014 | UK (2) | ● | | | ● | ● | | S | ● | ● |
| Banfill, et al. | 2013 | UK (2) | ● | | | ● | ● | | S | ● | ● |
| Gupta, et al. | 2013 | UK (1) | ● | ● | ● | ● | | | MS | | ● |
| Total studies = 39 | | Most=UK (13) | 29 | 12 | 19 | 28 | 5 | 9 | 31 | 19 | 11 |

# RESILIENT DESIGN MODELING

| Residential | Commercial | Multiple Building Sub-Types | EUI or Similar | Heating & Cooling Energy | Energy Cost | Heating / Cooling Degree Days | Adaptive Comfort Model | Indoor Operative Temp. | Fanger Comfort Model | Indoor Air Change Rate | Consec. Days/Hours Overheat | Custom Metric |
|---|---|---|---|---|---|---|---|---|---|---|---|---|
| Bldg. | | | | Metrics | | | | | | | | |
| | ● | | ● | ● | | | ● | ● | | ● | | |
| | ● | | | | | | | | | ● | | |
| ● | | | ● | | | | | ● | | | | |
| ● | | | | ● | | | | ● | ● | | | |
| ● | | ● | | | | | | ● | | | ● | |
| | | | | | | | ● | ● | | | | |
| ● | | | | | | ● | ● | ● | | | | |
| ● | | | | | | | | ● | | | | |
| ● | | | | | | | ● | ● | | | | |
| ● | | | | | | ● | | | | | | |
| ● | | ● | | ● | | | | | | | | ● |
| ● | | ● | | | | | ● | ● | | | | ● |
| ● | | ● | | | | | ● | ● | | | | |
| ● | ● | ● | ● | ● | | ● | | ● | | | | |
| | ● | ● | | | | | ● | ● | ● | ● | | |
| ● | ● | ● | | | | | | ● | | | | |
| ● | | | | | | | | ● | | | ● | |
| ● | | | | | | | | ● | | | | |
| ● | | ● | | | | | | ● | | | | |
| 27 | 15 | 10 | 19 | 16 | 3 | 10 | 11 | 19 | 3 | 2 | 2 | 4 |

Table 2.2  Comparison of Literature Review Papers for Energy Conservation or Resilient Design Measures.

| Paper | Year | Location (City Qty) | Roof Solar Absorptance | Roof Conductance | Wall Solar Absorptance | Wall Conductance | Infiltration / permeability |
|---|---|---|---|---|---|---|---|
| Andrić, et al. | 2017 | EU (3), CAN (2) |  | ● |  | ● | ● |
| Taleghani, et al. | 2014 | Netherlands (1) |  |  |  |  |  |
| Hosseini, et al. | 2018 | Canada (1) | ● | ● |  |  |  |
| Triana, et al. | 2018 | Brazil (2) | ● | ● | ● | ● |  |
| Karimopour, et al. | 2015 | Australia (1) | ● | ● | ● | ● |  |
| Wang, et al. | 2017 | USA (5) |  |  |  |  |  |
| Shen | 2017 | USA (4) |  |  |  |  |  |
| Holmes and Reinhart | 2013 | USA (2) |  | ● |  | ● | ● |
| Glassman and Reinhart | 2013 | USA (3) |  |  |  | ● |  |
| Ascione, et al. | 2017 | Italy (1) | ● | ● | ● | ● |  |
| Pagliano, et al. | 2016 | Italy (1) |  | ● |  | ● | ● |
| Invidiata and Ghisi | 2016 | Brazil (3) | ● | ● | ● | ● |  |
| Wang and Chen | 2014 | USA (15) |  |  |  |  |  |
| Huang and Hwang | 2016 | Taiwan (1) |  | ● |  | ● |  |
| Nik, et al. | 2015 | Sweden (1) |  | ● |  | ● |  |
| Chinazzo, et al. | 2015 | Italy (1) |  | ● |  | ● | ● |
| Cellura, et al. | 2018 | Europe (15) |  | ● |  |  |  |
| Nik | 2017 | Sweden (1) |  |  |  |  |  |
| Huang and Gurney | 2016 | US (925) |  |  |  |  |  |
| Santamouris | 2016 | Global (12) |  |  |  |  |  |
| Lomas and Ji | 2009 | UK (2) |  |  |  |  |  |
| Kalvelage, et al. | 2015 | US (1) |  |  |  |  |  |

ECM or RDM Considered

| WWR | External Shading | Window U-Value | Window SHGC | Natural Vent (Window Area) | Natural Ventilation (On/Off) | Thermal Mass | Lighting | Non Occupant Internal Loads | HVAC Efficiency | Orientation |
|---|---|---|---|---|---|---|---|---|---|---|
| | | ● | | | | | | | | |
| ● | ● | | | ● | | | | | | |
| | | ● | ● | | | | | | | |
| | | | | | ● | | ● | | ● | |
| ● | ● | ● | ● | ● | ● | | | | ● | |
| ● | ● | | | | | | | | | |
| | | ● | ● | | | | | | ● | |
| | | ● | ● | | | | ● | | ● | |
| | ● | | | | | | | | | |
| | | ● | ● | | | | | | | |
| | ● | | | | | ● | | | | |
| | | | | | | | ● | | | |
| ● | | | | | | | | | | |
| ● | ● | | ● | ● | | ● | | | | ● |
| | | ● | | | | | | | | |

*(Continued)*

Table 2.2 Continued Comparison of Literature Review Papers for Energy Conservation or Resilient Design Measures.

| Paper | Year | Location (City Qty) | Roof Solar Absorptance | Roof Conductance | Wall Solar Absorptance | Wall Conductance | Infiltration / permeability |
|---|---|---|---|---|---|---|---|
| | | | ECM or RDM Considered | | | | |
| Ozkan, et al. | 2018 | CAN (2), TUR (1) | | ● | | ● | ● |
| O'Brien | 2016 | Canada (1) | | | | | |
| Porritt, et al. | 2013 | UK (1) | ● | ● | ● | ● | ● |
| Van Hoof, et al. | 2015 | Netherlands (1) | ● | ● | ● | ● | |
| Din and Brotas | 2017 | UK (1) | | | | | |
| McLeod, et al. | 2013 | UK (1) | | | | | ● |
| Mulville, et al. | 2016 | UK (2) | | ● | | ● | ● |
| Baniassadi, et al. | 2018 | USA (15) | | ● | | ● | ● |
| Symonds, et al. | 2016 | UK (3) | | ● | | ● | ● |
| Hamdy, et al. | 2017 | Netherlands (1) | | ● | | ● | ● |
| Taylor, et al. | 2015 | UK (1) | | ● | | ● | ● |
| de Wilde and Tian | 2012 | UK (1) | | | | ● | ● |
| Barclay, et al. | 2012 | UK (1) | | | | | |
| Jenkins, D. et al. | 2014 | UK (2) | | | | | |
| Patidar, et al. | 2014 | UK (2) | | | | | |
| Banfill, et al. | 2013 | UK (2) | | | | | |
| Gupta, et al. | 2013 | UK (1) | | | | | |
| **Total studies = 39** | | Most = UK (13) | 7 | 20 | 6 | 20 | 13 |

utilize either morphed or synthetic weather files to simulate future climate change scenarios. However, only 19 studies use multiple climate change scenarios, with the remaining 14 only analyzing one future scenario. As many of the papers note, given the uncertainty surrounding future emissions, a more robust climate simulation should address multiple emissions scenarios, ideally the current RCP

| WWR | External Shading | Window U-Value | Window SHGC | Natural Vent (Window Area) | Natural Ventilation (On/Off) | Thermal Mass | Lighting | Non Occupant Internal Loads | HVAC Efficiency | Orientation |
|---|---|---|---|---|---|---|---|---|---|---|
| ● | ● | ● | ● | | | | | | | |
| ● | ● | ● | ● | | | | | | | |
| | ● | | ● | ● | ● | | | | | |
| | ● | | | | ● | ● | | | | |
| ● | ● | | | | | ● | | | | |
| ● | ● | | | ● | | ● | | ● | | |
| ● | ● | ● | ● | ● | | ● | | | | ● |
| | ● | ● | | | ● | | | | | ● |
| ● | ● | ● | ● | | | | ● | ● | | ● |
| | | ● | | | | | | | | |
| | | ● | ● | | | | ● | | ● | |
| | ● | | | ● | | | | | | |
| ● | | | | | ● | | | ● | | |
| ● | | | | | ● | | | ● | | |
| 13 | 18 | 13 | 13 | 7 | 7 | 6 | 5 | 4 | 5 | 4 |

scenarios. Another noticeable trend is that 29/39 papers utilize TMY, TRY, or equivalent weather files in the simulation studies, while 10/39 use synthetic weather from a weather generator (i.e. UKCP09). Six of the nineteen overheating studies simulated using both TMY-type and synthetic weather files. Though both TMY and synthetic weather files use is acceptable, TMY usage is likely greater as they are native to most energy modeling tools. Only 10/39 studies used probabilistic future weather files, all for European locations mostly in the UK. This finding is not surprising as probabilistic future weather data is still relatively new.

Regarding buildings and metrics, most studies (27/39) examine housing, less than half (15/39) examine commercial properties, and 9/39 examine multiple property types. When filtered for housing priority, overheating studies focus more on housing (15/19) than energy-focused studies (12/20). This finding is likely due to commercial properties having greater mechanical cooling capacity and uniform occupant type (adults) than residential properties, which often utilize passive ventilation and have more vulnerable populations (young children, infirm, and elderly). Regarding analysis metrics for the 20 energy-focused papers, the EUI metric is used most frequently (16/20), followed by heating/cooling energy consumption (12/20). Other notable energy metrics include HDD/CDD (7/20), adaptive comfort (4/20), and energy cost (3/20). Given the wide use of the EUI metric in energy efficiency simulation and its direct relationship to cooling and heating loads, this easily overlaps with energy resilience analysis. For the 19 papers focused on overheating, the indoor operative temperature ($T_o$) (17/19) and adaptive comfort criteria (7/19) metrics are utilized most frequently. This finding is likely due to the ASHRAE 55 and BS EN 15251 standards utilize these metrics for overheating assessment and energy models natively outputting operative temperature. Other notable overheating metrics include CDD (3/19), PMV/PPD (3/19), indoor air change rate (2/19), and the number of consecutive days/hours overheated (2/19). Many papers note that the lack of a robust overheating and/or PS metric makes simulating climate-related heat impacts very difficult and increases uncertainty.

Table 2.2 lists the ECMs and RDMs evaluated by 15 of the energy studies and 17 of the overheating studies (the remaining studies did not evaluate these variables). For energy-focused studies, the leading ECMs considered were roof (12/15) and wall (11/15) conductance, while overheating studies considered roof (9/17) and wall (8/17) conductance less frequently. Given that roofs cause significant heat gain in buildings, it is surprising that more energy-focused studies (5/15) examine roof solar absorption than overheating studies (2/17). Furthermore, overheating studies examined external shading more frequently (11/17), compared to energy-focused studies (7/15). Overheating studies evaluate internal thermal mass dampening more frequently (5/17) than energy-focused studies (1/15). Similarly, orientation of the building is examined four times by overheating studies, while none of the energy-focused studies consider orientation; this may be due to energy-focused studies being more focused on retrofitting existing buildings. In all but one of the overheating studies, natural ventilation is always present; however, the manipulation of natural ventilation (window operability or size) is not frequently evaluated (5/17). Finally, window U-value and solar heat gain are examined in roughly 35%–40% of the energy-focused projects as well as the overheating focused case studies.

In general, this literature review indicates several interesting trends and possibilities. Though the prospects of simulating for an infinite number of futures for a building seem daunting, the recent development of the probabilistic future weather data and Low Carbon Futures project's regression tool offers hope that the process will be more easily achieved. With that said, the methods of communicating probabilistic information in this setting is still nascent and requires further development and refinement. Additionally, there is a need for more probabilistic weather datasets outside of Europe; this literature review did not uncover a single case study that used probabilistic weather data outside of Europe and the UK. Probabilistic analysis of future weather does appear the more accurate way forward, as the morphing of traditional TMY-type weather files does not filter for historic averaging, and traditional DSY-type summer weather files may not capture heatwave events. Probabilistic weather analysis resolves these issues as the simulator selects the desired percentile for the study (i.e. 90th percentile hot summer, or 50th percentile emissions scenario, or 10th percentile warm winter). Furthermore, as the emissions scenarios utilized by GCMs and RCMs get more advanced, the need for more probabilistic evaluation and simulation will undoubtedly increase and become more streamlined between climate models and weather generators.

Another interesting finding is that the EUI and adaptive comfort criteria are the most widely used metrics for energy-focused studies and overheating studies, respectively. Though the heating and cooling energy total metric was used somewhat in energy-focused studies, it may require more attention; *all* the studies examined that use the heating/cooling energy total metric indicate increased cooling loads and decreased heating loads under all future climate scenarios. Additionally, as adaptive comfort criteria become more widespread, the overlap between the energy-focused and overheating-focused studies should increase, ideally leading to wider use of mixed-mode cooling design. For overheating studies, the adaptive comfort model is acceptable given the current state of heat-health evaluation. However, many of the overheating studies recommend that more research is needed to evaluate indoor heat-health, particularly regarding PS. The adaptive comfort model does not fully integrate heat-health thresholds as they relate to the complete combination of air temperature, humidity, radiant temperature, air-speed, occupant health, metabolic rate, and clothing levels. Though it is likely improbable that one "silver-bullet" metric exists for evaluating buildings to this level, some greater consensus between building science and epidemiological professionals is necessary in order to evaluate TA and PS.

Though the metrics used are consistent across the studies analyzed, the energy conservation and RDM are less consistent and more wide-ranging across otherwise similar studies. Though many of the design solutions analyzed could be considered either an ECM or an RDM, it is interesting that a common measure did not appear across all the analyses. Natural ventilation came close to uniform assessment, as it is considered in all but one overheating study; however, roof conductance would seem critical for both energy conservation and overheating analysis, yet only half of the overheating studies considered this design measure. Understandably, the overheating studies focus significant attention on airflow, ventilation, and solar gain through windows; however, the operative temperature metric does incorporate surface radiant heat, and therefore conductive and radiative heat gain from the building envelope. This point is strengthened by the observation from several overheating studies that an evenly distributed internal thermal mass helps reduce indoor overheating from conductive and radiant gains.

## Conclusion

The 39 papers analyzed in this literature review describe a spectrum of methods to simulate buildings for climate change impacts and building resiliency. In order to incorporate the vast spectrum of climate uncertainty, simulation studies range from the simple (simulate a historic heatwave) to the complex (examine 3,000 probabilistic futures). Though the more complex approach in this case is likely more precise, the need for precision must be weighed against the requirements of the analysis (i.e. estimating a life cycle energy analysis of an office building vs. developing national elder-care regulations). The studies presented indicate a strong preference to continue the use of the EUI and adaptive comfort metric in resilient design simulation as it relates to climate change; however, several other metrics are being generated such as a variety of robustness indices. Similarly, many standard ECM also serve as RDM, particularly in relation to indoor overheating. Though natural ventilation is understandably the focus of overheating studies, future research should expand solar impacts on the envelope and the percentage of indoor thermal mass. Overall, this review only captures a portion of the recent progress in this ever-growing library of climate resilient building simulation; though this author wishes he could have been more thorough and all-encompassing in his search, he is thankful so many researchers are making the pool of knowledge that much deeper.

## References

Andrić, Ivan, André Pina, Paulo Ferrão, Jérémy Fournier, Bruno Lacarrière, and Olivier Le Corre. 2017. "The impact of climate change on building heat demand in different climate types." *Energy and Buildings* 149: 225–234.

Ascione, Fabrizio, Nicola Bianco, Rosa Francesca De Masi, Gerardo Maria Mauro, and Giuseppe Peter Vanoli. 2017. "Resilience of robust cost-optimal energy retrofit of buildings to global warming: A multi-stage, multi-objective approach." *Energy and Buildings* 153: 150–167.

ASHRAE. 2013. "ANSI/ASHRAE Standard 55:2013-Thermal Environmental Conditions for Human Occupancy." American Society of Heating, Ventilation, Refrigeration, and Air-Conditioning Engineers.

Banfill, P. F. G., D. P. Jenkins, S. Patidar, M. Gul, G. F. Menzies, and G. J. Gibson. 2013. "Towards an overheating risk tool for building design." *Structural Survey* 31 (4): 253–266.

Baniassadi, Amir, and David J. Sailor. 2018. "Synergies and trade-offs between energy efficiency and resiliency to extreme heat – A case study." *Building and Environment* 132: 263–272.

Barclay, Michael, Steve Sharples, Jian Kang, and Richard Watkins. 2012. "The natural ventilation performance of buildings under alternative future weather projections." *Building Services Engineering Research and Technology* 33 (1): 35–50.

Belcher, S. E., J. N. Hacker, and D. S. Powell. 2005. "Constructing design weather data for future climates." *Building Services Engineering Research and Technology* 26 (1): 49–61.

BSI. 2007. *BS EN 15251:2007 Indoor Environmental Input Parameters for Design and Assessment of Energy Performance of Buildings Addressing Indoor Air Quality, Thermal Environment, Lighting and Acoustics*. London: British Standards Institution.

Burroughs, Steve. 2017. "Development of a tool for assessing commercial building resilience." *Procedia Engineering* 180: 1034–1043.

Cellura, Maurizio, Francesco Guarino, Sonia Longo, and Giovanni Tumminia. 2018. "Climate change and the building sector: Modelling and energy implications to an office building in southern Europe." *Energy for Sustainable Development* 45: 46–65.

Chinazzo, Giorgia, Parag Rastogi, and Marilyne Andersen. 2015. "Robustness assessment methodology for the evaluation of building performance with a view to climate uncertainties." *Building Simulation 2015: 14th Conference of International Building Performance Simulation Association*. Hyderabad, India: International Building Performance Simulation Association, 947–954.

City of New York. 2013. "A Stronger More Resilient New York." The City of New York: PlaNYC, 445.

de Wilde, Pieter, and Wei Tian. 2012. "Management of thermal performance risks in buildings subject to climate change." *Building and Environment* 55: 167–177.

Din, A., and L. Brotas. 2017. "Assessment of climate change on UK dwelling indoor comfort." *Energy Procedia* 122, 21–26.

Enterprise Green Communities. 2016. "Strategies for Multifamily Building Resilience." Enterprise Green Communities.

Glassman, Elliot J., and Christoph Reinhart. 2013. "Facade optimization using parametric design and future climate scenarios." *Building Simulation 2013: 13th Conference of the International Building Performance Simulation Association*. Chambéry, France: International Building Performance Simulation Association, 1585–1592.

Gul, Mehreen S., and Gillian F. Menzies. 2012. *Designing Domestic Buildings for Future Summers: Attitudes and Opinions of Building Professionals*. Elsevier, 752–761. https://doi.org/10.1016/j.enpol.2012.03.046.

Gupta, R., and M. Gregg. 2012. "Climate change. Adaptations." In *International Encyclopedia of Housing and Home*, by R. Gupta and M. Gregg. Elsevier, 164–179.

Gupta, Rajat, Matthew Gregg, Hu Du, and Katie Williams. 2013. "Evaluative application of UKCP09 based downscaled future weather years to simulate overheating risk in typical English homes." *Structural Survey* 31 (4): 231–252.

Hacker, Jake, Stephen Belcher, and Andrew White. 2014. "Design Summer Years for London Design Summer Years for London." The Chartered Institution of Building Services Engineers.

Hamdy, Mohamed, Salvatore Carlucci, Pieter Jan Hoes, and Jan L. M. Hensen. 2017. "The impact of climate change on the overheating risk in dwellings—A Dutch case study." *Building and Environment* 122: 307–323.

Holmes, Seth H., and Christoph F. Reinhart. 2013. "Assessing future climate change and energy price scenarios: Institutional building investment." *Building Research & Information* 41 (2): 209–222.

Holmes, Seth H., Thomas Phillips, and Alex Wilson. 2016. "Overheating and passive habitability: Indoor health and heat indices." *Building Research and Information* 44 (1): 1–19.

Hosseini, Mirata, François Tardy, and Bruno Lee. 2018. "Cooling and heating energy performance of a building with a variety of roof designs; the effects of future weather data in a cold climate." *Journal of Building Engineering* 17: 107–114.

Huang, Jianhua, and Kevin Robert Gurney. 2016. "The variation of climate change impact on building energy consumption to building type and spatiotemporal scale." *Energy* 111: 137–153.

Huang, Kuo Tsang, and Ruey Lung Hwang. 2016. "Future trends of residential building cooling energy and passive adaptation measures to counteract climate change: The case of Taiwan." *Applied Energy* 184: 1230–1240.

Invidiata, Andrea, and Enedir Ghisi. 2016. "Impact of climate change on heating and cooling energy demand in houses in Brazil." *Energy and Buildings* 130: 20–32.

Jenkins, David P., Sandhya Patidar, Phil Banfill, and Gavin Gibson. 2014. "Developing a probabilistic tool for assessing the risk of overheating in buildings for future climates." *Renewable Energy* 61: 7–11.

Jentsch, Mark F., Matt E. Eames, and Geoff J. Levermore. 2015. "Generating near-extreme Summer Reference Years for building performance simulation." *Building Services Engineering Research and Technology* 36 (6): 701–721.

Jones, Keith, Api Desai, Noel Brosnan, Justine Cooper, and Fuad Ali. 2017. "Built asset management climate change adaptation model." *International Journal of Disaster Resilience in the Built Environment* 8 (3): 263–274.

Kalvelage, Kelly, Michael Dorneich, and Ulrike Passe. 2015. "Simulating the future microclimate to identify vulnerable building interior conditions." *Building Simulation 2015: 14th Conference of International Building Performance Simulation Association*. Hyderabad, India: International Building Performance Simulation Association, 2507–2514.

Karimpour, Mahsa, Martin Belusko, Ke Xing, John Boland, and Frank Bruno. 2015. "Impact of climate change on the design of energy efficient residential building envelopes." *Energy and Buildings* 87: 142–154.

Lomas, Kevin J., and Stephen M. Porritt. 2017. "Overheating in buildings: Lessons from research." *Building Research and Information* 45: 1–18.

Lomas, Kevin John, and Yingchun Ji. 2009. "Resilience of naturally ventilated buildings to climate change: Advanced natural ventilation and hospital wards." *Energy and Buildings* 41 (6): 629–653.

McLeod, Robert S., Christina J. Hopfe, and Alan Kwan. 2013. "An investigation into future performance and overheating risks in Passivhaus dwellings." *Building and Environment* 70: 189–209.

Mulville, Mark, and Spyridon Stravoravdis. 2016. "The impact of regulations on overheating risk in dwellings." *Building Research and Information* 44 (5–6): 520–534.

Nik, Vahid M. 2017. "Application of typical and extreme weather data sets in the hygrothermal simulation of building components for future climate – A case study for a wooden frame wall." *Energy and Buildings* 154: 30–45.

Nik, Vahid M., Érika Mata, and Angela Sasic Kalagasidis. 2015. "A statistical method for assessing retrofitting measures of buildings and ranking their robustness against climate change." *Energy and Buildings* 88: 262–275.

O'Brien, William O. 2016. "Simulation-based evaluation of high-rise residential building thermal resilience." *ASHRAE Transactions* 122: 1–14.

Ozkan, Aylin, Ted Kesik, Ayse Zerrin Yilmaz, and William O'Brien. 2018. "Development and visualization of time-based building energy performance metrics." *Building Research and Information* 4 (11): 1–25.

Pagliano, Lorenzo, Salvatore Carlucci, Francesco Causone, Amin Moazami, and Giulio Cattarin. 2016. "Energy retrofit for a climate resilient child care centre." *Energy and Buildings* 127: 1117–1132.

Patidar, Sandhya, David Jenkins, Phil Banfill, and Gavin Gibson. 2014. "Simple statistical model for complex probabilistic climate projections: Overheating risk and extreme events." *Renewable Energy* 61: 23–28.

Porritt, Stephen M., Paul C. Cropper, Li Shao, and Chris I. Goodier. 2013. "Heat wave adaptations for UK dwellings and development of a retrofit toolkit." *International Journal of Disaster Resilience in the Built Environment* 4 (3): 269–286.

Santamouris, Mat. 2016. "Cooling the buildings – Past, present and future." *Energy and Buildings* 128: 617–638.

Shen, Pengyuan. 2017. "Impacts of climate change on U.S. building energy use by using downscaled hourly future weather data." *Energy and Buildings* 134: 61–70.

Sousa, Joana. 2012. "Energy Simulation Software for Buildings: Review and Comparison." *Information Technology for Energy Applications 2012*, 57–68.

Stocker, Thomas F., and Dahe Qin. 2013. *Climate Change 2013 The Physical Science Basis*. Cambridge: Cambridge University Press.

Symonds, Phil, Jonathon Taylor, Zaid Chalabi, Anna Mavrogianni, Michael Davies, Ian Hamilton, Sotiris Vardoulakis, Clare Heaviside, and Helen Macintyre. 2016. "Development of an England-wide indoor overheating and air pollution model using artificial neural networks." *Journal of Building Performance Simulation* 9 (6): 606–619.

Taleghani, Mohammad, Martin Tenpierik, and Andy van den Dobbelsteen. 2014. "Energy performance and thermal comfort of courtyard/atrium dwellings in the Netherlands in the light of climate change." *Renewable Energy* 63: 486–497.

Taylor, Jonathon, A. Mavrogianni, M. Davies, P. Das, Clive Shrubsole, P. Biddulph, and E. Oikonomou. 2015. "Understanding and mitigating overheating and indoor PM2.5 risks using coupled temperature and indoor air quality models." *Building Services Engineering Research and Technology* 36 (2): 275–289.

Triana, Maria Andrea, Roberto Lamberts, and Paola Sassi. 2018. "Should we consider climate change for Brazilian social housing? Assessment of energy efficiency adaptation measures." *Energy and Buildings* 158: 1379–1392.

Van Hooff, T., B. Blocken, J. L. M. Hensen, and H. J. P. Timmermans. 2015. "On the predicted effectiveness of climate adaptation measures for residential buildings." *Building and Environment* 83: 142–158.

Wang, Haojie, and Qingyan Chen. 2014. "Impact of climate change heating and cooling energy use in buildings in the United States." *Energy and Buildings* 82: 428–436.

Wang, Liping, Xiaohong Liu, and Hunter Brown. 2017. "Prediction of the impacts of climate change on energy consumption for a medium-size office building with two climate models." *Energy and Buildings* 157: 218–226.

Young, Rachel. 2014. "Global Approaches: A Comparison of Building Energy Codes in 15 Countries." *ACEEE Summer Study on Energy Efficiency in Buildings*, 351–366.

# 3
# PLANNING FOR A CHANGING CLIMATE WITHOUT ACCURATE PREDICTIONS

*Parag Rastogi and Mohammad Emtiyaz Khan*

## Introduction

The built environment, particularly homes and offices, is a key component of mitigating or adapting to climate change. Estimating the usage and thermal characteristics of buildings is crucial to planning for extreme events such as heat waves or broader changes in climate such as those in rainfall and average summer temperatures. Having estimates of how common building types will behave under different probable future weather conditions, especially extreme events, provides the ability to conduct what-if analyses, which are powerful tools for policy-making. Being able to model the energy demand of buildings also informs the planning of the energy grid.

Simulation is a useful tool for estimating the performance of a system where real data is unavailable, like new buildings and systems, changes to existing buildings, or existing infrastructure operating under future (unknown) operating conditions. Currently, tools to simulate the energy performance of buildings are deterministic, i.e., they assume that the inputs are fixed and known. This is an issue when we do not know the exact values of some inputs, such as the future climate. Using statistical models, we can only estimate certain characteristics, e.g., average indoor temperature and its uncertainty, or how much this estimate might vary. This is often expressed as an 'error bound' on an estimate. We describe a method to obtain such error bounds on outputs by running simulations with multiple realistic estimates of future weather and climate (Rastogi and Andersen 2015; Rastogi 2016; Rastogi, Khan, and Andersen 2017). The principle of simulating with a variety of inputs to construct a less precise but potentially more accurate picture of unknown future conditions is well-established (Davison and Hinkley 1997; Hastie, Tibshirani, and Friedman 2009). The method described here could be used to estimate the responses of a building or system under different future weather conditions.

In this chapter, we demonstrate this method using simulations (calculations) of the energy performance of buildings. We use a simulator called EnergyPlus that calculates the state of the indoor environment based on building construction and materials, outdoor climate, and human interactions and presence (LBNL 2017). The simulator outputs temperature, moisture levels, and other parameters of the indoor environment. These conditions can be used to estimate the level of human comfort indoors, and the energy needed to achieve this comfort if conditions are not as desired. The simulator is, therefore, useful for estimating the behavior of buildings under different usage and environmental conditions like a changing climate. We can calculate the probability of issues like overheating and obtain useful proxies for demand on energy grids.

## The Problem

So far, we have introduced the major issue that affects preparation or planning for the impacts of climate change on buildings and energy infrastructure, namely the unavailability of precise and accurate predictions. In this section, we describe how having precise or exact predictions is not necessarily a good thing since we have no way of verifying their accuracy. We also discuss one source of these predictions, climate model outputs, and how they may be used.

Precision and accuracy are often used interchangeably, but in the context of mathematical models, they mean different things. Using the target analogy illustrated by Figure 3.1, the goal of planning is to hit the bullseye of a target (some social, environmental, or technical goal) with every arrow fired (every action or policy). In the context of planning for climate change, our arrows are estimates of climate trajectories or pathways into the future. The precision of the estimated trajectories is up to us (number of arrows), but we cannot verify the accuracy of our estimates because *we cannot see the target*, i.e., the future climate. We are planning in the present for the future, but we cannot wait for that future to be realized before acting on a plan. In addition, the target is always moving; our actions and the earth's complex feedback loops change the trajectory of the climate. So, if we act on a prediction now, e.g., electrify domestic heating, we may change the evolution of the climate because the electrification of a large enough number of heating systems might significantly reduce the use of natural gas and associated greenhouse gas (GHG) emissions. Or if we promote reforestation and better urban/building design, and improve emergency response, we might be able to reduce the impact of heat waves even if they are meteorologically more extreme than what we have seen so far. The upshot is that if we do not know where the target is, then a small number of precise arrows are not useful because we have no way of verifying that they landed near enough to the target. For planners and designers, being wrong with complete precision (one estimate, probably incorrect, impossible to

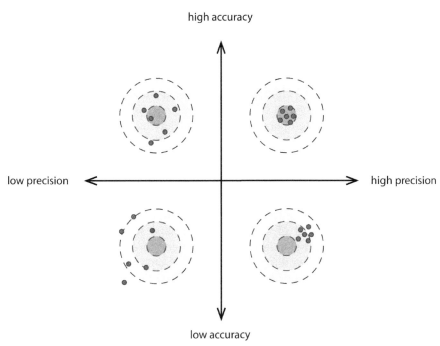

Figure 3.1 Precision versus accuracy, as illustrated by shooting at a virtual target. High precision implies getting most of one's arrows to land in a small area, regardless of whether that is on or near the bullseye. High accuracy implies getting most of the arrows near the bullseye, even if they are spread out over a large area. Ideally, climate change forecasts should be both precise and accurate, but we have no way of verifying accuracy since we cannot see the real target (i.e., know the future climate in advance).

verify accuracy) is not as useful as being approximately right (many estimates, one of which is likely to be correct).

Currently, the only way to estimate future values of weather parameters for simulation is to use climate models. These are mathematical models of global and regional climate that are 'tuned' using historical data (trained/fit) and then set to forecast with potential future conditions (prediction). The inputs to these models could be natural, e.g., the uptake of carbon dioxide ($CO_2$) by the ocean, or related to humans, e.g., the number, efficiency, and usage of cars. The outputs of these models are sensitive to errors and assumptions about these natural and social processes. Thus, these outputs of climate models can only be regarded as probable future pathways that the climate could take. Recent advances in climate modeling have made long-term climate and weather forecasts more precise, both spatially and temporally. We can have predictions over small, well-defined cells of less than a degree latitude/longitude on either side, and we can have these for every day of the rest of the century. However, the social and technological assumptions underlying the model and lack of knowledge mean that the precision of these models is not an indication of their accuracy.

## Availability of Climatic Data for Simulating Dynamic Systems

The results of future climate simulations on a global scale are freely available for use, e.g., daily mean outputs from the CORDEX collaboration (WRCP 2017). These simulated time series can be used to simulate individual systems and buildings, once modified to have an appropriate temporal and spatial resolution.

For building simulation, the temporal resolution of the data needs to be reasonably high since dynamic models of human-scale systems generally work with inputs and outputs that change several times a day. These dynamic models are required to accurately simulate the changing nature of energy flows in buildings and systems and the effect of transient phenomena such as heat waves and clouds. Most simulation models need more than one reading per day, usually working at frequencies from one per hour to one per second. Methods have been proposed to convert low-resolution weather data to a higher resolution suitable for building simulation and renewable energy generation (e.g., Belcher, Hacker, and Powell 2005; Crawley 2007, 2008; Magnano, Boland, and Hyndman 2008; Remund et al. 2012; Rastogi and Andersen 2015, 2016; Rastogi 2016; Grantham, Pudney, and Boland 2018). These methods can either work from records that are only available as summary data, e.g., daily historical means, or from the outputs of climate change models.

Building simulation also requires data at a high geographical resolution since the effects of natural features, such as mountains, and artificial features, such as cities, can change microclimates. Microclimate refers to the climate over a very small area, such as a valley, a street, or a city block. This means that the results of global-scale climate simulations must be 'downscaled' to smaller areas. The CORDEX collaboration, for example, gives outputs from multiple Regional Climate Models (RCM), each of which is based on a Global Climate Model (GCM). As the name suggests, to simulate buildings, we use the outputs of RCMs, not those of GCMs directly. Another method, called statistical downscaling, may also be used to downscale the results of GCMs to a small region. This involves using local climate statistics to shift the GCM results to match the local climate.

The time series data from these simulations describes a probable future pathway of temperature and other weather variables (sunshine, pressure, wind, and humidity). The models are based on both natural and human inputs; while the physical, biological, and chemical interactions of the climate form the core of the simulation, the effect of human activities is also included. These include population changes, deforestation/afforestation, GHG emissions, improvements in energy grids and technologies, policies, and economic growth. Since these models contain several interactions that cannot be calculated directly, because they are poorly understood or measured, the models must contain approximations, assumptions, and simplifications. The approximations are often represented by solvable mathematical relationships that contain parameters that must be estimated using some 'ground truth'. To ensure that the models are as correct as can be, these parameters are tuned on the only ground truth available to us: historical weather. Each model is tuned slightly differently on historical data and then assumes a certain path for the future conditions of the climate based on assumptions about human activities. In the current iterations of the models published through the Intergovernmental Panel on Climate Change (IPCC 2014), four pathways are used, designated as RCP 2.6, 4.5, 6.0, and 8.5. RCP stands for Representative Concentration Pathway and the number for each represents the radiative forcing expected at the end of the present century (circa 2100) in W/m$^2$ (Vuuren et al. 2011).

> The Representative Concentration Pathways (RCPs) … describe four different 21st century pathways of GHG emissions and atmospheric concentrations, air pollutant emissions and land use. The RCPs include a stringent mitigation scenario (RCP2.6), two intermediate scenarios (RCP4.5 and RCP6.0) and one scenario with very high GHG emissions (RCP8.5). Scenarios without additional efforts to constrain emissions ('baseline scenarios') lead to pathways ranging between RCP6.0 and RCP8.5… RCP2.6 is representative of a scenario that aims to keep global warming likely below 2°C above pre-industrial temperatures.
> 
> (IPCC 2014)

## Climate Change Data for Building Simulation

The state of the art in incorporating climate change into building design and simulation is focused on two themes: how to generate future climate files and how to adapt buildings to unknown future climates. Guan (2009) divides work on predicting future climate data into two categories: one that relies on historical data and the other on fundamental physical models. The historical data category includes extrapolation, imposed offset methods, and stochastic generation. Extrapolation is the straightforward extension of recent historical trends into the future, usually used with a simplified energy calculation like the Degree Day method (e.g., Cox et al. 2015). Imposed offset methods include the 'morphing' procedure (Belcher, Hacker, and Powell 2005), based on shifting and/or stretching weather variables one-at-a-time, and others that deal with two variables – temperature and humidity – by postulating some assumption on the future values of relative humidity, e.g., Guan (2009). Finally, stochastic generation would include the weather generators (e.g., Eames 2016; Rastogi and Andersen 2015, 2016). Guan (2009) themselves suggest a mixture of imposed offset and a 'diurnal modeling method', which uses current diurnal patterns with expected future statistical characteristics like daily minimum and maximum, like morphing. The alternative to these data-based approaches is the use of numerical climate models such as RCMs and GCMs, as discussed above. The physics-based approaches are assumed to be closer to the truth, since they encode causal, dynamic relationships. However, currently, limitations on knowledge and computation mean that the data-based approaches continue to have wide applicability.

Morphing is the most popular method for creating time series of future weather conditions to test buildings (e.g., Crawley 2007, 2008; Coley and Kershaw 2010; Du, Underwood, and Edge 2011, 2012; Eames, Kershaw, and Coley 2011, 2012; Jentsch et al. 2013; Cox et al. 2015; Nik 2016; Troup and Fannon 2016). This method of shifting existing weather files can be applied to a measured year from the past or a composite typical year (Wilcox and Marion 2008). Since the most common practice in simulation-based studies to inform building design is the use of a single year of 'typical weather' composed of months taken from the historical record, most future climate studies have tended to morph (shift) historical typical years as well. Some studies, particularly those from the UK, extend the use of morphing by applying it to many years and selecting 'extreme years'. The concept of an extreme year is usually based on temperature, such as those recommended by the Chartered Institute for Building Service Engineers (CIBSE) for estimating summer overheating (Eames 2016) or described by Crawley and Lawrie (2015). For example, the Design Summer Year in the UK uses a criteria based on exceedance of a temperature threshold (a heat wave) and its impact on indoor comfort in a nominal, simplified building (Eames 2016; Bonfigli et al. 2017). For a wider review of impact studies see Rastogi (2016, Section 2.2).

Each of these methods proposes the use of a single or a small number of future weather outcomes, and tries to improve the representativeness and quality of the weather inputs. That is, we are improving the arrows we use, but still relying on a small number of shots. The issue with validating these methods, therefore, is that if we are working from the premise that the climate is changing, then we cannot know if historical extremes will remain extremes in the future, or whether they will become normal or common. In other words, we do not know if we are aiming at the correct target. For example, will the hottest summer in the past 20 years also be the hottest summer in the next 20 years, or will it become just an above-average summer? Another issue with morphing or selecting a historical extreme is that we cannot have variations in sequences of temperatures or combinations of values of different weather parameters like temperature and solar radiation. These are important to stress-test dynamic systems, asking questions like: "after how many hours of temperatures above 30 degrees Celsius does the buildup of heat inside a care home surpass the ability of the occupants to adapt?"

## Proposed Solution

We will use a model of a generic apartment building located in New York City to demonstrate the effect of choosing weather input for simulation. The model is a simplified, realistic representation of a new construction or renovation in the EnergyPlus software (NREL and USDOE 2017). We use the concept of 'ideal loads' to show nominal energy use for space conditioning. The model represents a mixed-demographic residential complex, i.e., with a variety of household types and preferences, including usage, temperature setpoints, appliances, lighting, and ventilation. Realistic random usage profiles were generated using the methods described in Flett and Kelly (2016, 2017). For details about the simulation, see Agarwal et al. (2016). The buildings were simulated with historical and typical weather data from John. F. Kennedy (JFK) Airport, La Guardia Airport, and Central Park Observatory. They were also simulated with plausible synthetic future weather generated using the algorithms described in Rastogi and Andersen (2015, 2016); Rastogi (2016). We first present graphs of simulated energy use (estimated thermal performance of the buildings) using the Central Park weather station, and finally compare the simulations from all three stations.

## Why Simulations with a Diverse Sample of Inputs Are Better than Typical Inputs

In Figure 3.2 we show the results from simulating two different typical files (Wilcox and Marion 2008; Remund et al. 2012), based on two different algorithms and periods of record, against the measured weather from 1991 to 2017. The weather files are for one station, New York City – John F. Kennedy International Airport. We see that regardless of the method or number of years used to select a 'test year' for simulation, the time-varying performance of a building is poorly described when the future operating conditions (climate only in this case) are unknown. Figure 3.3 shows the same plots for another station nearby (New York City – Central Park Observatory). The similarity in the coverage of the typical files is to be expected. While some stations do show less intra- and inter-annual variability than others, e.g., the low seasonal variation of temperature in tropical climates, there are too many plausible future pathways of weather.

In some cases, like New York City, multiple weather stations are available, and the same station may have many typical files available as well, based on different generating algorithms or source periods of record. We see from Figure 3.4 that using a small number of files is better than using one, but coverage may still be inadequate. The problem lies in the fact that we are interested in knowing the extent of energy used throughout the year, and the driving input for this energy use is a very variable natural phenomenon that we do not understand well. This means that we need a very large number of samples to adequately describe this highly variable future condition. A small sample

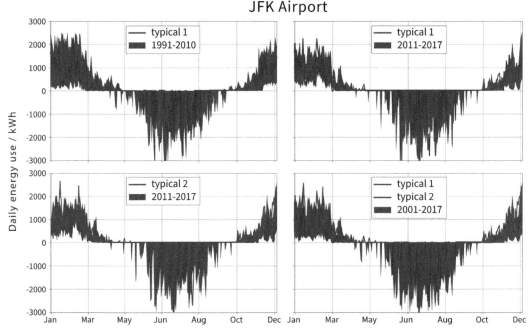

Figure 3.2 Energy use for heating and cooling simulated with a composite typical year versus actual complete years from several decades, New York City – John F. Kennedy International Airport weather station. Negative values of energy represent cooling (total heat removed per day) and positive represent heating. Two typical files were used, the first of which (typical 1) is composed of years from the 1970s, 1980s, and 1990s, and the second (typical 2) from 2000–2010. They are plotted separately, with their corresponding 'future years', and together [bottom-right]. For typical 1, the time period 2000–2016 represents the 'future', while for typical 2, 2010–2016 is the future. Using only the typical file at any time, e.g., in 2000, does not give a sufficient estimate of the variety of loads seen during the subsequent decade. This illustrates our argument that using one weather file input only represents some portion of the actual weather experienced by a building, regardless of the quality of the input file. The further out one gets from the source years of the typical file, the worse its coverage of extremes and even broad trends. A noticeable trend is that the number of days that require cooling is increasing with each decade, another aspect that cannot be represented by a typical file composed from historical data.

of files may describe the overall headline figures acceptably, but they fail when it is important to know time-sensitive quantities such as peak loads.

The most effective strategy for finding out the extent of future values is to use as large a sample of weather inputs as possible, as shown in Figure 3.5. In this case, we have the measured data from three stations from 1991 to 2017. So, if we had, in 2000, used all available historical data for New York City, we would have 10 years * 3 stations = 30 files. This number of files approaches the coverage required for robust planning. However, using only historical data means that future samples will diverge further and further from historical data, since, by using only historical data, the effect of climate change is not explicitly included. In the case of New York City, we have many files available,

PLANNING FOR A CHANGING CLIMATE 43

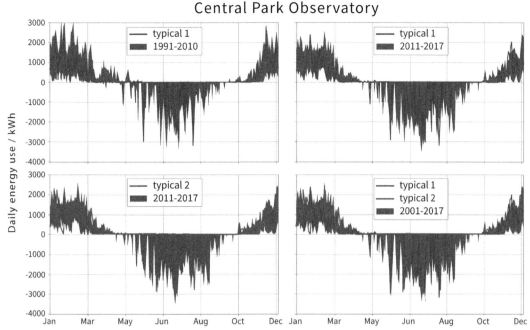

Figure 3.3 Energy use for heating and cooling simulated with a composite typical year versus actual complete years from several decades, New York City – Central Park Observatory station. This plot shows a similar result as the plot for the JFK Airport station – that a single 'typical' file does not give adequate coverage of plausible future outcomes (in this case, energy demand for space conditioning).

which is a best-case scenario for the use of historical data only. The plots presented in Figure 3.5 are only 1–17 years out from the date of planning. If one is interested in planning for several decades, then the extent of possible outcomes is larger. The further into the future we plan for, the less we know about the climate then because it will have changed further, in unknown ways. Even if we were to extrapolate current trajectories and emissions, as discussed above, the extent and magnitude of changes would not be clear.

In Table 3.1, we present a final comparison of the summary statistics from simulations of heating and cooling load using historical data, i.e., the conditions that a building actually experienced over the period of record (1991–2017), to the simulations using two typical files (both based on pre-2000 data). The statistics we compare are the 1st, 50th, and 99th percentiles of the annual, monthly, and daily sums of heating and cooling loads. Typical files were not designed to replicate extreme conditions, so only using them is not a reliable way to assess risks or estimate summary statistics. This is a classical problem, i.e., having one or only a small set of samples gives no indication of the accuracy of estimated statistics. For example, the high and low percentiles (1st and 99th) of the annual heating load in the period of record are about 33% different from the median value (±30,000 kWh), while cooling percentiles are off by 90% (36,000 kWh) and 60%

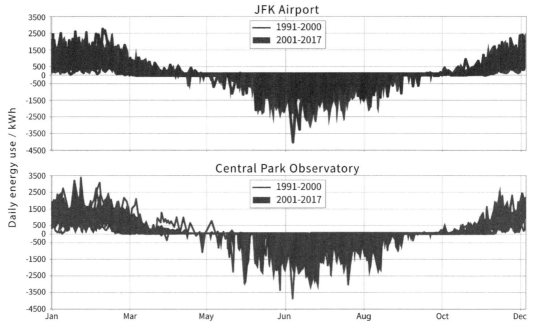

Figure 3.4 Heating and cooling loads from measured weather from JFK Airport (top) and Central Park Observatory (bottom), plotted with typical files from three stations each – JFK Airport, Central Park Observatory, and La Guardia Airport. Using multiple typical files from nearby stations improves the coverage of potential future weather patterns but, in most cases, this is still an inadequate sample.

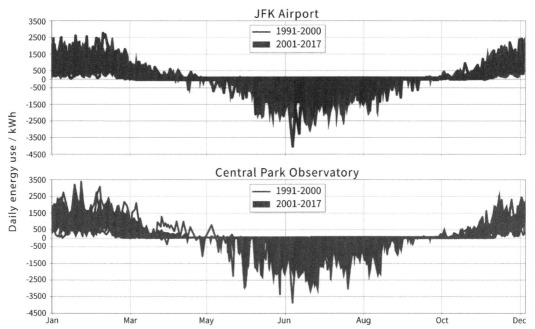

Figure 3.5 A large sample of historical data showing good coverage of the 'future' climate (2001–2017) using nearby stations, to provide the best coverage. When planning several decades into the future, the potential boundaries of plausible outcomes are much larger due to the uncertainty in quantifying the magnitude of climate change.

Table 3.1 Summary Statistics of Heating and Cooling Load Calculated from Typical and Historical Files for the JFK Airport Station. The Annual, Monthly, and Daily Columns Represent the Annual, Monthly, and Daily Sums, Respectively. Each Figure is the Quantile for the Sums of That Time Period.

|  | Quantile | Historical |  |  | Typical |  |  |
| --- | --- | --- | --- | --- | --- | --- | --- |
|  |  | Annual | Monthly | Daily | Annual | Monthly | Daily |
| Heating | 0.01 | 60,700 | 0 | 0 | 97,387 | 0 | 0 |
|  | 0.5 | 90,316 | 1,395 | 5 | 98,646 | 870 | 2 |
|  | 0.99 | 110,381 | 44,874 | 2,503 | 99,905 | 32,768 | 1,987 |
| Cooling | 0.01 | −76,387 | −32,988 | −2,767 | −66,106 | −28,732 | −2,549 |
|  | 0.5 | −40,370 | −521 | 0 | −65,608 | 0 | 0 |
|  | 0.99 | −16,078 | 0 | 0 | −65,110 | 0 | 0 |

(24,000 kWh) of the median, respectively. These are significant range of annual consumption for cooling by an apartment building: year-on-year the cooling load could be double or half of the long-term average. Moving on to the sub-annual figures, we see that the extreme monthly and daily figures are estimated better by a typical file. This is because even a single year-long simulation provides 12 monthly or 365 daily data points, and we have used two typical files here. For planning the day-to-day loads on average days, the typical files do an acceptable job. Estimating the factor of safety to meet demand on extreme days is what cannot be accomplished with typical files alone.

## Conclusion

In this chapter, we have described how our proposals could improve planning for the impacts of climate change on buildings. We showed that a small number of precise predictions are not useful if they do not describe the probable range of future outcomes. With modern computing, simulating many potential paths of future climate to obtain an idea of the limits of the capacity of a building or system is feasible and provides a ready tool for planning. We have proposed methods to reduce this computational time (Rastogi, Khan, and Andersen 2017) that make these simulations even more practical.

Knowing the likely response of a system under a range of conditions allows operators and planners to be proactive. The value of being able to plan for heat waves or other extreme conditions in terms of avoided fatalities, loss of productivity and economic output, and the direct costs of repair and rehabilitation is, however, as difficult to estimate as the exact future climate conditions themselves. This is because the problem with preparing an engineering system for an extreme event is that the event may not actually occur in the operational lifetime of the system. Planning will consume resources now, like collecting information about the building stock, but the benefits of using that planning may or may not materialize, and we have no way of knowing except waiting. This does not mean that the planning failed or that the preparation was unnecessary. The tools we propose in this chapter allow planners to model the behavior of the built environment and estimate under what conditions the buildings and systems will fail, but a decision must eventually be made about how robust we can afford to make the systems and when we must plan around failures.

By proposing the use of simulation, we make the case for creating and maintaining a database of the construction, condition, and usage of buildings and energy systems. This should include the construction of buildings, their condition, and age; information about the materials, systems, and equipment used in buildings; and the patterns of usage and preferences among occupants or users. An accurate representation of the built environment is crucial for informative what-if analysis. This can help designers and planners of energy networks and the built environment prepare for a changing climate. Not having enough information about the underlying causes of the complex demand profiles that are met by a grid can, at worst, lead to black-outs, or, at best, lead to oversized systems that tie up more capital expenditure and resources than necessary.

The power of simulating with a reasonable variety of inputs, like with the Monte Carlo method, is that it exposes many more variations and scenarios than a small number of deterministic simulations would. They allow a planner to think probabilistically, to determine the robustness of their designs against plausible future outcomes, and to decide up to what plausible future level a system should continue to operate. For example, the misestimation of annual figures could be an indication of the changing distribution of days in the weather stations. Current trends, including those seen in this dataset, suggest that we should expect to see more warm days in the future. The current decade has some of the warmest years on record globally. It is outside the scope of this study to determine whether the recently increased intensity and frequency of extreme events is an outcome of a changing climate or not. Rather, we demonstrate the changing distribution of weather parameters over years and decades, and the inability of a deterministic simulation to capture the distribution.

The decision to plan for a range of future climate change impacts is akin to buying insurance. You may never need it and year-on-year, the common, small-impact events may make it feel worthless. However, if there is a probable event that can have calamitous outcomes with great human, environmental, or economic costs, then we have a duty of care to be prepared.

## References

Agarwal, Minu, Parag Rastogi, Margaux Peltier, Luisa Pastore, and Marilyne Andersen. 2016. 'Examining Building Design Decisions Under Long Term Weather Variability and Microclimate Effects: A Case Based Exploratory Study'. In *Proceedings of PLEA 2016*. Los Angeles, USA.

Belcher, S. E., J. N. Hacker, and D. S. Powell. 2005. 'Constructing Design Weather Data for Future Climates'. *Building Services Engineering Research and Technology* 26 (1): 49–61. https://doi.org/10.1191/0143624405bt112oa.

Bonfigli, Cecilia, Marguerita Chorafa, Susie Diamond, Chris Eliades, Anastasia Mylona, Becci Taylor, and Dane Virk. 2017. *TM59 Design Methodology for the Assessment of Overheating Risk in Homes*. TM 59.

Coley, David, and Tristan Kershaw. 2010. 'Changes in Internal Temperatures within the Built Environment as a Response to a Changing Climate'. *Building and Environment*, International Symposium on the Interaction between Human and Building Environment Special Issue Section, 45 (1): 89–93. https://doi.org/10.1016/j.buildenv.2009.05.009.

Cox, Rimante A., Martin Drews, Carsten Rode, and Susanne Balslev Nielsen. 2015. 'Simple Future Weather Files for Estimating Heating and Cooling Demand'. *Building and Environment*, Special Issue: Climate Adaptation in Cities, 83 (January): 104–114. https://doi.org/10.1016/j.buildenv.2014.04.006.

Crawley, Drury B. 2007. 'Creating Weather Files for Climate Change and Urbanization Impacts Analysis'. In *Proceedings of BS 2007*, 7: 1075–1082. Beijing, China. http://www.ibpsa.org/proceedings/BS2007/p455_final.pdf.

Crawley, Drury B. 2008. 'Estimating the Impacts of Climate Change and Urbanization on Building Performance'. *Journal of Building Performance Simulation* 1 (2): 91–115. https://doi.org/10.1080/19401490802182079.

Crawley, Drury B., and Linda K. Lawrie. 2015. 'Rethinking the TMY: Is the "Typical" Meteorological Year Best for Building Performance Simulation?' In *Proceedings of BS 2015*. Hyderabad, India.

Davison, A. C., and D. V. Hinkley. 1997. *Bootstrap Methods and Their Application*. 1st ed. Cambridge University Press.

Du, H., C. P. Underwood, and J. S. Edge. 2011. 'Generating Test Reference Years from the UKCP09 Projections and Their Application in Building Energy Simulations'. *Building Services Engineering Research and Technology* 33 (4): 387–406. https://doi.org/10.1177/0143624411418132.

Du, H., C. P. Underwood, and J. S. Edge. 2012. 'Generating Design Reference Years from the UKCP09 Projections and Their Application to Future Air-Conditioning Loads'. *Building Services Engineering Research and Technology* 33 (1): 63–79. https://doi.org/10.1177/0143624411431775.

Eames, Matt. 2016. 'An Update of the UKs Design Summer Years: Probabilistic Design Summer Years for Enhanced Overheating Risk Analysis in Building Design'. *Building Services Engineering Research and Technology*, February. https://doi.org/10.1177/0143624416631131.

Eames, Matt, Tristan Kershaw, and David Coley. 2011. 'On the Creation of Future Probabilistic Design Weather Years from UKCP09'. *Building Services Engineering Research and Technology* 32 (2): 127–142. https://doi.org/10.1177/0143624410379934.

Eames, Matt, Tristan Kershaw, and David Coley. 2012. 'A Comparison of Future Weather Created from Morphed Observed Weather and Created by a Weather Generator'. *Building and Environment* 56 (October): 252–264. https://doi.org/10.1016/j.buildenv.2012.03.006.

Flett, Graeme, and Nick Kelly. 2016. 'An Occupant-Differentiated, Higher-Order Markov Chain Method for Prediction of Domestic Occupancy'. *Energy and Buildings* 125 (August): 219–230. https://doi.org/10.1016/j.enbuild.2016.05.015.

Flett, Graeme, and Nick Kelly. 2017. 'A Disaggregated, Probabilistic, High Resolution Method for Assessment of Domestic Occupancy and Electrical Demand'. *Energy and Buildings* 140 (April): 171–187. https://doi.org/10.1016/j.enbuild.2017.01.069.

Grantham, A. P., P. J. Pudney, and J. W. Boland. 2018. 'Generating Synthetic Sequences of Global Horizontal Irradiation'. *Solar Energy* 162 (March): 500–509. https://doi.org/10.1016/j.solener.2018.01.044.

Guan, Lisa. 2009. 'Preparation of Future Weather Data to Study the Impact of Climate Change on Buildings'. *Building and Environment* 44 (4): 793–800. https://doi.org/10.1016/j.buildenv.2008.05.021.

Hastie, Trevor, Robert Tibshirani, and Jerome Friedman. 2009. *The Elements of Statistical Learning: Data Mining, Inference, and Prediction*. 2nd ed. Springer.

IPCC. 2014. 'Climate Change 2014 Synthesis Report: Summary for Policymakers'. Geneva, Switzerland: Intergovernmental Panel on Climate Change (IPCC). http://epic.awi.de/37530/.

Jentsch, Mark F., Patrick A. B. James, Leonidas Bourikas, and AbuBakr S. Bahaj. 2013. 'Transforming Existing Weather Data for Worldwide Locations to Enable Energy and Building Performance Simulation under Future Climates'. *Renewable Energy* 55 (July): 514–524. https://doi.org/10.1016/j.renene.2012.12.049.

LBNL. 2017. 'References for EnergyPlus v8.8'. Berkley, CA, USA: Lawrence Berkeley National Laboratory.

Magnano, L., John Boland, and R. J. Hyndman. 2008. 'Generation of Synthetic Sequences of Half-Hourly Temperature'. *Environmetrics* 19 (8): 818–835. https://doi.org/10.1002/env.905.

Nik, Vahid M. 2016. 'Making Energy Simulation Easier for Future Climate – Synthesizing Typical and Extreme Weather Data Sets Out of Regional Climate Models (RCMs)'. *Applied Energy* 177 (September): 204–226. https://doi.org/10.1016/j.apenergy.2016.05.107.

NREL, and USDOE. 2017. 'EnergyPlus'. November 2017. https://energyplus.net/weather.

Rastogi, Parag. 2016. 'On the Sensitivity of Buildings to Climate: The Interaction of Weather and Building Envelopes in Determining Future Building Energy Consumption'. PhD, Lausanne, Switzerland: Ecole polytechnique fédérale de Lausanne. EPFL Infoscience. https://doi.org/10.5075/epfl-thesis-6881.

Rastogi, Parag, and Marilyne Andersen. 2015. 'Embedding Stochasticity in Building Simulation Through Synthetic Weather Files'. In *Proceedings of BS 2015*. Hyderabad, India. http://infoscience.epfl.ch/record/208743.

Rastogi, Parag, and Marilyne Andersen. 2016. 'Incorporating Climate Change Predictions in the Analysis of Weather-Based Uncertainty'. In *Proceedings of SimBuild 2016*. Salt Lake City, UT, USA. http://infoscience.epfl.ch/record/208743.

Rastogi, Parag, Mohammad Emtiyaz Khan, and Marilyne Andersen. 2017. 'Gaussian-Process-Based Emulators for Building Performance Simulation'. In *Proceedings of BS 2017*. San Francisco, CA, USA: IBPSA.

Remund, Jan, Stefan Mueller, Stefan Kunz, and Christoph Schilter. 2012. 'METEONORM Handbook Part II : Theory'. http://meteonorm.com/download/software/mn70/.

Troup, Luke, and David Fannon. 2016. 'Morphing Climate Data to Simulate Building Energy Consumption'. In *Proceedings of SimBuild 2016*. Salt Lake City, UT, USA. https://www.researchgate.net/publication/311715661_Morphing_Climate_Data_to_Simulate_Building_Energy_Consumption.

Vuuren, Detlef P. van, Jae Edmonds, Mikiko Kainuma, Keywan Riahi, Allison Thomson, Kathy Hibbard, George C. Hurtt, et al. 2011. 'The Representative Concentration Pathways: An Overview'. *Climatic Change* 109 (1–2): 5–31. https://doi.org/10.1007/s10584-011-0148-z.

Wilcox, S., and W. Marion. 2008. 'Users' Manual for TMY3 Data Sets'. http://www.nrel.gov/docs/fy08osti/43156.pdf.

WRCP. 2017. 'CORDEX'. World Climate Research Programme CORDEX. 1 April 2017. http://www.cordex.org/.

# 4
# TOOLS FOR COMMUNITY ENERGY EMPOWERMENT

## A Co-Design Approach

*Bess Krietemeyer*

### Introduction

#### The Role of Climate Data Visualization

How can visualization tools empower community members to better understand and contribute to building and urban adaptation strategies in the face of climate change? Communicating anticipated climate change impacts and adaptive measures to a wide audience is important yet challenging due to the vast amount of climate data, the complexity of climate models, and global scale issues. In the context of the built environment, information visualization has the capacity to convey and interpret complex climate data into applicable knowledge and actionable information for varying audiences, including researchers, architectural and urban design professionals, policy makers, and individual energy consumers.

In recent years a focus on climate change visualization tools has grown to foster environmental knowledge and literacy while supporting policy making as well as citizen engagement (Rosenow-Williams 2018). These include climate data visualization web sources such as the U.S. Climate Resilience Toolkit Climate Explorer (NOAA 2020) and Global Assimilation of Information for Action (GAIA) project. Both have a global focus and draw connections between climate change and issues such as health and food security (Strong et al. 2011). Other tools for detailed disaster preparedness use information and communication technologies to visualize and anticipate natural hazards and related uncertainties (Kunz, Gret-Regamey, and Hurni, 2011), which can be used in the city planning process. Geographic information systems (GIS) software has incorporated utility networks for city planners and government officials preparing for emergency response (ESRI 2020). One of the challenges across many climate visualization tools is that they tend to have a global focus, making it difficult to relate at a local level within a geographically defined community. Many are aimed at enhanced understanding rather than actionable measures.

Additionally, the knowledge produced for the tools is largely expert-driven, without necessarily considering its applicability for those who could directly benefit from the tool's feedback (Shaw et al. 2009). The increasing complexity of climate models and amount of climate-related data call for interactive map-based tools that support communication, exploration, and analysis for a broad user profile (Neset et al. 2016). As a result, a small but growing number of web-based tools aimed at novice users are being designed to support adaptation actions and individual decision processes more locally. Interactive visualization tools that target individual homeowners aim to both assess climate change risks and also identify adaptation measures specific to their location and house type (Johansson et al. 2015). Such online tools can help homeowners and tenants increase resilience by visualizing resilience indicators at the home and community levels (Fannon and Laboy 2018).

Incorporating user feedback to inform tool development is another challenge. User-focused studies of visualization tools supporting climate change adaptation are limited and, with the exception of those aimed at novice users, generally address the knowledge base and interests of experts. However, lessons learned emphasize the importance of ease of use, clarity of information, varying degrees of interactivity, and actionable feedback. The scarce number of climate visualization tools that do offer feedback on adaptive measures for a range of knowledge bases demonstrates a need for tools that go beyond illustrating global or regional climate issues toward those that provide local and actionable feedback. In order to make environmental data and adaptation measures meaningful, the data must be contextualized, visibly accessible, and capable of cultivating citizen engagement. For both emergency management situations and for long-term sustainable behaviors—data visualization that supports open, informed conversation, and understanding across stakeholders is crucial.

## *Energy Feedback Technologies*

Tools that tailor environmental feedback and adaptation measures are readily available for the individual energy consumer. Energy feedback technologies—from smart thermostats to web portals to customized mobile applications—can assist in both immediate and long-term energy conservation and planning. These technologies can play a role in reducing resource consumption in buildings by giving individuals information about their energy consumption patterns, including personalized tips, that can be used to reinforce and suggest behavior change. Advances in data sensing, storage, and dissemination have made it possible to collect information about energy consumers' behaviors, and to represent this data in the form of ambient displays, gamification systems, and dashboard designs for both mobile and web platforms (Karlin, Ford, Squirers 2014). Customized mobile application and dashboard products have the capability to integrate directly with the local utility and can alert the individual consumer about their energy consumption in ways that might alleviate grid pressures and increase customer savings. Tailored feedback might include real-time data on multiple energy-consuming devices, daily, weekly, or monthly energy consumption patterns, real-time cost, as well as actions that can be taken to increase financial savings or alleviate stresses on the grid (Suen and Hershkowitz 2015).

Individual and household-centered applications offer valuable device-specific feedback and customizable tips for saving energy. However, they focus on the energy consumer who receives information through the privacy of their personal device, thus placing the onus to actually change behaviors on the individual themselves. Incentives focus on financial gain or other egoistic concerns, with little to no exposure or comparison to others' energy use, motivations, or collective impacts on grid reliability or the environment. The presentation of the data within many existing energy feedback technologies is not necessarily tied to a geographically defined space, making it difficult for a person to situate oneself relative to familiar or otherwise vulnerable areas. Within the isolated experience of such energy feedback systems, questions of visibility, accountability, and social consciousness also come into play. How can feedback technologies support a dialogue between individuals and their community, making the experience a social one? How can they enable the development and delivery of environmentally beneficial feedback through alternative modes and across spatiotemporal scales?

### *Sociotechnical Energy Feedback*

A unique category of sociotechnical energy feedback systems is emerging that recognizes the integral roles that technology, community participation, and identity creation can play in addressing issues of sustainability and resilience. These systems, which are largely informed by social psychology, aim to reintroduce feedback at multiple scales to motivate and empower conservation, promote systems thinking, and build pro-environmental identity, at both individual and community levels (Petersen 2016). Petersen et al. (2014) argue that we can build more sustainable and resilient communities and cultures by engineering new information flows that realign our thinking and behavior with the realities of the ecosystems that support us. Peterson et al. (2016) has developed a variety of novel approaches focused on sociotechnical feedback systems that have the potential to reconnect humans to nature and motivate behaviors that are more attuned to ecological constraints and opportunities (Petersen, Frantz, Shammin 2014). The approaches have included real-time energy monitoring and display systems in public buildings, environmental 'orbs' that communicate energy consumption through dynamic ambient lighting, and an environmental dashboard website that incorporates multiple scales and dimensions of feedback, including building consumption, citywide energy flows, and a 'community voices' social media webpage to engage more stakeholder participation. Eco-visualization tools that merge art and technology are another thread of the sociotechnical approach to communicate climate change issues through creative uses of media and real-time energy performance data. A common aim with these approaches is to establish longer-term ecological and behavioral change (Holmes, 2007).

Other sociotechnical approaches build on the concept of creative citizenship, which has the capacity to strengthen and support community through tools that promote social interaction and co-creation (Lee 2015). Over the last decade, creative citizenship has been used to promote citizen engagement within political decision-making, especially in the context of smart cities. The use of e-participation tools, such as open data websites or the use of social media platforms, are aimed at assisting governments in smart cities planning by creating public virtual spaces for collaboration and participation (Bolívar 2018). They demonstrate strong potential for community users to provide valuable feedback and insights and contribute to the co-production of public services, particularly energy production and distribution (Granier and Kudo 2016). One of the main challenges for creative citizenship is understanding how to design tools to facilitate deliberation from all stakeholders and support collaborative working environments (Bolívar 2018), signifying a need for tools that enable deeper, more meaningful interactions between users. This raises questions about the social implications of virtual interactions versus the benefits of interacting with other stakeholders in a shared physical space and context.

The advancement of interactive platforms for collaborative design and data feedback can be seen in recent work such as MIT's CityScope project, a data-driven tangible user interface (TUI) for enabling iterative, evidence-based decision-making between traditionally siloed stakeholders (Alonso et al. 2018). Similarly, Cool Cities is a TUI game for children to design environmentally friendly cities around different social and financial objectives (Doshi et al. 2017). ColorTable, another TUI, supports stakeholder discussions of urban projects through constructing mixed reality scenes (Maquil 2015). Results from recent TUI research demonstrates the promise of novel data visualization methods and intuitive interfaces to promote energy awareness and stakeholder engagement. One of the challenges is achieving candid engagement from large groups of participants without the presence of authorities. Current methods to incorporate user feedback can be somewhat limited to observations or recordings in controlled lab settings where user identities are exposed to researchers and decision-makers, and a moderator is typically present to assist users.

Although the focus of existing TUIs has not necessarily been on climate adaptation and actionable feedback at local levels, the growing interest in interactive platforms that promote energy awareness, citizen engagement, and shared visualization experiences suggests a fundamentally new type of environmental feedback approach that connects rather than separates humans from each other, with a focus on community-level participation. What they also suggest is the need for tools that create a meaningful social experience through interactive processes that not only motivate action, but sustain user engagement over time.

## Objectives: Toward Co-Designed Climate Adaptation

Research focused on participatory capacity building in the context of climate change demonstrates that the effective ways to holistically communicate climate science include the ability to contextualize climate change impacts on the regional and local level by means of geographically defined communities. This allows people to 'encounter' the possible impacts and make them more meaningful. Another key component to effective communication is the ability to visualize links between climate change impacts and behavioral change and action. Finally, the co-production of knowledge can improve ownership and social robustness of problems and solutions (Shaw et al. 2009). Based on these essential capabilities, recommendations for participatory capacity building for climate change action at the local level point toward new explorations into the science-art interface for the creation of scenarios, visuals, and narratives that address issues in a credible and compelling way, to "overcome the politics and behavior 'as usual'" (Shaw et al. 2009). Building on the recent sociotechnical approaches and recommendations for effective communication, this research asks: how can climate adaptation tools visually contextualize data about energy and our built environment to engage a wide audience on the impacts of climate change at a local level? And how can energy feedback tools empower community members to better understand and contribute to the co-production of building and urban climate adaptation strategies?

In addressing the questions above, the research presented here emphasizes a co-design approach for collective energy awareness, empowerment, and behavioral change. Building on Petersen's concept of pro-environmental identity, and inspired by goals of creative citizenship relative to climate adaptation, this work focuses on developing an interactive energy visualization platform as both an educational and a design tool for the community. The objectives are to engage community members in collectively visualizing climate conditions and simulating design adaptation strategies. The platform focuses on three critical capabilities not yet integrated within existing climate visualization and energy feedback tools: (1) interactive visualization of existing and anticipated climate conditions within a geographically defined community, making data accessible and familiar to users; (2) comparison of energy resource and demand in a spatial and temporal way to augment the integration of building-scale renewable energy systems; (3) exploration of existing and future scenarios of climate-responsive building and urban design conditions through energy simulation workflows. It seeks to make the interaction with energy data a social experience by enabling users to view and overlay the results of their visualizations with other users' selections in a shared setting. Critically, this platform combines climate, urban, and building data into a collaborative, user-driven visualization experience, where community participants can explore datasets to understand their local conditions while co-creating strategies for building and neighborhood climate adaptation (Figure 4.1).

In contrast to virtual e-participation tools and data visualization websites, the platform presented here is a physically located interactive installation with digitally projected media displayed on a 3D-constructed model that includes buildings, streets, parks, and infrastructure. The digital media is activated through gestural movements and uses projection mapping for the dynamic display of information onto the model surfaces. The platform is designed to incorporate climate data into a 3D geospatial visualization experience to observe existing and anticipated climate conditions, including typical weather and extreme events. It also supports the dynamic display of building and urban data, whereby users can view data layers related to existing building and city performance, such as hourly energy use, locations of green infrastructure, and utility networks. The platform provides a data visualization framework for users to selectively view datasets and strategies to explore combinations of building designs,

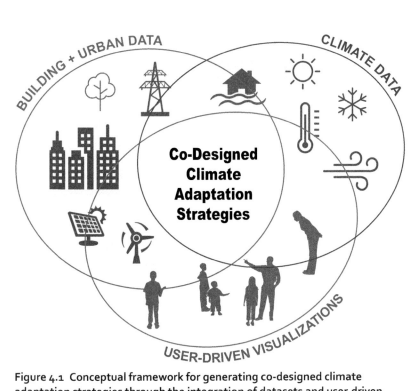

Figure 4.1 Conceptual framework for generating co-designed climate adaptation strategies through the integration of datasets and user-driven visualizations.

energy systems, and energy management across different temporal scales and spatial zones.

Designed for multiple users to interact simultaneously, the platform seeks to invite participants to collectively shape the types of feedback and design adaptation that is made visible, contributing to community-level identity formation. It aims to encourage the community to participate as an active, coordinated, and informed agent with the ability to visually explore relationships between energy resource, demand, and the impacts of future building and urban design scenarios. The ultimate goal is to understand how tools like this one might empower community members and enable a co-design process—one that offers architects, urban planners, and policy makers new insights on the values and design opportunities for strengthening the adaptive qualities of a mid-sized city.

## MethoDS: Development of an Interactive Energy Visualization Platform

### Testbed: Syracuse, New York

Focusing on the Central New York climate, the City of Syracuse presents a useful testbed to develop the platform for the co-design process because of its challenging climate, infrastructure, and scale. Syracuse experiences extreme precipitation falling in heavy events, in particular lake effect snowfall (DEC 2015), and two to three times more heating degree days than most northeastern coastal cities. Like other mid-sized rustbelt cities, it requires adaptive management of extreme weather events within a 20th-century aging infrastructure—including buildings, bridges, roads, water and sewer lines, and other utility services—representing a need for smart and efficient solutions to designing, maintaining, and repairing its city fabric. As one of 12 U.S. cities selected to participate in the expansion of its Innovation Teams program,[1] Syracuse has government initiatives to engage citizens in human-centered and data-driven approaches to create solutions that offer meaningful results for residents. These have taken the form of open-source city data websites, community-driven workshops, data hackathons, and ideation meetings, led by the city's Innovation Team (i-team 2020). With a recent focus on housing and infrastructure issues, the combined human-centered and data-driven approach has paved a pathway for community ideas to reach policy decision-making. Here lies potential to bring community co-designed climate adaptation priorities and ideas to city planners and policy makers.

Two prototypes of the platform have been installed in Syracuse, New York: one located at the Syracuse Center of Excellence for Environmental and Energy Systems (SyracuseCoE), an academic and industry research facility for Central New York. Here the platform prototype is developed in the Interactive Design and Visualization Lab (IDVL) by

[1] The Bloomberg Philanthropies program aims to improve the capacity of City Halls to effectively design and implement new approaches that improve citizen's lives—relying on data and open innovation to help mayors address urban challenges. https://www.bloomberg.org/press/releases/bloomberg-philanthropies-expands-innovationteam-program-12-new-american-cities/.

a team of faculty and students from the Syracuse University School of Architecture, led by Bess Krietemeyer and Amber Bartosh, in collaboration with visual artist and interactive software developer Lorne Covington of NOIRFLUX. At the IDVL and with NOIRFLUX, data visualizations and interaction methods are created and simulated on the prototype before testing in a public setting. A larger prototype was installed at the Milton J. Rubenstein Museum of Science and Technology (MoST), located in the downtown Syracuse area. Being situated at the MoST, the platform is open to interpretation, play, and exploration by visitors of all ages and backgrounds. It is also where the research team can gather the most candid feedback on the content being displayed and usability of the interactive system. In this museum setting, the platform steps out of the black box of the research lab and into the public realm for continuous user testing and input on how to make it more engaging and meaningful—an iterative, community-driven approach to discovering effective ways to communicate climate-related information.

## An Interactive Experience with Energy Data

The digital-physical experience with the platform is possible through a combination of projectors, depth sensors, and interactive design software, creating a novel encounter with climate and energy data in the context of one's own community. Multiple projectors are positioned to display digital media on all surfaces of the scaled physical model of the downtown area. A large screen provides an informational display of icons, graphics, and directions for users to select and view datasets with a wave of a hand. Users can make a selection which gets mapped to the 3D model as an information spotlight. In this way, data is not only viewed on a single screen by an individual user; instead, multiple users' data selections, browsing patterns, and overlays can be dynamically mapped, overlapped, and made visible to each other in the same physical space, creating potentially unexpected connections between people and data. This sets the stage for participatory engagement in creating layers of shared visual mappings that illustrate environmental and energy use conditions specific to the local geography and climate.

The user experience sequence is intended to be simple and straightforward: when a person approaches the platform from a few feet away, a depth sensor picks up that person's presence, which triggers an icon to pop up on the screen, signaling to them to point and select from the display menu screen. When they do, the icon directs them to point to the model below. By extending one's arm to the model and moving it around, a visitor can point to different buildings or neighborhoods and view the area's energy or climate data spotlight dynamically mapped across the 3D buildings (Krietemeyer et al. 2019). The spotlight follows that person's hand as they explore different areas around the model until they select a different dataset or step out of the user tracking zone. The spotlight can illustrate a particular type

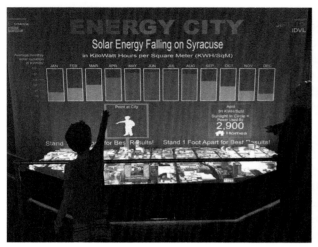

Figure 4.2 Images of the interactive energy visualization platform installation at the Milton J. Rubenstein MoST in Syracuse, NY.

of climate or energy resource through graphics and color, such as a false color heat map of solar radiation hitting that area of the city. In this example, the average monthly solar radiation data is calculated as kWh/m², which gets converted into information that is more widely understood, such as the number of homes that could be powered by harnessing solar energy in that zone (Figure 4.2). Through this interactive experience, the personal spotlight provides a lens through which to explore energy data that is contextually specific, comparable to other datasets at the same scale, and spatial. The data is not only mapped onto the flat horizontal ground surfaces, but can be mapped onto building facades and roofs. This has the advantage of comparing different datasets or design strategies on one or more 3D buildings, such as green roofs combined with façade retrofits, to explore the potential energy savings of multiple systems and their impacts at different scales.

## Software Workflow and Development of Spatiotemporal Data Visualizations

The workflow utilizes both open-source and commercially available software, and is intended to be applicable to any community. It combines data from GIS tools, urban building energy simulations, and climate analyses. The applicability of GIS tools is becoming more widespread across disciplines; for the architecture and urban design community, access to building and city data, such as land use, building type, and building age, can be mapped with other demographic and climate data in order to draw connections between information such as building energy use, renewable resources, urban surface temperatures, green infrastructure, or air quality. The growing number of geospatial datasets, resources, and mapping tools is expanding the possibilities, responsibilities, and potential impact of communicating these data. How the collapse of this information gets viewed, translated, and understood by the non-expert in a meaningful way is something this research seeks to explore.

To construct the digital model used for generating simulation-based visuals, a computer model of the downtown Syracuse neighborhood was created in the Rhinoceros 3D CAD modeling software. Model surfaces were mapped with textures representing building and ground surfaces, which provide the base imagery for new data projection overlays. The climate data visualizations were simulated through the DIVA plug-in for Rhinoceros, which uses the 3D model geometry and typical meteorological year (TMY) weather data to generate monthly maps of incident solar radiation. Future spatialized weather datasets could also be simulated using morphed weather data files based on downscaled climate and hydrology projection models to show anticipated climate conditions, like increasing temperatures or precipitation. Even extreme weather scenarios, such as severe winds, ice, and heavy snowfall accumulation, could be visualized with morphed weather data files to highlight neighborhood zones in need of snow removal or at risk of power outages.

## Designing the Interactive User Experience

Well-designed interactive and user experience sequences are essential to attracting and sustaining visitor engagement. The interactive experience designed through this platform is based on a novel workflow that links custom coding in interactive design software with 3D depth sensors that capture user locations and gestures as 3D data 'pointclouds.' The custom-coded environment, called 'vvvv,' is a live programming environment (vvvv 2020), which enables a full viewing of the pointcloud depth data that drives the selection of datasets projected on the model (Figure 4.3). It also provides a useful record of how users are engaging the platform including which selections were made and when (Figure 4.4). Through this programming environment, updates to the system can be made on the fly and immediately visible to platform participants (Krietemeyer et al. 2019).

The interactive workflow presents new opportunities for data collection and user observation in the actual context of use. It simultaneously provides methods to test the usability of the gestural interaction sequences, the activity levels of the platform, and the types of content being generated. Prior user studies with the platform have demonstrated the value of utilizing this approach to collect unbiased user feedback. The user behaviors can be viewed in real-time or recorded, which creates a fluid process between modifying the content and receiving immediate feedback (Krietemeyer et al. 2019). Thus, designing and refining the platform continues to be an ongoing iterative process, as new dataset options or gestural interaction sequences get introduced to the system, and users' responses to those changes are easily viewable to the design programmer. Both the research process

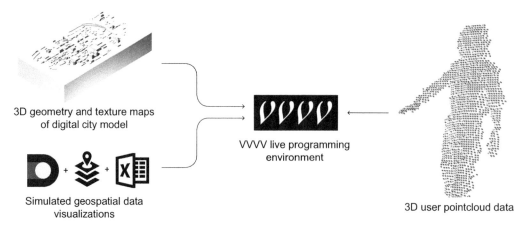

Figure 4.3 Diagram of the software workflow integrating a 3D digital model, simulated geospatial data visualizations, and 3D user pointcloud data into the vvvv live programming environment.

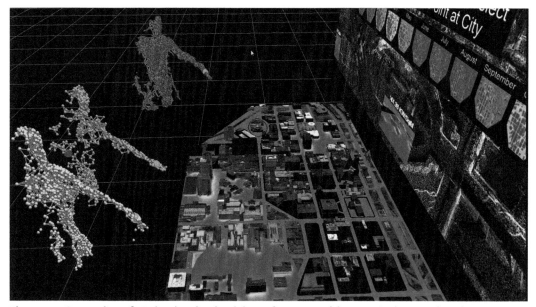

Figure 4.4 Screenshot of 3D depth pointcloud data of museum visitors gesturing to select datasets to view within the installation. Courtesy NOIRFLUX.

and information produced are enhanced by real-time multi-user feedback that is continuous and ongoing, so that improvements to the design of the overall user experience can be made more quickly, which increases the amount of time each user spends engaging with it.

### Opportunities for Co-Designed Climate Adaptation Strategies

The spatiotemporal mapping of typical and future energy and climate conditions provides the basis for visualizing different forms of adaptation, ranging from building- to urban-scale strategies, and from immediate response to long-term planning and design. With the ongoing development and integration of geospatial visualizations into the software workflow, new opportunities for co-designed climate adaptation strategies are possible. A key aspect to the projective nature of the visualization platform is the ability for users to explore datasets and adaptation strategies that can be collectively compared and layered in unexpected ways. This could allow for the visualization of multiple environmental hazards simultaneously, which may drive solutions that are not limited to isolated incidents but rather tackle various scales and phases of adaptation. Impacts on power, traffic patterns, and access to safety resources could be viewed alongside data such as sociodemographic information, building age, and predicted energy use. Many types of spatialized building and urban data can be overlaid and related in ways that might not have occurred to any one individual before, leading to deeper insights and to the potential for emergent interactions between different layers of information. The convergence of multiple user's values, perspectives, and creations might lead to strategies that would otherwise not be considered in isolation (Figure 4.5).

At the building scale, the platform has the potential to demonstrate adaptation through design or behavioral changes in relationship to energy use. Users could select from a menu of building-scale design or retrofit strategies such as altering the window to wall ratio (WWR), glazing materials, or exterior insulated finishing systems (EIFS), to selecting behavioral changes such as energy consumption

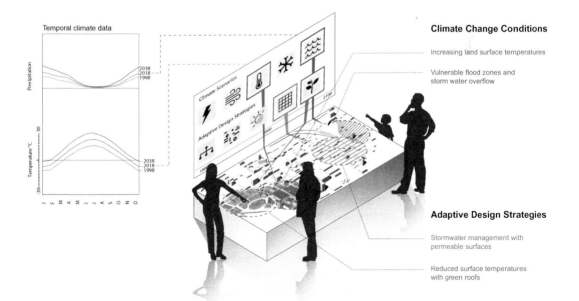

Figure 4.5 Diagram illustrating the translation of temporal climate data charts into spatiotemporal climate change visualizations.

load-shifting, and the use of smart appliances and thermostats. One way to view the impacts of those strategies is to simulate the building energy use intensity (EUI), expressed as energy per square foot per year, using a 3D color-coded map. Urban building energy modeling software such as the Rhino-integrated Urban Modeling Interface (umi) simulates building EUI by assigning model attributes like building use type, materials, occupancy schedules, and equipment schedules. Based on those parameters, the simulations can illustrate when and how much energy buildings of a certain type or size typically use to maintain comfortable inhabitable conditions. The 3D EUI maps can be compared or viewed with other data through the platform, such as climate data, which could highlight opportunities for matching renewable resources with building energy demands, or for identifying strategies for load-shifting based on building type and land use. Renewable energy resources could be better portrayed as assets with potential to be harnessed for passive environmental control strategies and renewable energy use, rather than forces incompatible with human comfort and building performance. Certain buildings or neighborhoods in the city might have greater potential for harnessing solar energy and daylight through passive strategies such as thermal mass and building orientation, or actively through thermal solar heating or building-integrated photovoltaics. Spatializing the impacts of building-scale strategies at the community level provides insights as to how surrounding buildings or infrastructure might impact a building's exposure to renewable resources, like solar or wind. Incorporating building-level adaptation could also indicate the potential of certain buildings to perform, during extreme weather events, as grid-interactive efficient buildings to avert system stress.

Alternative 'what if' scenarios could be explored at the urban scale, where users might choose to visualize the proliferation of green infrastructures such as green roofs, rain gardens, or permeable pavement in place of parking lots, and learn how those design strategies impact urban heat island, air quality, storm water runoff, and community-level energy consumption. For public stakeholder acceptance of urban scale strategies, it is essential to have community engagement to help people understand the trade-offs of such design interventions, and to see environmental and sociocultural benefits (Culligan 2018). The platform aims to provide a mechanism for stakeholders to engage with design strategies by exploring the trade-offs in a familiar context. It also provides a mode of documenting user-driven visualizations to identify priority areas and design ideas.

Because multiple users have the opportunity to choose datasets and view them on the 3D projected model using gestural interactions that stay with them, platforms such as this could produce a dynamic collage of diverse interests, datasets, explorations, and attitudes, allowing viewers to collectively explore and imagine design futures (Figure 4.6). Recordings of visitor actions and user-driven visualizations create a unique method of documentation of how people are

TOOLS FOR COMMUNITY ENERGY EMPOWERMENT    63

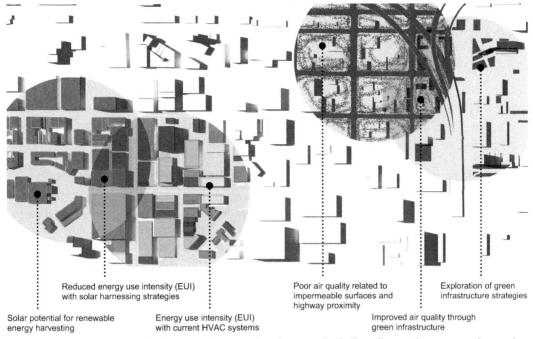

Figure 4.6 Diagram illustrating layers of intersecting datasets, including climate data, strategies, and potential impacts.

making selections, what data gets compared, which strategies get the most attention, and the emergence of strategies that might result from unexpected layering of spatiotemporal information. Thus, the user-driven visualization approach has the potential to create an evolving library of co-designed solutions, ones which inform the platform for further viewing and investigation. With the ongoing evolution of data visualizations depicting future building and urban design scenarios, a co-design process may emerge, whereby users engage in design exploration, collaboration, and debate about what the future of their community might hold. But rather than resolving a singular and ideal design solution, the aim is to empower community members by providing collective awareness, curiosity, communication, and creative design exploration made visible to others.

## Discussion and Future Directions

The interactive energy visualization platform is an ongoing experimental process, a sociotechnical approach to climate visualization and adaptation intended to communicate diverse values and generate ideas. It takes advantage of creating and debating in a physical social setting, much like a community meeting, but with interactive technologies that enable an open process of participation with visual evidence of interests and ideas. With multiple ways to observe and explore the projected content, the platform offers a spectrum of interactive options that might cater to different learning styles and paces. It is an approach toward participatory capacity building, behavioral shifting, and citizen engagement that is fundamentally different from the individually focused online tools in energy feedback or e-participation. The interactive social setting and the continually evolving visual outputs could potentially motivate and sustain user engagement over longer periods of time because of the unique experience each time one visits the platform. By allowing individual users to leave their imprint in the platform's memory, whether it is a navigational pathway through climate data or a series of adaptation strategies, the platform creates a hub for collective ideation and citizen science that could lead to better informed decision-making.

With the computational framework and physical prototype in place and with methods for continuous user data collection underway, new directions for future work seek to incorporate more geospatial visualizations, integrate climate model projection data, and conduct user studies with key stakeholders. The integration of future microclimate data and extreme weather event data is necessary moving forward. There are many projective climate model approaches, and considerations should include validity of the model and data formatting that aligns with simulation capabilities and the platform software workflow. Downscaling is a critical factor for visualizing the impact of design strategies at the neighborhood level. Incorporating downscaled TMY and projective climate data that take into consideration microclimatic conditions will yield more valuable results in terms of potential impacts of combined strategies. Expanding the software framework to utilize big data and the Internet of Things could inform methods for modeling future microclimates, as well as the design strategies that could mitigate or adapt through distributed smart sensing systems in and around buildings. By providing a framework to visualize future scenarios, the platform could inspire innovative data collection techniques, such as distributed GPS sensors on vehicles, or other crowdsourcing techniques that would increase the resolution of data available and thus improve adaptation approaches that are increasingly specific to local contexts. This work also demonstrates the need for more holistic modeling frameworks that support the visualization and management of multiscalar infrastructural systems like utility networks as they relate to building performance. This could enable the visualization of strategies for power grid storage and delivery, vulnerability assessment, and emergency response at different scales.

Obtaining key stakeholder participation and developing pathways to decision-making are important areas for the ideas and discussions generated through platforms such as this to be applicable in the real world. Part of this challenge could be addressed through the platform's method for tracking and documenting user feedback, which includes records of user actions and their selected data visualizations and strategies. An important consideration relative to the user sensing and tracking approach deals with potential ethical and security concerns that may impact agreements to continuously document user-generated visualizations. Although the individual's identity remains anonymous through the current depth sensing settings, the resolution of the user pointclouds is optimized to facilitate interaction with the platform and has potential to increase. Future work should examine issues of ownership and control over the documentation of participants' actions in regard to the level of pointcloud detail that gets recorded. Further studies are also needed to develop methods to streamline and package the data collection and analysis of participant input in order to effectively communicate this information to municipal and decision-making entities. Studies that involve structured user evaluations and interactions with key stakeholders could leverage the platform for identifying the most pressing climate change concerns, prioritization of strategies, and co-designed solutions for certain neighborhoods. The integration of behavioral science and environmental psychology methods could bring valuable insights to understanding how various stakeholders respond to information and assess appropriate scales of action, as well as how they identify possible barriers and pathways to desirable futures for the community. Finally, as with any climate visualization or energy feedback tool, accessibility to the platform is key both for gathering feedback for improvement, and more importantly for making the co-design process more widespread. Methods to make the platform easily replicable and accessible to other communities, cities, and rural areas across diverse climate regions is an important step in the design research. Enabling expansive use of the platform through web-based extensions could enable many voices to be represented and continuously informed, thus empowering a broad range of users from diverse backgrounds to build on the evolving collection of co-designed strategies and values that are critical to climate change awareness and effective adaptation.

## Acknowledgments

This research was supported by the New York State Department of Economic Development through the Syracuse Center of Excellence (SyracuseCoE) in Environmental and Energy Systems, the Syracuse University School of Architecture, and the Milton J. Rubenstein MoST. The work would not be possible without the contributions of collaborators such as Lorne Covington of NOIRFLUX, Amber Bartosh of the Syracuse University School of Architecture, and Kevin Lucas of the MoST. Special thanks go to Syracuse University graduate students Raward El Contar, Harshita Kataria, Katharina Koerber, and Chenxie Li for their contributions to the data simulations and visualizations.

## References

Alonso, Luis, Zhang, Yan Rya, Grignard, Arnaud, Noyman, Ariel, Sakai, Yasuchi, ElKatsha, Markus, Doorley, Ronan, and Kent Larson. 2018. "CityScope: A Data-Driven Interactive Simulation Tool for Urban Design.

Use Case Volpe." In *Unifying Themes in Complex Systems IX. ICCS 2018. Springer Proceedings in Complexity.* Edited by Morales A., Gershenson C., Braha D., Minai A., and Bar-Yam. Springer: 253–261.

Bolívar, Manuel Pedro Rodríguez. 2018. "Creative Citizenship: The New Wave for Collaborative Environments in Smart Cities." *Academia Revista Latinoamericana de Administración* 31(1): 277–302.

Culligan, Patricia. 2018. "Green Infrastructure and Urban Sustainability: Recent Advances and Future Challenges." *Proceedings of the 7th International Building Physics Conference (IBPC2018): Healthy, Intelligent and Resilient Buildings and Urban Environments*, September 23–26, Syracuse, New York, USA. https://doi.org/10.14305/ibpc2018.

Doshi, Sonia, Hojjat, Kimiya, Lin, Anita, and Paulo Blikstein. 2017. "Cool Cities: A Tangible User Interface for Thinking Critically about Climate Change." *Proceedings of the 2017 Conference on Interaction Design and Children*, June 27–30, Standford, CA, USA.

ESRI. n.d. "ArcGIS for Emergency Management." Accessed February 1, 2020. https://www.esri.com/en-us/arcgis/products/arcgis-for-emergency-management.

Fannon, D., and Michelle Laboy. "Resilient Homes Online Design Aid: Connecting Research and Practice for Socially Resilient Communities." *Design and Resilience: Proceedings of the 2018 AIA/ACSA Intersections Symposium*, Washington, DC, USA.

Granier, Benoit, and Hiroko Kudo. 2016. "How Are Citizens Involved in Smart Cities? Analysing Citizen Participation in Japanese 'Smart Communities'." *Information Polity* 21(1): 61–76.

Holmes, Tiffany. 2007. "Eco-visualization: Combining Art and Technology to Reduce Energy Consumption." *Proceedings of the 6th ACM SIGCHI Conference on Creativity & Cognition*, June 13–15, Washington DC, USA: 153–162.

Johansson, Jimmy, Opach, Tomasz, Glaas, Erik, Neset, Tina-Simone, Navarra, Carlo, and Jan Ketil Rod Bjorn-Ola Linner. 2015. "VisAdapt: A Visualization Tool to Support Climate Change Adaptation." *IEEE Computer Graphics and Applications* 37(2): 54–65.

Karlin, Beth, Ford, Rebecca, and Cassandra Squiers. 2014. "Energy Feedback Technology: A Review and Taxonomy of Products and Platforms." *Energy Efficiency* 7(3): 377–399.

Krietemeyer, Bess, Bartosh, Amber, and Lorne Covington. 2019. "A Shared Realities Workflow for Interactive Design Using Virtual Reality and 3D Depth Sensing." *International Journal of Architectural Computing* 17(2): 220–235.

Kunz, M., Gret-Regamey, A., and L. Hurni. 2011. "Customized Visualization of Natural Hazards Assessment Results and Associated Uncertainties through Interactive Functionality." *Cartography and Geographic Information Science* 38: 232–242.

Lee, Stephen. 2015. "Creative Citizenship and the Public Policy Process: A Flibbertijibbet, a Will-O-The-Wisp, a Clown?" *Cultural Science Journal* 8:1, 85–90.

Maquil, Valerie. 2015. "Towards Understanding the Design Space of Tangible User Interfaces for Collaborative Urban Planning." *Interacting with Computers* 28(3): 332–351.

National Oceanic and Atmospheric Administration (NOAA). n.d. "U.S. Climate Resilience Toolkit Climate Explorer." Accessed February 1, 2020. https://toolkit.climate.gov/.

New York State Department of Environmental Conservation (DEC). 2015. "Observed and Projected Climate Change in New York State: An Overview." *Final Report for the Community Risk and Resiliency Act (CRRA) Drafting*

*Teams*. http://www.dec.ny.gov/docs/administration_pdf/climbkgncrra.pdf.

Neset, Tina-Simone, Opach, Tomasz, Lion, Peter, Lilja, Anna, and Jimmy Johansson. 2016. "Map-Based Web Tools Supporting Climate Change Adaptation." *The Professional Geographer* 68(1): 103–114.

Petersen, John. 2016. "Bringing Environmental Dashboard to Your Community." https://environmentaldashboard.org/bring-dashboard-to-your-community.

Petersen, John, Frantz, Cindy, and Rumi Shammin. 2014. "Using Sociotechnical Feedback to Engage, Educate, Motivate, and Empower Environmental Thought and Action." *The Solutions Journal* 5(1): 79–87.

Rosenow-Williams, K. 2018. "Visualizing Climate Change Adaptation." *Visual Methodologies* 5(2): 21–34.

Shaw, Allison, Sheppard, Stephen, Burch, Sarah, Flanders, David, Wiek, Arnim, Carmichael, Jeff, Robinson, John, and Stewart Cohen. 2009. "Making Local Futures Tangible—Synthesizing, Downscaling, and Visualizing Climate Change Scenarios for Participatory Capacity Building." *Global Environmental Change* 19(4): 447–463.

Suen, Ka-Chuan, Hershkowitz, and J. Cole. 2015. "Real-Time Monitoring and Analysis of Energy Use." U.S. Patent 2015/0112617 A1.

Strong, Shadrian, Schaefer, Robert, Kaushiva, Alpana, Paxton, Larry, and Andrew Higgins. 2011. "Visualizing the Impact of Climate Change with GAIA." https://www.researchgate.net/publication/258471299_Visualizing_the_Impact_of_Climate_Change_with_GAIA.

Syracuse Innovation Team (i-team). n.d. *Innovation Team.* Accessed February 1, 2020. http://www.innovatesyracuse.com/.

vvvv. n.d. "vvvv-a multipurpose toolkit." Accessed February 1, 2020. www.vvvv.org.

# 5
# RHOnDA

## An Online Tool to Help Homeowners and Tenants Increase Resilience

*Michelle Laboy and David Fannon*

### Introduction

Resilience of the residential fabric in the face of disasters—particularly enabling residents to shelter-in-place—is essential to adapt the built environment to the new normal caused by global climate change. This is a significant challenge; as in the United States alone, there were approximately 120 million units of housing in 2015, of which nearly 70% were single-family homes (United States Census Bureau 2015). Historical homeownership rates fluctuate, but trends suggest nearly two thirds of residents are homeowners (United States Census Bureau 2011) representing highly diffuse-control. Climate disasters generate significant losses in property, with global insured losses constituting close to $135 billion in 2017, half of which took place in the United States (Munich Re 2018). Beyond property value, emergency measures cannot shelter the entire population, and damage or loss of a home causes severe life disruptions, particularly in the repetitive residential fabric of small buildings in urban areas. The US Census records 81% of the US population in "urban" areas; however, this combines cities and suburbs into one category. Recent efforts to disaggregate the figures indicate that the fastest growing cities in the United States are majority suburban, that the boundaries between urban and suburban may not align with the political boundaries of city governments, and that the national rate of growth of suburban areas is faster than urban areas (Kolko 2015). Another strategy to add granularity to the census data uses the population size of the jurisdiction, finding that 75% of the urban population lives in small towns (Berg 2012). These findings suggest that a large portion of the existing, under-designed, and vulnerable housing units are found in suburban or exurban areas with ad-hoc or poor planning, or in small towns, which may also have limited access to the resources of large city centers currently planning for climate change adaptation. These facts, combined with the reversing trend of the wealthy moving to prosperous city centers, the suburbanization of minorities, and predominant and fast-growing white population of the exurbs (Frey

2011), further complicate the intersection of social vulnerability, race, and disaster risk.

Shelter-in-place requires action from a resilient population of homeowners and tenants. In turn, these residents need the support of social, economic, and organizational system domains to implement, operate, and maintain technical means of mitigation and adaptation. That is why studies in socio-ecological resilience suggest that resilience in the built environment is fundamentally about *people* and *systems*, rather than property alone (Laboy and Fannon 2016). For example, Keenan points to the duality of buildings as material (object) and social construction (managers/users) as critical to understating the adaptive capacity to climate change (Keenan 2014). Similarly, Adger emphasizes increasing the ability of individuals, groups, or organizations to adapt to changes, and to implement adaptation decisions by taking action (Adger, Arnell, and Tompkins 2005). Ironically, post-disaster responses that do not reach the most-affected people and/or that focus on the "political and economic will to reconstruct quickly" may not only exclude vulnerable and marginalized communities from post-disaster assistance, but may in fact inhibit increasing physical and social resilience through recovery (Bosher and Andrew 2011). In sum, the success and sustainability of future adaptations depend on socio-cultural measures, complicating the mathematically idealized "recovery curves" often used to illustrate resilience (Bruneau et al. 2003).

By building resilience against specific hazards into critical or high-value buildings, architects, engineers, and other experts make important contributions to urban resilience, providing shelter during an event, and enhancing recovery and reconstruction by adapting them to new conditions. However, we argue that dramatic increases in urban resilience will be achieved only by addressing the existing urban fabric of repetitive, residential buildings that these professionals have historically neither designed nor studied (Fannon and Laboy 2019, 6). Historic estimates suggest that only between 2% and 5% of buildings worldwide are designed by architects, although higher percentages of up to 40% are estimated to occur in developed countries like the United Kingdom (Doxiadis 1963, 69–77). Recent industry surveys suggest that the housing sector constitutes only 4% of the billings from the top ranking architecture and engineering firms in the United States (Building Design + Construction 2016). A survey of professional architects by the American Institute of Architects (AIA) showed that only 11%–14% of presumably licensed members engage in residential work, and industry advisors estimate that architects only design about 2% of custom houses in the United States (Dickinson 2016). These figures also illuminate the deeply ingrained fragmentation of those who plan, design, construct, research, and regulate the building industry—which among other problems impedes integrated disaster risk reduction (Bosher and Andrew 2011). And yet, 17% of the building stock in the United States will be demolished, 50% will be remodeled, and an additional 50% will be added by 2035 (Architecture2030.org

2010). These estimates represent a dramatic opportunity to expand the reach of professional and academic research to enhance resilience in a significant portion of the urban fabric.

Addressing the sheer number of residential buildings—particularly given the relatively limited access to professional guidance—demands new partnerships, policies, and tools to connect people with research on mitigation and adaptation strategies. These data and even these strategies exist; however, the large and growing body of information available about climate resilience risks tends to be dispersed, redundant, and/or designed for a professional audience. Experts tend to study and present data about one type of hazard, independent of others, requiring residents to know in advance what they seek. Once found, the publicly available information may be abstract or difficult for non-experts to translate. For example, users may find their location on a flood map, but not know the elevation relative to the datum, much less how to use the data to assess the impacts to their specific home or building construction. Similarly, resources like the Social Vulnerability Index developed by the Center for Disease Control and Prevention (CDC) are specifically written as metrics to guide the policies and plans of government agencies or emergency responders, even though the data is invaluable for individuals or groups seeking to enhance resilience and aid the vulnerable. A recent report categorized the multitude available tools, metrics and guidelines for the design of resilient buildings as either *technical*—those that focused on the physical/technical aspects of buildings—or *holistic*—those that include social and other human effects (Wright, Whitehouse, and Curti 2017). Notably, most of these guidelines are top-down, hazard- or event-focused, and/or assume new construction, even though residents exert diffuse-control, experience multiple hazards, and reside in millions of existing buildings. Considering these points reaffirms that the most pressing needs and highest potential impact of resilience research may be related to implementation, technology transfer, and diffusion of existing knowledge in new contexts—especially if more widespread—not necessarily in discovering or creating new knowledge *per se* (Bosher and Andrew 2011).

While government regulations could—in theory—mandate technical improvements based on the available guidance, the top-down and expert-focused approach is at odds with the scale of the problem, realities of individual ownership, and the goal of building greater social resilience. On the other hand, Bosher and Andrew (2011) describe community-based disaster risk reduction, based on shared information, local ownership, capacity building, robust evaluation, and positive relationships founded on dialogue. This approach replaces legislative "sticks" with the "carrot" of public education and outreach, and

> shifts away from punishment as a primary motivator and instead points toward a community-based imperative that emphasizes

users and builders who are educated sufficiently to take the lead in voluntary compliance and in developing a critical mass providing leadership from the grass roots up.

(Glass 2008, 195)

Given their limited role in this type of housing, what role (if any) should architects and researchers play in enhancing community-based resilience of the residential building fabric? This chapter argues that architecture researchers and professionals can meaningfully contribute to climate adaptation by translating their expert knowledge about resilience to engage a broad audience, and by leveraging new tools for community engagement to generate a feedback loop that informs future planning and design practice, research directions, and policy initiatives.

In sum, increasing urban resilience demands resilience research shift from performing highly specific, detailed analysis of an exceptional, high-value building aimed at an expert audience, to identifying a broadly applicable set of probabilistic trends based on sampling, modeling, and centralizing public data. The work presented here describes one attempt to do so through the mechanism of an online tool that addresses both the extent of repetitive residential urban fabric, and the limited professional engagement with it. The early testing of the Resilient Homes Online Design Aide (RHOnDA) with various stakeholders indicates the potential to engage in climate adaptation planning by communicating with the widest possible audience, customizing the approach through downscaled vulnerability assessments, connecting specific risks and incentive programs, and obtaining new data about the human response to this information to further inform new initiatives. Consistent with the goals and limits of climate adaptation planning found in the literature, preliminary field research with user focus groups of residents and municipal planners showed the tool has potential for research-enabled community resilience, to guide priorities of public/private incentivization efforts, and inform public policy.

## Background: The Limits of Climate Adaptation Planning

### *The Existing Residential Fabric: Mandates or Incentives*

Bedsworth and Hanak, authors of a 2010 policy synthesis study on climate adaptation planning, identified the "areas of planning concern" as water supply, flood control, electricity, coastal resources, air quality, public health, and ecosystem resources. While all these factors impact housing function and dwellers' health, climate adaptation planning often occurs at the infrastructural level, protecting centralized resources, defensive measures, or delivery mechanisms to ensure general urban resilience to anticipated events. In fact,

Bedsworth and Hanak (2010) say little about housing—and nothing at all about the existing residential fabric—noting only that new development should be away from areas of high hazard. This is particularly striking given their assumption that large portions of the population will shelter-in-place.

For this chapter, we identified key actions that local and regional planners must take, including: identifying and using the best science, deciding on goals and early actions, locating relevant partners, identifying and eliminating regulatory barriers, and encouraging the introduction of new mandates and guidelines, all in a timely manner. We argue that top-down planning approaches must also promote community-based measures to reduce stress on central services and infrastructure, allow residents to safely shelter-in-place, and organize community-based emergency response. Approaches include: presenting science to promote risk literacy, aligning residents' goals and agency for action with those of government programs, understanding and overcoming non-regulatory barriers, and motivating individual action through mandates or incentives.

By focusing on the existing residential fabric, our work engages a particular challenge to top-down adaptation planning; by definition, most urban residents live in existing homes, where limits on political and statutory authority often preclude mandatory changes. Building codes—the primary instrument for building-scale regulation—are generally based on national model codes, adopted by state-level legislation, and ultimately enforced locally, complicating a bottom-up resilience. Moreover, because existing laws and policies may inhibit resilience planning, code revisions often occur during the limited period of "disaster thinking" immediately following an event, when exceptions are made and bureaucracy streamlined (Nachbur et al. 2017). Unfortunately, this approach too often reacts to the immediate effects of that event, while failing to anticipate other effects and other events, much less the possibility of creating *better* conditions post-recovery. Fragmentation and decentralization in the post-disaster period exacerbate the problem by compressing desirable policy and legislative changes and coordination among citizens and various levels of government. Whatever resilience measures do become code are not always mandated or uniformly implemented across all jurisdictions, a fact tracked and scored by the insurance industry (Insurance Institute for Business & Home Safety 2018). Furthermore, building codes almost never affect existing buildings; only a substantial renovation or addition, prompting the application for a new building permit, will trigger upgrades to current code. Even post-disaster reconstruction up to the new code may not be covered by insurance, leading the market to offer a special type of coverage for post-disaster recovery.

There are a few examples of mandates that are enacted and enforced on entire populations (including existing buildings) without a permit trigger, such as Los Angeles requirements for seismic retrofits of buildings with soft stories (Xia and Schleuss 2016). These exceptions prove the rule, and illuminate some policy and practical challenges related to mandating upgrades, such as cost sharing, rental properties, and wide-scale municipal assessment. Even with expedited assessment methods, these programs ultimately rely on owners hiring licensed professionals to do detailed assessment to determine which retrofits are needed and to implement them. On the other hand, planners and policy makers who adopt optional incentive programs replace those challenges with others, particularly raising awareness. For example, homeowners may not be aware of current policies and available incentives, may not connect such programs with various climate change risks, and much less understand how local actions contribute to broader community resilience. Whether through mandates or incentives, local and regional planners must partner with the homeowners, tenants, and landlords to increase the resilience of the existing housing stock.

Economic interests make institutions, like utilities, the home-financing industry, and insurance companies, into strategic partners in motivating change. In recent years the United States experienced the property loss, business disruption, and health costs of a record number of major climate disasters—totaling $306.2 billion in 2017, and exceeding the previous record of $214.8 billion (NOAA National Centers for Environmental Information (NCEI) 2018). These growing losses are driven not only by the increased frequency and severity of natural hazards, but more by the number, location, value, and above all, the vulnerability of various assets—especially buildings—to these hazards (Smith and Katz 2013). Governments and insurance companies bear the brunt of the direct financial costs, and signs indicate these public and private actors understand the value of mitigation, and will continue sponsoring research and innovation in resilience, as well as incentivizing implementation. A 2018 report by the National Institute of Building Science (NIBS) showed that every dollar spent in mitigation on buildings produces $6 in savings when spent through federal mitigation grants, and $4 in savings when spent in private investments, with the benefits extending beyond reduced property losses to include health and economic productivity (Multihazard Mitigation Council 2018), illuminating both the substantial risk and significant financial opportunity. Put another way, natural hazard events are not a disaster; rather, disaster results from the lack of preparedness for those events. Among the least-prepared groups are occupants of the small and unmanaged residential buildings that comprise the vast majority of the built environment. Unfortunately, research shows that often the least-prepared are also the most socially vulnerable.

## *Vulnerable Populations: Challenges of Access to Knowledge and Agency*

In the built environment, the economic value of pre-disaster mitigation illustrates the lack of preparedness in apparently objective terms; however, it inherently minimizes the impacts on low-value assets where poor populations live. The NIBS report cautions that financial accounting cannot capture all impacts or all hazards, acknowledging that "Disasters clearly disrupt populations in ways that are difficult to articulate, let alone assign monetary worth." However, just as some adverse impacts are difficult to quantify, but no less real, so too the benefits of efforts to mitigate vulnerability—for example by improving the resilience of the built environment—inherently address these other, non-quantified impacts as well. Experts project that the poorest populations will be disproportionately affected by climate change, in large part because of access, quality, and preparedness of housing (Intergovernmental Panel on Climate Change 2007). The Federal Government's Interagency Concept for Community Resilience (ICCR) focused on community resilience indicators, assessments, and measures that include well-being factors like income, housing condition and affordability, and healthcare (U.S. Department of Homeland Security, and Mitigation Framework Leadership Group 2016). While it sought to align state and federal metrics, the concept has been criticized for not identifying performance thresholds or providing guidance for local communities (Wright, Whitehouse, and Curti 2017). Non-Governmental Organizations (NGOs) like Enterprise, who work to make affordable housing more sustainable, may include resilience as a secondary goal, but often focus on larger multi-family buildings to maximize impact for effort invested. All this evidence underscores the difficulty of addressing the situation and interests of a broad segment of the public, especially those living in the existing, small residential building stock that is both underprepared and under-researched. Climate adaptation planning efforts, which empower communities to self-assess, reorganize, and rebuild, will develop broad social resilience, becoming better prepared for all kinds of uncertainties beyond climate change. As a critical first step, communities need localized risk information accessible to all residents. Adaptation planners make that information more useful by explaining mitigation and adaptation strategies for multiple risks, and by offering general recommendations connected with local resources, policies, or incentives.

As described above, research about resilience of the built environment historically focused on critical infrastructure, consistent with a 2013 presidential directive (Obama 2013), setting priorities for federal research and funding. Building-specific resilience research follows funder priorities: with government entities focusing on critical assets that provide essential services during a disaster (e.g. shelters, emergency response facilities, hospitals) while private support emphasizes high-value assets (highest losses in property value or economic productivity). Thus, resilience guidelines and metrics for building owners tend to focus on large and commercial buildings against specific hazards or in specific regions, for example guidelines for large commercial buildings in Boston (Wright, Koo, and Belden 2015). New developments of large multi-family housing in high-value urban areas may benefit; however, these guides do little for the owners or managers of the existing fabric of small, repetitive, residential structures, who lack the capital and organization of large developers. While insurance companies and other industry sectors have developed research-based guidelines at the scale of smaller properties, the metrics and guidelines focus property *value* while leaving out many aspects of building community resilience, such as hazards to health and social well-being. In fact, a study of 117 countries by the World Bank estimates that losses to well-being of people are *greater* than net asset losses in disasters, especially those affecting the poor (Hallegatte et al. 2017). In short, however essential or expensive, individual critical and high-value buildings represent only a small percentage of the urban fabric, by number, area, and even dollar value of harm. Even acknowledging their disproportionate importance in emergencies, we believe widespread improvements to the homes and neighborhoods housing most of the population contribute the greater portion to long-term social resilience in the face of increasingly common disruptions.

Taken together, these challenges show that while they differ on some motivations and goals, both climate adaptation planners and private industry can benefit from rapid, inexpensive, and broadly available evaluations of common residential buildings, particularly when coupled with education about vulnerabilities, and connected to promote voluntary mitigation strategies. Based on the process for climate adaptation planning introduced by the International Council for Local Environmental Initiatives (ICLEI) in 2010, the United States Green Building Council (USGBC) suggested four steps to incorporate climate adaptation into existing buildings: understanding regional impacts, evaluating current operations and maintenance targets, conducting a scenario analysis of how the building will respond to climate impacts, and implementing adaptation strategies (Larsen et al. 2011). Municipalities working on climate adaptation planning are mostly focused on the first step, and the findings may not necessarily reach building owners. Until now, the following two steps were rightly seen as requiring detailed, building-specific analysis and expert advice, resources many homeowners do not have. Efforts to circumvent the need for detailed analysis often result in a frustrating lack of specificity. For example, the same USGBC document lists a menu of useful recommendations but neither sets priorities nor connects specific recommendations to specific vulnerabilities. Although the list has simple filters like *climate*, it does not account for significant differences like building type, age, and location; indeed, it seems written for the sort of expert audience that can discern those nuances. Meanwhile, the fourth step—and indeed the whole effort to incorporate climate adaptation into existing buildings—depends on owners' and managers' initiative or incentive, a highly individual, poorly understood, and difficult to influence set of motivations.

A holistic approach to communicating risks, one that provides specific recommendations and better understands the effect on human behavior, will likely result from a multi-sector, public-private effort to simultaneously address social well-being and collective action through public education and calibrated incentives for property owners. The RHOnDA presented here is an attempt to do just that: create a tool that disseminates information about risks, provides semi-customized recommendations, and gathers research data about user motivations and values to inform future policy and programs.

## Motivation and Foundational Research for RHOnDA

### Prior Research and Applications on Multi-Hazard Resilient Buildings

This work builds on decades of research about designing for multi-hazard resilience in new high-value buildings. Funding agencies like the National Science Foundation supported numerous research teams to develop frameworks that can support decisions about multi-hazard resilience and sustainability in buildings (Flint et al. 2017). A Northeastern University-led team used particular buildings—hospitals, large offices, elementary schools—to investigate resilience and sustainability in facilities essential to life safety, economic recovery, and for short-term community shelters during an event (Fannon 2018). Efforts like this, while yielding substantial and valuable contributions, typify the single-building focus for expert audiences, and prompted the practical translation of that research to a generalized model of repetitive and similar existing buildings. Further, our own theoretical research on socio-ecological resilience in architecture shaped this present effort to develop a framework for community engagement that feeds future investigations about the human factors of building resilience—knowledge, agency, and systematic-thinking. By translating the latest in technical knowledge while simultaneously engaging beyond conventional technical disciplinary boundaries, we seek to holistically address the political, social, economic, and technical domains of resilience (see Figure 5.1).

### Shifting Research Priorities

The work on RHOnDA represents a shift from theoretical, speculative, and fundamental research towards a form of applied research, driven by the conviction that building resilience is about building knowledge and capacity in people who will ultimately implement mitigation and adaptation strategies in buildings. This work tests methods to sample, model, and predict the resilience performance of a large segment of the built environment; explores the design of interfaces to disseminate this information to a broad audience; and measures the effect of providing customized information to many and different types of users. Our goal is to determine the data different stakeholders involved in the climate adaptation planning process need, to translate

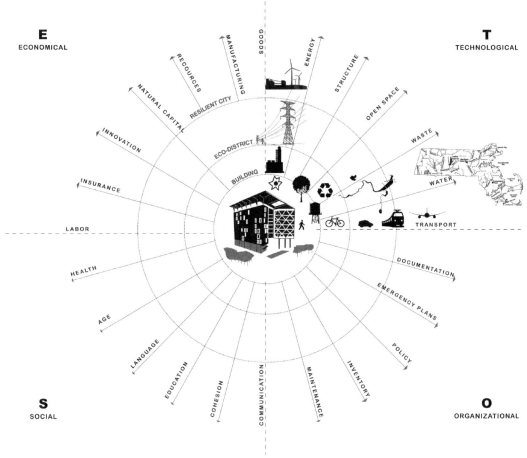

Figure 5.1 Graphic adaptation of the MCEER TOSE model of resilience expanded to multiple hazards and mapped to scales of the built environment (Laboy and Fannon, 2016).

research into information through educational and data gathering platforms, and finally to increase communities' resilience by enabling effective application of knowledge.

This work aligns with global and national shifts in research priorities that seek to expand the reach and relevance of resilience research. In the inaugural meeting of the interdisciplinary Global Research Network (GRN), hosted by the Global Resilience Institute (GRI) at Northeastern University, leading researchers from around the world identified the three top priorities for transdisciplinary research as (1) Risk Literacy & Education, (2) Baking in Resilience through Design & Urban Planning, and (3) Governance & Incentives (Global Resilience Institute 2018), all immediate objectives in developing RHOnDA. Researchers' increased attention to education and incentives as parallel to and equally important as design echoes emerging interest areas of multi-sector groups like NIBS, which engage the AEC community, insurance, finance, and government to identify best practices for inspiring action. Recent calls for research funding at the federal level demonstrate increased emphasis on human factors of resilience and community participation, especially among socially vulnerable populations. Our work seeks to collaborate directly with those stakeholders in the research, meeting them where they are, rather than merely "engaging" through mechanisms such as focus groups.

## Stakeholders' Motivations and Concerns

Our preliminary research identified potential partners and cataloged their need for, interest in, and thoughts about tools for education, community engagement, and decision support. All of the stakeholders—public and private—share an interest in education and incentives, although their target audiences and specific goals naturally vary. A common question emerged from preliminary discussions with representatives from these stakeholders, taking different forms but the same thrust: "what information and incentives work best to inspire broad, voluntary adaptation?" We hypothesize that this question will be answered through applied research focused on community engagement, using tools like RHOnDA to share information and evaluate user responses to it.

The first stakeholders are local governments involved in climate adaptation planning, and increasingly concerned about the most vulnerable communities and individuals. Supported by the Rockefeller Foundation's 100 Resilient Cities program, cities like Boston appointed Chief Resilience Officers to focus on social resilience and cohesion to overcome inequity. These efforts target youth workers, the poor, and other governmental counterparts, to work on initiatives in education and economic opportunity, youth empowerment, changes in zoning for more affordable and higher-quality development of new communities, and regional cooperation through entities like the Metropolitan Area Planning Council (MAPC) (Transatlantic Policy Lab 2016). We presented the RHOnDA tool to the Climate Preparedness Task Force of the Metropolitan Mayors Coalition of Greater Boston, a group of 15 member-municipalities in the Boston area who, with support from the MAPC, work to coordinate regional climate mitigation and adaptation activities, as well as state and federal agencies ("Metro Mayors Climate Preparedness Taskforce" n.d.). The MAPC members are testing RHOnDA as a tool for their community planning efforts, and their planners and constituents are providing feedback to refine its design. For example, climate adaptation planners in the City of Cambridge, MA, have completed downscaled vulnerability assessments for some hazards, but are seeking ways to communicate their findings and to encourage residents to use them. Planners need to know what motivates owners, tenants, or landlords to implement mitigation action in homes, inform further research, shape new policies, enhance communication, and forge connections to existing programs. These are nuanced issues; for example, planners in the MAPC expressed concern about the emotional impact of individuals more directly understanding risks, particularly for unaided users discovering information for the first time. Some suggested the tools be used in guided community workshops to provide professional expertise and emotional support when receiving information about vulnerabilities.

The second stakeholders are NGOs, including community development corporations and organizations interested in advocacy for voluntary/community action, such as Neighborhood of Affordable Housing, Inc. (NOAH) in East Boston. Non-profit organizations like this strive to assess, map, and communicate risks to their communities. Like city governments, the challenge lies in determining what information people care about, and will stimulate residents to translate into action; however, these groups are primarily concerned with dissemination of information that empowers communities to generate collective, rather than individual action. This is particularly important when the majority of community residents are tenants rather than owners. In both cases, making information accessible to non-experts depends on *language*, not only avoiding jargon, but indeed translating for non-English speakers, especially in many urban areas like East Boston that have high risk and social vulnerability. As in other areas, NGOs and local governments both benefit from collaboration because deeply embedded community groups represent the trusted local actors most capable of introducing and explaining available resources, and of reaching marginalized populations such as the disabled, undocumented, the old, and those with language barriers. Organizations like NOAH already engage youth as the on-the-ground-workers in their planning and research efforts, and we are exploring partnerships to apply that model to resilience. The premise is young citizen-researchers conducting door-to-door home visits testing the tool with a diverse range of residents, including those who cannot speak English, while producing a fine-grained assessment of risks in the community.

Design and consulting firms supporting adaptation planning and vulnerability assessments for governments and companies represent a third stakeholder. Firms engaged in this work have contributed to audit protocols for developers of multi-family housing (Chase, Baumann, and New Ecology, Inc., n.d.), menus of resilience strategies, and manuals for specific cities (e.g. Kleinfelder in the City of Cambridge). However, these remain one-off efforts serving the government client, rather than citizens directly, thus reinforcing the need for research and tools that better engage the public in understanding risks and potential actions to mitigate and adapt. Design firms see increased community participation in their design process as adding value—to the client and the professional services—so seek platforms to explain design strategies and connect across multiple hazards. In preliminary discussions with firms, an area of interest is increasing design literacy in the population they engage through effective and simple graphic illustrations, technical explanations, cross-references between strategies, and potentially finding ways of linking those with existing incentive programs. Like their clients in government, design firms are particularly interested in working with residents living in areas identified as vulnerable or high hazard, out of a pragmatic need to prioritize. We interviewed professionals at these firms, and they are testing RHOnDA for its ability to gather feedback and application to these unique problems.

The residential insurance and real-estate industries comprise the fourth stakeholder group, with economic motivations to promote adaptation beyond current code in order to reduce industry's exposure to claims resulting from future natural hazards. Concomitantly, the industry has financial resources to invest in and incentivize adaptation, including by helping owners pay for upgrades. Their audience includes their customers, the owners of insured properties, as well as potential customers attracted by resilience-focused insurance or financing products. For example, the Multihazard Mitigation Council of the National Institutes of Building Sciences proposed the "resilience mortgage" to incentivize and finance resilience improvements to the residential buildings (Multihazard Mitigation Council 2015). This council called for the development of software tools to aid a "resilience evaluator"—a job similar to the role of a home inspector during home purchases or an energy auditor for energy retrofits—who would conduct a home-visit (Fannon and Laboy 2019, 10). Industry representatives, imagining paths to commercialization, suggested that tools like RHOnDA could serve those functions. Beyond the direct benefits, collecting a large body of user responses to risk information and recommendations (from homeowners and tenants) might also reveal motivations interest or action, helping identify ways to manage risk, develop incentives, and connect existing or new customers with these new products.

## Methodology: Developing and Testing RHOnDA

We first developed and tested the methods to translate high-quality research, conduct sophisticated analysis, and communicate expert judgment to a wide audience of non-expert users in one region: the Boston metro area (Fannon and Laboy 2019). From the start, this pilot was defined using a scalable organization and repeatable method that would apply across the country, to serve the vast urban residential fabric.

### *Geographic-Based Database of Natural and Social/Infrastructural Hazards*

We began by identifying hazards, specifically those with sufficient publicly available data, with which to assess risk for a specific property. These included highly dispersed data from government, industry, and NGO sources—such as FEMA, NOAA, DOE, SurgingSeas, and the Insurance Institute for Business and Home Safety—mostly directed at expert audiences. To organize, we classified hazards to buildings and people into 12 types (high wind storms or hurricanes, drought, tornadoes, earthquakes, power failure, indoor air quality, hail, coastal and inland flooding, wild fire, high-heat, extreme cold, and ecological effects of climate change). Even after identifying the best data sources available, localizing these multiple hazards at a spatially constant resolution presented a significant challenge. While an imperfect geographic measure—especially for downscaled hazards such as hot spots of urban heat island for extreme heat—we chose to develop a zip code-based national database to address multi-hazard resilience in a format most homeowners and tenants know, and could share without privacy concerns. This intermediate scale (bigger than a house, smaller than a city) helps translate abstract hazards into local risks based on user responses. Zip code also helps bridge between human and natural systems, connecting natural hazards with the risks posed by the social and infrastructural context, for example, accessibility scores, ecological factors like urban canopy, and Social Vulnerability Index (which includes socio-economic status, household composition and disabilities, minority status and language barriers, and housing/infrastructure quality). The resulting localized hazards become personalized risks through the lens of the *household* to connect the physical home and the people dwelling in it to the effects of the natural hazards, socio-ecological factors of resilience at the community scale. This zip code-based database also incorporates climate zone data drawn from the Building America Optimized Climate Solutions (U.S. Department of Energy n.d.).

## Sample of Cities, Climates, and Hazards

One benefit of a repetitive built environment is that it becomes reasonable to use statistical approaches to evaluate general trends for the physical characteristics of housing by sampling urban regions that represent relatively large regions. Of course, these characteristics change according to climate, cultural traditions of construction, and environmental risks; to characterize this variation, we expanded our Boston-based development and sampled buildings from three major metropolitan areas with different climates and hazards: Boston (cold climate, primary hazard: flooding), San Francisco (temperate marine environment, primary hazard: seismic), and Miami (hot humid climate, primary hazard: hurricane/strong winds). This resulted in different building typologies and parameters for each, for example, single-family homes exist in all three, but with vastly different distributions for year of construction, construction type, exterior materials, and proportions. As part of building the database, we researched critical historical dates for major building code developments, and the main mechanisms of failure for residential buildings in historical events, especially in these three regions, for example soft stories in California housing. This information was supplemented in the database with information from code enactment and compliance scores in hurricane-prone states, developed by the insurance industry (Insurance Institute for Business & Home Safety 2018) to provide key dates for various states and jurisdictions to translate into zip code-based data with the risk information mentioned above.

## Random Sample of Identified Residential Building Typologies

Rather than collect finely resolved information about each property, sampling from assessor databases within each repetitive building stock yields results with acceptable, albeit commensurably lower, fidelity (Fannon and Laboy 2019, 6). To that end we evaluated, sorted, and clustered the entire database of residential buildings under five stories in each of these three cities into types, for example single family, triple-deckers, duplexes, and row houses in Boston, as illustrated in Figure 5.2. We conducted research on construction types and typical methods and evolving building technologies by building age in each city. The five or six types for each city were held to be sufficiently similar that findings from one could be generalized across the group with only minor adjustments, for example scaling by floor area. We then drew random, equally sized samples of each type from the assessor's data and mapped them to ensure a well-distributed sample. The information in the assessors' data was combined with measurable data taken from publicly available aerial photography and street views, including measurements of window-to-wall ratio, overall footprint, orientation, wall and roof materials, as shown in Figure 5.2.

## Data Model and Machine-Learning Algorithm

We developed a detailed data model of each of the sample buildings, including basic systems information, year of construction and/or renovation, size, envelope characteristics, and other factors (Fannon and Laboy 2019, 6). We analyzed the performance of each sample building using these data and looked at the findings across the sample as representative of the whole type in that city. In some cases where

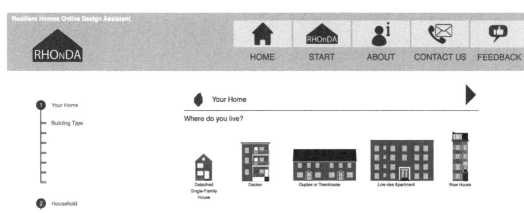

Figure 5.2 Representative diagrams of the five building types based on sampling the Boston residential building under five stories. From left: single-family, triple-decker, duplex, low-rise multi-family building, and row house.

precise values were unknown, a range of plausible values in each critical parameter consistent with the findings in the type were used, accounting for uncertainty and variation. These data models are used to simulate the comfort, energy use, response to natural hazards, and other performance metrics for the sample buildings, which are then used to train a machine-learning algorithm. This generalizable multivariable algorithm allows any other house of the type (even one we did not model) to be approximated based on user input.

We modeled each sample building in BEopt, an interface for the industry-standard EnergyPlus simulation engine. Geometry, materials, and systems data were determined by combining assessor data, visual inspection of photographs and other sources, or imputed when unavailable based on building age and typical practice. To address the many unknowns and promote comparisons across the study, we held many things like internal load schedules constant. We reduced other variables to parameters by simulating them across a (finite) range of values (e.g. wall insulation). Simulating each combination yields a dataspace with an average of 71 unique versions of each building (2,840 per type), with the assumption that the true building performance lies somewhere within that range. The model provides heating and cooling and total energy use, and, thanks to the large solution space, an estimate of the potential for energy conservation measures.

To apply these findings beyond the 40 sample buildings of each type, we adopted a series of machine-learning algorithms, which are "trained" to identify patterns and relationships between the inputs (from users and the assessors' data) and the outputs (energy consumption). When a user provides unique inputs, the algorithm calculates an output based on the pattern. In this case, the data were randomly divided into two tranches, 75% (2,134 runs) were used to train the multi-variable regression model how to predict energy use from the inputs. The remaining 25% (711 runs) were used to validate the model, by comparing the simulated values for the 25% testing set with the outputs of the prediction model based on the values of independent variables from that tranch.

### *Inventory, Combinations, Translation, and Illustration of Recommendations*

One key feature of this statistical or generalized approach is that small variations in users' answers about their homes do not necessarily yield vastly different recommendations unless they occur at specific thresholds (e.g. a specific year of construction in relationship to adoption of new code provisions). That stability allowed us to develop a database of recommendations in advance based on the range of buildings in the sample. Over 100 recommendations were drawn from an extensive literature review of research papers, insurance industry guidelines, resilience metrics, government programs, and new and developing standards. These were combined using expert judgment into simple descriptions and illustrations accessible to a non-expert audience. The text and graphics are tagged by climate zone, risk, and construction type; and cross-linked with others that either reinforce or contradict them to support presentation to users.

### Critical User Questions and Interface

In parallel with developing the risk and preparedness data model and the machine-learning algorithms, we identified the input variables necessary to personalize the responses to specific users. We generated a list of simple questions, with explanatory graphics, for users to answer about their home through an accessible web interface. In the background, we connected the possible responses with the data models (to assess risk) and the potential strategies (to offer recommendations). As a user completes the survey, their responses about the home, occupants, expectations, and preparedness determine if each recommendation applies, and at what level, depending on the severity of the risk and the level of preparedness. Users can filter and screen the resulting recommendations based on tags and other conditional statements. Each recommendation combines simple text and illustration, and cross-references related hazards, links to other recommendations, and cites extensive references for additional information should users wish to dive more deeply. While the current interface is linear, the team has engaged a game design expert and designed a serious game, currently entering a beta-testing phase, that engages users in various decision-making scenarios.

### Stakeholder Testing

A key aspect of the development process is soliciting feedback from partners involved in climate adaptation to understand its usefulness and potential applications, and to test it with real users. As described above, we engaged stakeholders working across domains and scales to support the development of tools. An initial conversation with climate adaptation planners in the City of Cambridge, MA, prompted us to consider local customizations of the tool to meet the specific needs of climate adaptation planning in a jurisdiction. For Cambridge, the first objective was incorporating the higher resolution of parcel-level hazard data. Second, they hoped to help citizens find, interpret, and understand their eligibility for the existing programs available. For example, rather than general recommendations such as trees planting or photovoltaic (PV) installations, a customized version of the web tool could deliver links to specific local programs where residence could request a sidewalk tree, or information about incentives for PV assessment and installation, among others (Fannon and Laboy 2019, 10). A second meeting was organized as a workshop attended by nearly two-dozen residents: a mix of homeowners, renters, experts, and non-experts, to test the tool and solicit feedback on the interface, its usefulness to residents, and potential opportunities to expand its communicative power. Similarly, we presented to the MAPC climate task force, and provided the planners in attendance with a private link to beta-test RHONDA, as well as survey to collect feedback. As with the Cambridge workshop, these data will improve the tool, and are a first step towards public workshops in additional communities, each with unique priorities, information needs, and demographics.

## Conclusion and Future Directions

RHOnDA represents a modest effort in both scale and scope. The challenge of engaging across all levels of the built environment and all the domains of resilience is better known, but still present. In some ways, the work on RHOnDA raises more questions than it answers, and in that regard, may be useful in identifying directions for future research, and productive methods and avenues to conduct it. Based on our effort, we believe resilience, including promoting climate change adaptation in the built environment, will ultimately require the scale and scope of effort witnessed over the past three decades to increase the sustainability of the built environment. Working together, we will discover new knowledge, develop new tools, create new jobs, invent new products, establish new standards, and write new policies. Each change will demand new research to inform and shape it. To that end, we offer the following six knowledge challenges:

1. Knowing what we have (documenting current conditions through survey and audits)
2. Knowing what is coming (downscaling future hazards to identify risks)
3. Knowing what will happen (predicting building performance under hazard, not only at failure)
4. Knowing how to choose (evaluating and comparing interventions on a life-cycle basis)
5. Knowing how it is working (measuring effectiveness of programs, incentives, and regulations)
6. Knowing how to communicate (educating a wide populace about risk and response)

These challenges fit squarely within the social, if not the technical, domain; and as such bear uncertainty and complexity, but also contain the promise of broader impact and relevance.

## References

Adger, W., Nigel W. Arnell, and Emma L. Tompkins. 2005. "Successful Adaptation to Climate Change across Scales." *Global Environmental Change* 15 (2): 77–86. https://doi.org/10.1016/j.gloenvcha.2004.12.005.

Architecture2030.org. 2010. "Architecture 2030." http://architecture2030.org/files/2010_handout.pdf.

Berg, Nate. 2012. "U.S. Urban Population Is Up… But What Does 'Urban' Really Mean?" *CityLab*, March 26, 2012. https://www.citylab.com/equity/2012/03/-us-urban-population-what-does-urban-really-mean/1589/.

Bosher, Lee, and Andrew Dainty. 2011. "Disaster Risk Reduction and 'Built-in' Resilience: Towards Overarching Principles for Construction Practice." *DISA Disasters* 35 (1): 1–18.

Bruneau, Michel, Stephanie E. Chang, Ronald T. Eguchi, George C. Lee, Thomas D. O'Rourke, Andrei M. Reinhorn, Masanobu Shinozuka, Kathleen Tierney, William A. Wallace, and Detlof von Winterfeldt. 2003. "A Framework to Quantitatively Assess and Enhance the Seismic Resilience of Communities." *Earthquake Spectra* 19 (4): 733–752. https://doi.org/10.1193/1.1623497.

Building Design + Construction. 2016. "2016 Giants 300 Report: Ranking the Nation's Largest Architecture, Engineering, and Construction Firms." https://www.bdcnetwork.com/2016-giants-300-report-ranking-nations-largest-architecture-engineering-and-construction-firms.

Chase, Thomas, Lauren Baumann, and New Ecology, Inc. n.d. "Multifamily Housing Resiliency Audits," 12.

Dickinson, Duo. 2016. "Architects Design Just 2% of All Houses–Why?" *Common Edge*, April 7, 2016. http://commonedge.org/architects-design-just-2-of-all-houses-why/.

Doxiadis, Constantinos A. 1963. *Architecture in Transition*. New York: Oxford University Press. https://archive.org/stream/architectureintr002017mbp#page/n73/mode/2up/search/percent.

Fannon, David. 2018. *Evaluating Resilient & Sustainable Buildings*. Washington, DC: National Institute of Building Sciences.

Fannon, David, and Michelle Laboy. 2019. "Resilient Homes Online Design Aide: Connecting Research and Practice for Socially Resilient Communities." In *Intersections of Design and Resilience*, 8. New York: ACSA Press.

Flint, M., G. Warn, J. van de Lindt, D. Fannon, and M. Sasani. 2017. *Multi-Hazard Resilient and Sustainable Buildings*. Duluth, MN: ASCE.

Frey, William H. 2011. "Melting Pot Cities and Suburbs: Racial and Ethnic Change in Metro America in the 2000s." State of Metropolitan America. Brookings Institution.

Glass, J. 2008. "Facing the Future by Designing in Resilience: An Architectural Perspective." In *Hazards and the Built Environment: Attaining Built-in Resilience*, edited by Lee Bosher. London and New York: Taylor & Francis.

Global Resilience Institute. 2018. "Thriving, Not Just Surviving: Solutions for Global Resilience." The Inaugural Global Resilience Reseach Network Summit. https://www.grrnsummit.org.

Hallegatte, Stephane, Adrien Vogt-Schilb, Mook Bangalore, and Julie Rozenberg. 2017. "Unbreakable: Building the Resilience of the Poor in the Face of Natural Disasters." Overview Booklet. Climate Change and Development Series. Washington, DC: The World Bank. https://openknowledge.worldbank.org/bitstream/handle/10986/25335/211003ovEN.pdf?sequence=3.

Insurance Institute for Business & Home Safety. 2018. "Rating the States: 2018: An Assessment of Residential Building Code and Enforcement Systems for Life Safety and Property Protection in Hurricane-Prone Regions." Insurance Institute for Business & Home Safety. http://disastersafety.org/wp-content/uploads/2018/03/ibhs-rating-the-states-2018.pdf.

IPCC. 2007. "Climate Change 2007: Synthesis Report. Contribution of Working Groups I, II and III to the Fourth Assessment Report of the Intergovernmental Panel on Climate Change." [Core Writing Team, Pachauri, R.K and Reisinger, A. (eds.)]. IPCC, Geneva, Switzerland, 104 pp.

Katryn Wright, Jeremy Koo, and Andy Belden. 2015. "Enhancing Resilience in Boston A Guide for Large Buildings and Institutions." A Better City. http://abettercity.org/about/publications.html.

Keenan, Jesse M. 2014. "Material and Social Construction: A Framework for the Adaptation of Buildings." *Enquiry : The ARCC Journal of Architectural Research* 11 (1).

Kolko, Jed. 2015. "How Suburban Are Big American Cities?" *FiveThirtyEight* (blog). May 21, 2015. https://fivethirtyeight.com/features/how-suburban-are-big-american-cities/.

Laboy, Michelle, and David Fannon. 2016. "Resilience Theory and Praxis: A Critical Framework for Architecture." *Enquiry: A Journal for Architectural Research* 13 (2). https://doi.org/10.17831/enq:arcc.v13i2.405.

Larsen, L., N. Rajkovich, C. Leighton, K. McCoy, K. Calhoun, E. Mallen, K. Bush, et al. 2011. "Green Building and Climate Resilisence: Understanding Impacts and Preparing for Changing Conditions." University of Michigan; U.S. Green Building Council. http://www.usgbc.org/resources/green-building-and-climate-resilience-understanding-impacts-and-preparing-changing-conditi.

"Metro Mayors Climate Preparedness Taskforce." n.d. MAPC. Accessed July 24, 2018. https://www.mapc.org/our-work/expertise/climate/mmc/.

Multihazard Mitigation Council. 2015. "Developing Pre-Disaster Resilience Based on Public and Private Incentivization." NIBS. http://www.nibs.org/resource/resmgr/MMC/MMC_ResilienceIncentivesWP.pdf.

Multihazard Mitigation Council. 2018. "Natural Hazard Mitigation Saves: 2017 Interim Report." National Institute of Building Sciences. http://www.nibs.org/page/mitigationsaves.

Munich Re. 2018. "Natural Catastrophe Review: Series of Hurricanes Makes 2017 Year of Highest Insured Losses Ever." January 4, 2018. https://www.munichre.com/en/media-relations/publications/press-releases/2018/2018-01-04-press-release/index.html.

Nachbur, James, Irina Feygina, Elise Lipkowitz, and Darshan Karwat. 2017. "Climate Change Resilience: Governance and Reforms." Arizona State University. https://cspo.org/wp-content/uploads/2017/01/Resilience-Governance-Reforms-Report-With-Logos.pdf.

NOAA National Centers for Environmental Information (NCEI). 2018. "U.S. Billion-Dollar Weather and Climate Disasters." 2018. https://www.ncdc.noaa.gov/billions/.

Obama, Barack. 2013. "Presidential Policy Directive – Critical Infrastructure Security and Resilience." Office of the Press Secretary. https://www.whitehouse.gov/the-press-office/2013/02/12/presidential-policy-directive-critical-infrastructure-security-and-resil.

Rosanna Xia, and Jon Schleuss. 2016. "L.A. Releases Addresses of 13,500 Apartments and Condos Likely to Need Earthquake Retrofitting." *Los Angeles Times*, April 15, 2016. http://www.latimes.com/local/california/la-me-quake-risk-20160415-story.html.

Smith, Adam B., and Richard W. Katz. 2013. "US Billion-Dollar Weather and Climate Disasters: Data Sources, Trends, Accuracy and Biases." *Natural Hazards* 67 (2): 387–410. https://doi.org/10.1007/s11069-013-0566-5.

Transatlantic Policy Lab. 2016. "Advancing Equity for Boston's Resilience." Bertelsmann Foundation, Open Society Foundations, 100 Resilient Cities Initiative and the German Marshall Fund of the United States. https://www.bfna.org/wp-content/uploads/2017/12/Boston-Lab-Recommendations-2016-01-15.pdf.

United States Census Bureau. 2011. "Historical Census of Housing Tables – Homeownership." 2011. https://www.census.gov/hhes/www/housing/census/historic/owner.html.

United States Census Bureau. 2015. "American Housing Survey: 2015 National General Housing Data." https://www.census.gov/programs-surveys/ahs/data/

interactive/ahstablecreator.html#?s_areas=a00000&s_year=n2015&s_tableName=Table1&s_byGroup1=a3&s_byGroup2=a4&s_filterGroup1=t1&s_filterGroup2=g1&s_show=S.

U.S. Department of Energy. n.d. "Optimized Climate Solutions | Building America Solution Center." Accessed July 26, 2018. https://basc.pnnl.gov/optimized-climate-solutions/.

U.S. Department of Homeland Security, and Mitigation Framework Leadership Group. 2016. "Draft Interagency Concept for Community Resilience Indicators and National-Level Measures." Federal Emergency Management Agency. https://www.fema.gov/media-library-data/1466085676217-a14e229a461adfa574a5d03041a6297c/FEMA-CRI-Draft-Concept-Paper-508_Jun_2016.pdf.

Wright, Kathryn, Kalee Whitehouse, and Julie Curti. 2017. "Voluntary Resilience Standards: An Assessment of the Emerging Market for Resilience in the Built Environment." Meister Consultants Group. http://www.mc-group.com/wp-content/uploads/2017/05/Final-Report_VoluntaryResilienceStandards_v1.pdf.

# 6

# RESILIENCE HUBS

## Shifting Power to Communities through Action

*Kristin Baja*

### Introduction

Resilience should be holistic and comprehensive; it is not about "bouncing back" after a disruption to the status quo, but an opportunity to proactively reimagine systems, center on human everyday needs, build in redundancy, and increase the capacity to adapt and thrive amidst changing conditions.

Unfortunately, the way resilience is defined has been controversial for at least the last decade. An archaic definition developed and supported by many federal government agencies is that resilience is "the ability of a community to bounce back after hazardous events" (NOAA, 2020). This definition is not only short-sighted, but also concentrates resilience on disruptions and hard infrastructure solutions that attempt to control nature rather than on holistic options that work with nature, center human needs, shifts power into neighborhoods, and emphasize systems that enhance quality of life (Baja, 2020a).

Communities should be resilient year-round, not just in the event of a major disturbance but in the face of all stressors, challenges, and disruptions. However, to create resilient communities, acknowledgment of power dynamics, systemic racism, and intentional disenfranchisement must be at the core of the work; centering healing, reparative action, power shifting, and community health and well-being.

This chapter describes a way to operationalize equity in resilience work and shift power from government to community members and partners through the development of neighborhood Resilience Hubs. Communities that have suffered decades of disenfranchisement and systemic racism have learned to distrust government and institutions that continue to prioritize economic benefits over human equality of life. This chapter identifies Resilience Hubs as an actionable solution to increase community self-determination while working at the intersection of climate resilience, greenhouse gas (GHG) mitigation, human health, and emergency management.

DOI: 10.4324/9781003030720-6

This chapter begins by reframing resilience and utilizing a more comprehensive and human-centered approach to increasing community resilience by introducing the concept of Resilience Hubs. It is then broken into six sections:

1. What Resilience Hubs are and what they are not;
2. How Resilience Hubs came to be and were co-developed with community members;
3. The five foundational elements that establish a Hub;
4. How Hubs can be utilized for both short-term shocks and long-term disruptions including a global pandemic;
5. Potential sources of funding and financing; and
6. Examples of communities actively working to establish a Resilience Hub.

Ideally, Resilience Hubs are neighborhood-determined and managed sites that enhance community adaptive capacity and ability to thrive, improve community well-being and connectivity, and reduce risk year-round.

## *Reframing Resilience for Hubs*

Resilience requires community capacity to plan for, respond to, and recover from everyday stressors and both short- and long-term disruptions (Baja, 2019b). Short-term disruptions such as heat waves, hurricanes, and other extreme weather events—often intensified by climate change—may seemingly be short-term, but also have long-term cascading impacts, especially for low-income and communities in high-risk areas who may be unable to recover from a loss of wages or damage to property.

Long-term disruptions, such as a global pandemic or an extended wildfire season, can stretch from months to years and often exacerbate everyday stressors and short-term disruptions, and vice versa. At all times, people and their communities need the ability to anticipate, accommodate, adapt, and thrive.

However, resilience is not disaster response and recovery; resilience is not "bouncing back". A resilient community is a community that is resilient year-round, not just in the event of a disruption. There is a critical need to reframe the way we talk about resilience and determine which approaches and actions to prioritize. Rather than focusing primarily on technical solutions, we need to reframe resilience holistically and focus on meeting the needs of people year-round.

Many people, especially Black Indigenous and People of Color (BIPOC), experience a constant struggle to meet their everyday needs such as putting food on the table, getting from one location to another safely, and having access to clean water. This is due to centuries of racism and white supremacy that are institutionalized into our systems and structures and have led to inequitable stressors for BIPOC communities.

Stressors refer to the everyday challenges that make people and communities more vulnerable to disruptions and climate change, including epidemic drug use, poverty, aging infrastructure, and unemployment—all of which are exacerbated by disruptions and make it more difficult to proactively plan, respond, and recover.

Re-centering resilience on community needs and self-determination can improve social cohesion and strong partnerships while providing greater access to resources such as food, water, childcare, internet, and other services. A more resilient community also includes consideration of foundational elements of community quality of life, such as greater access to jobs, more affordable housing, strengthening infrastructure, and stronger social support systems.

## Prioritizing Marginalized Communities

Government in the United States was designed around a single user group: white male landowners (Williams-Rajee, 2020). This intentional design was based on extraction from both people and the environment, and provided resources, access, and power to a subset of the population while withholding opportunities and power from all others. As a result, the United States has massive wealth gaps, inequitable power structures, and unequal access to resources.

BIPOC communities bore and continue to bear the outcome of unjust systems, but they are also the populations impacted most by a rapidly changing climate. Climate change is also connected to other crises, such as the current COVID-19 pandemic. As disaster events increase in frequency and intensity around the world, humans push further into habitats primarily inhabited by other species and increase likelihood of future global pandemics. COVID-19 has already shown us that "Pacific Islanders, Latino, Black and Indigenous Americans all have a COVID-19 death rate of double or more that of White and Asian Americans" (APM, 2021). Therefore, Resilience Hubs should be prioritized in BIPOC and low-income communities that have been intentionally disregarded for centuries.

Resilient communities are ones that thrive every day, during disruptions, and as they recover from disruption. A critical component of thriving in day-to-day life is having a community that values a person's life and a government and institutions that are accountable for supporting that individual's well-being.

Investing in and supporting Resilience Hubs provides an opportunity for government to collaborate with communities to dismantle our unjust systems and shift power to residents and community-based partners to design and influence decision-making and resource distribution, and self-determine future opportunities.

They can create both a physical space and also a culture and relationships that support all residents and work to dismantle inequities and their root causes. Resilience Hubs reject the "one size fits all" approach and "one user group" design and prioritize funding, resources, and community benefits in disenfranchised communities. The development process captures the unique characteristics and needs of each neighborhood, and provides an opportunity to openly acknowledge and repair our broken systems while benefiting community well-being and enhancing adaptive capacity.

## *What Is a Resilience Hub?*

Resilience Hubs are community-determined and community-serving facilities enhanced to support residents, provide programming, coordinate communication, distribute resources, connect people to nature, and reduce carbon pollution while enhancing social cohesiveness and quality of life (Baja, 2019a). They provide an opportunity to effectively work at the nexus of community resilience, emergency management, human health, climate change mitigation, and social equity while also offering opportunities for communities to become more self-determining, socially connected, and successful year-round.

Resilience Hubs use a physical space—a building and its surrounding infrastructure—to meet numerous physical, ecological, and social goals. These physical spaces are rooted in place (typically neighborhoods) to ensure reliability, coordination, and accessibility. Some of the most successful Hubs utilize existing well-trusted spaces such as community centers, recreation facilities, faith-based buildings, or multi-family housing common areas where members already gather and value the site. Often existing buildings require retrofitting to meet newly identified service and programming needs along with improving redundancy and reliability of systems. In addition, sites are intended to act as a focal point for resource distribution, access to parks and open space, heating, cooling, clean air and water, and power needs as well as a range of other services. In some cases, new construction is an option as long as community members are involved as partners in site determination and co-design (Figure 6.1).

Kristin Baja @USDN

**Figure 6.1 Resilience Hub.**

## What Resilience Hubs Are Not

Resilience Hubs are not emergency shelters. They are not spaces opened only in the event of a disruption. They are also not solely buildings with backup power systems and generators. Hubs can emerge in a variety of ways, but they must be centered on a comprehensive vision of resilience and shifting power to communities to increase neighborhood self-determination. Therefore, Hubs are not intended for use only in the event of disruption and emergency and should not center around hazards for planning. Finally, Resilience Hubs are community-driven and co-designed. They should not be identified or selected by government or organizational partners without community collaboration and support.

## *How Was the Concept of a Resilience Hub Developed?*

Resilience Hubs were born out of a series of community preparedness meetings with residents in Baltimore City. At the time, I was serving as the Climate Resilience Planner for the City of Baltimore and was responsible for development and implementation of the city's *Make a Plan. Build a Kit. Help Each Other* and *Every Story Counts* campaigns (Peltier 2016). As the city's resilience lead, I attended over 40 community meetings in neighborhoods still reeling from the impacts of redlining, segregation, environmental injustice, and the city's racist policies and practices.

At these meetings, I guided community members in learning about climate change and natural disasters, creating emergency plans, and building emergency kits. (All materials were provided to participants.) However, as part of "help each other element" I focused on listening and asking questions about people's lived experiences (Akerlof, 2016).

In these listening sessions, people voiced a lack of trust in government, lack of support in their daily needs being met, and a lack of resources. While we had reduced resilience to simply setting aside cans of food and backup water, people's stories demonstrated that the need was far greater than a plan or kit. We needed to do better, to go deeper, and to better understand why community members refused to go to emergency shelters even if they desperately needed assistance. The need for support was tremendous and yet, so were the damaging effects of decades of systemic racism.

Based on these early listening sessions and campaigns, I worked with neighborhood community leaders to revamp the city's resilience efforts. Instead of using the archaic "one size fits all" structure provided by both federal and state agencies, we decided to continue with community member interviews and listening sessions. Through these sessions we heard stories of government neglect and discrimination that opened my eyes.

Residents shared that discrimination and racism were alive and thriving in the city; community members no longer wanted to rely on government support, they wanted autonomy. Together, we conducted in-depth vulnerability assessments, identified challenges and shortcomings, and ultimately co-developed the community's preferred solution: Resilience Hubs.

Community members wanted support to retrofit existing buildings, improve services and programming, and increase community self-sufficiency year-round. With generous support from the Town Creek Foundation, we were able to collaborate, co-design, and test different options in four neighborhoods in Baltimore City. Each had different specific needs, but the overall desire was clear: residents wanted to be more well-resourced, aware, accurately informed, and self-determined without government oversight or reliance.

These pilot sites brought a number of challenges to light but also allowed us to experiment with co-developed solutions. The concept of Resilience Hubs grew in popularity through presentations, information sharing sessions, and peer learning opportunities. As interest grew, I transitioned to a new position with the Urban Sustainability Directors Network (USDN) which allowed me to work more directly with cities and counties across North America.

USDN is a network of over 240 local government sustainability, climate, and racial equity leaders focused on centering racial equity in all climate and sustainability work. Through a series of network collaboration opportunities and collective action groups with community members and other city leaders, the Resilience Hub concept became more refined and structured. I have written several documents including a white paper and guidance document along with development of a public website to ensure materials were (and still are) available to all interested parties. USDN continues to collaborate with regional and national partners as well as directly with local community-based organizations to support the development of Resilience Hubs across North America.

## Location of Hubs

Resilience Hubs tend to be in urban areas or more dense suburban spaces. Although they can also be utilized in rural areas, rural Hubs are more likely to serve a response and recovery purpose rather than year-round gathering location or node for community resources. For example, Wellington, New Zealand, has a network of Community Emergency Hubs that activate in the event of a disaster, such as an earthquake. These local community hubs are managed and supported by residents; however, they are often not within walking distance and are only activated in a disruption.

Urban Resilience Hubs are intentionally located in more densely populated areas where people have been made more vulnerable due

# RESILIENCE HUBS: SHIFTING POWER TO COMMUNITIES

to discriminatory zoning, redlining, and intentional citing of non-desirable uses. These areas are often referred to as *sacrifice zones* (Lerner, 2010) which denote low-income and BIPOC communities that have permanent impacts from pollution and economic disinvestment. In addition, these communities often have crumbling infrastructure, inadequate housing, lack of access to resources, green space and transportation, and poor health conditions. They are often the last neighborhoods to be supported in a disruption and are certainly the neighborhoods that continue to be overlooked by developers and decision-makers. Thus, the greatest need for Resilience Hubs are primarily in lower-income BIPOC neighborhoods that are still dealing with historic and current inequities and discrimination.

Hubs can also act as safe spaces for undocumented persons, those experiencing homelessness and other marginalized groups. There should not be identification or insurance requirements for services and/or use of a Resilience Hub. Instead, community members can collectively determine the service area (geographical range) for the site and have resources available for those seeking additional support such as sheltering or medical services that are not provided at the Hub.

## Three Modes for Resilience Hubs

In order to meet community needs year-round, Resilience Hubs function in three modes or operating conditions: (1) everyday (non-disruption), (2) response (both short- and long-term disruption), and (3) recovery (Figure 6.2).

Everyday (non-disruption) mode encompasses everyday stressors such as access to childcare, healthy food and water, or appropriate

## RESILIENCE MODES

USDN urban sustainability directors network

| | |
|---|---|
| Everyday (non disruption) | • All infrastructure and services are available.<br>• No major disruptions are present.<br>• Primary focus is on community services and programming and relationship-building. |
| Disruption | • Disruption to normal everyday function for any duration.<br>• Disruptions can include natural disasters, health-disasters (pandemic) and human-influenced disruptions.<br>• Disruption can vary from minutes to months or years. |
| Short-term | • Related to shocks or events that hit relatively quickly such as a hurricane or tornado |
| Long-term | • Related to disruptions that last longer and impact "everyday mode" such as global pandemic or war |
| Recovery | • Process of returning to everyday mode.<br>• The aftermath of the disruption during which the community works to restore normal or better conditions.<br>• Can last days to years. |

Kristin Baja @USDN

Figure 6.2 Three modes.

programming for seniors and youth. Essentially, the everyday mode is when no major disruption influencing the entire neighborhood is present but services and resources can still be provided through the Hub. Although individuals may have personal or familial disruptions such as loss of a job or divorce, those are not disruptions for the entire community.

In everyday mode, Resilience Hubs act as trusted neighborhood spaces that provide a range of community-determined services and programming and access to community spaces such as gardens, recreation, or green spaces. They are also the location to bring in proactive planning and preparedness services so the community can co-design and co-develop culturally appropriate solutions that help guide and support external partners in response and recovery modes.

Response mode, also referred to as disruption mode, is when a disruption is present and impacting the majority of the community. Disruptions vary in scale and impact and can be either short- or long-term.

Short-term disruptions like a hurricane, snowstorm, or tornado may have long-term impacts even when the disruption itself is short-lived. This is often when communities are experiencing loss of resources, capacity, assets, and, in some cases, lives. This is also when emergency response and recovery services are necessary and when community members can actively engage in supporting each other and ensuring those with less capacity are prioritized.

For short-term disruptions, Resilience Hubs provide a location where emergency response partners can drop off supplies and provide additional resources to those with the most need, channeled through a space they trust, feel safe, and have a sense of ownership. Hubs also provide a space to organize community search and rescue, post information and updates, and center communications and coordination efforts.

Long-term disruptions impact the entire community and lead to changes in access to resources and quality of life such as a pandemic. Short-term and long-term disruptions can occur simultaneously and often are threat multipliers. For example, the COVID-19 pandemic required physical distancing and shutting down of several service providers. Essential workers such as agricultural, health, and transportation still were necessary for a functioning society, however; when wildfires started burning along states in the west coast, those workers were put in harm's way due to poor air quality and extreme temperatures. These individuals were more risk to the virus because they couldn't afford to lose wages and the threats to their health multiplied with the wildfires.

Resilience Hubs can help coordinate a variety of services during long-term disruptions. They are locations to access trusted information; for community members to receive treatments, access to testing, and/or vaccines; to connect service providers with those in need for resources such as food, water, and supplies; and to translate and disseminate information in culturally respectful ways and in a resident's primary language.

Recovery mode can have an extensive timeline that differs based on individual and community circumstances. It is the period of time when resources, materials, and support are often available but may have barriers to access or coordination challenges. Typically, national and/or regional partners come into communities through federal programs that have long timelines such as federal buy-out programs which can take years to come to fruition (Zavar, 2019). Resilience Hubs provide an opportunity to bring in support services and translators to assist with arduous processes and better support residents in need of additional capacity and support.

## Five Foundational Areas

Resilience Hubs are unique, just like the neighborhoods they serve, and there are no two that are exactly alike. However, over the last seven years of supporting Resilience Hubs it has become clear that there are five foundational elements that make each of them successful:

1. Services and Programming;
2. Communications;
3. Building and Landscape;
4. Power Systems; and
5. Operations.

Most Hubs do not and may never have full completion in each of these areas. However, neighborhoods are encouraged to set ambitious goals for all three resilience modes (everyday, disruption, and recovery) in the five foundational areas (Figure 6.3).

When identifying community needs and goals in the five foundational areas, it is important to provide a range of options from baseline to ideal. That is, what elements a site must have to be considered a Resilience Hub (baseline); what elements the community would like to have and strive towards over time (optional); and what the most idealized version of a Resilience Hub would be.

I have facilitated exercises to identify community needs and goals over 40 times with communities throughout the United States. This workshop provides an opportunity for community members and community partners to identify criteria for their Resilience Hub and then ground their expectations around funding, capacity, and timeline.

Typically, this workshop is designed to be a collective vision board exercise. Each of the five foundational areas is listed as headers (or circles) situated around a community building. Within each box, the three modes of resilience (everyday, disruption, recovery) are positioned along the top and the three range of options (baseline, optional, and

| Resilient Services and Programming | Resilient Communications | Resilient Building and Landscape | Resilient Power Systems | Resilient Operations |
|---|---|---|---|---|
| The Hub has additional services and programs that build relationships, promote community preparedness, and improve residents' health and well-being. | Building relationships and respect within the neighborhood (service area) year-round. Ensuring the ability to communicate within and outside the service area during disruptions. | Strengthening the resilience of the facility to ensure that it meets operational goals in all conditions. Identify opportunities to utilize surrounding landscape for resilience benefits. | Ensuring uninterrupted power to the facility during a hazard while also improving the cost-effectiveness and sustainability of operations in all three resilience modes. | Ensuring personnel and processes are in place to operate the facility year-round and also continue operating during disruption and recovery. |
| Examples:<br>• Maker Space<br>• How To Courses (ex. computers)<br>• Job Trainings and Recruitment<br>• Health Services<br>• Nutrition Services | Examples:<br>• CERT Training with extra section for proactive outreach<br>• Radio<br>• Translated Info<br>• Culturally relevant | Examples:<br>• Air Filtration<br>• Water Capture and reused<br>• Weatherization<br>• Earthquake-proof<br>• Urban Gardening | Examples:<br>• Hybrid Power Solutions include battery-back up and generator<br>• Solar Panels | Examples:<br>• Site Leadership<br>• Accessibility<br>• Site Retrofits and Assigned Task Management<br>• Roles in all Modes |

Kristin Baja @USDN

Figure 6.3  Foundational areas.

ideal) are positioned on the left. Using the board, community members and partners begin to co-design the community Resilience Hub and prioritize services, design components, and needs. Beginning with baseline needs and desires often works best so communities can be realistic about funding and timelines (Figure 6.4).

### Resilient Services and Programming

Community members determine which services are needed to meet a range of community needs. Site services and programs will differ from neighborhood to neighborhood based on a range of factors such as percentage of persons of advanced age, desire for maker spaces and job training, or need for coordinated childcare. Programs may include performing and visual arts, senior connection services, cooking classes, horticulture courses, children's before and/or after school programs, or proactive Community Emergency Response Team (CERT) training. Services may include a tool checkout, computer and Wi-Fi access, access to mental health experts and social workers, trainings on how to manage finances, meal services, potable water refill stations, access to showers and restrooms, or other services that improve community members health and well-being.

Services and programming must be adaptable and fluid. They need to be able to adjust based on community needs and the way a community grows over time. For example, if a large number of community members are new mothers who desire a space for gathering that has safe and comfortable spaces for children and that supports their ability to gather, talk, run their own business, then the site will need

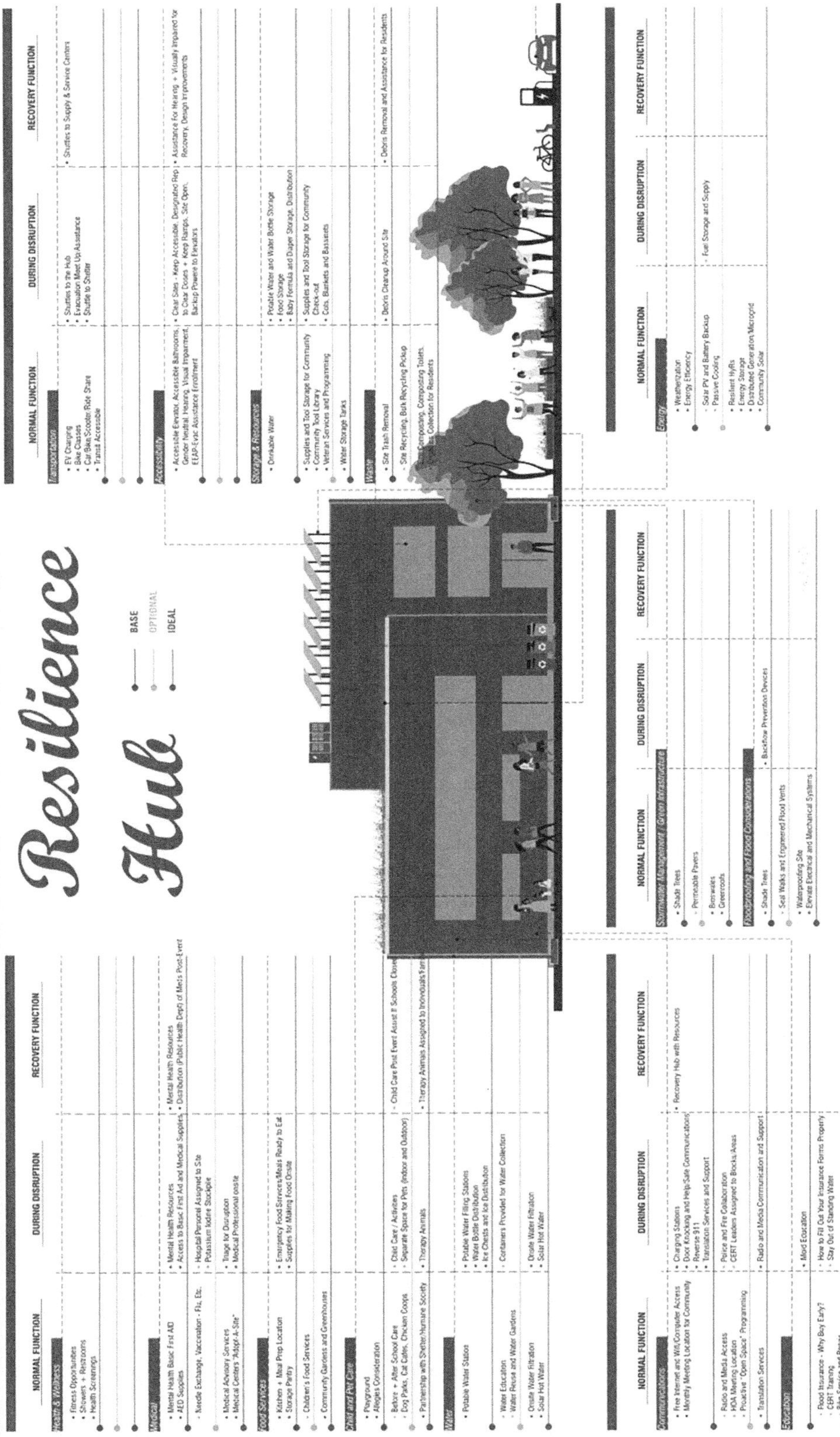

RESILIENCE HUBS: SHIFTING POWER TO COMMUNITIES    99

**Figure 6.4 Workshop facilitation.**

structure in the everyday to support their needs. After five years, the needs may change and community members may seek more educational programming and services for seniors on a daily basis.

An example is Boyle Heights Arts Conservatory (BHAC) in Los Angeles. BHAC provides media, creative arts, and technology programming that is inclusive of members of the community so they can learn and pursue careers in arts and creative industries. The team at BHAC prioritizes supporting young people in writing, recording, editing, songwriting, and much more so they can pursue careers while also having a place to connect with others and feel supported. The youth-led radio station is an element of programming that connects to resilient communication by also ensuring residents have access to information from trusted sources and in Spanish which is important since 94% of the population of Boyle Heights is Hispanic or Latino (LA Times, 2021).

### *Resilient Communications*

Accessible, reliable, and easily understood information is essential to community cohesion and connectivity in all three resilience modes. Although communication is often thought of as electronic and printed materials or scheduled meetings, the core of resilient communication is trust and relationships.

The Chicago heatwave of 1995 taught us how important social connectivity and cohesiveness is. In an interview with Eric Klinenberg, author of *Heat Wave*, he stated that "the death toll was the result of distinct dangers in Chicago's social environment: an increased population of isolated seniors who live and die alone: the culture of fear that makes city dwellers reluctant to trust their neighbors…" (Klinenberg, 2002). Essentially, the causes of death in the Chicago heatwave were isolation, lack of connectivity, and lack of trust because neighbors didn't know each other or check in on each other. Thus, enhancing and supporting opportunities to connect with neighbors and building stronger relationships is a key to community resilience, and Resilience Hubs provide a node for interactions, healing and trauma support, trainings, and continuous relationship-building.

In addition, Hubs can be utilized as a center for distributing and receiving information year-round. It is often said that people are unaware of risk and that education campaigns are a way to increase community resilience. However, in my experience, there are often a large number of campaigns happening simultaneously from different government departments, community organizations, and institutional partners which leads to community champions and information channels being overrun.

Resilience Hubs provide a neighborhood node for information sharing where community members can co-develop the type of information they would like access to, identify how they would like to be supported, and determine what languages the information needs to be in to make it accessible. This challenges all stakeholders to listen to community needs, streamline and translate information for ease of use, translate to multiple learning levels and through different mediums, and to take direction from community members in how to support dissemination of information.

Proactive relationship building is key; well-organized and coordinated communication pathways based on trust can then be utilized more effectively in disruption and recovery. This includes hosting events and providing trainings for community members as well as proactively setting up connections with the local Emergency Operations Center (EOC) and other service providers. Additionally, structuring internal communications is important, including role designation, use of walkie-talkies, monitoring of the radio, and coordinated search and rescue.

Wellington, New Zealand, community emergency hubs provide an excellent framework for internal communications in the event of a disruption. Although their model is based around the disaster rather than community resilience year-round, they have developed a set of resources including community emergency hub kits and structure for how to work as a team onsite.

Increasing the community's adaptive capacity through proactive communications and relationship building will help reduce strain on resources, better support emergency service providers, and increase community adaptive capacity.

## Resilient Building and Landscaping

Resilience Hubs provide architects, landscape architects, and engineers with unique opportunities and significant challenges. Typically, the most successful Hubs are located in existing buildings that can range in age, materials, and use. In many cases, the communities most in need of Hubs are those that have been disenfranchised and intentionally ignored for decades. In the United States, this tends to be in BIPOC and low-income neighborhoods impacted by redlining and sacrifice zones (Lerner, 2010). Hubs work best when located in already trusted community spaces; most often those spaces are older buildings with unique layouts and/or sites managed on small budgets which can make them difficult to retrofit and upgrade.

Despite these challenges, community members should lead the selection of the Resilience Hub site and be active participants in co-designing new spaces or retrofitting existing spaces (Baja 2019b). For example, if the community determines that having a food pantry and community kitchen is the most critical need, the design team will need to focus on retrofitting the interior space for storage and commercial kitchen use rather than focusing on external landscaping or upgrading electrical for solar energy systems.

Ideally, the physical building(s) that acts as the Hub node will have access to clean and filtered air, healthy and potable water, nutritious food, heating and cooling, power for lighting and charging, and sanitation. Depending on the additional services determined by the community, the Hub can also include amenities such as shower and locker facilities, entertainment spaces, and maker spaces which translates to a wide range of scale and cost. On a basic level, considerations for electric and plumbing upgrades, roof replacement, weatherization, and security are often primary considerations. Commonly, designers face challenges that are related to lack of storage space or battery backup systems.

Similarly, landscape architects may face challenges in retrofitting outdoor spaces for community uses that help improve resilience while meeting programming needs. The most common landscaping alterations include opportunities to grow food such as community gardens, greenhouses, or aquaculture; increased shade and cooling such as increasing tree canopy or integrating shade structures; multi-use spaces that capture and release water such as underground cisterns with above ground raingardens or bioswales; and access to recreational opportunities such as parks, fields and courts.

Connection to nature and outdoor space has also been found to improve mental health in addition to physical health (White, 2019). Ideally, Hubs recognize and integrate mental and physical health considerations and the benefits of nature and green spaces as critical components. Landscaping can provide space for community connectivity, improve human health, support ecosystem services, and reduce risk. Based on projected climate impacts, regionally specific concerns, and specific neighborhood needs, landscape retrofits vary considerably from site to site.

For example, development of Resilience Hubs in the East Bay of California has led to specific programming for a network of "resilient spaces" that connect to the Hub. These spaces can include community gardens, community-supported green infrastructure, tool-banks in community sheds, or personally owned spaces that are converted to community use (NorCal Resilience Network, 2021).

### Resilient Power Systems

Access to power is critical year-round. With the increased dependence on handheld devices and the internet as sources of information, connection, and communication, having a community space to utilize Wi-Fi, computers, and charging stations is important in all resilience modes. In addition to communications and connectivity, refrigeration, heating, cooling, and lighting are important for human health and well-being. Each of these services requires electricity and a functioning power system.

Generators rely heavily on proactive maintenance practices and knowledge of the system. Unfortunately, backup generators not only contribute to GHG emissions, they also rely heavily on servicing, right-sizing, and human intervention, and if neglected, lead to increased likelihood of failure in emergency situations (Marqusee and Jenket, 2020). For example, several hospitals in New York City had to evacuate patients after their backup generators failed during Hurricane Sandy (CBS, 2012). Even with warnings about the storm and time to prepare, human error led to putting patients' lives in danger.

Resilience Hub's power solution must meet social, operational, financial, and environmental goals. Although there are many renewable energy solutions, to date, the majority of resilient power projects connected to Resilience Hubs are solar and storage solutions and Hybrid Resilience Systems (HyRS). HyRS is a generation and storage system that utilizes grid generation, solar photovoltaic generation, and batteries to meet the Hubs goals in all three modes while remaining fiscally sensible (Oxnam & Baja, 2019).

Putting solar and backup battery storage or a HyRS system on a building helps to make that building more resilient. The system provides renewable energy and stores energy for use in the event of grid failure and/or disruption. However, installing a resilient energy system does not translate to enhancing community resilience. If community members are unaware of the resilient energy system or distrust the building and/or owner of the site, they won't go to it. They won't receive benefits of the resilient power daily or in the event of a disruption. Ensuring reliable backup power to a facility while also improving cost-effectiveness and sustainability of operations in all three resilience modes is the goal with integrating renewable energy (solar) systems with storage (battery backup).

Installing resilient power systems on Hubs provides an opportunity to partner with local solar partners, offer technical skills training to community members from the neighborhood, and potentially require local job generation. USDN partners with national level organizations such as Clean Energy Group (CEG) and American Microgrid Solutions (AMS) to provide energy audits and solar and storage feasibility assessments and to design preliminary solutions that meet the community's specific power needs. These partners then work with local trainers and organizations to help identify financing solutions, train local workers, and install the systems.

For example, USDN and the Southeast Sustainability Directors Network (SSDN) collaborated to provide a grant and direct support to Fulton County, Georgia, for the development of several Resilience Hubs. USDN brought in CEG and AMS to provide funding and technical support for feasibility assessments on four potential sites and then worked with local partners such as Southface Institute and local energy partners to begin designing actionable solutions.

Beyond reliable and resilient power, Resilience Hubs also provide potential economic benefits. Renewable energy and storage systems can reduce power bills, generate revenue for utilities by generating power onsite, and potentially even provide additional savings if regulations allow for community solar benefits.

## Resilient Operations

Resilience Hubs require a capable team that supports different elements of the Hub in different operating conditions. The most reliable Hubs are ones with personnel and processes in place to ensure continued operations, adaptable services and programming, and ongoing support. Additionally, the site must be safe and accessible for all people within the neighborhood. This requires Americans with Disabilities Act (ADA) compliance, consideration of security measures, and ongoing maintenance. For example, it may be important to create spaces exclusively for children and people with children, and to have those spaces separated from other adult-only spaces to proactively ensure all parties feel safe and spaces are designed to support different uses and/or needs.

Site operations also include elements around trainings, personnel, and contractor specifications. Resilience Hubs are intended to support disenfranchised communities but they also have the ability to help create a more equitable market by prioritizing contracts with women-owned and BIPOC-owned businesses, hiring local contractors, and demanding external contractors to consider all five foundational areas and a holistic approach.

Lastly, site operations must proactively consider site activation. How will community members be continuously involved in both design and decision-making around the Hub? What differences will there be in hours of operation and resources in different operating modes? How will community members who have difficultly leaving their homes be supported proactively?

USDN is working with partners to develop resources and guidance to help answer some of these questions such as creating an additional level to CERT training focused on proactive outreach and support for those with additional needs. However, each community is unique and operations considerations must be made with community leaders and partners.

## Networks of Resilience Hubs

As previously mentioned, no two Resilience Hubs are exactly alike. In my time working on Resilience Hub development in communities across the country, I have seen a number of different sites utilized or developed as Hubs.

In some areas, population density or socio-cultural differences generate a "network of Hubs" approach rather than a focus on one Resilience Hub. A networked approach has the same core considerations and foundational areas: "soft elements" such as community cohesiveness, adaptive capacity, and connectivity as well as retrofits to "hard elements" such as buildings, community spaces, and infrastructure. However, these elements must be considered at a larger scale and integrated into a larger community resilience vision.

Certain sites may have higher capacity for one foundational area such as a site with a radio tower and radio station may be a stronger "communications site" whereas other site may have more space and storage for community gardens and food growth, thus making them a "food distribution site". Although it is ideal for all Resilience Hubs to have all five foundational areas, networks of Hubs are likely to serve different niches and coordination will be a critical element for optimal function. Currently, networks of Resilience Hubs are being considered in Houston, Hawaii, Oakland, Puerto Rico, and southeast Florida.

## Resilience Hubs in a Pandemic

Throughout the COVID-19 pandemic it has become increasingly clear that our systems need to change. It is critical that community members have access to trusted information, safe community spaces, and easily accessible parks and green spaces to support social connections, mental and physical health support, civic discourse, and emergency response—all keys to resilience.

Resilience Hubs can help coordinate these services; reduce strain on hospitals and first responders; improve dissemination of resources, supplies, and critical information; and even serve as sites for testing and vaccinations. Hubs are set up to support communities in the event of a disruption.

The World Health Organization (WHO) has warned that the COVID-19 global pandemic will not be our last (DW, 2020). Early in the COVID-19 pandemic, I outlined six ways that Resilience Hubs could help in responding to the pandemic including acting as:

1. Community-based testing sites;
2. Neighborhood distribution centers;
3. Locations to coordinate childcare and meals;
4. Virtual platform and mutual aid organization;
5. Equity-centered proactive planning sites; and
6. Redundant and reliable systems (Baja, 2020b).

## The Hub Funding Puzzle

It is critical for federal, state, and local governments to invest in neighborhood-based Resilience Hubs and to shift power to the hands of communities that have been intentionally ignored and diminished for decades. Investments in Hubs help communities become more self-determining while also improving coordination and connectivity, and increasing adaptive capacity.

From their prior site uses and conditions to their primary goals and functions, funding Resilience Hubs projects is like putting together a complex puzzle. Just as houses span from tiny homes to large mansions, Resilience Hubs range in size and sophistication. Because Hubs bring together so many different fields of practice and areas of specialty, there is no one source of funding for these sites at this time.

Ideally, Resilience Hubs will be classified as critical facilities and critical neighborhood functions and eventually be fully funded and supported by federal funding. The United States Federal Emergency Management Agency (FEMA), Department of Housing and Urban Development (HUD), and Health and Human Services (HHS) all have funding resources and interest in community resilience and well-being. Hubs could help reduce barriers among funding sources and also ensure resources were going into community-supported projects.

While USDN and partners are working towards this type of coordination and support from the federal government, current forms of funding come from a combination of philanthropic support or one-time pilot grants. Thus, when seeking out funding for a Resilience Hub it is easiest to organize sources into two buckets: financial mechanisms and grants.

Financial mechanisms include sources of funding that local governments can utilize such as revolving loans, bonds, loan programs, or other debt financing. Examples include public benefit bonds, impact investing partnerships, and power purchase agreements (PPAs). USDN has partnered with Climate Resilience Consulting to develop a funding and financing resource guide for Resilience Hubs. That guide will be available online[1] in mid-2021.

Grants can come from several different sources including philanthropy, state or federal government, and utilities. Grants are often preferred because repayment is not expected. However, they also tend to be short-term support or for single projects rather than continuous operations. Grants tend to fall into two categories: proactive preparedness which supports everyday mode and post-disaster funding which supports in disruption and recovery mode.

Successful grant applications for Resilience Hubs usually include seeking grants within the five foundational areas. Because different sectors have different funders and investors, it is easiest to seek funding for the resilient power system separately from ADA retrofits or communications support. For example, the City of Minneapolis and Little Earth of United Tribes collectively sought funding to support a Resilience Hub. The City was able to provide support for peer learning and training and in-home health assessments through existing programs while also bringing in funding from philanthropy and USDN partners to support the resilient power system work. They also brought in partner such as the Center for Energy and Environment to work on site retrofits to reduce energy and water use and help save the site money (USDN, 2021).

## Communities Actively Working to Establish Resilience Hubs

Resilience Hubs provide investors and businesses interested in supporting community resilience, equity, and proactive climate action with an implementable solution that's flexible and has social, environmental, and economic benefits over time. Communities throughout North America are actively working to establish neighborhood Resilience Hubs. Most have started based on community input or community demand for neighborhood resilience projects; however, others have started from initiatives identified in resilience plans or through disaster risk reduction efforts.

## Conclusions

When optimally designed, Resilience Hubs provide services that strengthen community resilience not simply in the face of disruption, but on a daily basis. Shifting power and capacity to communities through the development of Hubs can help reduce stress on systems and infrastructure such as public safety, hospitals, and transportation while increasing community adaptive capacity.

Resilience Hubs can become community cornerstones where neighbors come together to better understand one another, cooperate toward common goals, and bolster the health of their shared community. They can also help expedite and improve logistics for support networks and other relief agencies in the event of a disruption by providing established and well-trusted sites where people can access relief materials and resources easily and efficiently.

In closing, this chapter highlighted nine key recommendations for enhancing community resilience:

1. *Redefine resilience*. Resilient communities are resilient year-round. It is critical to acknowledge power dynamics, systemic racism, and intentional disenfranchisement of BIPOC communities and to shift to reparative action, power shifting, and centering human health and well-being.
2. *Prioritize marginalized communities*. The United States continues to suffer from white supremacy and systemic racism. Resilience Hubs must prioritize BIPOC and low-income communities and ensure that marginalized people have access to the resources, support, and power to increase self-determination and community adaptive capacity.
3. *Focus at the intersection of climate resilience, GHG mitigation, human health, and emergency management*. Resilience Hubs provide an opportunity to work at the intersection of many fields of practice while improving social, ecological, and technological systems holistically.

4. *Resilience Hubs should be community identified, designed, and supported.* Hubs work best when located in already trusted community spaces. Community members should lead site selection, participate in design, and identify community needs to be served in all resilience modes.
5. *Resilience Hubs must support community in all three resilience modes.* Hubs serve the community year-round: daily, during short-term disruptions and long-term disruptions, and throughout recovery.
6. *Communities should identify Hub criteria for baseline, optional, and ideal situations.* An important part of establishing a Hub is visioning and developing criteria for what a site must have, what elements it should have in the near future, and what the most idealized version would be.
7. *Resilience Hubs should include all five foundational areas.* To be a Resilience Hub, sites must have community services and programming, resilient power systems, building(s) and landscape, proactive communications, and strong operations.
8. *Federal and state government agencies and programs should support the development of Resilience Hubs.* Existing agencies have funding and initiatives aimed at enhancing community resilience, improving human health, reducing risk to climate impacts, and curbing GHG emissions. Hubs are an opportunity for funding and resources to be put into action.
9. *Resilience Hubs should be designated as critical facilities.* Neighborhood resilience should come from the bottom-up, not the top-down. Hubs as critical facilities would provide reliable funding and resources to local governments and communities, and increase neighborhood resilience.

## References

Akerlof, K. (2016). *Perceptions of Community Resilience: A Maryland Community Pilot Study, 2016.* Fairfax, VA: Center for Climate Change Communication, George Mason University.

American Public Media Research Lab. (2021). Accessed online 1/22/21 from https://www.apmresearchlab.org/covid/deaths-by-race.

Baja, K. (2020a). *Climate Resilience: Centering Racial Equity and Shifting Power.* Keynote Speaker, CannonDesign. Virtual Presentation, October 16, 2020.

Baja, Kristin. (2020b). *How Resilience Hubs in Cities Could Help Coronavirus Response.* Reuters, March 27, 2021. https://news.trust.org/item/20200327105242-0pnw2.

Baja, Kristin. (2019a). *Resilience Hubs. Shifting Power to Communities and Increasing Community Adaptive Capacity.* Urban Sustainability Directors Network.

Baja, Kristin. (2019b). *Guide to Developing Resilience Hubs.* Urban Sustainability Directors Network.

CBS (2012). *What Caused Generators to Fail at NYC Hospitals?* CBS News. Retrieved 12/27/20 from https://www.cbsnews.com/news/what-caused-generators-to-fail-at-nyc-hospitals/.

DW. 2020. *COVID-19 Will Not Be the Last Pandemic: WHO*. DW News. Retrieved 1/2/2021 from https://www.dw.com/en/covid-19-will-not-be-last-pandemic-who/a-56065483.

Klinenberg, Eric. 2002. *Dying Alone. An Interview with Eric Klinenberg Author of Heat Wave: A Social Autopsy of Disaster in Chicago*. University of Chicago Press. Retrieved 1/12/21 from: https://press.uchicago.edu/Misc/Chicago/443213in.html.

Lerner, Steve. 2010. *Sacrifice Zones: The Front Lines of Toxic Chemical Exposure in the United States*. Cambridge: MIT Press.

*Los Angeles Times*. Mapping LA > Rankings > Ethnicity by Neighborhood. Accessed online 1/20/21 from: http://maps.latimes.com/neighborhoods/ethnicity/latino/neighborhood/list/.

Marqusee, Jeffery and Jenket, Don. 2020. *Reliability of Emergency and Standby Diesel Generators: Impact on Energy Resiliency Solutions*. Applied Energy, 268, 114918. https://doi.org/10.1016/j.apenergy.2020.114918.

National Oceanic and Atmospheric Administration (NOAA). (2021). Retrieved on 12/24/20 from: https://oceanservice.noaa.gov/ecosystems/resilience/.

NorCal Resilience Network. 2021. *Resilient Spaces*. Retrieved 1/12/20 from: https://norcalresilience.org/resilient-hub-initiative/.

Oxnam, G. and Baja, K. (2019). *Powering Community Resilience: A Framework for Optimizing Resilience Hub Power Systems*. Urban Sustainability Directors Network.

Peltier, L. (2016). *Baltimore's Kristin Baja Honored by the White House for Climate Leadership*. Baltimore Fishbowl. July 14. Retrieved at: https://baltimorefishbowl.com/stories/baltimores-kristin-baja-honored-white-house-climate-leadership/.

USDN Progress Reports. (2021). *Minneapolis Resilience Hub Progress Report*. http://resilience-hub.org/.

White, M.P., Alcock, I., Grellier, J. et al. (2019) *Spending at least 120 minutes a week in nature is associated with good health and wellbeing*. Scientific Reports, 9, 7730. https://doi.org/10.1038/s41598-019-44097-3.

Williams-Rajee, D. (2020). *Equity and Climate Theory of Change*. Kapwa Consulting (K. Baja, Interviewer)

Zavar, E. (2019, May 28). *After Disaster: Why Home Buyout Programs Fizzle Out*. Gov1, pp. 1–3.

# 7
# CLIMATE CHANGE AND HEALTH

## Connecting the Dots, Building a Resilient Future

*Kim Knowlton and Yerina Mugica*

### Introduction

Climate change is a matter of public health, community health, and planetary health. This chapter, "Climate Change and Health: Connecting the Dots, Building a More Resilient Future" touches upon one of the most pressing aspects of climate change, namely society's uncertainties around what to anticipate in the ways of future extreme weather, changing environmental and social dynamics, and the degree to which our buildings and our communities will respond in a way that is resilient, just, and healthy for all.

### Climate Change and Human Health

#### *Connecting the Dots: Climate Change Is a Matter of Health in NY State Today and into the Future*

Climate change has been the topic of significant, if intermittent, media attention for decades in the United States, and yet only in recent years has it been recognized as a pressing public health issue. It's been 30 years since Dr. James Hansen, then director of NASA's Goddard Institute for Space Studies in New York City, told Congress that "The greenhouse effect has been detected, and it is changing our climate now" (Krajick 2018). It took decades longer for the human health effects to become more widely apparent to the scientific community and to the public. In 2010, the American Public Health Association (APHA) annual meeting offered only about a dozen talks on the topic of climate change. By 2017, climate change was the overarching theme of APHA's annual meeting, with over 300 talks, panel discussions, and posters offered on the topic (APHA 2018). Not only are public health professionals advocating more vocally for responding to climate change's threats to health; over 170 international schools that train medical, nursing, and public health professionals have committed to include climate change in their educational curricula (GCCHE 2018).

DOI: 10.4324/9781003030720-7

In recent years, warming of the atmosphere and oceans has had global effects with very local impacts in New York State, the Northeast, and the Great Lakes. More frequent, more intense, and longer-lasting heat waves plague the region, causing acute increases in reported heat-related illnesses and deaths and respiratory, cardiovascular, and kidney ailments and mortality. Rising temperatures exacerbate air pollution as they speed the rate of formation of ground-level ozone smog; contribute to drought conditions that enhance windblown dust, wildfire, and smoke conditions; and lengthen the seasons over which airborne allergenic pollen is produced (USEPA 2008; Horton et al. 2014a; NYSDOH 2015). Not only is outdoor air quality threatened by climate change: indoor air quality is reduced when moisture-damaged residential and business infrastructure harbors mold growth (IOM 2011). Warmer atmospheric temperatures have contributed to changing precipitation patterns, and over the last 60 years extreme rainfall has increased in the Northeast (Melillo, Richmond, and Yohe 2014). The NCA3 report's *Highlights* show a 71% change in the amount of precipitation falling in very heavy events (the heaviest 1%) from 1958 to 2012 in the Northeastern US, which includes New York, part of a national trend toward greater amounts of precipitation being concentrated in very heavy events.

Those extreme rains increase the extent of inland flooding across the state, even as climate change-fueled sea level rise and coastal storms with higher maximum wind speeds, more rainfall, and higher storm surge heights increase the extent of coastal flooding. This flooding affects the state's buildings via direct threats to building integrity and access, and moreover to indoor air quality.

Climate change is increasing the range and biting behavior of vectors like mosquitoes that can carry infectious diseases including West Nile virus, dengue fever and chikungunya, or Lyme disease and other tick-borne illnesses. With all these multiple climate-health threats, mental health is becoming more frequently cited as a public health concern that threatens personal well-being, workplace and school productivity, and community stability (Luber et al. 2014). The projected impacts of climate change on the health of the people of New York state have been described elsewhere (APHA 2016), in reports like the New York State Department of Health's 2015 BRACE (Building Resilience Against Climate Extremes) report (NYSDOH 2015), the 2014 update of ClimAID (Horton et al. 2014a), the 2014 Third US National Climate Assessment (NCA3)'s *Northeast* chapter (Horton et al. 2014b) (or the soon to be released NCA4 report), and numerous peer-reviewed journal papers.

## Climate-Health Vulnerabilities Are Increasing at the Same Time as Exposures to Extreme Weather Events

While climate change continues to fuel more frequent, intense, and extensive extreme weather events, there's also an increasingly large number of people especially vulnerable to its harmful health effects. Older adults are among the most climate-vulnerable groups since they have a greater prevalence of pre-existing conditions like cardiovascular, respiratory, or kidney ailments that can be worsened with poor air quality, extreme heat, or the needs of emergency response. With the aging of Baby Boomers, the number of people aged 65 and over in the United States is projected to grow from 43.1 million in 2012 to 78.0 million by 2035, for the first time ever surpassing the number of Americans under the age of 18. In 2050, the projected population aged 65 and older is 83.7 million, almost double today's (Ortman, Velkoff, and Hogan 2014; US Census Bureau 2018). Economically disadvantaged households, some communities of color, young children, pregnant women, and people with limited physical mobility are among those especially vulnerable to climate change's effects. Recent work shows that climate change's effects can further exacerbate wealth inequities that already exist, by increasing wealth inequality between white communities and communities of color after extreme weather disasters, as disaster relief funding flows unequally to their different areas (Howell and Elliott 2018). As extreme weather events like storms and wildfires become more destructive with climate change, one can expect that inequalities could become worse. If steps are taken to improve the resilience of buildings in an equitable way, it could lessen the responses required to restore all communities post-disaster.

## Adapting to Climate Change Affords Opportunities to Protect and Promote Health, Equity, and Environmental Justice

Addressing climate change resilience also provides an opportunity to address health inequities. For example, urban heat islands (UHIs) are higher-temperature areas within cities where manmade pavement and building materials absorb and later re-radiate the sun's daytime heat, warming the urban environment relative to the surrounding countryside, sometimes with more than 20°F differences. Low income and communities of color are more likely to be located in UHIs, which also have "fewer trees, less green space, more buildings, higher energy use, and more impervious asphalt and concrete" (Rudolph et al. 2018). Developing strategies to reduce UHIs can thus simultaneously address current-day health and residential inequities and enhance community resilience to climate change-fueled warming. Energy usage can be reduced in ways that promote equity: for example, building retrofits to upgrade multi-family affordable housing and increase energy efficiency can use readily available, non-toxic, healthier materials in insulation and sealing, which would simultaneously enhance energy equity and protect residents' health (Energy Efficiency for All 2018). Climate change has been called "the greatest health threat" and "the greatest health opportunity" of the 21st century in two subsequent iterations of The Lancet Commission's reports on climate change (Costello et al. 2009; Watts et al. 2015). It now remains for us as a global society to develop the projects that will take the opportunity to listen to people's lived experience of environmental health today, which will then inform the creation of strategies to help communities equitably respond to increasing uncertainties and challenges of climate change.

## Building Sector and Climate Resilience

### The Building Sector Is Central to Improved Health and Equity and Advancing Climate Resilience Can Ensure We Support Those Outcomes

Housing quality, affordability, location, and social and community attributes all influence people's capacity to lead healthy lives and build wealth. Each of these elements plays an important role in ensuring that people are not exposed to health risks and that they have opportunities to thrive.

Housing that is safe, dry, clean, maintained, adequately ventilated, and free from pests and contaminants, such as lead, radon, and carbon monoxide, can reduce the incidence of negative health outcomes such as injuries, asthma, cancer, neurotoxicity, cardiovascular disease, and poor mental health. Affordable housing enables people to have stable homes, avoid displacement, and pay for other basic needs such as utilities, food, and medical care, which can reduce the incidence of negative health outcomes such as malnutrition, diabetes, anxiety, and depression.

Housing location is also key to increasing resiliency in residential buildings. Easy access to public transportation, parks and recreation, quality schools, good jobs, healthy foods, and medical care can help reduce the incidence of chronic disease, injury, respiratory disease, mortality, and poor mental health. Neighborhoods that nurture diversity and value people of color, that support efforts to eliminate concentrated poverty, and in which residents have close and supporting relationships with one another can improve physical and mental health by reducing stress and exposure to violence and crime as well as improving school performance and civic engagement.

Finally, housing inequality is the primary driver of economic inequality. All of these factors are important. Planning for adaptation and climate resilience necessitates multidisciplinary approaches (Keenan, Hill, and Gumber 2018). Given the range of factors within the building sector that affect a community's resiliency, we need to take a multidisciplinary approach that reflects and heeds those factors in designing for climate solutions. Climate change is impacting our lives in a myriad of ways. Perhaps most important of those is how climate change will likely impact the geography of human settlements and the property markets that support the development and redevelopment of our collective built environment. Understanding the potential impacts and the unique vulnerabilities within a communities' building sector requires interconnected and multidisciplinary approaches.

We need to design our climate resiliency actions to work at multiple scales and to realize multiple benefits rather than focus on single needs or single processes. Within the building sector, this includes combining adaptation with mitigation activities to optimize co-benefits while also working to advance equity and justice.

Below, we highlight three opportunities on how we might combine our thinking on climate resilience and the building sector.

1. To create climate resilience, we will need to plan for our building infrastructure to last centuries and to outlast climate impacts (Black in Design 2017).

Infrastructure should be built, rebuilt, and/or retrofitted with climate change in mind. Infrastructure investments need to take into account climate science and to prepare for conditions 100 years in the future. Given the timeline of this infrastructure, efforts to address climate resilience in the built environment must start with the inequalities inherent in the existing building sector. In order to strengthen our communities and ensure that we are not perpetuating past injustices, initiatives to build resilience must be coupled with policies, financing, and initiatives aimed at reducing inequality and health vulnerability in our building sector.

2. Our buildings need to be upgraded and built to mitigate the growing health impacts of a hotter climate.

In communities where extreme heat is becoming the norm, residents struggle with the health impacts of extreme heat. At the same time, extreme heat also means higher energy bills as families try to keep their homes cooled. The resultant rising energy costs threaten the health of children and seniors as families struggle to pay their utility bills, often making difficult choices between paying their energy bill and buying sufficient food or medication. In fact, low-income residents already pay the highest percentage of their income on energy bills, and these energy burdens are compounded by areas experiencing housing crises. It's no surprise that utility shutoffs are skyrocketing further endangering residents. Existing mechanisms for upgrading buildings often disadvantage low-income owners and residents from accessing financing and services, and leave them vulnerable to cost increases designed to pay for upgrades that do occur. Upgrading buildings allows us to balance improved living conditions now and greater resilience to climate extremes in future.

3. We need more affordable housing, and to ensure affordable housing is built quickly post-major storm events.

Affordable housing is often a major casualty of monster storms. The failure of communities to invest in or replace their damaged public housing is a recurring problem that is exacerbated by climate change. According to a report by Harvard's Joint Center for Housing Studies, there are only 35 affordable rental units for every 100 extremely low-income households in the United States. That gap widens in many coastal cities, where each extreme weather event causes housing stock to dwindle further, pushing low-income people permanently out of their communities.

As a recent article on Houston affordable housing crisis post-Hurricane Harvey points out, there is a resistance in cities across the nation to rebuild affordable housing after they've been destroyed by climate chaos. Many affordable housing experts remain skeptical of the outlook for those pushed out by storm-related difficulties. There is often a lack of commitment by city mayors and agencies to replace public housing. This exacerbates the housing crisis. "There's absolutely an agenda to eliminate and not replace public housing in this country," says Matthew Lasner, an associate professor of urban policy and planning at the City University of New York's (CUNY) Hunter College.

In the aftermath of severe hurricanes—including Katrina, Harvey, and Ike—officials often say they continue to support public housing, Lasner contends, while in reality "they're often happy to see public housing go."

Affordable housing activists are pushing back and organizing around displacement, evictions, and gentrification. They are also resisting the rent hikes that the U.S. Department of Housing and Urban Development has proposed for public housing residents. These issues of affordability are intricately linked with climate resiliency and efforts to rebuild. By recognizing the interconnectivity, we can begin to address the challenge holistically.

## Facing and Addressing Larger, More Systemic Issues Comprehensively

How might we start thinking about how to do this? It is fundamental to begin by ensuring that climate resilience integrates social resilience at its core. Enhancing the resilience of the built environment can be a strong demonstration of this.

The two great challenges facing communities worldwide in the decades to come are rising inequality and the increasing likelihood we will see more severe impacts of climate change. Yet the two challenges, and the two sets of political infrastructures that prioritize them, largely operate in isolation from each other. Often, it is argued or assumed that actions to redress social and environmental challenges

## Case Study 1: Centering Health and Equity While Enhancing Climate Resilience in Our Building Sector

WE ACT for Environmental Justice is a community-based environmental justice organization based in Northern Manhattan whose mission is to build healthy communities by ensuring that people of color and/or low-income residents participate meaningfully in the creation of environmental policies and practices.

In 2015, with help from a grant from the Kresge Foundation, WE ACT undertook a six-month participatory planning initiative to create a community-driven and needs-based climate resiliency plan for Northern Manhattan. Over that period, over 500 New Yorkers from the neighborhoods of Inwood, Washington Heights, West Harlem, Central Harlem, and East Harlem participated in workshops designed to gain feedback on community resilience priorities and challenges. The workshops included a suite of "serious games," simulations of climate-related environmental crises likely to occur in New York.

Inputs synthesized from this process of community prioritization were synthesized into a set of community infrastructure and policy recommendations collectively known as the Northern Manhattan Climate Action Plan, or NMCA. Operationalizing the plan centered on two main concepts: emergency preparedness and energy democracy.

Workshop participants' prioritizing of energy democracy for NMCA reflected the deep disparity in climate-related disruption recovery times experienced by residents of Northern Manhattan in relation to their neighbors downtown, whereby the neighborhoods with more people of color and low-income residents had longer recovery times. Northern Manhattan residents collectively expressed the desire to have a reliable, resilient, and affordable source of energy in the face of climate-related chaos like an extreme heatwave or storm. The participants also recognized the increasing issue of disparities in energy affordability, and the higher energy burdens faced by low- to moderate-income New Yorkers. To facilitate the plan's energy-related work moving forward, WE ACT formed the Climate Justice Working Group, comprised of community volunteers and WE ACT staff liaisons.

As part of the NMCA visioning process, WE ACT volunteers and staff recognized the benefit of proliferated rooftop solar and efficiency measures on affordable housing. With a small grant from the City of New York administered by Sustainable CUNY (SCUNY), and with support from the Energy Foundation, the

> Energy Democracy Working Group undertook the effort to improve buildings in Northern Manhattan through energy efficiency and onsite generation of energy. To operationalize NMCA, WE ACT and partners such as Solar One, SCUNY, and the Urban Homesteaders Assistance Board (UHAB) began an outreach, technical support, and infrastructure initiative known as Solar Uptown Now (SUN). The project currently has 13 completed solar installations, 11 of which are in affordable multi-family buildings, and a green jobs worker training/employment component. WE ACT has engaged in weatherization, retrofitting, and cool roofs outreach as well as further planning and development efforts involving community solar and microgrids. These efforts have sought to advance the key concepts developed through the community workshops.
>
> Throughout this initiative, stakeholders emphasized the goal of improving upon existing socio-economic conditions, not simply maintaining the status quo, while addressing climate resilience and preparedness. To be able to support communities and follow through on these ideas, resiliency needs to include both political and economic powers. That means facing and addressing larger, more systemic issues comprehensively and engaging community stakeholders directly, to keep in mind when thinking about the resiliency of communities and neighborhoods.

are in tension; however, they must be balanced if we are going to achieve a just sustainable transition to a climate resilient future.

The best strategy to slash carbon emissions and adapt to the inevitable climate-linked disasters we cannot prevent is for public authorities working with community-based groups and movements to take immediate action to reduce urban and housing inequality. In short, the best way to prevent climate impacts is to democratically pursue climate policies that prioritize and reduce social inequality. This is an important objective of adaptation, which allows communities to be in a stronger position to withstand shocks and stressors of greater unpredictability.

Evidence suggests that climate change will cause some property to be more or less valuable by virtue of its capacity to accommodate a certain density of human settlement and its associated infrastructure. The resulting impacts from climate change will further existing trends toward gentrification in cities. There is now realization that cities need to invest in infrastructure that can withstand increasing temperatures, more extreme storms, and the uncertainty that climate change brings. The surge of green development has resulted in dramatic increase in housing costs, pricing long-time residents out of their homes, and further away from these environmental benefits. This will exacerbate existing inequalities even as climate change erodes even more value from low-income communities and communities of color who already face discrimination biases in the proper valuation of their communities.

Climate policies often lack a strong foundation in justice, raising ethical and political concerns about who drives climate emissions, who is most impacted, and who makes decisions about responding to climate change and how problems of inequity and socially just development can be addressed by these policies.

As climate change and resilience strategies become adopted, interpreted, and implemented by cities, the built environment will be the central conduit for investing in climate resilience. Increasing investments in this space without attention to existing inequalities and changing the patterns of development that created them will only increase them.

Implementing climate resilience solutions offers an opportunity to change course, to create a more just and sustainable future.

### *A Holistic Approach That Links Climate Resilience and the Building Sector Can Lead to a More Resilient Social Safety Net That Reinforces Equity and Improved Health Outcomes*

Health and equity in our communities are inextricably linked to the building sector. Buildings are a fundamental part of thriving, healthy communities and must be considered in that context. If we are to center the health and safety of people in our resiliency efforts, we must connect the dots between equity, health, and resilience. Improving resiliency goes beyond fortifying physical infrastructure and includes investing in holistic solutions that strengthen communities by supporting healthy, affordable homes and work places and recognizing the economic challenges that lead to climate vulnerability.

While clearly climate change creates real and dire challenges, it also creates an opportunity to correct past inequities and invest in both infrastructure and new approaches that improve livability and economic opportunities, while reducing losses to climate-change impacts and promoting a low-carbon future. We must seize this once-in-a-multi-generational transformation of the way we build our homes and other buildings and the way we invest and include low-income communities in creating the solutions that we need to thrive in a climate-changed world. We can break the cycle of underinvestment and inequitable economic growth while also building climate resilient cities by centering the goals of health and equity for all.

To be sure there are many questions to be addressed. How can we align project financing with social, environmental, and economic

## Case Study 2: Placing Equity at the Center of Our Work

In the Great Lakes Region, and in Chicago, Illinois, specifically, small and local developers, municipal leaders, and community groups are helping to build more resilient communities. They are leveraging housing, transit, and community cultural resources to reverse a legacy of racial and economic segregation and advance more equitable and resilient development. As these strategies continue to be adopted and implemented, there is the opportunity to examine their efficacy in addressing the critical development gaps to help communities and governments manage their climate risks.

Locally, one organization helping to manage climate risk in Chicago is LUCHA, Latin United Community Housing Association. LUCHA is a housing rights advocacy and affordable housing development organization, working within and across communities to preserve and strengthen housing in Chicago's neighborhoods. LUCHA is a strong proponent of energy efficiency and climate resilience, advocating for more efficient buildings as means of making housing affordable for low-income tenants. Tierra Linda, a 45-unit LUCHA development, includes the first multi-family affordable passive flats built in the City of Chicago. The development, which was completed in 2018 and fully occupied since 2019, is located along the 606-trail, a linear multi-use park connecting several Chicago neighborhoods. Tierra Linda represents a larger commitment to equitable housing by bringing decreased energy costs and higher-quality housing to renters. This commitment builds towards community resilience both by reducing exposures to climate impacts like heat or air pollution, by ensuring residents can reliably cool or heat their homes, and also by protecting human health by ensuring that homes remain affordable and are made with better building materials.

LUCHA, along with other mission developers like Ghian Foreman, who is working to advance local business opportunities in disinvested areas, has advocated for better housing policies that address issues of displacement. In the North Side, for example, the 606-trail has become an asset for the surrounding Logan Square neighborhood. The planning and development of the trail, however, has spurred an increase in nearby housing costs by approximately 50%, including dramatic increases in property taxes, causing strain and economic and cultural stress to long-time renters, homeowners on fixed incomes, and small businesses. Mission-driven developers have become a part of the advocacy for community stabilization by advocating for better polices that preserve affordable housing and prevent displacement. This work is being done in addition to striving to implement the highest energy efficiency standards and solar into their developments. Engaging at both the building and city policy level has proven critical to ensuring low-income residents can access environment and resilience benefits like social cohesion and cleaner air that comes with greener development.

Regionally, the Metropolitan Planning Council (MPC) is a committed partner in advancing equity by bringing better data to policy solutions that address racial inequality in the city. In conjunction with the Urban Institute, MPC released the Cost of Segregation report, demonstrating that segregation costs billions of dollars in lost income and quality of life. From a resilience perspective, more segregated communities are often less civically engaged and have less influence on land-use decisions. MPC is using the data from the report to explore a set of interventions, including housing and equitable development policies that will address segregation and improve safety and well-being.

Statewide, the Future Energy Jobs Act (FEJA), passed by the state of Illinois in 2016, directs energy efficiency and renewable energy to underserved communities. FEJA is a landmark bill that funds job training for renewable energy, reduces energy burdens for low-income residents, requires utilities to become more efficient, and provides incentives for green energy investments. The divestment from fossil fuels and reinvestment in clean energy fits into a larger vision for a just transition for communities and local economies.

These city and state initiatives to reduce urban inequalities resulting from legacies of segregation and disinvestment characterize the opportunity in Chicago and in the State of Illinois of building a more sustainable future. These investments begin to address the underlying inequities, and as they begin to align at the state, regional, and local levels, there begins to be path forward towards changing the pattern of development towards more equitable *and* climate resilient outcomes.

goals? How will/should our social safety net respond to changes in the way we produce, distribute, transmit, use, and price energy? How will these changes influence how we finance the creation and preservation of affordable housing? What do the changes implied by efforts to improve residential efficiency, indoor air quality, and improved standards on adequacy and building materials mean for our health system in a moment of political crisis and transition?

## Key Adaptation Research, Strategies to Reduce Climate-Health Vulnerabilities, and Research Gaps/Needs

There is a growing body of research addressing these questions, but also gaps in research to be filled.

### Key Existing Research

a. CDC BRACE, green building codes, climate & health outreach, and education and research on adaptation.
b. Three Cubed study on weatherization and health outcomes.
c. ACEEE study on the health impacts of energy efficiency.

### Key Research Gaps—What Research Would We Want to See Undertaken?

a. Research on the costs of NOT investing in resilience and climate adaptation, by conducting valuation studies of the effects of adaptation in diminishing the avoidable health impacts and building community resilience to climate change. Research on the cost-benefit ratio on existing building adaptation strategies.
b. Research on the efficacy of climate resilience funds. Looking at the extent to which particular strategies have actually achieved resiliency goals.
c. For post-Sandy funds that were distributed to support recovery and preparedness, how equitably were those funds distributed? What is the break out of to which communities the funding flowed?
d. Mapping of adaptation investment versus need (geographic and demographic).
e. Describe best practices in adaptation and developing social resilience strategies in collaboration with vulnerable populations/communities.
f. Investigate the deep disparities in climate-related disruption recovery times experienced by residents of Northern Manhattan in relation to their neighbors downtown, whereby the neighborhoods with more people of color and low-income residents had longer recovery times.
g. Evaluate the differences in indoor versus outdoor temperatures in residential buildings, in particular during heat waves, to inform the development of overall heat-protective building guidelines and to help target public heat-health alerts.
h. Develop a consistent framework for monitoring and responding to indoor air quality problems that can threaten human health, in particular after flooding events.
i. Consider of the optimal scale of adaptation and energy interventions, in collaboration with vulnerable populations/communities.

## Conclusion

The two great challenges facing communities worldwide in the decades to come are rising inequality and the increasing likelihood we will see more severe impacts of climate change. We can address both of these challenges by acknowledging their interconnectedness. Climate change while clearly creating real and dire challenges, also creates an opportunity to correct past inequities and invest in both infrastructure and new approaches that improve livability and economic opportunities, while reducing losses to climate-change impacts and promoting a low-carbon future. The building sector is central to improved health and equity, and advancing climate resilience can ensure we support those outcomes. Investing in buildings for climate resilience represents a huge opportunity to improve community health, and begin to address inequities within those communities. Buildings are where we spend our hours, what we see when we come to home, work, or school. They affect our greenhouse gas footprint and have an impact on our economic well-being. Under a changing climate, we must ensure that our technologies and programs make our infrastructure, our buildings, and our communities healthier, stronger, and safer.

## Acknowledgments

NRDC wishes to gratefully acknowledge the contributing authors of this chapter, Marissa Ramirez, Pamela Rivera, Khalil Shahyd, and Cai Steger. We are also grateful for review and contributions by Stephan Roundtree of WE ACT, and Lindsay Robbins and Maria Stamas of NRDC.

## References

APHA (American Public Health Association). 2016. "Successfully peparing for climate change in New York state." Accessed September 14, 2018. https://apha.org/-/media/files/pdf/topics/climate/climatechangeny_2016.ashx?la=en&hash=E34F609BF0D03BD8DE6DDE6A329757F026A92EF2.

APHA (American Public Health Association). 2018. "Climate change." Accessed September 14, 2018. https://www.apha.org/topics-and-issues/climate-change.

Black in Design. 2017. "Designing resistance, building coalitions." Conference, Harvard University Graduate School of Design African American Student Union, Cambridge, MA, October 6–8, 2017.

Costello, Anthony, Mustafa Abbas, Adriana Allen, Sarah Ball, Sarah Bell, Richard Bellamy, Sharon Friel, Nora Groce, Anne Johnson, Maria Kett, Maria Lee, Caren Levy, Mark Maslin, David McCoy, Bill McGuire, Hugh Montgomery, David Napier, Christina Pagel, Jinesh Patel, Jose Antonio Puppim de Oliveira, Nanneke Redclift, Hannah Rees, Daniel Rogger, Joanne Scott, Judith Stephenson, John Twigg, Jonathan Wolff, and Craig Patterson. 2009. "Managing the health effects of climate change." *The Lancet* 373(9676):1693–1733. Lancet and University College London Institute for Global Health Commission (May 16, 2009). Accessed September 14, 2018. https://doi.org/10.1016/S0140-6736(09)60935-1.

Energy Efficiency for All. 2018. Making Affordable Multifamily Housing More Energy Efficient: A Guide to Healthier Upgrade Materials (September 2018). Accessed September 14, 2018. http://www.energyefficiencyforall.org/resources/making-affordable-multifamily-housing-more-energy-efficient-guide-healthier-upgrade.

GCCHE (Global Consortium on Climate and Health Education). 2018. "Mission." Accessed September 14, 2018. https://www.mailman.columbia.edu/research/global-consortium-climate-and-health-education.

Horton, Radley, Daniel Bader, Cynthia Rosenzweig, Art DeGaetano, and William Solecki. 2014a. Climate Change in New York State: Updating the 2011 ClimAID Climate Risk Information. New York State Energy Research and Development Authority (NYSERDA), Albany, New York.

Horton, Radley, Gary Yohe, William Easterling, Robert Kates, Matthias Ruth, Edna Sussman, Adam Whelchel, David Wolfe, and Fred Lipschultz. 2014b. *Ch. 16: Northeast. Climate Change Impacts in the United States: The Third National Climate Assessment.* Jerry M. Melillo, Terese (T.C.) Richmond, and Gary W. Yohe, eds. Washington, DC: U.S. Global Change Research Program, 16-1-nn.

Howell, Junia, and James R. Elliott. 2018. "Damages done: the longitudinal impacts of natural hazards on wealth inequality in the United States." *Social Problems* 072018:1–20 (14 August 2018). Accessed September 14, 2018. https://doi.org/10.1093/socpro/spy016.

IOM (Institute of Medicine). 2011. *Climate Change, the Indoor Environment, and Health.* Washington, DC: The National Academies Press. https://www.nap.edu/catalog/13115/climate-change-the-indoor-environment-and-health.

Keenan, Jesse M., Thomas Hill, and Anurag Gumber. 2018. "Climate gentrification: from theory to empiricism in Miami-Dade County, Florida." *Environmental Research Letters* 13(5) (April 2018):1–11. https://doi.org/10.1088/1748-9326/aabb32.

Krajick, Kevin. 2018. "James Hansen's climate warning, 30 years later." State of the Planet: Climate. Earth Institute, Columbia University (June 26, 2018). Accessed September 14, 2018. https://blogs.ei.columbia.edu/2018/06/26/james-hansens-climate-warning-30-years-later/.

Luber, George, Kim Knowlton, John Balbus, Howard Frumkin, Mary Hayden, Jeremy Hess, Michael McGeehin, Nicky Sheats, Lorraine Backer, Charles B. Beard, Kristie L. Ebi, Edward Maibach, Richard S. Ostfeld, Christine Wiedinmyer, Emily Zielinski-Gutiérrez, and Lewis Ziska. 2014. *Ch. 9: Human Health. Climate Change Impacts in the United States: The Third National Climate Assessment.* Jerry M. Melillo, Terese (T.C.) Richmond, and Gary W. Yohe, eds. U.S. Global Change Research Program, 220–256. https://doi.org/10.7930/J0PN93H5.

Melillo, Jerry M., Terese (T.C.) Richmond, and Gary W. Yohe, eds. 2014. *Highlights of Climate Change Impacts in the United States: The Third National Climate Assessment.* U.S. Global Change Research Program. https://www.globalchange.gov/browse/reports/highlights-climate-change-impacts-united-states-third-national-climate-assessment.

NYSDOH (New York State Department of Health). 2015. Building Resilience Against Climate Effects (BRACE) in New York State: Climate and Health Profile (June 2015). Accessed September 14, 2018. https://www.health.ny.gov/environmental/weather/docs/climatehealthprofile6-2015.pdf.

Ortman, Jennifer M., Victoria A. Velkoff, and Howard Hogan. 2014. An Aging Nation: The Older Population in the United States—Population Estimates and Projections. Current Population Reports.

Rudolph, Linda, Catherine Harrison, Laura Buckley, and Savannah North. 2018. Climate Change, Health, and Equity: A Guide for Local Health Departments. Oakland, CA and Washington DC, Public Health Institute and American Public Health Association. Accessed September 14, 2018. https://www.phi.org/uploads/application/files/h7fj0u01i38v3tu427p9s9kcmhs30xsi7tsg1fovh3yesd5hxu.pdf.

The Pew Charitable Trusts. 2016. "The Relationship Between Housing and Health." Accessed September 2018. https://www.pewtrusts.org/en/research-and-analysis/data-visualizations/2016/the-relationship-between-housing-and-health.

US Census Bureau. 2018. "Older People Projected to Outnumber Children for First Time in U.S. History." Release Number CB18–41 (March 13, 2018). Accessed September 14, 2018. https://www.census.gov/newsroom/press-releases/2018/cb18-41-population-projections.html.

USEPA (US Environmental Protection Agency). 2008. Review of the Impact of Climate Variability and Change on Aeroallergens and Their Associated Effects. EPA/600/R-06/164F.

Watts, Nick, W Neil Adger, Paolo Agnolucci, Jason Blackstock, Peter Byass, Wenjia Cai, Sarah Chaytor, Tim Colbourn, Mat Collins, Adam Cooper, Peter M Cox, Joanna Depledge, Paul Drummond, Paul Ekins, Victor Galaz, Delia Grace, Hilary Graham, Michael Grubb, Andy Haines, Ian Hamilton, Alasdair Hunter, Xujia Jiang, Moxuan Li, Ilan Kelman, Lu Liang, Melissa Lott, Robert Lowe, Yong Luo, Georgina Mace, Mark Maslin, Maria Nilsson, Tadj Oreszczyn, Steve Pye, Tara Quinn, My Svensdotter, Sergey Venevsky, Koko Warner, Bing Xu, Jun Yang, Yongyuan Yin, Chaoqing Yu, Qiang Zhang, Peng Gong, Hugh Montgomery, and Anthony Costello. 2015. "Health and climate change: policy responses to protect public health." *Lancet* 386(10006):1861–1914 (June 22, 2015). Accessed September 14, 2018. https://doi.org/10.1016/S0140-6736(15)60854-6.

# 8
# INCREASING ADAPTIVE CAPACITY OF VULNERABLE POPULATIONS THROUGH INCLUSIVE DESIGN

*Jordana L. Maisel, Brittany Perez and Krista Macy*

### Who Is Most Vulnerable?

Older adults (i.e., individuals ≥ 65 years of age) and people with disabilities are regularly identified as populations that are more vulnerable to environmental stressors due to climate change than the general population (Gamble et al. 2013; Rhoades, Gruber, and Horton 2017). Approximately 14.5% of the U.S. population are currently 65 years and older (Colby and Ortman 2017). Projections indicate that the number of older adults is expected to double from 43.1 million in 2012 to an estimated 83.7 million by 2050 (Ortman, Velkoff, and Hogan 2014). This population shift is largely due to the aging baby boom generation, as well as advances in medicine and technology that contribute to increased longevity among older Americans. This is particularly apparent in the projected increase in the population of 85 years and older (Pray et al. 2010). Moreover, most of the nation's oldest population is clustered in the Northeast; 8 of the top 11 states with the oldest populations are in the Northeast, with many of the most senior-heavy areas located in the Great Lakes region. Projections indicate this trend will continue and grow rapidly since this region has been losing residents, particularly younger people, to other places for generations (Kotkin 2016; Wilson 2013).

The rapidly aging population will further increase the prevalence of disability. About 13% of the civilian non-institutionalized US population (about 41 million people) report having a severe disability (Brault 2012). Among the total population, 44 million (13.9%) have difficulty with self-care, independent living or ambulation, 19.1 million (6%) have difficulty with vision or hearing, and 15.5 million (4.9%) have difficulty with cognitive functioning (Lauer and Houtenville 2018). In the past 30 years, there has been a sixfold increase in wheeled mobility device users—up to 4 million. Another 12 million people use walking aids (U.S. Census Bureau 2012). People with disabilities and their families are particularly in need of adaptation and coping strategies to minimize the harmful effects of climate change and ensure they have access to basic necessities, health care, social support, and opportunities for social participation.

Older adults and people with disabilities, who also belong to other minority groups based on gender, race, or ethnicity, may experience greater exposure to climate stressors. They may also face additional disadvantages in having their needs met during and/or after a weather-related event (GPDD and The World Bank 2009). For example, race—specifically African American—is frequently cited as an indicator of reduced adaptive capacity (Shirley, Boruff, and Cutter 2012). Gerontologists point out that older African American women are exposed to a triple threat to their quality of life. Each demographic category—gender, minority status, and age—increases the likelihood that a person will have lower disposable income, worse health, and other low quality of life outcomes (Washington, Moxley, and Taylor 2009). Older adults and people with disabilities living in poverty may not only experience greater exposure to the effects of extreme temperatures and other climate stressors (e.g., lack of resources for an air conditioner, poor housing conditions, etc.), but may also lack the financial resources to prepare for and respond to climate-related events (e.g., insurance, purchasing supplies, home repairs). Thus, older adults and people with disabilities, who are further marginalized by gender, race, ethnicity, or income, may experience more significant and complex barriers in response to climate stressors. The disproportionate impact of climate change on these groups will worsen unless municipalities adopt inclusive strategies to increase building and community resilience.

## Additional Factors Contributing to Vulnerability

Numerous physiological, psychological, and contextual factors further increase the sensitivity and exposure of older adults and people with disabilities to climate stressors, and impair their ability to cope with the adverse impacts of climate change. Although many older adults are healthy and active, aging is often accompanied by an increased risk of certain diseases and disorders such as impaired breathing, increased susceptibility to infectious diseases, and cardiovascular disease (Gamble et al. 2013). Early exposure to air pollution and toxins may compromise individuals' immune systems and cause respiratory impairments. For example, air pollution can exacerbate asthma and symptoms of Chronic Obstructive Pulmonary Disease (COPD). Individuals with diabetes are at a greater risk for heat-related morbidity and mortality than the general population. This is particularly concerning since the prevalence of diabetes is growing among older Americans, with projections suggesting it could double by 2050. Older adults with cardiovascular impairments (e.g., heart disease, hypertension) are also more sensitive to extreme temperatures since they have greater difficulty regulating their body temperature (Gamble et al. 2013).

Individuals, both young and old, with mobility, sensory, and cognitive limitations have reduced ability to respond to climate stressors. For example, people with mobility impairments (e.g., impaired balance, decreased motor strength, wheeled mobility device users) may face additional physical challenges during extreme weather events if emergency response plans do not adequately anticipate and address the specific needs of these populations (e.g., accessible transportation and shelters) (World Health Organization 2013). Individuals with poor hearing may not hear or comprehend important warnings or instructions related to climate stressors. Similarly, individuals with Alzheimer's and other cognitive impairments may experience difficulty receiving and comprehending warnings, as well as challenges with navigating complex recovery processes (Rhoades, Gruber, and Horton 2018).

Social isolation also impacts individuals' adaptive capacity to certain climate stressors (Gamble et al. 2013; Zimmerman et al. 2009). Individuals with more social capital and stronger social networks are better equipped to manage climate stressors because they have better access to information, social support, and resources (Dolan and Walker 2006, Ebi and Semenza 2008). Consequently, older adults and individuals with disabilities who live by themselves may not receive critical emergency information; they may underestimate the severity of a climate event; and/or they may be unaware of social services and community supports available to them (Gamble et al. 2008). Even some individuals with strong social support systems experience loneliness and reduced adaptive capacity due to climate change stressors. For instance, natural disasters often disrupt social networks, eroding a key coping resource. Weather-related events may reduce the capacity of caregivers to provide for and support individuals with disabilities. In response, common psychological reactions to extreme weather disasters include depression, post-traumatic stress disorder (PTSD), anxiety, and heightened family tension (Evans 2018).

Geographic factors may also influence the exposure and degree to which climate change affects older Americans and individuals with disabilities. For example, some locations with growing older adult populations are likely to experience greater climate stressors, such as hurricanes, floods, infectious diseases, and extreme temperatures. Approximately 20% of older Americans resided in a county where a hurricane or tropical storm was likely to make landfall between 1995 and 2005. Moreover, there appears to be a higher concentration of low-income older adults in these at-risk locations (Filiberto et al. 2010; Zimmerman et al. 2009). The large numbers of older adults in urban locations is also considered a risk factor for vulnerability to climate stressors since these areas are more prone to exacerbated summer heat; the lack of open land combined with buildings and impermeable surfaces creates a 'heat island effect' (Gamble et al. 2008). The growing population of older Americans in the Northeast may be particularly vulnerable to extreme temperatures, coastal flooding/sea level rise, the decline of air quality, and the spread of infectious disease/pests—climate stressors predicted to increase and intensify in these regions.

## Climate Stressors Impacting the Northeast

The Northeastern region of the U.S. is home to densely populated urban centers such as New York City, Boston, and Washington D.C., along with vast rural landscapes, supporting more than 180,000 farms (Horton et al. 2014; U.S. Global Change Research Program 2014). With a population of over 64 million people, this unique region is largely covered by forest, but is also well known for its bodies of freshwater, coastal zones, beaches, wetlands, and grasslands (U.S. Global Change Research Program 2014). Although the built and natural environments vary greatly throughout this part of the U.S., weather events and climate stressors have exposed significant vulnerabilities that require attention. The most relevant climate stressors to this region include extreme temperatures; coastal flooding, sea level rise, increased precipitation; air quality; and infectious disease, invasive species, and pests.

### *Extreme Temperatures*

The global land and ocean surface temperature in 2017 was recorded to be 0.38°C–0.48°C above the 1981–2010 average, making 2017 warmer than any year in recorded history prior to 2015 (Blunden et al. 2018). This shift in temperature has led to an increase in the frequency, duration, and severity of heat waves (Meehl and Tebaldi 2004). One study, which collected temperature and mortality data globally from 400 communities, found that high temperatures create a substantial health burden. Variations in the observed mortality rates related to heat waves between communities and regions demonstrate the importance of employing local heat wave response plans along with heat mitigation strategies in every community, even those thought to be low risk (Guo et al. 2017). While existing data illustrates an increase in average temperatures globally, extreme cold events remain prevalent and pose health and safety risks. Temperatures are not expected to drop as a result of climate change; however, winter storm frequency and severity are expected to increase as a result of higher ocean temperatures and an increased amount of moisture in the air (National Oceanic and Atmospheric Administration 2014). For example, the frequency of severe snowstorms in the latter half of the 20th century is almost twice that of the previous 50 years in the U.S. (National Oceanic and Atmospheric Administration 2014). Western New York's 2014 winter storm 'Snowvember' serves as an example of a severe winter storm that brought with it increased amounts of snow, ice, and gusting winds. This resulted in power outages, building and infrastructure damage, and increased risk of travel.

## Coastal Flooding/Sea Level Rise/Increased Precipitation

Flooding accounts for 90% of all natural disasters in the U.S. This is increasingly due to coastal flooding, storm surge, and rising sea levels (Horton et al. 2014; Rajkovich et al. 2018). Sea levels have risen approximately 1 foot since 1900, and are projected to rise another 1–4 feet by 2100. This, combined with the predicted increases in precipitation, makes flooding a major concern going forward (Blunden et al. 2018; Meehl and Tebaldi 2004). Approximately, 1.6 million Northeasterners reside within the Federal Emergency Management Agency's (FEMA) 100-year coastal flood zone, further increasing vulnerabilities to building stock, infrastructure, economies, and, most importantly, the health and wellness of individuals residing in this region (Horton et al. 2014).

## Air Quality

Changing temperatures, precipitation, atmospheric allergen levels, and humidity levels, along with natural disasters such as storm events, can strain mechanical equipment, increase the risk of mold growth indoors and out, and change vapor and pollution transmission through the building envelope. Indoor air quality is a critical issue because the configuration of the building envelope, building systems, and the choice of materials can lead to pollution concentrations that are between 2 and 100 times greater than they are outdoors (U.S. Environmental Protection Agency 2016b). Compounding the problem, people in industrialized countries spend as much as 90% of their time indoors (Klepeis et al. 2001). Finally, many people have chronic respiratory or cardiovascular diseases exacerbated by certain toxins (U.S. Environmental Protection Agency 2016a).

## Infectious Disease/Invasive Species/Pests

The changing climate has resulted in impacts on the ecosystems and habitats of animal and pest populations, leading to shifts towards new or expanded habitats (U.S. Drug Administration 2014). This shift will continue to cause the increased spread of disease and invasive species to both vegetation and animal populations, leading to an increased health risk to humans, animals, and agriculture products alike (U.S. Drug Administration 2014). These climatic changes will influence the invasion and establishment of non-native diseases and agricultural pests (U.S. Drug Administration 2014).

## Inclusive Design and Resilience

Inclusive design serves as a useful tool for addressing the needs of vulnerable populations in response to intensifying climate stressors and increasing individual, building, and community resilience. Inclusive design is a holistic approach to the process of developing and creating

[1] Inclusive design and universal design are interchangeably used terms.

products, buildings, landscapes, systems, and cities. Designing for human diversity—in regard to age, gender, race, religion, personality, and other factors—is central, particularly in addressing the wide spectrum of physical, sensory, and cognitive abilities that comprise society. Longer life spans, trends in disease and disability, and general demographic diversification of societies prompt the need for alternative design processes and strategies. Significant changes in climate behavior are also demanding the need to rethink traditional design and policy practices. Inclusive design, or universal design,[1] must be used in conjunction with other sustainable planning and design practices moving forward in order to reduce the risk factors, exclusionary practices, and even neglect that vulnerable populations encounter in the midst of climate change.

The aim of inclusive design is frequently described in terms of outcomes, e.g., a product or building being functional for and usable by the greatest percentage of the population possible. Recognizing the need for a new, cross-cultural framework, Steinfeld and Maisel (2012) defined universal design as "A process that enables and empowers a diverse population by improving human performance, health and wellness, and social participation." What this definition adds to this outcomes-oriented framework is a view of inclusive design *as a process*, rather than as an end product or feature. The intention of inclusive design, seen through this lens, then, is to identify and refine architectural ways of thinking and working that improve the self-efficacy and self-actualization of all built environment users.

To accompany and support this definition, Steinfeld and Maisel (2012) developed the eight Goals of Universal Design. The first four goals—Body Fit, Comfort, Awareness, and Understanding—incorporated research from anthropometry (the study of the size and movements of human bodies), human factors (ergonomics and sensory perception), and the health sciences (e.g., rehabilitation sciences). The fifth goal—Wellness—emerged from growing science on how the materials and forms of products, buildings, and environments not only affect usability but also affect health and well-being. The last three goals—Social Integration, Personalization, and Cultural Appropriateness—leveraged social-science research toward the recognition that individuals have diverse needs, preferences, and aspirations, and that norms, taboos, and values differ across geographies and cultures, as do building codes and conventions.

The development of inclusive design research and practice is contemporaneous with that of sustainability or 'green building,' and the two share considerable intellectual space. The concept of social sustainability is a sizeable area of overlap. Ultimately, social injustices and inequalities will have negative economic and environmental impacts. Another key similarity between inclusive design and green building is the emphasis on design process, including careful thinking about the formation of the design team and its consultants and stakeholders, the sources and research used to guide decisions, and the steps for identifying hidden consequences and improving the likelihood of success. Inclusive design can be a powerful tool to build up a community's adaptive capacity in general, and specifically to address the vulnerabilities of people with disabilities and older adults across various climate stressors. Responding to the needs of these communities requires more holistic and inclusive strategies that shift the paradigm from traditional design practices that have isolated and left behind these groups in the past.

## Building Adaptive Capacity through Inclusive Design

The primary challenge for stakeholders engaged in climate resilience, such as inclusive designers, policy makers, and advocates, is to build environments, develop communication and education programs, and implement policies that meet people's evolving needs over the course of their lives. This is particularly true when addressing the needs of vulnerable populations before, during, and after climate-related events. Given that resilient strategies, plans, and policies are limited and often focus on the needs of able-bodied adults, the reward for these stakeholders is collaborating with climate resilience experts to expand standard practices and the populations they serve.

### *Built Environment*

Some existing resilient strategies not only address climate hazards facing the Northeast, but also illustrate opportunities to integrate inclusive design. While some of these strategies serve to mitigate climate change, others result in increased resiliency. Regardless, the ultimate goal of identifying these approaches is to increase the capacity for adaptation so that climate-related events do not impose a greater risk to often marginalized, vulnerable populations. The list of strategies is not exhaustive. Therefore, it should not serve as a manual; rather, its primary purpose is to provide designers and practitioners with guidance to more thoughtfully incorporate inclusivity into the design of climate resilient strategies.

Although resilient building and planning strategies may vary between hot and cold temperature extremes, health and safety risks to vulnerable populations, specifically those with limited resources and decreased thermal regulation, are exacerbated in both scenarios. Implementing inclusive design strategies can help minimize the negative impacts of these climate stressors. For example, in extreme heat or cold events government and community agencies often provide cool or warm safe havens for individuals at risk. However, existing barriers, such as lack of accessible transportation or lack of awareness, leave a large percentage of the vulnerable populations for which these services exist, unable to utilize these resources. Programs such as these can improve their effectiveness by considering the varying abilities of the targeted populations and putting in place systems that increase access to services. For example, they should improve their communication efforts and provide accessible transportation. Other inclusive resilient strategies to addresses extreme temperatures include:

*Increase vegetation and tree cover*: This strategy provides added shade and increases permeable surfaces, which help to reflect heat rather than absorb it, making the outdoors more usable during warm events. Conversely, during winter weather events, trees and vegetation help to decrease the effects of wind gusts and blowing snow.

*Increase accessible permeable pavement*: This strategy mitigates the effects of the urban heat island effect, similar to vegetative ground cover. However, it also provides accessible pathways for those with limited mobility.

*Install accessible, easy to use, operable windows with shading devices*: This strategy provides building users with the ability to utilize passive methods of cooling independently, with the added benefits of decreased energy use, increased ventilation, and improvements to indoor air quality.

Health and wellness risks from flood events related to water damage, mold growth, air quality, and water contamination due to strain on aging infrastructure often last long after floodwaters have subsided. While it is important to implement mitigation strategies to limit this damage, recovery and emergency response actions should be designed to better support vulnerable populations following these events. For example, resilient recommendations, following the 2012 Superstorm Sandy, are called for the raising of coastal buildings well above storm surge levels. While this is an effective means to protect coastal building stock, it poses accessibility barriers and increases risk for those with mobility impairments. Therefore, the organizations and agencies responsible for these recommendations need to consider and recommend accessible and inclusive features, such as ramps and site planning to allow for on grade entry, in order to better serve and protect all building users. Other inclusive resilient strategies to address coastal flooding/sea level rise/increased precipitation include:

*Install automatic solar- and/or battery-powered emergency lighting*: This strategy provides additional visibility during power outages, which often occur concurrently with flood events. Individuals with vision impairments may have difficulty maneuvering through a non-illuminated space while looking for additional safety lighting, or may have difficulty seeing with the limited illumination of a flashlight.

*Implement permeable planters, pavement, and rain gardens along paths of travel*: This strategy mitigates excess storm water, combined sewage overflow (CSO), and standing water following heavy precipitation events. Standing water and CSOs along paths of travel can create barriers to accessible mobility.

*Utilize natural grading and slope*: While this strategy may take more time and effort at the early stages of a design, it has the added benefits of maximizing natural drainage and minimizing required site work and grading. Accessible building features should be designed around these natural elements to better improve safety and access.

Individuals with limitations that make them unable to leave their homes or individuals who are institutionalized may be disproportionately exposed to poor indoor air quality due to the various conditions previously described. Designers should consider how the building envelope and mechanical systems in these homes and facilities will perform over time as the atmosphere continues to warm and storm events become more frequent (Ilacqua et al. 2015; Institute of Medicine 2015). Resilient recommendations suggest improving air quality through increased building ventilation. However, institutional buildings, and in some cases homes and apartments, lack easy to use operable windows. If planners recommend increased ventilation, details within this strategy must also include the installation of more usable windows; otherwise, the most vulnerable populations will more acutely suffer the consequences of poor air quality.

Integrated Pest Management (IPM) serves as an example of a universally designed resilience strategy. IPM is a mitigation strategy that focuses on prevention of harmful diseases, species, and pests through the use of the most effective, lowest risk options by considering risks to the applicator, building occupants, and environment (U.S. Environmental Protection Agency 2016c). Unlike traditional pest control, which relies primarily on the use of toxic pesticides, IPM programs take a more inclusive and holistic approach, by taking advantage of all appropriate pest management methods. For example, it factors in sanitation, building maintenance, removal of standing water, installation of pest barriers, and the judicious use of pesticides (Kass et al. 2009). IPM is not limited to just one method, but rather involves identifying the specific problem (the problematic pest, disease, or species), and determining the best preventative measure with the lowest risk of harming humans and/or the surrounding ecosystem (U.S. Environmental Protection Agency 2016c).

## Education and Communication

As climate stressors continue to increase and intensify, education and communication efforts targeting vulnerable populations must also increase in order to build stronger community-based adaptive capacity. Older adults and individuals with disabilities, previously unaffected or minimally affected by climate stressors, may be underprepared for future intensifying stressors. They are often unaware of how climate stressors could affect their short-term and long-term health outcomes. Consequently, few seek educational information to help them prepare for and/or recover from weather-related events. In addition, people living with certain health conditions require more specific educational information than what is typically distributed to the general public (Ebi and Semenza 2008). For example, people who have high-level spinal cord injuries often have difficulty or the inability to perspire, putting them at greater risk during a heat wave. Educational materials for this population should include information about better climate control in the home, nearby accessible cooling shelters, and accessible transportation to access the cooling shelters. Similarly, individuals who use mobility devices may require information about wheelchair accessible shelters or shelters that will have other medical necessities available if the need to evacuate arises. Beyond educating vulnerable populations, planning and policy stakeholders should also improve their own education efforts to learn more about the vulnerable communities they serve and represent.

To educate both the general public and vulnerable populations effectively, stakeholders must have access to relevant, accurate, and accessible weather-related information for their specific needs (World Health Organization 2013). An inclusive education and communication strategy involves diverse users in the development process. Engaging community residents helps ensure that messages reflect the needs and abilities of both the general public and specific vulnerable populations (Ebi and Semenza 2008). Stakeholders charged with developing and disseminating critical information can collaborate with different accessibility experts; area agencies for aging; senior centers; disability advocacy organizations; and/or independent living centers, local governmental disability offices, and community advocacy organizations to develop and review education and communication strategies. Partnerships with these organizations can help provide professional trainings on the specific needs of different populations.

Ongoing education and emergency-related communication efforts must also be available in multiple formats so that people who have varying communication needs receive critical information related to living in a changing climate, preparing for emergencies, and recovering from emergencies. At a minimum, all forms of public, climate stressor-related communication and information should comply with standards for information and communication technology (covered by Section 508 of the Rehabilitation Act and Section 255 of the Communication Act) (U.S. Access Board 2017). A more inclusive approach to effective communication ensures that all public communication is available in multiple written formats and languages and through diverse in-person, virtual, and media-based outlets. An inclusive communication strategy that integrates the Goals of Universal Design may help reduce the disproportionately negative impact of climate stressors for people with disabilities and older adults by equipping them early and often with useful information.

The weakened adaptive capacity of older adults and people with disabilities may not be due to insufficient educational resources or services, but instead due to a lack of awareness that these programs and education materials exist (Rhoades, Gruber, and Horton 2018). Communication is one of the most significant barriers for vulnerable populations related to climate stressors and weather-related disasters (Gamble et al. 2013, World Health Organization 2013). Climate-related communication efforts are often inaccessible to many populations, and predominantly disseminated only using mainstream media outlets. Using inclusive and participatory approaches to educational outreach strategies ensures effective dissemination of important information. Partnerships established to help develop education materials can also help facilitate community outreach.

Greater access to technology increases the potential range of adaptation options available to communities, and therefore increases their adaptive capacity (Dolan and Walker 2006). As education and communication efforts increasingly rely on technology for widespread dissemination, understanding and improving how communities and vulnerable populations access and utilize technology remains critical. This ensures that people with limited access to technology are not further alienated or put at greater risk of climate-related stressors and weather disasters. Community assessments can provide valuable insight into how technology use varies across age groups, income levels, geographic regions, etc., and how best to target specific populations. For example, in a community assessment of older adults in Erie County, New York, technology use for communication varied significantly by age. Older adults between the ages of 50 and 75 more frequently used mobile phones and text messaging, while older adults age 75 and over more frequently used postal mail and home telephones. Despite these differences, a majority of older adults reported frequent use of email, suggesting high access to the Internet across all old age cohorts (Age Friendly Erie County 2018). A similar study in Connecticut engaged older adults in community discussions and surveys and found that older adults preferred phone and in-person warnings for weather emergency information (Rhoades, Gruber, and Horton 2018).

## *Policy*

As policy makers throughout the Northeast and Great Lakes region continue to learn about escalating climate stressors affecting these areas, they need to evaluate and assess their current resilience policies and practices. An inclusive, community-based approach to resilience requires both a top-down and bottom-up approach to health, safety, and hazard policies (Ebi and Semenza 2008). In the top-down approach, policy makers must evaluate and confirm that existing mainstream emergency operations, disaster risk reduction services, and other resilience policies and practices address the needs of vulnerable populations. Analyzing disaggregated data from national, state, or local surveys can help identify and locate where older adults and people with disabilities live, if they use special equipment, and/or their transportation behaviors (McGuire, Ford, and Okoro 2007). This helps reduce the number of people excluded from needs assessments, outreach, and recovery efforts (World Health Organization 2013). Policy makers also have the opportunity to introduce and implement new policies and programs such as Complete Streets and Age Friendly Communities that enhance social resilience and improve a community's ability to respond to climate-related stressors. These policies provide built environment guidelines that support more inclusive and livable communities. In addition, policy makers can mandate tools like innovative solutions for Universal Design (isUD™), which is a set of strategies for creating more inclusive buildings, along with LEED or other sustainable design approaches, to increase a community's adaptive capacity during reconstruction.

Policy makers should not rely on secondary data or assume they know the unique and diverse needs of older adults and people with disabilities in their communities. Using a bottom-up approach, policy makers should work with the local community and people from vulnerable groups to review current policies and identify opportunities for integrating inclusive resilience strategies that address disaster events, emergency responses, and rebuilding and recovery efforts (Dolan and Walker 2006). Together, they must ensure that individualized support policies address the specific needs and requirements of older adults and people with disabilities (Lewis et al. 2011). Policy development and evaluation must therefore take a participatory approach that includes and empowers vulnerable populations to create solutions. Older adults and people with disabilities often have significant experience negotiating adversity and overcoming barriers; therefore, they have the lived expertise to critically inform resilience policies (Rhoades, Gruber, and Horton 2018). In addition to contributing to these adaptive capacity strategies, people in these vulnerable populations can also be powerful climate activists and help with climate mitigation efforts to reduce carbon emissions, climate change education, and emergency planning (Lewis et al. 2011).

A recent community-based research approach in Connecticut demonstrated the benefits of engaging diverse stakeholders in conversations about resilience. In-person participatory meetings asked older adults about their climate-related needs, as well as how these stressors affect them. Researchers also distributed a survey, in both English and Spanish, asking about older adults' levels of concern across various extreme weather-related issues. The results helped inform adaptation strategies and planning efforts in their community. The researchers plan to repeat this process, with various populations, to build an even greater inclusive adaptive capacity approach to resilience (Rhoades, Gruber, and Horton 2018). In Portland, Oregon, the City Repair Project engaged the community in implementing various interventions that addressed heat islands. Individuals who participated in the implementation efforts had higher self-reported ratings of health and social capital outcomes when compared to individuals who did not participate (Ebi and Semenza 2008).

## Conclusion

Climate stressors affecting the Northeast are increasingly exposing older adults and people with disabilities to health and safety risks. These vulnerable populations are already at greater risk due to physiological, economic, and geographic factors. Advocates and policy makers must understand and amplify the needs of older adults and people with disabilities in response to climate stressors in order to build stronger resilience strategies. Individual, built environment, and community-based approaches to building adaptive capacity are needed. Although research explores climate change and the factors contributing to vulnerability, limited research examines how inclusive design can address the needs of these vulnerable populations, while also providing resilient solutions for the general population. Integrating inclusive designs and practices in the built environment, communication and education efforts, and policies not only builds resilience for climate-related stressors and weather-related disasters, but also strengthens community resilience for a wider range of significant challenges that may arise.

## References

Age Friendly Erie County. 2018. Age Friendly Erie County Community Assessment. IDeA Center, Erie County Senior Services.

Blunden, Jessica, Derek S Arndt, and Gail Hartfield, Eds. 2018. State of the Climate in 2017. In *Bulletin of the American Meteorological Society.*

Brault, Matthew W. 2012. *Americans with Disabilities: 2010.* US Department of Commerce, Economics and Statistics Administration, US Census Bureau Washington, D.C.

Colby, Sandra L, and Jennifer M Ortman. 2017. "Projections of the Size and Composition of the US Population: 2014 to 2060: Population Estimates and Projections."

Dolan, AH, and IJ Walker. 2006. "Understanding Vulnerability of Coastal Communities to Climate Change Related Risks." *Journal of Coastal Research* 39:1316–1323.

Ebi, Kristie L, and Jan C Semenza. 2008. "Community-Based Adaptation to the Health Impacts of Climate Change." *American Journal of Preventive Medicine* 35(5):501–507. doi: 10.1016/j.amepre.2008.08.018.

Evans, Gary W. 2018. "Projected Behavioral Impacts of Global Climate Change." *Annual Review of Psychology* 70:449–474.

Filiberto, David, Elaine Wethington, Karl Pillemer, Nancy Wells, Mark Wysocki, and Jennifer Parise. 2008. "Older People and Climate Change: Vulnerability and Health Effects." *Generations* 33:19–25.

Gamble, Janet L, Bradford J Hurley, Peter A Schultz, Wendy S Jaglom, Nisha Krishnan, and Melinda Harris. 2013. "Climate Change and Older Americans: State of the Science." *Environmental Health Perspectives* 121(1):15.

Gamble, JL, KL Ebi, DH Grambsch, FG Sussman, and TJ Wilbanks. 2008. "Analyses of the Effects of Global Change on Human Health and Welfare and Human Systems: Final Report, Synthesis and Assessment Product 4.6." *Report by the US Climate Change Science Program and the Subcommittee on Global Change Research*. Washington, D.C., US, p. ix [204 p].

Global Partnership for Disability & Development (GPDD) and The World Bank (Human Development Network – Social Protection/Disability & Development Team). 2009. *The Impact of Climate Change on People with Disabilities*.

Guo, Yuming, Antonio Gasparrini, G Armstrong Ben, Benjawan Tawatsupa, Aurelio Tobias, Eric Lavigne, Stagliorio Coelho Micheline de Sousa Zanotti, Xiaochuan Pan, Ho Kim, Masahiro Hashizume, Yasushi Honda, Leon Guo Yue-Liang, Chang-Fu Wu, Antonella Zanobetti, D Schwartz Joel, L Bell Michelle, Matteo Scortichini, Paola Michelozzi, Kornwipa Punnasiri, Shanshan Li, Linwei Tian, Osorio Garcia Samuel David, Xerxes Seposo, Ala Overcenco, Ariana Zeka, Patrick Goodman, Ngoc Dang Tran, Van Dung Do, Fatemeh Mayvaneh, Nascimento Saldiva Paulo Hilario, Gail Williams, and Shilu Tong. 2017. "Heat Wave and Mortality: A Multicountry, Multicommunity Study." *Environmental Health Perspectives* 125(8):087006. doi: 10.1289/EHP1026.

Horton, R, G Yohe, W Easterling, R Kates, M Ruth, E Sussman, A Whelchel, and D Wolfe. 2014. "Ch. 16: Northeast." In *Climate Change Immpacts in the United States: The Third National Climate Assessment*, edited by JM Melillo, Terese (TC) Richmon, and G Yohem. Washington, D.C.: U.S. Global Change Research Program.

Ilacqua, Vito, John Dawson, Michael Breen, Sarany Singer, and Ashley Berg. 2015. "Effects of Climate Change on Residential Infiltration and Air Pollution Exposure." Journal of Exposure Science & Environmental Epidemiology 27, 16–23.

IOM (Institute of Medicine). 2011. *Climate Change, the Indoor Environment, and Health*. Washington, D.C.: The National Academies Press. https://www.nap.edu/catalog/13115/climate-change-the-indoor-environment-and-health.

Kass, Daniel, Wendy McKelvey, Elizabeth Carlton, Marta Hernandez, Ginger Chew, Sean Nagle, Robin Garfinkel, Brian Clarke, Julius Tiven, Christian Espino, and David Evans. 2009. "Effectiveness of an Integrated Pest Management Intervention in Controlling Cockroaches, Mice, and Allergens in New York City Public Housing." *Environmental Health Perspectives* 117(8): 1219–1225.

Klepeis, Neil E, William C Nelson, Wayne R Ott, John P Robinson, Andy M Tsang, Paul Switzer, Joseph V Behar, Stephen C Hern, and William H Engelmann. 2001. "The National Human Activity Pattern Survey (NHAPS): A Resource for Assessing Exposure to Environmental Pollutants." *Journal of Exposure Science and Environmental Epidemiology* 11(3):231.

Kotkin, Joel. 2016. "America's Senior Moment: The Most Rapidly Aging Cities." *Forbes*, February 16, 2016. https://www.forbes.com/sites/joelkotkin/2016/02/16/americas-senior-moment-the-most-rapidly-aging-cities/#34af716353e5.

Lauer, EA, and AJ Houtenville. 2018. "2017 Annual Disability Statistics Compendium." Institute on Disability, University of New Hampshire.

Lewis, David, Strategic Programmes Director, CBM Australia, Kath Ballard, and Inclusion Matters. 2011. "Disability and Climate Change: Understanding Vulnerability and Building Resilience in a Changing World." *Development Bulletin*.

McGuire, Lisa C, Earl S Ford, and Catherine A Okoro. 2007. "Natural Disasters and Older US Adults with Disabilities: Implications for Evacuation." *Disasters* 31(1):49–56.

Meehl, GA, and C Tebaldi. 2004. "More Intense, More Frequent, and Longer Lasting Heat Waves in the 21st Century." *Science* 305(5686):994–997. doi: 10.1126/science.1098704.

National Oceanic and Atmospheric Administration. 2014. Climate Change and Extreme Snow in the U.S. Accessed 2018. https://www.ncdc.noaa.gov/news/climate-change-and-extreme-snow-us.

Ortman, Jennifer M, Victoria A Velkoff, and Howard Hogan. 2014. *An Aging Nation: The Older Population in the United States*. United States Census Bureau, Economics and Statistics Administration, US Department of Commerce.

Pray, L, C Boon, EA Miller, and L Pillsbury. 2010. *Providing Healthy and Safe Foods as We Age: Workshop Summary*. Washington, D.C.: National Academies Press.

Rajkovich, Nicholas B, Michael E Tuzzo, Nathaniel Heckman, Krista Macy, Elizabeth Gilman, Martha Bohm, and Harlee-Rae Tanner. 2018. *Climate Resilience Strategies for Buildings in New York State*, edited by New York State Energy Research Development Authority (NYSERDA). Albany, New York.

Rhoades, Jason L, James S Gruber, and Bill Horton. 2017. "Developing an In-Depth Understanding of Elderly Adult's Vulnerability to Climate Change." *The Gerontologist*: 58(3):567–577.

Rhoades, Jason L, James S Gruber, and Bill Horton. 2018. "Developing an In-Depth Understanding of Elderly Adult's Vulnerability to Climate Change." *The Gerontologist* 58(3):567–577. doi: 10.1093/geront/gnw167.

Shirley, W Lynn, Bryan J Boruff, and Susan L Cutter. 2012. "Social Vulnerability to Environmental Hazards." In *Hazards Vulnerability and Environmental Justice*, 143–160. Edited by Susan L. Cutter. Routledge.

Steinfeld, Edward, and Jordana Maisel. 2012. *Universal Design: Creating Inclusive Environments*. John Wiley & Sons.

U.S. Access Board. 2017. "Architectural and Transportation Barriers Compliance Board 36 CFR Parts 1193 and 1194 RIN 3014–AA37 Information and Communication Technology (ICT) Standards and Guidelines AGENCY: Architectural and Transportation Barriers Compliance Board. ACTION: Final Rule." *Federal Register* 82(11).

U.S. Census Bureau. 2012. Anniversary of Americans with Disabilities Act: July 26. In *Profile America Facts for Features*. https://www.census.gov/newsroom/facts-for-features/2021/disabilities-act.html.

U.S. Drug Administration. 2014. USDA Animal and Plant Health Inspection Service Climate Adaptation Plan 2014, edited by Animal and Plant Health Inspection Service.

U.S. Environmental Protection Agency. 2016a. "Emergency Response for Drinking Water and Wastewater Utilities." Last modified May 20, 2016, accessed July 5, 2016. https://www.epa.gov/waterutilityresponse.

U.S. Environmental Protection Agency. 2016b. "Indoor Air Quality." Accessed May 13, 2016. https://www.epa.gov/indoor-air-quality-iaq.

U.S. Environmental Protection Agency. 2016c. "Introduction to Integrated Pest Management." [web page]. U.S. Environmental Protection Agency, last modified April 20, 2016, accessed July 11, 2016. https://www.epa.gov/managing-pests-schools/introduction-integrated-pest-management.

U.S. Global Change Research Program. 2014. 2014 National Climate Assessment. Washington, D.C.

Washington, OGM, DP Moxley, and JY Taylor. 2009. "Enabling Older Homeless Minority Women to Overcome Homelessness by Using a Life Management Enhancement Group Intervention." *Issues in Mental Health Nursing* 30:86–97.

Wilson, Reid. 2013. "The Northeast is Getting Older, and It's Going to Cost Them." *The Washington Post*, September 12, 2013, GovBeat. https://www.washingtonpost.com/blogs/govbeat/wp/2013/09/12/the-northeast-is-getting-older-and-its-going-to-cost-them/?noredirect=on&utm_term=.c09b96199037.

World Health Organization. 2013. "Guidance Note on Disability and Emergency Risk Management for Health." *Geneva: World Health Organization.* Available at http://www.who.int/hac/techguidance/preparedness/disability/en 5: 2013.

Zimmerman, Rae, Carlos E. Restrepo, Becca Nagorsky, and Alison M. Culpen. 2007. "Vulnerability of the Elderly During Natural Hazard Events." In *Proceedings of the Hazards and Disasters Researchers Meeting*, pp. 38–40.

# 9
# PASSIVE SURVIVABILITY

## Understanding and Quantifying the Thermal Habitability of Buildings during Power Outages

*Alex Wilson*

## Introduction

*Passive survivability* refers to the idea that certain buildings, especially houses and apartment buildings, should be designed and built to maintain habitable temperatures in the event of an extended power outage or interruption in heating fuel.

This design criterion emerged following Hurricane Katrina in the Gulf Coast in the fall of 2005 when several chapters of the United States Green Building Council (USGBC) organized and led a series of design charrettes on how to make the Gulf Coast more sustainable through the reconstruction and planning following this storm event. More than 100 designers, planners, municipal officials, and others, including more than 30 from the Gulf Coast, were brought together at the 2005 Greenbuild Conference in Atlanta for several days of brainstorming about the Katrina response.

Among the outcomes of these charrettes was a document, *The New Orleans Principles*, that articulated ten principles that could guide this process of recovery in New Orleans, see Table 9.1 (Wilson, 2005).

The concept of passive survivability occurred to charrette organizers who remembered seeing New Orleans residents evacuated to the Superdome in the City and then, a day or two later, being evacuated from the Superdome because it was too hot inside. The building wasn't designed to maintain habitable temperatures without mechanical systems supplying cooling.

Similarly, among homes on the Gulf Coast that lost power for an extended period of time (but weren't flooded), there were reports that *older homes*, built prior to the advent of air conditioning, were more livable than newer homes that were built after air conditioning systems became ubiquitous. Those older homes were built using *vernacular architecture*—architecture that made sense for the hot, humid bioclimate of the American Southeast. These older homes had features like wrap-around porches that shaded the windows from direct

**Table 9.1** The New Orleans Principles.

| | The New Orleans Principles |
|---|---|
| 1 | *Respect the rights of all citizens of New Orleans.*<br>Displaced citizens who wish to return to New Orleans should be afforded the opportunity to return to healthy, livable, safe, and secure neighborhoods of choice. |
| 2 | *Restore natural protections of the greater New Orleans region.*<br>Sustain and restore the coastal and floodplain ecosystems and urban forests that support and protect the environment, economy, communities, and culture of southern Louisiana, and that contribute greatly to the economy and well-being of the nation. |
| 3 | *Implement an inclusive planning process.*<br>Build a community-centered planning process that uses local talent and makes sure that the voices of all New Orleanians are heard. This process should be an agent of change and renewal for New Orleans. |
| 4 | *Value diversity in New Orleans.*<br>Build on the traditional strength of New Orleans neighborhoods, encourage mixed uses and diverse housing options, and foster communities of varied incomes, mixed age groups, and a racial diversity. Celebrate the unique culture of New Orleans, including its food, music, and art. |
| 5 | *Protect the city of New Orleans.*<br>Expand or build a flood protection infrastructure that serves multiple uses. Value, restore, and expand the urban forests, wetlands, and natural systems of the New Orleans region that protect the city from wind and storms. |
| 6 | *Embrace smart redevelopment.*<br>Maintain and strengthen the New Orleans tradition of compact, connected, and mixed-use communities. Provide residents and visitors with multiple transportation options. Look to schools for jumpstarting neighborhood redevelopment and for rebuilding strong communities in the city. |
| 7 | *Honor the past; build for the future.*<br>In the rebuilding of New Orleans, honor the history of the city while creating 21st-century buildings that are durable, affordable, inexpensive to operate, and healthy to live in. Through codes and other measures, ensure that all new buildings are built to high standards of energy, structural, environmental, and human health performance. |
| 8 | *Provide for passive survivability.*<br>Homes, schools, public buildings, and neighborhoods should be designed and built or rebuilt to serve as livable refuges in the event of crisis or breakdown of energy, water, and sewer systems. |
| 9 | *Foster locally owned, sustainable businesses.*<br>Support existing and new local businesses built on a platform of sustainability that will contribute to a stronger and more diverse local economy. |
| 10 | *Focus on the long term.*<br>All measures related to rebuilding and ecological restoration, even short-term efforts, must be undertaken with explicit attention to the long-term solutions. |

sunlight, tall ceilings that resulted in temperature stratification, geometries, and fenestration that channeled cooling summer breezes through the occupied space, and outdoor living spaces where residents could spend time during the hottest weather.

Once mechanical cooling (air conditioning) systems came along, the principles of vernacular architecture were left behind. The same ranch houses began to be built everywhere, and designs that maintained reasonable comfort passively were forgotten.

Participants of the Atlanta design charrettes reasoned that Hurricane Katrina wouldn't be the last storm event to cause a prolonged power outage, and they argued that homes (and certain other buildings) should be designed and built to keep occupants safe if they are unable to evacuate and have to shelter in place during an extended power outage. They also recognized that certain events, such as power outages that result from equipment failures, usually don't lead to evacuations.

Providing for passive survivability was a way to help ensure that people would remain safer. It was a life-safety priority not only for homes and apartment buildings, but also for schools and other public buildings that are designated to serve as emergency shelters.

## Initiatives to Address Passive Survivability

The issue of passive survivability has begun attracting significant attention in some cities as well as research initiatives and national resilience programs.

### *New York City Greening the Codes Task Force, 2008–2010*

In advancing the PlaNYC initiative to make New York City more sustainable and reduce its carbon footprint 30% by 2030, Mayor Michael Bloomberg and City Council Speaker Christine Quinn engaged the Urban Green Council in 2008 to lead an effort to "green" the City's building codes. The NYC Green Codes Task Force, with over 200 members, was assembled by the Urban Green Council to carry out this initiative, and their final report was issued in February 2010 (Urban Green Council, 2010). The Resilient Design Institute (RDI) was represented on this Task Force and argued for passive survivability to be incorporated into the City's building code.

There are 111 proposals included in the final report, divided into ten categories. One of the nine proposals in the Building Resilience category (BR6) is to "Analyze Strategies to Maintain Habitability During Power Outages." The specific recommendation in BR6 is to "Undertake a comprehensive study of passive survivability and dual-mode functionality, then propose code changes to incorporate these concepts into the city's building codes. Also include a study on refuge areas in sealed buildings." While the recommendation was really to just study the issue, at least it got the concept onto the agenda.

### *Addressing Metrics of Passive Survivability*

While the RDI had been advancing the concept of passive survivability since 2005, we only had a vague sense of what passive survivability actually meant. We reasoned that more energy-efficient buildings would maintain habitable temperatures better than conventional buildings, but we didn't really know what "habitability" meant or even how it should be measured. In an effort to answer these questions, RDI convened a one-day workshop in New York City in May 2013 (Resilient Design Institute, 2013).

Eighteen leading engineers, architects, and other experts addressed these questions, as well as others, in a full, intensive day of brainstorming and discussion. While the workshop itself did not result in specific answers to these questions, it led to a technical paper by two of the participants and a third coauthor in the peer-reviewed journal *Building Research & Information*: "Overheating and passive habitability: indoor health and heat indices" (Holmes, Phillips, and Wilson, 2016).

## New York City's Building Resiliency Task Force, 2012–2013

Following Superstorm Sandy in the fall of 2012, New York City sought to address resilience through a wide range of measures. As with the Greening the Codes initiative several years earlier, Mayor Bloomberg and City Council Speaker Quinn engaged the Urban Green Council to convene a task force to address resilience. The Building Resiliency Task Force, with over 200 members, including a representative from the RDI, was convened in late 2012, and their final report was issued in June 2013 (Urban Green Council, 2013).

The final report of the Building Resiliency Task Force includes 33 specific proposals organized into four categories: Stronger Buildings; Back-up Power; Essential Safety; and Better Planning. The section on Essential Safety includes six proposals, including two that relate specifically to passive survivability: Ensure Operable Windows in Residential Buildings (#26) and Maintain Habitable Temperatures Without Power (#27). Relative to operable windows, New York currently has a requirement for operability, but it is in conflict with a law relating to child safety (fall protection) that limits the window opening size. The proposal for ensuring that habitable temperatures are maintained during power outages has not been addressed by the City to date.

## Baby It's Cold Inside Report

In February 2014 the Urban Green Council published *Baby It's Cold Inside*, a concise report of thermal modeling conducted for Urban Green by the engineering form Atelier Ten (Urban Green Council, 2014). In the report, six different residential building types were examined relative to interior temperature conditions during week-long power outages during typical (not extreme) summer and winter conditions. Separately, these buildings were modeled assuming typical building stock and energy code compliance.

The results of this modeling showed that standard buildings quickly reach unsafe conditions during extended power outages, both in winter and in summer, while more energy-efficient buildings maintain more habitable conditions. Temperature charts from the report for winter conditions are shown in Figures 9.1 and 9.2. This report

**Typical Building**

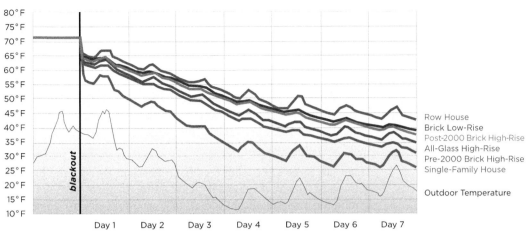

Figure 9.1 Indoor drift temperatures for different types of buildings based on thermal modeling by Atelier Ten, assuming typical construction practices for existing buildings in New York City (Urban Green Council, 2014).

**High-Performing Building**

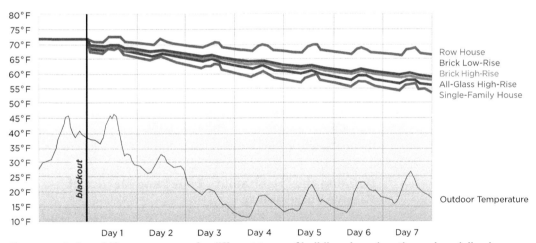

Figure 9.2 Indoor drift temperatures for different types of buildings based on thermal modeling by Atelier Ten, assuming energy-efficient construction practices for the buildings in New York City (Urban Green Council, 2014).

helped to convey the seriousness of this issue and the importance of addressing passive survivability—not just in New York City, but in any location.

## *LEED Pilot Credits on Resilient Design*

In November 2015 the USGBC rolled out a suite of three LEED pilot credits on Resilient Design. The LEED Rating System (Leadership in

Energy and Environmental Design) has helped advance green building worldwide since its introduction in 2000, but it hadn't addressed resilient design. The RDI led an effort to change that through a two-year process to develop pilot credits on resilient design. The pilot credits were available for one year, then taken down as the USGBC moved toward adopting the RELi Rating System as its resilience platform (see below). There remained strong interest in the LEED community for addressing resilience directly in LEED, and revised versions of the three pilot credits became available again in November 2018, including "Passive Survivability and Back-Up Power During Disruptions" (USGBC, 2018a).

There are three LEED pilot credits on Resilient Design: the first requires assessment of vulnerabilities at a site; the second requires mitigating the most significant threats (allowing a project two earn up to two points for addressing the greatest threats at the project location); and the third credit can be earned by addressing passive survivability (thermal safety) and providing back-up power (earning one point for each). The different compliance paths that can be used to demonstrate passive survivability are addressed later in this chapter.

### RELi Rating System

RELi is the resilience platform that Green Business Certification, Inc. (GBCI) and USGBC have adopted (GBCI, 2018). It is a wide-raging and comprehensive rating system that addresses an extensive of resilience issues, including thermal safety (RELi's terminology for passive survivability). Prior to the re-release of the LEED pilot credits on resilient design, the RELi Steering Committee worked on aligning the requirements for those aspects of resilience that are addressed in the pilot credits. As a result, the compliance paths for demonstrating thermal safety in RELi are identical to those of the pilot credits.

### Defining the "Habitability Zone" and Metrics of Passive Survivability

A key aspect of demonstrating that a building will maintain conditions of passive survivability is defining what constitutes habitable, or safe, conditions in buildings that lose power. How hot is too hot, and how cold is too cold? This is a far different question than what constitutes comfort—it is about survivability. Just as energy engineers refer to a "comfort zone" in designing mechanical systems for buildings, we can think of a "habitability zone" as those conditions that will generally keep people safe are buildings during power outages. This habitability zone has much wider temperature boundaries than does a comfort zone.

When the group of experts convened by the RDI considered this issue in May 2013, they quickly realized that those habitable conditions are not only about air temperature (dry-bulb temperature); they are also about relative humidity and mean radiant temperature. During an extended power outage, a building at 90°F in Phoenix, with 15% relative humidity, will be far different than a building at 90°F in Atlanta with 95% relative humidity, because the cooling effect of evaporation of moisture from an occupant's skin is impeded by higher relative humidity.

For this reason, experts who focus on passive survivability prefer less-common thermal metrics that factor in relative humidity and mean radiant temperature. These include Standard Effective Temperature (SET), Wet-Bulb Globe Temperature (WBGT), and—for high temperatures—Heat Index. These metrics of thermal conditions are used in the different compliance paths for demonstrating that a building will achieve passive survivability.

Unfortunately, these metrics were created primarily for outdoor conditions; they are not ideal metrics of indoor climatic conditions—but for now, they are what we have to work with.

Using the SET metric for thermal conditions, the developers of the LEED pilot credit on passive survivability identified a *habitability zone* for adults of average stature and physical condition as follows: a low of 54°F SET and a high of 86°F SET (12°C SET to 30°C SET)—and the pilot credit defines how much deviation there can be from this range. Another compliance path in this pilot credit provides not-to-exceed temperatures using either WBGT or Heat Index.

Note that maintaining temperatures and relative humidity within these boundaries will not guarantee safety for everybody. Differences in age, physical health, and physiology can mean that one person does fine at the high or low end of this thermal habitability range, while another individual is at great risk during a prolonged period of time in those conditions. Individuals with higher Body Mass Index (BMI), for example, may do fine at temperatures well below this thermal habitability zone, while being at risk in hot weather at temperatures well within the thermal habitability range.

## Methodologies for Assessing Passive Survivability

Both the revised 2018 LEED pilot credit on resilient design and the RELi Rating System v.2.0 provide three compliance paths for demonstrating passive survivability. The first two of these methodologies require thermal modeling specific to passive survivability. Requirements are laid out in a technical appendix to the LEED pilot credit Passive Survivability and Back-Up Power During Disruptions (USGBC, 2018b).

### *Compliance Path 1: Psychrometric Analysis*

The first compliance path relies on psychrometric analysis and establishes not-to-exceed temperatures using either Heat Index or WBGT metrics; these thresholds differ by building type and season. For summer conditions, thermal modeling must demonstrate that residential buildings will not exceed the "Extreme Caution" threshold in the Heat Index metric, or approximately 90°F (32°C) Heat Index. With non-residential buildings, that threshold is increased to the Extreme Danger threshold, or about 103°F (39°C) Heat Index.

With the WBGT metric (which differs somewhat from Heat Index, but also factors in relative humidity and mean radiant temperature) during summer conditions, thermal modeling must demonstrate that the building will not exceed 3°F WBGT (28°C WBGT). For non-residential buildings, those temperatures cannot exceed 88°F WBGT (31°C WBGT).

During the heating season (winter), relative humidity is less of a factor, and a standard air temperature metric (dry-bulb temperature) is used. Thermal modeling must demonstrate that the building temperature will not fall below 50°F (10°C)—for either residential or non-residential buildings.

### *Compliance Path 2: Standard Effective Temperature*

With the SET methodology, thermal modeling has to demonstrate that deviations from the "habitability zone" of 54°F SET to 86°F SET (12°C SET to 30°C SET) during winter and summer design weeks must be no greater than the referenced number of degree-days (or degree-hours). Those limits are as follows:

During peak summer conditions (cooling season) for residential buildings, the building can exceed 86°F SET for no more than 9°F SET-days (degree-days), or 216°F SET-hours, over a four-day period. In metric, residential buildings cannot exceed 30°C SET by more than 5°C SET-days (120°C SET-hours) over a four-day period. (Note that the LEED pilot credit on passive survivability originally established these allowable deviations over a one-week period, which is a more stringent requirement; there was not a consensus for changing that to four days.)

With non-residential buildings, greater deviation from the habitability zone is permitted, given the expectation that workers will leave the building and head home during an extended power outage. During peak summer conditions, the building cannot exceed 86°F SET for more than 18°F SET-days, or 432°F SET-hours. (In metric, non-residential buildings cannot exceed 30°C SET for more than 10°C SET-days (240°C SET-hours).

During the heating season, passive survivability requirements for residential and non-residential buildings are the same. Temperatures cannot fall below 54°F SET for more than 9°F SET-days (216°F SET-hours) during a four-day period in peak heating conditions. In metric,

# UNDERSTAND AND QUANTIFY THERMAL HABITABILITY

the building cannot fall below 12°C SET for more than 5°C SET-days (120°C SET-hours).

This terminology gets confusing. °F SET-days and °F SET-hours are degree-days and degree-hours in Fahrenheit degrees, using SET rather than air temperature as the metric. Here's how °F SET-hours are derived:

For the summer cooling season: Add up the difference between the building's modeled interior temperature (in SET) and 86°F, only if the interior SET is greater than 86°F, for all hours of the four-day period during the extreme hot week. For example, if on day 1 of that extreme week, there is an afternoon stretch where the temperatures rise to 87°F SET between 1 and 2 pm, to 90°F SET between 2 and 3 pm, to 88°F SET between 3 and 4 pm, before dropping below 86°F SET at 4 pm, you would come up with a total of 7°F SET-hours for that day. Those SET cooling degree-hours would be added up for each of the four days to come up with the total deviation. As long as the total is no more than 216°F SET-hours for that four-hour period (for a residential building), the passive survivability requirement would be met.

For the winter heating season: Add up the difference between the building's modeled interior temperature (in SET) and 54°F, only if the interior SET is less than 54°F, for all hours of the four-day period during the extreme cold week. The total SET heating-degree-hours for that four-day period cannot not exceed 216°F SET-hours or 9°F SET-days.

With metric, the calculations are the same, deriving °C SET-days and °C SET-hours for the four-day peak periods in summer and winter.

## *Compliance Path 3: Passive House Certification*

The third way in which the pilot credit point on passive survivability can be earned does not require separate thermal modeling. Instead, the project has to go through Passive House certification and demonstrate that natural ventilation can be achieved.

Passive House is a certification system for ultra-efficient buildings that was developed in Germany by the Passivhaus Institute (PHI) (Passivhaus Institute, 2015). To earn Passive House certification, a building must be extremely well-insulated, and such buildings typically include other passive features that help to minimize energy consumption, such as passive solar heating. The reasoning for including Passive House certification as a compliance path for demonstrating passive survivability is that such houses are so energy efficient that they are likely to maintain habitable temperatures for a power outage lasting many days.

In the LEED pilot credit on passive survivability, either the German Passive House standard may be used, or a modified version tailored for the U.S. may be used: Passive House Institute U.S. (PHIUS)

(Passive House Institute U.S., 2020). The rating systems are slightly different, with the PHIUS standard better factoring in cooling loads in U.S. climates, but either is a good indicator of a building that will maintain habitability in the U.S.

This is not to suggest that Passive House certification is easy. It is an arduous process and requires its own, sophisticated thermal modeling. But it is now a well-established system, and it is easier for design teams to understand than the complex methodologies employed in Compliance Paths 1 and 2.

In addition to Passive House certification, the pilot credit on passive survivability requires that *natural ventilation* be provided for the building. This requirement was added because it is possible to build a Passive House-certified building that relies 100% on mechanical ventilation that will not operate during a power outage. The natural ventilation requirement can be satisfied with operable windows or other means, and it is clearly described in the pilot credit appendix (USGBC, 2018b).

Other certification systems for net-zero-energy performance do not comply with the requirements of the LEED pilot credit on passive survivability, because net-zero-energy performance can be achieved by adding a lot of solar panels to a building with only mediocre energy performance. During a power outage, most solar systems do not operate, so the fact that a building achieves net-zero-energy performance is no guarantee that it will maintain habitable conditions.

These methodologies for assessing passive survivability are likely to evolve as we gain more experience in modeling passive conditions in buildings, but at least they provide a starting point for testing and comparing how we can track this important building performance criterion.

### Achieving Multiple Benefits: Synergies between Resilience and Sustainability

Buildings that achieve passive survivability will be far more energy efficient and, therefore, sustainable than typical buildings. It is very difficult to achieve the passive survivability performance, as defined here, without a highly energy-efficient building envelope as well as other features that will reduce operating energy use.

Passive survivability may also appeal to a wider audience than sustainability or green building. The motivation to achieve passive survivability can be one of life-safety, not just "doing the right thing." And although adaptation to climate change is an important motivation for pursuing passive survivability, one doesn't have to believe in global warming to want to keep his or her family safe.

As more frequent storms cause more frequent power outages, the motivation to design and build for passive survivability may grow.

Each new storm or outage-causing event—particularly Hurricane Katrina in 2005; Sandy in 2012; Harvey, Maria, and Florence in 2017; and Michael in 2018—builds motivation for creating buildings that will keep people safe. As the global climate warms, those motivations are likely to keep increasing.

Finally, while passive survivability is a climate *adaptation* response, the strategies for achieving this performance will save operating energy and therefore reduce carbon dioxide emissions. In other words, implementing passive survivability measures will help to *mitigate* climate change, even as it helps us adapt to it.

## The Path Ahead: The Research and Standards-Setting Agenda for Passive Survivability

There is tremendous need for additional research on key aspects of passive survivability.

From a human health and safety standpoint, we need a much better understanding of human physiology and how indoor thermal conditions during power outages can affect us. What is the *thermal habitability* zone in a building without power? How hot is too hot, and how cold is too cold? How does age (especially the very young and the elderly), illness, and body weight affect our ability to survive thermal extremes in buildings without power? How do relative humidity and mean radiant temperature affect human health and safety? How significant is our physiological adaptation to warmer and colder temperatures—in other words, if we live in a hot-humid climate will we do better in those conditions during a power outage?

We need to refine the metrics that can be used for assessing passive survivability in buildings. The metrics currently used to assess these thermal conditions, including SET, WBGT, and Heat Index, were all developed for use in assessing *outdoor conditions*. How should we model *indoor* thermal conditions in buildings that lose power? Can existing thermal modeling tools serve this function, or do new tools need to be developed?

We need to develop easy-to-use, clear methodologies for assessing passive survivability/thermal habitability. The methodologies developed for the LEED pilot credit on Passive Survivability (reported in this chapter) provide a good starting point, but these need much more thorough vetting and testing in real-world applications. Are these approaches realistic? Are they achievable? Are they understandable? What worksheets or calculators are needed to streamline this process?

Finally, we need to develop precise language and procedures for passive survivability so that these methodologies can be incorporated into building codes and/or other regulatory frameworks. If a municipality wants to incorporate passive survivability requirements into its building codes, as has been suggested in New York City, how does it go about doing that?

## References

GBCI, 2018: RELi Rating System. https://www.gbci.org/reli.

Holmes, Phillips, and Wilson 2016. "Overheating and passive habitability: indoor health and heat indices." *Building Research & Information*, 44(1): 1–19. http://dx.doi.org/10.1080/09613218.2015.1033875.

Passivhaus Institute, 2015. Passive House Certification System. https://passivehouse.com/.

Passive House Institute, U.S., 2020. PHIUS Certification for Buildings and Products. https://www.phius.org/home-page.

Resilient Design Institute, 2013. Resilient Design: Bouncing Back, Bouncing Forward: A Report from the Benchmarking Resilience Retreat on May 13, 2013. https://www.resilientdesign.org/resilient-design-strategies/rdi_benchmarking_resilience_summary-2/.

Urban Green Council, 2010. NYC Green Codes Task Force: A Report to Mayor Michael R. Bloomberg and Speaker Christine C. Quinn. https://www.urbangreencouncil.org/GreenCodes.

Urban Green Council, 2013. Building Resiliency Task Force: A Report to Mayor Michael R. Bloomberg and Speaker Christine C. Quinn. https://www.urbangreencouncil.org/content/projects/building-resilency-task-force.

Urban Green Council, 2014. Baby It's Cold Inside. https://www.urbangreencouncil.org/babyitscoldinside.

United States Green Building Council (USGBC), 2018a. LEED Pilot Credit: "Passive Survivability and Back-Up Power During Disruptions." https://www.usgbc.org/credits/passivesurvivability.

United States Green Building Council (USGBC), 2018b. LEED Pilot Credit: "Passive Survivability and Back-Up Power During Disruptions: Requirements Appendix." https://www.usgbc.org/credits/passivesurvivability?view=resources&return.

Wilson, 2005. "The New Orleans Principles Report". A report to the United States Green Building Council. Washington, DC.

# 10
# DESIGNING RESILIENT COASTAL COMMUNITIES WITH LIVING SHORELINES

*Wendy Meguro and Karl Kim*

## Introduction

### Coastal Flood Hazards

With climate change and sea level rise, coastal communities will experience increasingly frequent flooding. Coastal counties are home to over 126 million people, 40% of the nation's total population (NOAA Digital Coast 2015). Worldwide, insurers paid more than $300 billion for coastal storm damage in the 2000s (United Nations 2011). Routine events, such as high tides, regularly cause flooding and community disruptions. Nuisance flooding has increased tenfold over the past 60 years (Sweet and Park 2014). In Hawai'i, high wave events coupled with high tides threaten properties (Figure 10.1) eroding land beneath structures (Figure 10.2). With increased storms and flooding, policy makers and scientists recognize the need to take protective actions (Flavelle 2019). Hawai'i is implementing plans for 3.2 feet of sea level rise by mid-century (Caldwell 2018). On O'ahu, nearly 4,000 structures, 17 miles of major road, and 9,400 acres are likely to be chronically flooded with 3.2 feet of sea level rise (Hawaii CCMAC 2017).

When threatened by flooding, the typical response is to build seawalls or revetments. These tactics are expensive (US DOT 2019), lead to beach loss (Romine and Fletcher 2012), and separate people from the ocean. O'ahu has lost more than 5 miles of beaches due to seawalls with additional potential beach loss if armoring continues (Hawaii CCMAC 2017). Without armoring, over time, the width of a beach would remain approximately the same or the beach could move inland if there are sources of sand (NRC 2014). A living shoreline moves and changes over time.

### Background on Living Shorelines

Living shorelines integrate habitat restoration, coastal engineering, and conservation to reduce erosion, wave damage, and flood risks (NOAA 2015). Living shorelines and nature-based features include

DOI: 10.4324/9781003030720-10

Figure 10.1 Waves and elevated water levels during King Tides temporarily flood developed areas in Waikiki (University of Hawai'i (UH) Sea Grant King Tides Project n.d.). Photo courtesy of Andre Seale.

Figure 10.2 Large winter waves at Rocky Point on the North Shore of O'ahu cause severe coastal erosion, and sea level rise will accelerate beach loss (UH Sea Grant n.d.). Photo courtesy of Dolan Eversole.

# DESIGNING RESILIENT COASTAL COMMUNITIES

natural or constructed or restored salt marshes, wetlands, mangrove, coral, oysters, dunes, beach nourishment, berms, and maritime forests (US DOT 2019).

In this chapter, natural strategies are investigated to reduce erosion, dissipate wave energy, reduce wave forces, enhance habitat, and promote connection to the water. A hybrid approach combining constructed "gray" with natural "green" strategies is used to design "safe-to-fail or flood" environments as opposed to "fail safe" systems, which can result in larger disasters when thresholds are exceeded.

There is growing recognition that nature-based solutions and living shorelines can protect beaches and structures from storms and coastal flooding (Sutton-Grier, Wowk, and Bamford 2015). Increased acceptance is evidenced by the U.S. Army Corps of Engineers (USACE) shift towards green infrastructure and away from armoring (NRC 2014); major green design competitions such as Rebuild by Design; and federal funding for nature-based coastal resilience (NFWF 2018). These provide alternatives to armoring (Kittinger and Ayers 2010) and new technologies for adaptation (Klein et al. 2001). Living shorelines can offer a "low regrets" mitigation strategy with lower costs (US DOT 2019; Porro et al. 2020), shorter implementation times, and multiple co-benefits that complement efforts such as flood-proofing or relocation.

Figure 10.3 and Table 10.1 illustrate living shorelines. Coral reefs can dampen wave energy and reduce sediment transport and beach erosion. Beach nourishment, dune restoration, and vegetation can stabilize beaches and reduce wave run-up. Berms, culverts, swales, and other tools can divert and store water from storms. Complementary strategies include limiting run-off with rain gardens, pervious paving,

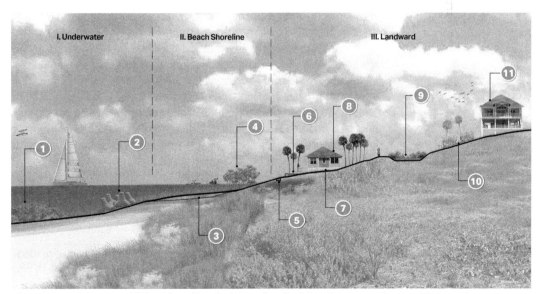

Figure 10.3 Elements of living shoreline design as flood mitigation strategies (AECOM 2020).

Table 10.1 Legend for Elements of Living Shoreline Design and Additional Flood Mitigation Strategies.

| Drawing Number | Strategy | Flood Mitigation Purpose |
|---|---|---|
| 1 | Coral reef restoration | Dissipate wave energy |
| 2 | Submerged breakwaters | Dissipate wave energy |
| 3 | Beach nourishment | Widen distance between shoreline and buildings |
| n/a | Dune restoration | Protective barrier; provide sand for beaches |
| 4 | Vegetation | Reduce wave run-up; mitigate erosion |
| 5 | Drainage | Divert water away from buildings |
| 6 | Permeable surfaces | Infiltrate water |
| 7 | Elevation of buildings | Accommodate water and protect building |
| 8 | Green roofs | Absorb and limit rainfall runoff |
| 9 | Detention/retention pond | Detain and infiltrate stormwater |
| 10 | Landscape design | Direct stormwater runoff to detention areas |
| 11 | Building relocation | Reduce exposure to flood hazard |

green roofs, detention ponds, and elevating or relocating structures. The cumulative impacts and synergistic effects of a combination of these different elements on habitat, activity patterns, and economic and social values should be considered when designing and building for resilience.

## Methods

### *Overall Approach*

There is growing but limited expertise as to when and where hybrid natural and built approaches to flood mitigation are best used (Sutton-Grier, Wowk, and Bamford 2015). More assessment of living shorelines is needed to support designers, planners, coastal managers, and property owners. This chapter addresses these needs based on research in Hawai'i. The method uses the first two steps in the Nature Conservancy's approach including: (1) assess risk and vulnerability; and (2) identify solutions (Nature Conservancy n.d.). It is also informed by NOAA's Conceptual Framework for Considering Living Shorelines (NOAA 2015) to understand the physical site conditions, habitats, and sea level rise, and balance appropriate green and gray infrastructure. The research informs practitioners by contributing to the understanding of how to integrate natural processes into coastal protection (Cooper and McKenna 2008) and improve urban ecological design (Steiner 2014).

### *Determine Study Areas*

Two different economically and culturally significant sites were identified: (1) a rural beach with detached residences (Sunset Beach) and (2) a dense urban resort destination (Waikiki Beach). The two sites enable comparison based on differing geological conditions, wave energies, development, building types, economic activity, and feasibility of in-place adaptation versus relocation. Additional resources to assess risk included information on social vulnerability (Climate Central n.d.; NOAA 2015), population characteristics (Climate Central n.d.), and risk assessment tools such as the Coastal Resilience decision support system (Nature Conservancy n.d.).

### Assess Risk and Vulnerability: Visualize Future Flooding

Future and current flooding are visualized through the Hawai'i Sea Level Rise Viewer (PacIOOS n.d.) map of flooded areas with 3.2 feet of sea level rise, annual high wave flooding, and coastal erosion (Figures 10.3 and 10.5) and photographs during high tides (UH Sea Grant King Tides Project n.d.). Estimated sea level rise depths at future dates (NOAA n.d.b.; Climate Central n.d.) as well as regional estimated flood frequencies (Sweet 2017) enabled the researchers to visualize flooding over time.

### Design and Plan for Living Shorelines

An interdisciplinary team of professionals identified, discussed, visualized, and evaluated site-specific living shoreline techniques based on reviews of scientific studies, regulatory policies, recent projects, and professional experience in marine science, coastal geology, engineering, architecture, and planning. The team identified types of living shorelines designs the sites could support, and assessed flood risk and habitat and recreational benefits, with consideration of monetary costs, long-term performance, and maintenance. Table 10.2 includes a summary of site characteristics and living shorelines strategies.

### Summarize Supporting Case Studies and Research

A literature review of living shorelines was conducted to identify case studies that demonstrated the effectiveness of proposed strategies in locations with similar wave energy, climate, and geology. Sources of information included scientific research, design competition proposals, and policies including NOAA's Guidance on Living Shorelines (NOAA n.d.a.); Systems Approach to Geomorphic Engineering (SAGE) Shoreline Stabilization brochure (SAGE 2015); The Nature Conservancy Coastal Resilience website (n.d.); U.S. Climate Resilience Toolkit Steps to Resilience (n.d.).

### Deliberate Alternatives with Stakeholders

The living shoreline strategies were visualized for discussion and critique in community meetings, conferences, and academic settings. A workshop and public exhibition entitled, "Living Shorelines on Tropical Islands: Creating and Maintaining Healthy Coastal Systems and Improving Community Resilience in the Face of Climate Change" was

**Table 10.2** Site Characteristics and Applicability of Living Shoreline Techniques, Sunset Beach and Waikiki.

|  | Sunset Beach | Waikiki |
|---|---|---|
| **Site Characteristics** | | |
| Activities, land use, character | Natural, rural setting<br>Low level of development<br>High recreational value | Urbanized resort destination<br>High-economic value<br>Tourism, jobs, activity center |
| Wave energy | High, 5 m significant wave height offshore buoy | Medium, 2 m significant wave height offshore buoy |
| Geology | Natural sandy beach with fringing reef | Man-made sandy beach with fringing reef |
| **I. Underwater** | | |
| Coral reef restoration | Not applicable<br>High wave energy would harm coral | Applicable in areas of low wave energy |
| Offshore breakwater<br>Groin, tombolo | Not applicable<br>High wave energy may damage breakwater and affect surfing conditions | May be applicable to reduce wave energy but may affect surfing conditions |
| **II. Beach/Shore** | | |
| Beach nourishment | Temporary sand mounds used to protect homes from coastal erosion | Applicable and currently used for periodic nourishment |
| Dune restoration | Applicable to slow erosion | Not applicable because of narrow beach widths |
| Vegetation, native planting | Applicable | Applicable |
| Drainage | Culverts, berms, landscaping | |
| Elevate structures | Applicable | Elevate critical equipment above ground floor. Use wet- or dry-floodproofing for ground floor |
| **III. Landward** | | |
| Porous surfaces | Applicable to roads, paths, hardscape | Applicable but needs integration with municipal drainage systems and consideration of shallow groundwater table |
| Green roofs, rain gardens | Applicable | Limited roof and garden area because of high-rise development with commercial and urban uses |
| Landscaping | Applicable | Applicable |
| Retention/detention | Potential for ponds and natural holding areas | Limited land availability, potential in parks, plazas, and underground parking facilities |
| Relocation of buildings and transportation | Applicable | Limited opportunities because of high densities and property values |
| Demolition/open space | Applicable | Limited opportunities |

hosted at the 2016 International Union for Conservation of Nature (IUCN) World Conservation Congress. Workshop participants evaluated living shorelines strategies visualized through interactive physical shoreline models, aquaria, an augmented reality sand box, and presentations of international case studies (see Figure 10.8).

## Results

The two study sites and the proposals for living shorelines and related flood mitigation projects are summarized in Table 10.2.

### Rural, Extreme/High Wave Energy: Sunset Beach, Oʻahu, HI

Sunset Beach is known for world-class surfing with sandy beaches, deeper fringing reefs, extreme seasonal (northern hemisphere) wave energy in winter months with 5 m offshore buoy significant wave heights (Vitousek and Fletcher 2008, 548), and a coastal slope of less than 20% (Fletcher et al. 2002, 53). The area is of importance for ocean recreation and tourism and residential development. Coastal dunes were graded, and many detached homes, roadways, and bicycle and pedestrian paths were built near the shoreline. Large winter waves eroded the bike path and threatened homes at Rocky Point (Figure 10.2), and over-washed more than 11 miles of main coastal highway forcing closure for days (USGCRP 2017).

Figure 10.4 shows the coastal flooding in the 3.2-foot sea level rise exposure area (SLR-XA) of coastal lands (in light blue), including significant stretches of the coastal road (in red).

Dune restoration with stabilizing vegetation was proposed to address wave run-up, overtopping, and erosion (US DOT 2019). Extensive dune restoration for Sunset Beach would require more space than is available between the shoreline and coastal road to allow for movement of the beach and dunes. Over the long term, relocation of the road and homes, and restoration of the dunes may be considered if maintaining the beach is a priority. The low density, rural setting makes relocation of more plausible than at Waikiki Beach. Relocation presents multiple challenges including acquiring land and compensating owners. Despite these difficulties, interest has been demonstrated in the recent Managed Retreat study. There have been coastal planning innovations including erosion-rate-based shoreline setbacks (Hwang 2005).

Figure 10.5 shows the physical model with the coastal road threatened by erosion (top image). The bottom image shows relocation of roads and homes landward, restoration of dunes with stabilizing vegetation (groundcover and shrubs), and an elevated pedestrian walkway to prevent foot compaction.

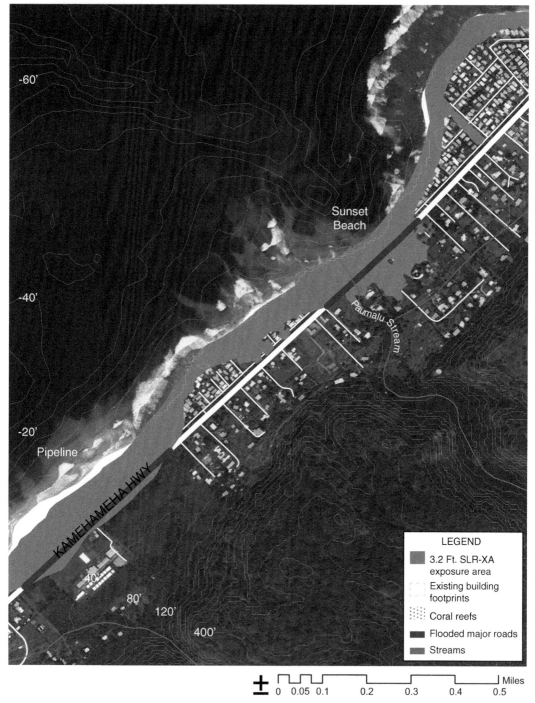

Figure 10.4 Sunset Beach map shows the projected 3.2-foot SLR-XA area (in light blue), including flooded stretches of the coastal road (in red). Image courtesy of PacIOOS.

# DESIGNING RESILIENT COASTAL COMMUNITIES

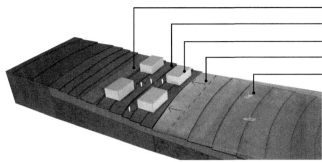

Existing condition scale model - Sunset Beach

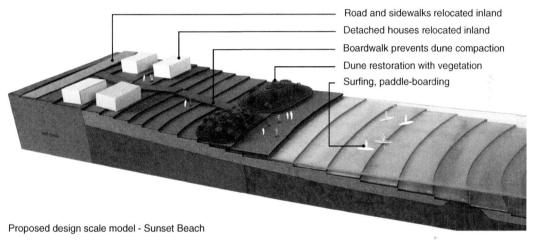

Proposed design scale model - Sunset Beach

**Figure 10.5** A scale model of Sunset Beach shows houses and a roadway threatened by erosion (top) and potential dune restoration after relocation of buildings and road (bottom).

Two other living shoreline strategies were considered: coral reef restoration and offshore breakwaters. While Hawai'i has experience with coral reef restoration, the high wave environment of Sunset Beach makes this approach unfeasible (Onat et al. 2018a, 2018b). Offshore breakwaters would be difficult to implement because of high wave energy and potential impacts on surfing, requiring more detailed planning, analysis, design, and engineering.

## Dense, Urban Coastal Development: Waikiki Beach, O'ahu, HI

Waikiki is an urban resort destination on the south shore of O'ahu and an economic hub for Hawai'i. Its hotels, condominiums, restaurants, shops, and attractions generate over $2.22 billion in annual visitor spending (Tarui, Peng and Eversole 2018). The study site is located near Fort DeRussy Beach Park, and has a sandy beach with tall buildings close to the shoreline and a two-lane road landward of the buildings. The area is at low elevation atop a filled wetland, adjacent to a two-mile long beach with shallow fringing coral reef and moderate wave energy exposure. Its low coastal slope makes it susceptible to tsunami, riverine flooding, storm surge, and seasonal high wave damage (Fletcher et al. 2002, 53). Waikiki has moderate wave energy, and 2-m significant wave height measured at an offshore buoy (Vitousek and Fletcher 2008, 548). High wave events from summer swells and high tides can overtop seawalls (Figure 10.1) and sand mounds, flood basements, and back-up sewers, so building owners deploy sandbags and temporary flood walls. The State in partnership with the Waikiki Beach Special Improvement District Association (WBSIDA) has implemented a program for beach nourishment and maintenance (Porro et al. 2020).

Figure 10.6 shows that with 3.2 feet of sea level rise, many buildings will likely experience flooding. With 6 feet of sea level rise, most of Waikiki will be inundated. With sea level rise, wave run-up will also increase, and less wave energy will be dissipated by nearshore reefs (PacIOOS n.d.). The density and high-economic values in Waikiki make retreat challenging. Living shorelines can minimize flooding impacts, enabling current activities to continue for as long as possible.

Living shorelines strategies to dampen wave energy and lessen wave run-up include coral reef restoration, offshore breakwaters to shelter coral reefs, coastal vegetation, and beach nourishment (US DOT 2019) (Figure 10.7). Most of the beach is not wide enough to accommodate dunes. Complementary strategies might include T-head groins tuned to the wave environment to create stable beach profiles, which can be filled with beach quality sand, elevated pedestrian boardwalks, below-grade temporary water storage, and floodable ground floor buildings (Figure 10.7).

Vegetation may reduce wave run-up while maintaining open sandy beach areas. An inventory of plant species for consideration in Waikiki was compiled, noting density as an indicator of ability to dissipate wave energy, native or low invasive risk, salt tolerance, and ability to thrive in coastal zones. Research (Francis, Kim, and Pant 2019) on stakeholder preferences found strong support for green infrastructure, beach replenishment, and coral reef restoration across diverse social, political, and economic groups.

## Supporting Case Studies

### *Coral Reef Case Studies*

Coral reefs are an important resource that offer benefits by dissipating wave energy, comparable to breakwaters (Ferrario et al. 2014). A study of coral reefs estimated annual coastal storm flood protection benefits at 32 square miles, over 18,000 people, and over $1.8 billion (Storlazzi et al. 2019, 1). Another found that the reefs reduce

# DESIGNING RESILIENT COASTAL COMMUNITIES

Figure 10.6 Map of Waikiki shows the projected 3.2-foot SLR-XA (in light blue), flooded stretches of a major road (in red), and existing coral reef. Image courtesy of PacIOOS.

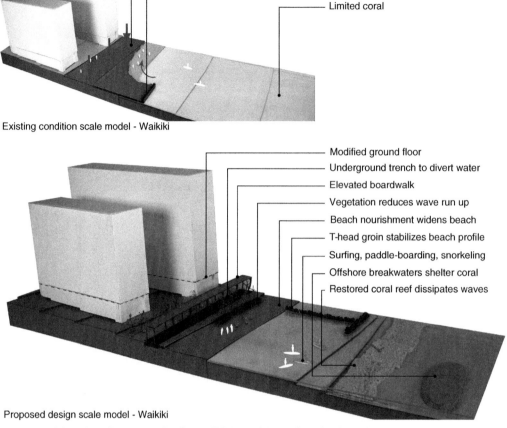

Figure 10.7 Living shoreline strategies for Waikiki to mitigate flooding including coral restoration, vegetated shorelines, and beach nourishment.

wave energy by 97% and wave heights by 84% (Ferrario et al. 2014, 3). Reefs closer to the surface, with higher surface complexity and hydraulic roughness, are most effective in dissipation of wave energy (Ferrario et al. 2014; Harris et al. 2018). Successful growing of corals in nurseries and transplanting into degraded reefs in low to medium wave energy locations has been implemented in Hawai'i (Piniak and Brown 2008; Rodgers et al. 2017) and the Florida Keys (Morin 2014). Coral reef restoration unit costs vary, but the median cost per linear foot is $393 (Ferrario et al. 2014, 3).

Marine and terrestrial conditions pose challenges to coral reef restoration. Moderate summer wave energy may damage newly transplanted coral, which might be addressed by transplanting during lower wave energy winter months and sheltering restoration areas with offshore submerged breakwaters. Other challenges include terrestrial pollution carried in stormwater runoff (Ferrario et al. 2014), invasive species, warmer ocean water temperatures, and beach erosion

(Sedensky 2003). Coral restoration, submerged breakwaters, T-head groins, and modifications to nearshore underwater environment could affect wave energy and sediment transport and impact surfing in Waikiki if not carefully designed. There must be comprehensive modeling and testing of proposed actions. Artificial low-crested detached breakwaters can reduce wave heights similarly to coral reef restoration, although construction of breakwaters is more expensive (Ferrario et al. 2014). In addition to the construction costs, permitting and environmental review also increase time and expenses.

Submerged breakwaters or T-head groins could also be designed to create habitat. The concrete can be designed and sited to grow and recruit biology, as done with the Living Breakwaters (Orff 2016, 226) or the Seattle waterfront project to improve marine habitats (Seattle 2020).

## Vegetation Case Studies

Vegetation can dissipate wave energy or stabilize sand dunes. Computer simulation of seagrass and mangroves has shown greater reductions in wave height, water level, and erosion as compared to non-vegetated areas (Guannel et al. 2015). Although the vegetation used in this study was not appropriate for Hawai'i, the methods are useful to Waikiki when considering vegetation types, location relative to the shoreline, and planting width. Physical modeling showed that vegetation reduced the loss of dunes by a factor of three compared to an unvegetated dune during a wave over-washing event (Bryant et al. 2018). Although studies on the wave dissipation effects of sea grass, mangroves, wetlands, and dune grass are available, more simulations and field studies are needed for coastal vegetation types in Hawai'i. The average cost per linear foot for vegetation is $63–113 with median $90 (US DOT 2019, 36).

## Beach Nourishment and Dune Restoration Case Studies

Beach nourishment is likely to continue in Waikiki. Dean (2000) found storm damage reduction from either widening a beach or moving infrastructure landward a similar distance. The average cost per linear foot for beach nourishment is $613–992 with median $802 (US DOT 2019, 36) and may re-occur and increase over time.

Sand dunes provide flood protection (USGCRP 2017), sand reserves for migrating beaches, buffers from waves and storm surge, and natural habitats. Dunes substantially reduced storm damage (Tomiczek et al. 2017) and flooding (Walling et al. 2014) from Hurricane Sandy in 2011.

Three dune restoration projects demonstrate feasibility. At the Patrick Air Force Base in Brevard County, Florida, beaches were restored with revetments, dune and beach re-nourishment, sand fences, and vegetation. Four projects over eight years added over one million cubic yards of sand to the beach (Judge et al. 2017). At Seaside Park in Ventura County, California, erosion was addressed by moving a parking lot and bicycle path landward, restoring 1,800 feet of shoreline with vegetated dunes, and adding a cobble berm and beach nourishment to mimic a neighboring naturally occurring beach (Judge et al. 2017). In South Milton, Devon, England, a parking lot was replaced with three restored dune ridges, each around 200 m long and 30 m wide, stabilized with dune grass (Hanley et al. 2014).

### Visual Communication to Deliberate Alternatives with Stakeholders

Maps, physical models (Figures 10.4–10.7), and interactive planning and design activities are invaluable for communicating adaptation options and ecological impacts. Visualizations support deliberation among professionals and stakeholders with local knowledge and understanding of construction practices and environmental and social concerns. The project included visualization of coral reef propagation, and coastal vegetation with an augmented reality sandbox, scale models, and videos and posters (Figure 10.8). Innovative technologies using i-clickers and smart phones make it possible to capture and record preferences among participants (Kim, Burnett, and Ghimire 2017).

### Discussion

Living shoreline approaches show much potential for reducing threats from flooding, sea level rise, and climate change. Wave energy, land use and density, and sediment volumes are key factors in determining the appropriateness of living shoreline strategies. Other factors include the availability of space and willingness to use new methods to protect properties, mitigate hazards, and adapt to long-term environmental change.

More research on performance, costs and benefits, and policy tools for implementation is needed. The biggest limitation to use of natural

Figure 10.8 Left to right: Coral reef propagation presented alongside the Waikiki scale model; augmented reality sandbox presented alongside the Sunset Beach scale model.

defenses is the lack of quantitative assessments of engineering performance and economic benefits (Storlazzi et al. 2019). Simulations showing wave dissipation from proposed living shorelines would help design teams. A useful tool is InVEST, which simulates site-specific wave dissipation with and without living shorelines (Natural Capital Project n.d.). Re-creation of shoreline profiles in wave tanks and modeling of treatments in laboratory settings from which site-specific models can be constructed support design.

Documentation of the faster pace of recovery associated with living shorelines would also assist designers and policy makers. Teams can learn from disasters and "design with nature" as Wagner, Merson, and Wentz (2016) did in Staten Island in the wake of Superstorm Sandy. Unlike hard infrastructure, living shorelines can be self-maintaining (Gedan et al. 2011) with potential to self-repair after damaging events (Ferrario et al. 2014).

There is need for greater awareness, training, and education. It is problematic that the protective services of natural defenses are overlooked because their value is not assessed like artificial defenses, such as seawalls (Storlazzi et al. 2019). Living shorelines' ecosystem services should be valued in planning and decision-making (NSTC 2015). Financing tools, value capture, property tax changes, and other ways to pay for coastal resilience should be considered (Parsons and Noailly 2004).

There are examples of the integration of living shorelines into policy. The President's Hurricane Sandy Rebuilding Task Force called for natural infrastructure options and required tools to measure and predict their effectiveness (Hurricane Sandy Rebuilding Task Force 2014). State examples include Virginia's policy (LIS 2011) to encourage the use of living shorelines and Hawai'i's Coastal Erosion Management Plan, which includes beach and dune management (DLNR n.d.). Community-based planning can also support development and funding. A regional beach master plan on Maui, Hawai'i (Baldwin Beach Park Master Plan 2019), included dune restoration and received federal funding for implementation (NFWF 2018). A policy-related challenge is the longer permitting times for living shorelines projects as compared to typical hard infrastructure (Sutton-Grier, Wowk, and Bamford 2015). Because of property rights and varying systems for management of development, the shared responsibilities for planning, financing, implementing, and maintaining living shorelines are complex and require new approaches and systems for governance.

## Conclusions

There is a need to encourage living shoreline planning and design to support flood risk reduction and adaptation. As Spaulding et al. (2014) have argued, more integration between ecosystem design, coastal protection, and adaptation to climate change is needed.

With living shorelines in Sunset Beach and Waikiki, the "sum is greater than the whole of the parts." The improved protection from flooding generates co-benefits such as creating habitat and improving ecosystem services. These benefits support recreational amenities, economic values, and quality of life.

There is need for more place-based approaches to resilience (Cutter et al. 2008), which enable designers and planners to enhance environmental conditions and protect valuable cultural and social assets. Indigenous knowledge, native plant species, and culturally appropriate practices are especially relevant to building and sustaining living shorelines in Hawai'i.

## References

AECOM. 2020. Living Shoreline Designs. Used with permission.

Baldwin Beach Park Master Plan. 2019. County of Maui. https://www.mauicounty.gov/2336/Baldwin-Beach-Park-Master-Plan.

Bryant, D., M. Bryant, J. Sharp, and G. Bell. 2018. "Erosion of Vegetated Dunes." *Proceedings of the 7th International Conference on the Application of Physical Modeling in the Coastal and Port Engineering Science*, Santander, Spain, 7.

Caldwell, K. 2018. "Mayor Issues Directive on Climate Change and Sea Level Rise in Response to Report from Climate Change Commission." Office of Climate Change, Sustainability and Resiliency City and County of Honolulu.

Climate Central. n.d. "Surging Seas." https://coastal.climatecentral.org/map.

Cooper, J., and J. McKenna. 2008. "Working with Natural Processes. The Challenge for Coastal Protection Strategies." *The Geographical Journal* 174(4): 315–331.

Cutter, S.L., L. Barnes, M. Berry, C. Burton, E. Evans, E. Tate, and J. Webb. 2008. "A Place-Based Model for Understanding Community Resilience to Natural Disasters." *Global Environmental Change* 18(4): 598–606.

Dean, R.G. 2000. "Storm Damage Reduction Potential via Beach Nourishment." *Proceedings of the 27th International Conference on Coastal Engineering*, ICCE 2000, 3305–3318.

DLNR (Department of Land and Natural Resources). n.d. "Coastal Erosion Management Plan." State of Hawaii, Land Division, Coastal Lands Program. https://dlnr.hawaii.gov/occl/files/2013/08/COEMAP1.pdf.

Ferrario, F., Beck, M.W., Storlazzi, C.D., Fiorenza, M., Shepard, C.C., Airoldi, L. 2014. "The Effectiveness of Coral Reefs for Coastal Hazard Risk Reduction and Adaptation." *Nature Communications* 5:3794.

Flavelle, C. 2019. "With More Storms and Rising Seas, Which U.S. Cities Should be Saved First?" *New York Times*, June 19, 2019. https://nyti.ms/2MUv2L0.

Fletcher, C.H., E.E. Grossman, B.M. Richmond, A.E. Gibbs. 2002. "Atlas of Natural Hazards in the Hawaiian Coastal Zone." U.S. Department of the Interior. U.S. Geological Survey.

Francis, O., K. Kim, and P. Pant. 2019. "Stakeholder Assessment of Coastal Risks and Mitigation Strategies." *Ocean and Coastal Management* 179: 104844.

Gedan, K.B., M.L. Kirwan, E. Wolanski, E. B. Barbier, and B.R. Silliman. 2011. "The Present and Future Role of Coastal Wetland Vegetation in Protecting Shorelines: Answering Recent Challenges to the Paradigm." *Climate Change* 106: 7–29.

Guannel, G., P. Ruggiero, J. Faries, K. Arkema, M. Pinsky, G. Gelfenbaum, A. Guerry, and C.-K. Kim 2015. "Integrated Modeling Framework to Quantify the Coastal Protection Services Supplied by Vegetation." *Journal of Geophysical Research-Oceans* 120(1): 324–345.

Hanley, M.E., S.P.G. Hoggart, D.J. Simmonds, et al. 2014. "Shifting Sands? Coastal Protection by Sand Banks, Beaches and Dunes." *Coastal Engineering* 87, no. C (May 2014): 136–146.

Harris, D.L., A. Rovere, E. Casella, R. Canavesio, A. Collin, A. Pomeroy, J.M. Webster, and V. Parravicini. 2018. "Coral Reef Structural Complexity Provides Important Coastal Protection from Waves Under Rising Sea Levels." *Science Advances* 4(2): eaao4350.

Hawaii CCMAC (Hawai'i Climate Change Mitigation and Adaptation Commission). 2017. "Hawai'i Sea Level Rise Vulnerability and Adaptation Report." Prepared by Tetra Tech, Inc. and the State of Hawai'i Department of Land and Natural Resources.

Hurricane Sandy Rebuilding Task Force. 2014. Hurricane Sandy Rebuilding Strategy Progress Report, Washington, DC. 55. https://monarchhousing.org/wp-content/uploads/2013/08/081913%20Hurricane_Sandy_Rebuilding_Strategy.pdf.

Judge, J., S. Newkirk, K. Leo, W. Heady, M. Hayden, S. Veloz, T. Cheng, B. Battalio, T. Ursell, and M. Small. 2017. "Case Studies of Natural Shoreline Infrastructure in Coastal California: A Component of Identification of Natural Infrastructure Options for Adapting to Sea Level Rise." The Nature Conservancy, Arlington, VA. 38 p.

Kim, K., K. Burnett, and J. Ghimire. 2017. "Integrating Fast Feedback and GIS to Plan for Important Agricultural Land Designations in Kauai County, Hawaii." *Journal of Land Use Science* 12(5): 375–390.

Kittinger, J., and A. Ayers. 2010. "Shoreline Armoring, Risk Management and Coastal Resilience Under Rising Seas." *Coastal Management* 38 (6): 634–653.

Klein, R., R. Nicholls, S. Ragoonaden, M. Capobianco, J. Aston, E.N. Buckley. 2001. "Technological Options for Adaptation to Climate Change in Coastal Zones." *Journal of Coastal Research* 17(3): 531–543.

LIS (Virginia's Legislative Information System). 2011. Senate Bill 964. http://lis.virginia.gov/cgi-bin/legp604.exe?111+ful+CHAP0885.

Morin, Richard. 2014. "A Lifesaving Transplant for Coral Reefs." *International New York Times*, November 26, 2014.

Natural Capital Project. n.d. "Integrated Valuation of Ecosystem Services and Tradeoffs (InVEST)." https://naturalcapitalproject.stanford.edu/software/invest.

Nature Conservancy. n.d. "Coastal Resilience." https://coastalresilience.org/.

NFWF (National Fish and Wildlife Foundation). 2018. "National Coastal Resilience Fund." https://www.nfwf.org/programs/national-coastal-resilience-fund.

NOAA (National Oceanic and Atmospheric Administration). n.d.a. "What Is a Living Shoreline?" Accessed November 23, 2018. https://oceanservice.noaa.gov/facts/living-shoreline.html.

NOAA. n.d.b "Sea Level Rise Viewer." https://coast.noaa.gov/slr.

NOAA Digital Coast. 2015. "2011 to 2015 American Community Survey (U.S. Census Bureau)." https://coast.noaa.gov/digitalcoast/data/acs.html.

NRC (National Research Council). 2014. *Reducing Coastal Risk on the East and Gulf Coasts*. Washington, DC: The National Academies Press. doi: 10.17226/18811.

NSTC (National Science and Technology Council). 2015. "Ecosystem-Service Assessment: Research Needs for Coastal Green Infrastructure." Office of Science and Technology Policy, 40 p.

Onat, Y., O. Francis, and K. Kim. 2018a. "Vulnerability Assessment and Adaptation to Sea Level Rise in High-wave Environments: A Case Study on Oʻahu, Hawaiʻi." *Ocean and Coastal Management* 157: 147–159.

Onat, Y., M. Marchant, O. Francis, and K. Kim. 2018b. "Coastal Exposure of the Hawaiian Islands Using GIS-based Index Modeling." *Ocean and Coastal Management* 163: 113–129.

Orff, K. 2016. *Toward an Urban Ecology*. New York: Monacelli Press.

PacIOOS (Pacific Islands Ocean Observing System). n.d. "Hawaii Sea Level Rise Viewer." https://www.pacioos.hawaii.edu/shoreline/slr-hawaii/.

Parsons, G., and J. Noailly. 2004. "A Value Capture Property Tax for Financing Beach Nourishment Projects: An Application to Delaware's Ocean Beaches." *Ocean and Coastal Management* 47(1): 49–61.

Piniak, G., and E. Brown. 2008. "Growth and Mortality of Coral Transplants (Pocillopora Damicornis) Along a Range of Sediment Influence in Maui, Hawaiʻi." *Pacific Science* 62: 1, 39–55.

Porro, R.K., D. Spirandelli, and K. Lowry. 2020. "Evaluating Erosion Management Strategies in Waikiki." *Ocean and Coastal Management* 188.

Rebuild by Design. n.d. "Hurricane Sandy Design Competition." http://www.rebuildbydesign.org/our-work/sandy-projects.

Rodgers, K.S., K. Lorance, A.R. Donà, Y. Stender, C. Lager, P.L. Jokiel, and J. Reimer. 2017. "Effectiveness of Coral Relocation as a Mitigation Strategy in Kāneʻohe Bay, Hawaiʻi." *PeerJ* 5:E3346.

Romine, B., and C. Fletcher. 2012. "Armoring on Eroding Coasts Leads to Beach Narrowing and Loss on Oahu, Hawaii." In *Pitfalls of Shoreline Stabilization: Selected Case Studies*, pp. 141–164. Edited by J.A.G. Cooper and O.H. Pilkey. Dordrecht: Springer Science+Business Media.

SAGE (Systems Approach to Geomorphic Engineering). 2015. "Natural and Structural Measures for Shoreline Stabilization." http://sagecoast.org/docs/SAGE_LivingShorelineBrochure_Print.pdf.

Seattle Office of the Waterfront and Civic Projects. 2020. "Seawall Project." https://waterfrontseattle.org/waterfront-projects/seawall.

Sedensky, M. 2003. "Waikiki Losing Its World-Famous Beach; Shoreline Has Been Receding into Ocean, Sand Filling Up Offshore Reefs." *The Washington Post*, July 27, 2003.

Spalding, M.D., S. Ruffo, C. Lacambra, I. Meliane, L.Z. Hale, C.C. Shepard, M.W. Beck. 2014. "The Role of Ecosystems in Coastal Protection: Adapting to Climate Change and Coastal Hazards." *Ocean and Coastal Management* 90: 50–57.

Steiner, F. 2014. "Frontiers in Urban Ecological Design and Planning Research." *Landscape and Urban Planning* 125: 304–311.

Storlazzi, C.D., B.G. Reguero, A.D. Cole, E. Lowe, J.B. Shope, A.E. Gibbs, B.A. Nickel, R.T. McCall, A.R. van Dongeren, and M.W. Beck. 2019. "Rigorously Valuing the Role of U.S. Coral Reefs in Coastal Hazard Risk Reduction." U.S. Geological Survey Open-File Report 2019–1027, 14 p.

Sutton-Grier, A.E., K. Wowk, and H. Bamford. 2015. "Future of Our Coasts: The Potential for Natural and Hybrid Infrastructure to Enhance the Resilience of Our Coastal Communities, Economies and Ecosystems." *Environmental Science and Policy* 51: 137–148.

Sweet, W.V. 2017. "Global and Regional Sea Level Rise Scenarios for the United States." NOAA Technical Report NOS CO-OPS 083.

Sweet, W.V., and J. Park. 2014. "From the Extreme to the Mean: Acceleration and Tipping Points of Coastal Inundation from Sea Level Rise." *Earth's Future* 2(12): 579–600.

Tarui, N., M. Peng, D. Eversole. 2018. Economic Impact Analysis of the Potential Erosion of Waikiki Beach. University of Hawai'i Sea Grant College Program

Tomiczek, T., A. Kennedy, Y. Zhang, M. Owensby, M.E. Hope, N. Lin, and A. Flory. 2017. "Hurricane Damage Classification Methodology and Fragility Functions Derived from Hurricane Sandy's Effects in Coastal New Jersey." *Journal of Waterway, Port, Coastal, and Ocean Engineering* 143(5): 1–17.

UH (University of Hawai'i) Sea Grant College Program. n.d. "Hawaii and Pacific Islands King Tides Project." http://seagrant.soest.hawaii.edu/coastal-and-climate-science-and-resilience/ccs-projects/hawaii-pacific-islands-king-tides-project/.

United Nations Office for Disaster Risk Reduction. 2011. *Global Assessment Report on Disaster Risk Reduction: Revealing Risk, Redefining Development.* New York: United Nations, 178 p.

U.S. Climate Resilience Toolkit. n.d. "Steps to Resilience." https://toolkit.climate.gov/#steps.

US DOT (US Department of Transportation). 2019. "Nature-Based Solutions for Coastal Highway Resilience: An Implementation Guide." Federal Highway Administration. Report No. FHWA-HEP-19–042.

USGCRP (U.S. Global Change Research Program). 2017. "Climate Science Special Report." In *Fourth National Climate Assessment*. Edited by D.J. Wuebbles, D.W. Fahey, K.A. Hibbard, D.J. Dokken, B.C. Stewart, and T.K. Maycock. Vol. I. Washington, DC: U.S. Global Change Research Program.

Vitousek, S., and C.H. Fletcher. 2008. "Maximum Annually Recurring Wave Heights in Hawaii." *Pacific Science* 62(4): 541–553.

Wagner, M., J. Merson, and E. Wentz. 2016. "Designing with Nature Key Lessons from McHarg's Instrinsic Suitability in the Wake of Hurricane Sandy." *Landscape and Urban Planning* 155: 33–45.

Walling, K., J. Miller, T. Herrington, and A. Eble. 2015. "Comparison of Hurricane Sandy Impacts in Three New Jersey Coastal Communities." *Coastal Engineering Proceedings*, 1(34). American Society of Civil Engineers. https://doi.org/10.9753/icce.v34.management.38.

# 11
# ADAPTING INLAND FLOODPLAIN HOUSING TO A CHANGING CLIMATE

## Disturbance, Risk, and Uncertainty as Drivers for Design

*Jamie L. Vanucchi*

### Introduction

Humans have long shared territory with rivers for provision of multiple resources. Floodplain soils are nutrient rich for agriculture and spring migrations of anadromous fish species, like shad and salmon, supplied a predictable and protein-rich food source. Rivers provided power with simple technologies for the milling of logs and grain, and easy transport of goods (relative to unpaved roads) to support trade. As early communities established themselves with more permanence, grew and industrialized, activities like river channelization and the filling of wetlands allowed development to migrate toward channel banks. Areas immediately adjacent to rivers were often occupied by factories, as they needed water for industrial processes and a conduit for effluent. A bit further away, housing developed in the floodplains, especially as flow became channelized and more predictable.

In 1968, Congress passed the National Flood Insurance Act to establish the National Flood Insurance Program (NFIP) and the Federal Insurance Administration (FIA) to address the economic burden to the nation as well as personal losses and hardships caused by flood disasters. At this time, Congress found that flood mitigation infrastructure, like levees and dams, constructed in the previous decades was not sufficient to address the growing threat of flood. The National Flood Insurance Act aimed to share the costs of flood losses by providing flood insurance to people living in communities that voluntarily adopted and enforced ordinances for floodplain management that met minimum NFIP requirements (FEMA 1997, 29–33). Flood insurance was always meant to be integrated with a unified national program of floodplain management.

Five years later, the Flood Disaster Protection Act (1973) expanded the flood insurance program by both substantially increasing limits of insurance coverage and by requiring known flood-prone communities to participate in the program. Homeowners in participating communities now had to purchase flood insurance as a condition of receiving federal financial assistance for acquisition, construction, or improvement of structures in special flood hazard areas (SFHAs). The Federal Emergency Management Agency (FEMA) was established in 1979, absorbing the FIA and several other federal agencies setup to address hazards and disasters (FEMA 2020, under "History of FEMA"). In 1994, one year after the Great Midwest Floods, the National Flood Insurance Reform Act required flood insurance for all mortgages secured by the Federal Government for homes located in a flood zone in communities participating in the NFIP (National Flood Insurance Reform Act of 1994).

Today, more than 30 million people live in US floodplains, flooding leads the list of costs for climate-based disasters, and Congress was recently forced to forgive a $16 billion debt to keep the besieged NFIP afloat (Gonzalez 2017; Peri, Rosoff, and Yager 2017; FEMA 2020, Under "Climate Change"). Created in part to dissuade floodplain development, the current NFIP leaves homeowners 'blind to dangers' or trapped in flood-prone homes (Palmer 2017). In the northeastern US, many municipalities are reckoning with keeping residents of floodplain housing safe while struggling with population loss and economic decline. At the same time, climate models predict increasing frequency of flooding due to larger and more intense storms (Northeast Regional Climate Center 2015, under "NY Projected IDF Curves").

Where do we go from here? While federal policy is important to direct how we manage changing risk, each community is unique in terms of

Figure 11.1 Living in the floodplain. A levee acts as a gate to a floodplain neighborhood.

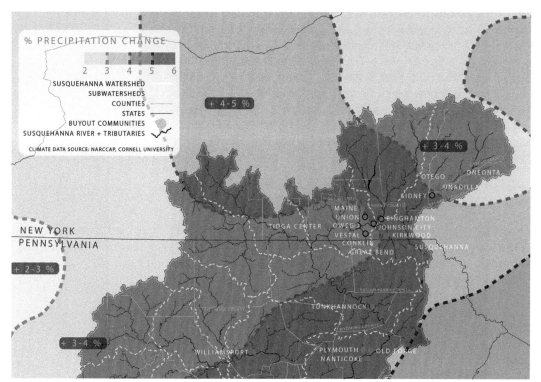

Figure 11.2 Study communities within the Susquehanna Basin, shown with projected precipitation change. Precipitation data courtesy of NARCCAP, Cornell University.

how they might apply policy directives based on their particular combination of watershed characteristics and flood regime, prior actions taken to address flood like the building of infrastructure, patterns of development, climate change projections, economic conditions, and the needs and values of its residents. Here, two upstream-downstream neighboring communities along the main stem Susquehanna River in the Southern Tier of central New York State provide a glimpse into some of the challenges facing inland, rural, and riverine communities as they struggle to adapt to climate change (Figure 11.2).

## Introduction to Study Geography, Communities, and Flood History

The Susquehanna River, known as America's Estuary, flows through the states of New York, Pennsylvania, and Maryland and then into the Chesapeake Bay. The Susquehanna Basin is home to over 4.1 million people, spans 27,510 square miles of mostly rural and forested lands, and contains 49,000 miles of surface waterways. Despite being described as 'a mile wide and a foot deep', the Susquehanna River is hydrologically notorious with a major flood every 14 years, annual flash flooding, and ice jams, all coupled with fairly common severe drought conditions that can have dramatic effects on low flow conditions even within the basin's main stem rivers (Susquehanna River Basin Coalition Annual Report 2013).

The focus of our study is the Upper Susquehanna sub-basin and five communities located along the main stem river. From the most eastern and upstream to the west and downstream, we have studied the communities of Sidney (Delaware County), Binghamton and Johnson City (Broome County), and Owego and Nichols (Tioga County). This area of New York State has a recent history of repeated extreme flooding events. During the period of June 25th–28th, 2006, opposing rotations of low and high pressure systems channeled tropical moisture over the area, causing flash floods and up to 15 inches of rain in 3 days. Classified as a '500-year' storm, this event caused $100 million in damage in New York State. The Susquehanna River crested at 25 feet at the Binghamton gauge, 11 feet over flood stage. Just five years later, from September 6th to 8th, 2011, Tropical Storm Lee moved north and interacted with moisture from a frontal system coming from the west and Hurricane Katia, resulting in up to 15 inches of rain in some areas within a 48-hour window. Over 20,000 residents were ordered to evacuate as waters overtopped floodwalls in some areas and crested at 25.73 feet. This event is the sub-basin's flood of record, causing the damage of $513 million.

## Two Communities along the Main Stem River, a Comparison

### Binghamton, NY

Located at the confluence of the Chenango and Susquehanna Rivers in Broome County, the small city of Binghamton is surprisingly urban. Over the past few decades, the city's population has stabilized at around 45,000 people, about half of what it was at its peak in the 1950s. Current residents inhabit a city where the named architecture, massive civic buildings, parks, public art, and hulking infrastructure of highways and levees suggest a community much larger in size. In 2011, 2,300 homes in the city were damaged in the flood, some when the city's 6.7 miles of earthen levees and concrete walls, constructed in the 1940s and 1950s to contain rising waters, were overtopped. Just a few months prior, FEMA had released its updated flood insurance rate maps (FIRMs) for the city—maps that met strong public backlash due to their broad expansion of the risk zone to include an additional 6,500 homes. FEMA had used 'natural valley' methods for risk modeling that ignored the presence of the city's extensive flood control infrastructure because it lacked adequate freeboard and needed to undergo a process of certification to be considered. City leaders refused to adopt the new maps since clearly the levees were providing some protection and to avoid what they saw as an unnecessary burden that newly designated risk zone residents would face in buying flood insurance, a mandate for NFIP community homeowners with federally backed mortgages. New York Senators Schumer and Gillibrand stepped in, and Congress declared that FEMA had to find a way to revise its model methodology (Wilber 2017). The outcome of this process is still unclear. Interestingly, the draft maps did a reasonably good job of predicting flood area extent in 2011.

## *Owego, NY*

About 20 miles downstream, one approaches the historic village of Owego from the south on the streetlamp-adorned Court Street Bridge leading over the Susquehanna, with its terminus at the stately brick Tioga County Courthouse and a well-manicured green. This quaint scene, along with a row of large, restored historic homes, leaves the impression of a well-planned and charming village nestled on the banks of the river. On second glance, signs of the familiar eastern US small-town struggle erode this image a bit with vacant storefronts and main street commercial buildings in disrepair. In Owego's neighborhoods, cheerful holiday decorations, mature street trees, and residents at ease reveal a persistent and resilient sense of community amid economic decline and disturbance. In this small village of 3,807 people, over half live in the 1% annual chance floodplain, and 85% of the village was flooded in 2011. Facing slow but steady population loss, Owego finds attracting new homeowners difficult given that existing single family housing stock still needs repairs for damage caused by earlier floods; prospective residents of floodplain housing face the added cost of flood insurance and suppressed property values (Owego Downtown Revitalization Initiative 2019).

## *Study Methods*

To understand these community cases, our methods include 30–90-minute interviews with a range of stakeholders involved in managing flood risk at the federal, regional, state, county, and community levels across three counties and five municipalities; risk mapping to identify populations with the greatest vulnerability and exposure to flood risk; experimental methods for capturing the uncertainty in mapping the floodplain; and fieldwork to characterize the floodplain landscape and to catalog buyout parcels, their current uses, and impact on neighborhoods. While close in proximity, Binghamton and Owego face very different situations of risk and prospects for addressing it. To adapt their housing to climate change, these communities will need to understand and acknowledge their (changing) risk and take some responsibility for protecting themselves, while tackling difficult equity issues like the varying vulnerability of residents and differentially felt effects of policy. Binghamton and Owego will also need to take action to consider and implement both short- and long-term strategies to mitigate or adapt to risk.

## Necessary Steps to Cultivating a Culture of Sustained Adaptation in Areas of Risk

We are interested in who takes responsibility for risk. Flood-related policies through time have shuffled responsibility for risk between federal government, local municipality, and homeowner. As disasters become even more costly due to the growing number of people living in coastal areas and inland floodplains, FEMA will increasingly struggle to cover costs to support everyone in need. Neoliberal policies shift responsibility from governments to individuals. If individuals do not have an accurate perception of their risk, the ability to afford to protect themselves with insurance, or the agency to seek other kinds of help the responsibility falls back on governments and nonprofit agencies (Stone 2012).

To adapt housing to flood risk, an informed citizenry is essential. There are good reasons why residents might be confused about their homes' susceptibility to inundation and their role in mitigating it. The terms we've used, such as '100-year flood', suggest that these events are rare. After experiencing two major flood events within a span of five years, one Binghamton resident said, "You know, they called it the '100-year flood', so we figured you're safe for quite a while" (Wilber 2017). Using only major events to define flood risk abstracts time-lived to statistical time and disassociates flood from the day-to-day experience.

Spatial disconnects are another part of the problem. We tend to think that floodplain residents live on the water, but for some who live in the floodplain of the Susquehanna, the river is not a nearby neighbor, but hidden beyond highways and levees and more than a mile away. This distance makes the proximity to water and the threat of flood easy to forget. Anyone with a federally backed mortgage should be made aware if they need to purchase flood insurance, but renters and those new to the area may not even be aware that they live in a risk zone.

Risk maps such as the FIRMs produced by FEMA are one of the primary tools used to understand an individual structure's risk in the event of a 1% or 0.02% annual chance storm. FEMA is currently updating these maps for communities around the country, often resulting in the expansion of special hazard areas to identify sometimes thousands more buildings at risk. This swelling of flood zones reflects both more precise modeling tools and data (such as LIDAR for topography), changing precipitation regimes, and the effects of land use changes that have occurred since the last maps were produced decades ago.

The rejection of the updated FIRMs in Binghamton highlights some of the issues related to using risk mapping as a primary tool to support adaptation to environmental threats. First, the conversations about mapping tend to focus on the price of risk—in terms of the cost of flood insurance for residents (and voters) and potentially declining property values. In his support of the rejection of Binghamton's new FIRMs, Senator Schumer called on FEMA to use "a more detailed approach to mapping [that] will put money back into businesses and homeowners pockets and ensure that future development is not stymied" (Wilber 2017). In the Southside neighborhood of Syracuse, about 75 miles north, Pralle found that costs of insurance dominated and politicized discussions of new FIRMs and that political leaders spent most of their energy supporting homeowners' denial of risk rather than trying to shift the focus to assisting them in mitigating it (Pralle 2019, 227–237).

Another issue is that risk maps have the difficult job of balancing our desire to clearly identify areas of risk with the need to acknowledge the uncertainty that always exists as part of the process. FIRM flood risk zones are drawn with clear boundaries, but changing climate and weather patterns coupled with a constantly shifting watershed landscape means that floodplains are not nearly as precise as that. New paved surfaces or ditches are constructed; stream channels are straightened, armored, or restored; levees are built; and precipitation patterns change. Floodplains occupy a *fuzzier* territory in constant flux. There is a clear tension between exposing this uncertainty and having to translate the maps for use in legal and regulatory action (Haughton and White 2018, 435–448). Some researchers suggest that we've been going about risk mapping all wrong, and rather than concealing uncertainty and using maps for 'discursive closure', we might open the mapping process to incorporate community knowledge (the 'lived experience of risk') and to "generate valuable opportunities to engage with communities in more creative policy making" (Soden, Sprain, and Palen 2017, 2042–2053; Haughton and White 2018, 435–448; Koslov 2019).

Finally, when it comes to acknowledging risk, it may just be human nature to forget. After the second extreme flood event in five years, residents in our study area were on edge. They monitored river gauges, discussed weather reports with neighbors online, and even recognized the uncertainty of living in an area of risk. But as years pass, most people prioritize more immediate concerns and forget about floods again. Flood insurance premiums feel more like a monthly financial burden than necessary protection. For municipalities, keeping a sustained interest in flooding can be difficult, and while money often flows generously after a disaster, funding for *pre*-hazard mitigation can be difficult to find. Political leaders are reluctant to adopt the maps amid citizen protest; as one interviewee said, "no mayor is going to do that" (County Planner 2018). It has been nine years since FEMA's draft risk maps for Binghamton were released but not officially adopted, and flood risk managers know that the maps that are legally enforceable are outdated. If we want to adapt to a changing climate, we'll need to find ways to break this cycle of inaction.

## Changing Risk Due to Climate Change

The threat of climate change to coastal areas is often in the news. In New York, large hurricanes like Sandy in 2012 can cause catastrophic damage due to a densely populated and lengthy urban coastline. These big events make national headlines for months (and rightly so!) and direct federal money to affected areas for rebuilding homes and infrastructure. Heightened concern after a disaster drives engineering and design studies to better understand storm surge and the potential effects of sea level rise.

Unlike the incremental and somewhat predictable trends coastal communities face with rising sea levels, inland communities cannot know when the next big storm will occur, although data from the last 80 years clearly shows an increase in storm magnitude and frequency for the northeastern US.

These hydrologic conditions suggest that predicting floods will only become more difficult in the future, especially in this region of the country. At the same time, communities need to understand how the flood regime will change in the coming years in order to help direct decisions about where to develop, where to undevelop, and where to construct or modify infrastructure. This need demands tools that help predict, mitigate, and adapt to change, and for these inland communities, those tools seem in short supply. One tool that is often misused as a future-oriented device to guide city planning is the FIRM. Designed to help adjusters establish insurance rates, FIRMs are stationary maps, representing *current* risks to structures for flooding (TMAC 2017).

New York's Southern Tier has seen one of the largest increases in precipitation over the past 50 years so that the amount of rainfall needed to cause a large flood is decreasing. For Broome County, NOAA recently lowered the 24-hour precipitation associated with the 1% annual chance storm from 6.3 to 6.15 inches. Other climate trends include hard-to-predict, sporadic, and intense cloudbursts affecting very small areas and causing flash flooding, and tropical storms that stall out and dump heavy rains over large areas. An Army Corps of Engineers representative familiar with the area predicted

> ... the evidence is there. You're going to see more of those little events like in Conklin. There's going to be these little thunderstorms that just park themselves over various areas, and that's really hard to model. Because most of the data that we have is on a much grander scale, so we can detect some trends, and you get into some of that whole economic analysis end of things. But I think climate change is going to be one of the biggest challenges in the future. I really do.
>
> (Risley 2018)

The inland communities along the main stem Susquehanna River are mostly small, rural, and conservative, with very limited development pressure, slow economic growth, and stagnant population trajectories. Using the term 'climate change' can be taboo in these small villages and towns. In some counties in the sub-basin, planners know not to use the term so that they can communicate with community members without triggering strong negative reactions. Our interviews reveal a struggle in working with community members to address climate change and its effects. One county planner told us, "So, we have never been able to say those words [climate change] to any of the municipalities. You don't have to say it. Just don't even say it" (Jardine 2018).

Nurturing a community's ability to adapt to climate change also requires finding ways to accept change and uncertainty—the only things we can really count on in a climate-changed future. Given the (partisan) politicization of climate change and risk and the need for community involvement in planning processes, how can rural, conservative communities acknowledge that the creeks and rivers they live alongside may be changing in the coming decades as they adjust to carry higher volumes of water?

## Equity

Both communities and residents vary in their capacity to adapt. Most municipal or county governments in our study communities are taking the important step to identify vulnerable residents, but we found no examples of proposals related specifically to these residents beyond 'prioritizing' them. Beyond assessments and maps, there are often no guidelines or strategies for ensuring that plans and policies do not place disproportionate burdens on these residents, nor to ensure that they are granted access to decision-making processes. This gap is important. A recent study found a wealth and racial divide in outcomes following a flood event—white homeowners see an increase in net worth after a flood, while Black and Latino homeowners mostly suffer economic losses—"federal disaster spending appears to exacerbate that wealth inequality" (Hersher and Benincasa 2019).

For floodplain residents, there are three options: protect, accommodate, or retreat (Kousky 2014, 9–20). Those who can afford to either sell their home and move out of harm's way (retreat) or pay to protect themselves by purchasing flood insurance. It's relatively easy for higher-income residents to protect their homes this way, but even the currently subsidized price of flood insurance is prohibitive for many who are lower or even middle income. Former mayor Kevin Millar called the cost of insurance an "extreme burden" for some Owego residents, such as the elderly with fixed incomes (Millar 2018). Even so, it is unclear how much longer the federal government will be able to suppress costs of insurance given the huge payouts required following several massive flood events (Hurricanes Katrina in 2005, Sandy in 2012, and Harvey, Irma, and Maria in 2017). Back in the Southside of Syracuse, Pralle noted that some residents expressed concern that their flood insurance premiums would be used to help wealthy owners of coastal properties (Pralle 2019, 227–237). These perceptions reveal a possible broader divide between wealthy/urban/coastal and lower-income/rural/inland populations.

Retreat, usually facilitated by the 'buyout' process where repeat-flood homes are purchased following a flood event, is more likely to occur in wealthier, more urban counties (Cartier 2019). Poorer and more rural populations could be at increased risk of becoming trapped in areas of high flood risk. Several interviewees addressed issues related to vulnerable populations, housing, and buyouts.

> But at the same time, at the beginning of when you first get your grant, you're just trying to get money out the door. Sometimes you don't even have access to the data that points you in the right direction in terms of those vulnerable populations.
> (Representative Governor's Office of Storm Recovery 2018)

> I call them 'our working poor'. These are families that both parents are probably working outside the home and they are barely making a living wage. Yet, they are waiting for this buyout so that they can move their kids to safer ground, hoping that it doesn't flood in the meantime, because they have no idea how they will rebuild a third time. That's what we're dealing with. We get sob stories every day, people calling saying 'I don't know whether to fix my roof or not, it's been leaking for a year and a half and is the buyout coming now? Or do I fix my roof and if I do I can't afford a down payment on a new house, when I have to move out so you can buy me out?'
> (Johnson-Bennett 2018) (County Planning)

> So, housing is at the bottom of that pyramid, there's not adequate housing. So, when you have a catastrophe like a flood, it just exacerbates that to an unmanageable point, but that population will dissipate into the kind of like… ether. They're already half invisible to us as institutions and when the disaster occurs, it's like New Orleans. Where did all those people go? We don't even know because we don't know where they were to begin with.
> (Costello 2018) (A former municipal official)

## Taking Action

As communities choose strategies to deal with specific threats, exposures, and vulnerabilities they must act, but which actions will prove best in addressing risk and the uncertainty associated with climate change? Policies and programs at the federal, state, and municipal level are important, but every community represents a unique case in terms of their application. Our case study communities present very particular physical conditions including geomorphology, land use, development patterns, infrastructure, and social conditions such as political climate, degree to which citizens are involved in decision-making, economic conditions, and level of vulnerability among residents. Together, these factors shape the range of future scenarios given a limited palette of mitigation and adaptation strategies.

Mitigation refers to activities that reduce risk and include the construction of flood control infrastructure, *undeveloping* the floodplain through buyouts. Adaptation requires finding ways to live with and accommodate risk we cannot change. Over the past several decades, the communities of Binghamton and Owego have utilized different approaches to mitigate or adapt to floods, and these decisions will continue to shape possible futures. Each strategy has impacts on quality of life for residents and their relationship to the river, equity, economics and community value, and the function and ecological value of the floodplain.

## Taking Action I: Mitigation

### Undeveloping (Buyouts)

Both Owego and Binghamton have made use of the buyout process to help relocate homeowners from repeat-flood properties. Federal money from FEMA or the Department of Housing and Urban Development (HUD), sometimes with a local match, funds the purchase (at pre-flood value) and demolition of flooded homes. Those we interviewed usually agreed that buyouts were a good idea to move people out of harm's way permanently, but complained that the process takes too long and lacks transparency, and that particular groups of homeowners can be hard to serve. Municipal governments sometimes resist this strategy, worried about the loss of tax base implied in *undeveloping* parts of their communities, and nearly all benefits of relocation (e.g. improvement of environmental quality in abandoned areas, and reduction in rescue costs, reconstruction costs, and costs related to social discomfort caused by emergency) are *potential*, related to risk of another disaster, and may not be realized if another disaster does not occur (Menoni and Pesaro 2008, 33–53).

Despite the fact that buyouts are now a common phenomenon around the country, there is no formal mechanism for communities to learn from one another and a lack of knowledge transfer means that the process is not improving (Greer and Brokopp Binder 2016). In addition, Congress mandated that municipalities coordinate buyout efforts and manage the application process. This could result in better outcomes over a piecemeal, individual homeowner-driven approach, as it suggests flood mitigation strategy could be grounded with data and evidence-based planning and design. However, our findings show that this mandate can exacerbate inequities in capacity across towns and cities and confirm that capacity at the municipal and county level varies greatly. In small communities, the management of buyouts has often fallen on the shoulders of municipal employees with little to no experience or training, and on top of existing job duties. Due to the size of these communities, homeowners are often neighbors or friends. One of our municipal interviewees discussed keeping a box of tissues on her desk as she consulted with residents on a day-to-day basis. Every interviewee directly involved in managing buyouts confirmed that the process had taken a toll on their mental or physical health.

FEMA requires that homes are demolished after buyout contracts have been signed, and that no new construction occurs on the property. A limited set of uses, such as parks or other recreation spaces, is allowed. Our research shows that some municipalities are maintaining post-buyout properties as lawn, while others are using non-FEMA funding sources in order to bypass this no-rebuild restriction. All buyouts are voluntary, and when some neighbors choose to stay and others leave, the neighborhood fabric is left with multiple gaps and municipal governments are still responsible for maintaining infrastructure like streets and sidewalks. The idea that vacated floodplains could become places of high community and ecological value seems to be overlooked.

The Floodplains by Design project in Washington State outlines a fairly broad set of possibilities for floodplains, including recreation and water access, habitat creation, and agricultural uses. The dispersed nature of buyout parcels can make floodplain reconnection challenging, but proposed use for buyout properties may be a significant factor in decision-making of property owners when considering a buyout. For example, following Hurricane Sandy, many homeowners on the eastern shore of Staten Island were willing to give up their home if the land was going to contribute to the larger community good (in that case, restored wetlands to provide a buffer for storm surge) (Koslov). Incentivizing buyouts this way, or by building new affordable housing nearby, might encourage more homeowners to consider this option.

### *Levees/Infrastructure (In Relation to Housing)*

Flood control infrastructure is typically only available to more densely developed communities where a cost-benefit analysis shows that the large federal expense for levees or flood walls is less than the price to replace the structures they will protect. For decades, Binghamton has benefited from the protection its levees and floodwalls provide, but now faces a crisis of sorts as the cost to certify the infrastructure is estimated at $1.5 million. To increase its height to provide adequate freeboard and to address other issues will be far more costly for a city already experiencing economic stress.

After a period of explosive dam and levee building around the U.S. in the 20th century, the Army Corps of Engineers has recently adopted a softer approach to flood mitigation, choosing options like bypass channels to direct floodwaters to undeveloped areas like farm fields for temporary storage. This shift reflects a growing body of research related to the negative effects of flood control on river ecosystems and the ecological value of the rhythmic pulses of flood. Binghamton's levees, built adjacent to the river's edge, constrict these benefits while disconnecting the river from the people who live nearby. Meanwhile, Owego's residents, located approximately 20 miles downstream, cannot shake the perception that their floods are made worse by their upstream neighbor's federally funded and protective infrastructure, knowing that their community is too small to ever have their own. The Army Corp of Engineers recently completed a two-year study of the hydrology of the Upper Susquehanna sub-basin, eventually finding no 'viable flood risk management alternatives', including for Owego, because "the cost to construct and maintain the project(s) outweighed the national economic development benefits the project(s) would provide if implemented" (33).

Decisions to build flood control infrastructure are difficult to undo, as development often quickly crowds in on newly protected waterfront land. Levees are not easily altered either. Raising an earthen levee means expanding horizontally as well, eating into lands formerly defended. Mitigating flooding with the construction of infrastructure can be a brittle strategy for reducing risk, while climate change demands more flexible options amidst growing uncertainty.

**Taking Action II: Strategies for Adaptation**

*Elevating*

Elevation is an adaptation strategy used to lift homes above the base flood elevation (BFE) established on FIRMs. While costly, funding from state agencies such as NY Rising have helped homeowners stay in place, but move out of harm's way. In the Town of Union nearby, a savvy town planner used community development block grant (CDBG) funding from HUD to rebuild homes with a full floodproofed first story used as a garage. This strategy helped the town avoid FEMA's forever green requirement to maintain its tax base.

With the option of flood control infrastructure off the table, Owego's primary strategy has been to adopt building codes for new floodplain development that exceed NFIP standards and represent the most stringent standards of any of the five study communities. A special permit is required for any new floodplain buildings, and the lowest floor elevation of new residential structures must be a minimum of 2 feet higher than the BFE. This 'freeboard' is the way engineers accommodate uncertainty, at a rate of $10,000 per foot. If future changes to the flood regime raise flood elevations beyond this built-in flexibility, changes will be costly. While Owego should be commended for its progressive code to regulate floodplain development, these standards are only effective if they are enforced. This strategy also begs the question: is the use of building standards that only affect new construction and major remodels the best adaptation strategy for a place with a declining population and very little new development?

## The Role of Planning

The Disaster Mitigation Act of 2000 made hazard mitigation plans a condition for mitigation assistance. Communities participating in the NFIP have to conduct this planning to identify hazards (flooding is just one) and propose actions to manage hazard-induced emergencies and reduce risk. Hazard mitigation plans can be boilerplate, seen as a hurdle to get over in order to receive funding. Our study found that community capacity can again be an issue, but in some cases planning and technical resources at the county level play a key role. In other places, towns and villages are reluctant to cooperate.

Communities commonly struggle to implement the actions proposed in these plans, and usually blame a lack of available funding. This common issue might be addressed by connecting the federally mandated hazard mitigation planning process to a municipality's comprehensive planning. In order to adapt to a climate-changed future, communities will have to face that floods are less likely to be rare events, and increasingly just part of life along a river. Integrating longer-term mitigation and adaptation actions with land use and infrastructure decisions, building codes, parks, housing, and economic development may be the only way to get things done.

Reviewing planning documents for our study communities reveals that this kind of future-forward planning often is not happening yet. Small communities lack capacity in planning, and some do not discuss future planning at all, resulting in a reactive rather than proactive position when managing flood risk. Owego adopted a new comprehensive plan in 2014, just three years after the village's flood of record caused by the remnants of tropical storm Lee. Despite acknowledging that nearly all the downtown area is located within the 100-year flood zone, the plan only mentions flooding a few times in the 64-page, consultant-prepared document and never directly connects future floods to village planning (Village of Owego Comprehensive Plan 2013).

## Risk, Uncertainty, and Disturbance as Drivers for Design

### Disturbance as a Driver for Design

Disasters create policy windows (Kousky 2014, 9–20), and coupled socio-economic and environmental disturbances can be drivers for experimental and adaptive design. While many flood risk managers we interviewed were frustrated by the many barriers to action, the convergence of factors in the months after a major flood event suggests a rare opportunity for more substantial change. Residents are most aware of their risk and wary of the post-flood process they have just experienced, including temporary dislocations, the loss of property and even loss of life, and difficult decisions about relocating or rebuilding. Cooperation among communities is strong and involves sharing of resources for emergency response and cleanup. Post-hazard mitigation funding from state and federal sources provides a rare influx of money to economically strapped and fiscally overlooked communities. If communities prepare in advance, the next disaster event could propel them forward instead of setting them back again.

### Risk as a Driver for Design

Disaster events and questions of risk expose community inequities. Heat waves in cities are hardest on poorer neighborhoods because they lack shade provided by mature street trees, pollution-emitting industries are often located nearby populations with the least political power, and vulnerable residents can often be found in floodplains.

Considering risk as a driver for adaptive design means working at larger and smaller scales. Our research suggests the need to engage upstream and downstream neighbors across watersheds, to develop community collaboration networks to formalize knowledge sharing and transfer, and to consider how one municipality's mitigation choices might impact its neighboring communities. It calls for work at the scale of the street block and household, to understand how decisions about strategies to manage flood risk impact the most vulnerable residents by asking them to be involved in planning processes and by incorporating community knowledge such as the 'lived experience' of risk into mapping and planning tools.

Elected and appointed officials come and go, but resilient communities need formal structures to ensure knowledge transfer. Sharing experiences with communities facing similar challenges is important for more isolated rural towns. Locally, the Upper Susquehanna Coalition is looking beyond town and county lines to coordinate activities of a group of 21 soil and water districts around the watershed. Further afield, Living City ATX is an organization that centralizes equity issues as they work to make Austin more resilient to climate change.

### Uncertainty as a Driver for Design

The need to break through barriers to action given growing climate uncertainty suggests that an adaptive management approach to addressing flood risk might be the best fit for communities along the Susquehanna River. Unlike risk-based approaches, adaptive management calls for the use of "provisional measures that can be adjusted or even reversed with learning from experiences" and "endorses flexibility and experimentation to enable policymakers to change course in response to new information" (Kucklicke and Demeritt 2016, 56–68). Adaptive management approaches also emphasize the value in planning processes that involve the participation of community members both in contributing valuable 'lived' information regarding flooding and in creating and evaluating possible futures. Strategies that address inequities, restore floodplain function, and build community value of the floodplain will provide benefits beyond mitigating or adapting to risk.

Building a culture of sustained adaptation means that individuals and governments share responsibility for risk. Cost-benefit analyses do not favor places with small populations, so small towns and cities are far less likely to be able to construct costly infrastructure to control and mitigate future floods and will have to be creative to imagine vibrant futures as risk and vulnerability increase. Is it possible that these inland, rural communities could become models for climate adaptation?

## Acknowledgments

I would like to acknowledge my colleagues, Dr. Amelia Greiner-Safi and Saumitra Sinha for their contributions to this research. We are grateful to all the smart, hardworking, and generous flood risk managers who took the time to share their thoughts and experiences with our research team. This work was funded by Federal Capacity Funds, USDA.

## Citations

Cartier, Kimberly. "Equity Concerns Raised in Federal Flood Property Buyouts." EOS. American Geophysical Union, October 9, 2019. https://eos.org/articles/equity-concerns-raised-in-federal-flood-property-buyouts.

"Climate Change." FEMA. U.S. Department of Homeland Security, September 1, 2020. https://www.fema.gov/emergency-managers/national-preparedness/climate-change.

Costello, Tom (2018, Oct 23). Personal interview.

County planner (2018, March 20). Personal interview.

Federal Emergency Management Agency (FEMA). 1997. The National Flood Insurance Act of 1968 as amended and the Flood Disaster Prevention Act of 1973 as amended. https://www.fema.gov/media-library-data/20130726-1545-20490-9247/frm_acts.pdf

Former managing director of research and strategic analysis at the Governor's Office of Storm Recovery (2018, August 10). Personal interview.

"History of FEMA." FEMA. U.S. Department of Homeland Security, August 14, 2020. https://www.fema.gov/about/history.

Gonzalez, Gloria. "House Passes Disaster Relief Bill Including NFIP Debt Forgiveness." Business Insurance, October 13, 2017.

Greer, Alex and Sherri Brokopp Binder (2016). "A Historical Assessment of Home Buyout Policy: Are We Learning or Just Failing?" Housing Policy Debate, DOI: 10.1080/10511482.2016.1245209.

Haughton, Graham and Iain White. "Risky Spaces: Creating, Contesting, and Communicating Lines on Environmental Hazard Maps." *Transactions of the Institute of British Geographers* (2018) 43:435–448.

Hersher, Rebecca, and Robert Benincasa. "How Federal Disaster Money Favors The Rich." NPR. NPR, March 5, 2019. https://www.npr.org/2019/03/05/688786177/how-federal-disaster-money-favors-the-rich.

Jardine, Elaine (2018, February 28). Personal interview.

Johnson-Bennett, Shelley (2018, July 9). Personal interview.

Koslov, Liz. "How Maps Make Time: Temporal Conflicts of Life in the Flood Zone." CITY, 2019. https://www.businessinsurance.com/article/20171013/NEWS06/912316519/House-passes-disaster-relief-bill-including-NFIP-debt-forgiveness. https://www.nab.usace.army.mil/Missions/Regulatory/Public-Notices/Public-Notice-View/Article/2079981/termination-upper-susquehanna-river-basin-comprehensive-flood-damage-reduction/.

Kousky, Carolyn. "Managing Shoreline Retreat: A US Perspective." *Climate Change* (2014) 124:9–20.

Kucklicke, Christian and David Demeritt. "Adaptive and Risk-Based Approaches to Climate Change and the Management of Uncertainty and Institutional Risk: The Case of Future Flooding in England." *Global Environmental Change* (March 2016) 37:56–68.

Menoni, Scira and Giulia Pesaro. "Is Relocation a Good Answer to Prevent risk?" *Disaster Prevention and Management* (2008) 17(1):33–53.

Millar, Kevin (2018, March 6). Personal interview.

National Flood Insurance Reform Act of 1994 (1994).

NY Projected IDF Curves. Northeast Regional Climate Center, 2015. http://ny-idf-projections.nrcc.cornell.edu/.

Owego Downtown Revitalization Initiative (2019). https://www.villageofowego.com/downtown-revitalization-initiative.

Palmer, Brian. "Our National Flood Insurance Program Is Going Underwater." March 13, 2017. https://www.nrdc.org/stories/our-national-flood-insurance-program-going-underwater.

Peri, Caroline, Stephanie Rosoff, and Jessica Yager. Rep. *Population in the U.S. Floodplains*. New York: NYU Furman Center, 2017. https://furmancenter.org/files/Floodplain_PopulationBrief_12DEC2017.pdf.

Pralle, Sarah. "Drawing Lines: FEMA and the Politics of Mapping Flood Zones." *Climatic Change* (2019) 152:227–237.

Risley, Daniel (2018, September, 13). Personal interview.

Soden, Robert, Leah Sprain, and Leysia Palen (2017). "Thin Grey Lines: Confrontations with Risk on Colorado's Front Range." In *Proceedings of the 2017 CHI Conference on Human Factors in Computing Systems*, ACM, 6–11 May, Denver, Colorado, 2042–2053.

Stone, Brian (2012). *The City and the Coming Climate: Climate Change in the Places We Live*. New York: Cambridge University Press.

Susquehanna River Basin Coalition Annual Report (2013).

The National Flood Insurance Act of 1968, as Amended, and the Flood Disaster Protection Act of 1973, as Amended, 42 U.S.C. 4001 et seq. § (1997).

TMAC (2017). TMAC 2017 Annual Report, December. https://www.fema.gov/media-library-data/1521054297905-ca85d066ddd84c975b165db653c9049/TMAC_2017_Annual_Report_Final 508(v8)_03–12–2018.pdf.

Village of Owego Comprehensive Plan (2013). https://www.villageofowego.com/sites/g/files/vyhlif1041/f/uploads/owego_comprehensive_plan.pdf.

Wilber, Tom. "Outdated Flood Maps Mean Many Binghamton-Area Homeowners Aren't Aware of Property Risks." Press & Sun-Bulletin. pressconnects.com, October 5, 2017. https://www.pressconnects.com/story/news/local/watchdog/2017/10/05/binghamton-flood-maps-outdated-homeowners-property-risk/717196001/.

# 4D! RESILIENT DESIGN IN FOUR DIMENSIONS

*Illya Azaroff*

### Rethinking Our Urban Footprint: Responding to Long-Term Change through Positive Adaption

The imperative of the 21st century is how cities respond to challenges presented by climate change. These challenges include short-term disturbances and long-term consequences that we can now project with a greater degree of accuracy. Urban resilience will be defined by those cities whose populations will be displaced en masse or by the cities that receive those displaced populations from around the globe. Forced migration, managed retreat, and strategic location are among the terms used to reference the current crisis.

Although migration to cities has been well underway for the past century, the acceleration of this migration is of concern. By 2050, it is estimated that 68% of the world's population will live in urban centers (UN DESA, 2018). Couple those statistics with historic locations of population centers on waterfront and riverine geographies, then the prospect of rising tides and increased disturbances due to climate change is quite alarming. The resulting impact scenarios are potentially uncontrollable and disastrous. Aside from population and location, cities are challenged with the fact that resilient measures being deployed in planning processes are based on the history of recent disturbances; therefore, we are in a constant state of reaction, rather than proactive positions that can anticipate future events. It is then understood that few cities can recognize when you need major surgery to attain long-term resilience rather than band-aids. And even when city agencies are clear in their planning and policy to meet these challenges, political will may fail to bring true resilient capacity into view.

What this means ultimately is that true resilience can only be found and achieved by a complete analysis and understanding of the top hazards and threats, not just for today, but projecting forward into the future using the best science available. What we are designing for today is for 30, 50, or even 100 years into the future. The scale of action appropriate to the growing hazards and threats must also be considered. Finally, respecting geographies rather than political boundaries is necessary to achieve resilience across natural and man-made systems, i.e., drainage basins and shared transportation networks. Overall, these scenarios provide an abundance of challenges; but they can be overcome with proper foresight and action.

Broader recognition of hazards such as extreme heat and extreme cold events being just as impactful as rising seas, often stressing already fragile systems and resources that ultimately may not be adequate. Scarcity of this type often triggers cascading events such as civil unrest, state conflict, degradation of the environment, and more. Recent conflicts around the globe have been linked to scarcity and stresses triggering forced migration (Podesta, 2019) (Wrathall, Van Den Hoek, Walters & Devenish, 2018). Those migrants find temporary homes that further stress resources in areas of flight creating friction and conflict. In recent years forced migration due to shocks, stresses, and disturbances has been upward of 70 million people annually worldwide. The projection of those numbers by 2050 is 200 million people displaced, and by 2100, the projected number of displaced is 550 million people (Brown, 2008). Cities are key to stemming the tide of climate refugees though comprehensive adaptation planning or being able to absorb these refugees.

### *Surgery Candidates*

One of the larger challenges faced by urban places is infrastructure and operations as it relates to a regional scale and further supply chains to global scale. These are the meta-scale pieces of resilience with intricate interdependencies that we should all recognize and engage in through comprehensive long-range planning. Organizations such as Next City, C40, and the now sunset 100RC have advanced programs engaging in such long range, shared data, and planning (C40, 2020) (NextCity, 2020) (The Rockefeller Foundation, 2019). Cities in the US are required to create a Hazard Mitigation plan to align with federal programs and aid in case a disaster occurs. The first step in risk reduction is to recognize your risks and plan for short-term response and long-term adaptation. These plans do have limitations, yet may be a key to identify how we begin to rethink our urban footprint.

We must examine the urban edge and how it abuts some of the most vulnerable areas and simultaneously intersects with critical areas of infrastructure and political boundaries that may inhibit true resilience. These three aspects of the urban edge simultaneously offer the greatest opportunity in achieving large-scale change to resilience. In the historic context, New York City's marginalized people have been pushed to the edge or in effect relocated as the city made its 20th-century progress. Land that was claimed from the sea or created by leftover infill from waste or construction, or claimed over 19th-century dumps and Ash-fields (in other words the least valued property) is the place inhabited by the poor at the edge or urban fringe (Blaszczak, N.D.) (Bowery Boys, 2013). Historic maps of the edge of New York City in the five boroughs reveal that reclaimed areas emerge as the city develops. These areas such as Redhook, Coney Island, the Rockaways, the lower Eastside, lower Manhattan, the Queens Ash fields that are now LaGuardia Airport in the surrounding area of college point are all areas of extreme vulnerability to climate change and stand as hurdles in attaining true urban resilience. For the most part these areas are economically and infrastructurally challenged, as they have been neglected for a great number of years. The urban edges, where definition and development of some type, offer great opportunity along with the stated vulnerabilities.

## LOW Zones

In part, examining how to redefine the urban edge and waterfront with respect to comprehensive resilience and the opportunities that arise in implementation (crosscutting benefits) is key. Additional examination of underserved waterfront communities at the nexus of these forces is necessary to empower them through community-based micro-grids and mesh-networks, as well as sustainable, circular economies. Defining these high-risk zones: LOW (low lying, low income, low rise). A resilient urban agenda must address long-term solutions in LOW zones across four dimensions, embracing social equity and community stakeholders as partners along with forecasting data over time to avoid disastrous, cascading consequences. A cautionary note is that a resilient urban agenda solely through social equity and community stakeholders may address much-needed criteria for sustainable urban security but may miss the large-scale view needed to achieve resilience.

## Treating the City as a Watershed

Water is the most precious resource in the world. Recent disturbances such as Super Storm Sandy in 2012, or the 2011 Tohoku earthquake and tsunami in Japan made people afraid of water. Walling off water seems to be a common response, yet is not the answer. Cities are interventions into natural systems, disturbing the environment and its processes. One essential approach to resilience is to align with sustainable strategies at the urban scale rather than continued history of disruption. Allowing the city to act as a watershed, as a sponge, and as a reservoir is the solution. Water management is key in this strategy and key to any city's long-term survival. When disturbances occur, such as a storm surge, tidal and/or riverine flooding, extreme precipitation, and drought, only a well-adapted and maintained hydrological system can provide a city and its residents continual functionality. Ultimately how any city deals with disturbance is tied to a large-scale systems approach that maintains mission critical functions including an integrated watershed approach.

### Wisdom from Everywhere

Best practices occur at all scales and from any place around the world. The tiny island of Saipan in the Northern Mariana Islands is a good example of meaningful proactive water management at a small scale. Being vulnerable to typhoons, daily rainstorms, and lacking drinking water springs has made Saipan proactive in its hydrological cycle design and management. Traditionally, all freshwater is delivered by tankers, making potable water the number one vulnerability. If a storm takes out the local seaport, or a seaport along the supply chain, then by extension delivery of water is interrupted for long periods of time. As part of the planning and governance solution for the island, the building code of the entire island requires rainwater harvesting (Sopac, 2004) (Horsley Witten Group, 2006). Every building, no matter the size, must harvest water into cisterns to sustain the island during periods where the port system or supply chain is interrupted. Ultimately tankers of water are not a long-term solution for an island surrounded by miles of ocean and seawater as well as substantial daily rainfall. Rethinking this mission critical system is underway.

In New York City, one of the easily attainable measures is leveraging the millions of square feet of flat roofs for rainwater catchment and harvesting. A nascent "blue roof" program is underway in the city to alleviate pressure on the aging infrastructure and to increase potable water capacity (Gerstein and Gilbride, 2013). Couple that measure with porous paving materials, catchment basins for recharging the aquifer, and bio-swales, and you have the New York City Green Streets Program aimed at making areas of the city a sponge. If cities can recognize the value of water and develop state-of-the-art waste treatment facilities that recycle water, we begin to see a complete "wetland" hydrological cycle that can address the future of cities in a proactive manner (Gunther and Jackewycz, 2010).

Further infrastructure reinvestment can be at the community scale with neighborhood ownership such as micro-grids or intelligently distributed micro-grids. These systems seem to be the logical next steps for New York and other cities with aging centralized infrastructures. Addressing community infrastructure in such a manner raises all boats; economic fortunes for all would change driving equity in LOW neighborhoods up.

### Managed Retreat Is Essential in Rethinking Our Urban Footprint

Retreat is not giving into climate change; it is recognizing that new ecological systems and restoration of natural systems are necessary to adapt to future challenges. The question is what benefits can a city attain and maintain when retreat is planned? As people move away from the coast and structures are removed there is an underlying natural system that is being restored. In the cases of the Jamaica Bay, Coney Island, and Redhook neighborhoods in New York, we should recognize that these are areas that are part of the freshwater estuary and wetlands contributing to the health of the New York Harbor. As these neighborhoods retreat, other amenities emerge that are allowed to flood, such as new grasslands, wetlands, and public. A new aquaculture and natural preserve can provide new ecologies and destinations that are different from what is there today, while helping to regenerate the city. In this managed retreat scenario, the footprint of New York City may remain the same, or migrate deeper on to Long Island and/or up the Hudson River. This could be combined with UpZoning, which would increase the density within the five boroughs as the edges are ceded to the natural environment.

The overall effect of restoration of natural areas, wetlands, dune systems, and coastal forests within the urban environment will have several positive and regenerative effects that combat climate-related disturbances. First and foremost, the city will restore a system that is well adept at slowing down, absorbing, and combating wind and water forces associated with hurricanes, tropical storms, and heavy rain events. In addition, extreme heat events, which are projected to increase over the next century, will be mitigated by the increased water or sponge effect from the urban edge and the other elements of green streets, such as the aforementioned bio-swales, creating an absorptive city rather than a city that rejects its water. Today it is not uncommon for dense urban environments, US cities in particular, to reject up to 85% of rainwater, the most precious resource on the planet (Strassler and Strellec, 1999). We need to rethink this strategy to adapt to a sustainable and resilient future.

A secondary effect of managed retreat is that people will no longer live within the immediate zone of risk in great numbers, maintaining the health, safety, and welfare of the public. There are many examples of rezoning, such as in Japan following the 2011 Tohoku disaster. Many of the towns and villages there have rezoned for commercial and industrial engagement at the waterfront, along with enhancement or expansion of public amenities such as beaches, wetlands, dunes, and those types of uses, whereas the living or residential zones are far out of harm's way. Sendai is the largest city in the region (one million residents), and their rezoning moved over 4,000 residential structures out of the tsunami hazard zones. The surgical relocation of 4,000 households was done in conjunction with a master plan to densify the urban center for an aging population, see Figures 12.1–12.4. On a smaller scale, coastal villages throughout the region follow similar strategies.

## Major Surgery

### Case Study: Tohoku Regional Recovery, Focus Onagawa Town, Japan

On March 11, 2011, a magnitude-9 earthquake shook northeastern Japan, unleashing a savage tsunami. The one-two punch of

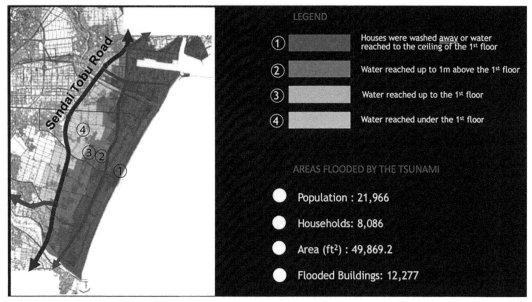

Figure 12.1 Rezoning Sendai City post-Tohoku disaster. Image Credit: +LAB Architect.

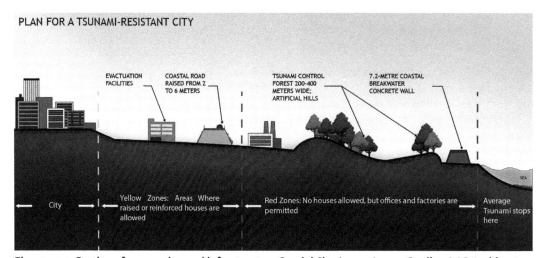

Figure 12.2 Section of new zoning and infrastructure Sendai City Japan. Image Credit: +LAB Architect.

earthquake and tsunami left a trail of devastation from which Japan is still recovering. In the wake of this disaster, one of the most popular resilient ideas was to build great sea walls across the entire region. Touring the region to review work on sea walls and plans for resilient measures noted several key elements. Some of these planned sea walls are as high as 45–50 feet (14 or 15 m). There is a precedent for these sea walls as prior walls did exist in coastal towns, but they were smaller and strategically placed to maintain visual and physical connections to the sea.

# 4D! RESILIENT DESIGN IN FOUR DIMENSIONS

Figure 12.3 New community housing Sendai City, Sendai Japan. Image Credit: Azaroff.

Figure 12.4 Final displacement and resettlement using social cohesion strategies. Image Credit: Azaroff.

Large, comprehensive sea walls may protect against a great future tsunami (Hyde, 2019), but they are undermining two key aspects of the Japanese coastal town in this region (McMurray, 2014). The Tohoku region is a favorite vacation-destination of many Japanese people. The region is a famed tourist destination for its beauty, ties to the land, coast, forests, and beaches. More directly, Onagawa is one of many small fishing villages and coastal towns in Japan that rely on the ocean as a way of life. Building these walls is at fundamental odds with sustaining the current economic and social models of coastal Japanese towns, as well as an ecological impact on wildlife, flora, and fauna.

Access to the sea directly fuels the local industries surrounding fishing, such as fish farming, transportation, nets, equipment, and maintaining boats. Furthermore, the local economy relies on access to a working waterfront. Fish processing and other economic generators are all at risk through a resilient measure that has not fully considered the sustainable industry that is central to the town's economic health and culture.

To address one of the economic and social concerns around the building of the seawalls, in some areas, entire villages are being elevated on fill to a new base plane that maintains the view of the sea (Figure 12.5). In Onagawa, the ground is being raised over 23 feet (7 m), equal to the height of the proposed sea wall. The top of the sea wall will be the major coastal highway, allowing a visual connection to the sea and allowing access directly to the waterfront through tunnels/gates beneath the roadway. Nearly 9 million cubic yards (7 million m³) of rock and soil were required to raise the village of 11,000 residents. Part

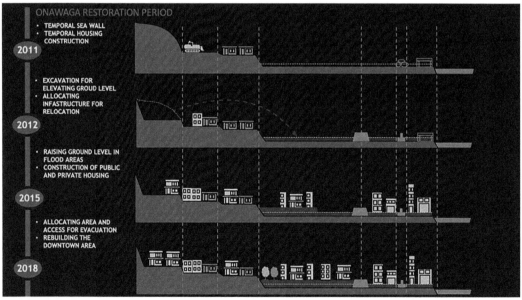

Figure 12.5 Sectional development to resilient Onagawa town, cut and fill coupled with rezoning residential and commercial districts. Image Credit: +LAB Architect.

of the master planning reimagines living patterns. The surrounding mountains supplied the material: their tops have been cut off, leaving flat plateaus where once peaks used to stand. Those flat plates are residential zones, well out of harm's way (Figures 12.6 and 12.7).

The outcome at Onagawa underlines how ecological disturbance and wholesale remaking of the landscape is not a sustainable practice, yet represents surgical thinking in reshaping urban places. There is no working with the environment in this case. Rather than replicating the lessons of the environment for protection, this project attempts to reshape the environment into an artificial landscape to attain resilience. History, culture, and society are disrupted. The relationship to the sea and the industry around it are disturbed, access is changed,

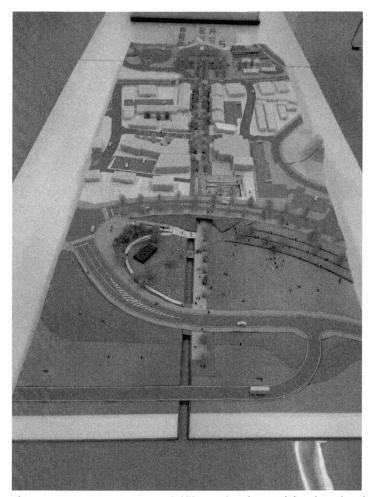

Figure 12.6 Onagawa town model illustrating the spatial and sectional relationship to the waterfront from the town center and coastal highway. Note the top of the model is the new train station with the main street to the water passing under the coastal highway with a flood gate positioned to close in case of disturbance. Image Credit: Azaroff.

Figure 12.7 Indicates extent of cut and fill. Image Credit: Azaroff.

creating a shift in the way a community operates and relates to its surroundings that may be every bit as damaging as the natural disaster itself.

> "We are more harmful to ourselves in the rebuilding than the disaster itself." Resident monk and custodian, Onagawa town

### Community Input and Alternate Plans

Residents in various villages proposed alternate plans, taking into account the history, culture, societal practices, and sustainable economy. Instead of supersized sea walls, some communities have elected to move entire residential areas of towns up and away from coastal zones, leaving in place only commercial and industrial uses in the traditional location of villages. This alternative will result in a commute to work, and it allows for the identity of the village and the relationship to the sea—with all its attendant values—to remain. The plan recognizes greater value for the land and sea, minimizing impacts.

From a sustainability standpoint, the sea wall ignores issues of ecological impact and the long-term sustainability of the coastal areas. The wall was built with the assumption that local ecologies and communities will adapt to new conditions, but the abrupt nature of these changes to the landscape and waterfront leaves little time for adaptation by either. The community is currently being forced to adapt, but its economic, cultural, and social systems were previously interwoven with an ecology that may not adapt quickly enough to prevent continued disruption and losses. These manmade disturbances to the community were created out of a reactionary response to the threat of future natural disturbances. In addition to the hydrological and habitat disruptions wrought by the sea wall fortifications, the human connection and the community's relation to the coast have been impacted in ways that cannot yet be fully understood. Only time will tell.

## Social Adaptive Models Ready for Retreat

Could New York City take a chapter again from the Japanese? Can New York and other cities relocate entire communities based on neighborhood registration roles in relation to new areas of the city aimed at maintaining cohesion of social groups, and relationships of extended family constructs? In this successful model, the community is not tied to physical attributes such as buildings, roads, or blocks; yet it is firmly embodied in the collective mass of people. Communities list surrounding families as part of emergency registration in Japan. Once collected, the immediate sheltering, then temporary housing, then final resettlement are calculated with respect to one's existing social network. This process keeps traditional family and neighbor relations together.

## Consequences and Paralysis

The consequences of inaction, or only treating the symptoms of these changes that are afoot, can be catastrophic. We are already seeing that the economic circumstances in insurance premiums and payouts do not balance, both in the US and worldwide. Therefore, will these LOW zone neighborhoods naturally disappear given the economic climate and public policy that is already in place? If so, then we are not practicing good governance, or looking to the distant future and making positive changes toward rethinking our urban footprint. The advantages of long-term planning relocation and managed retreat must be on the table for every coastal city in the world.

Impediments to resilience at the urban scale start with a community's history, cost of land, and the loss of wealth. Families in these LOW zone neighborhoods own their homes, and many have lived there for generations. It is difficult to dismantle neighborhoods with long-standing roots and, if it can be done, then the wealth or value of the property is being rezoned to have no value for residential use whatsoever. Hurricane Katrina in 2005 triggered a cascade effect in New Orleans' LOW neighborhoods, which have never fully recovered. How is that wealth redistributed, or those properties purchased (and from what funds), to allow this type of reimagining of the urban edge to occur and wealth to be maintained?

Back in Japan, this scenario plays out all along the region in the medium and smaller towns as well. Onagawa town is tabbed as the poster child for recovery in the region. Its urban resilience model is a simple formula of a new master plan that has a community park and commercial waterfront along a coastal road/sea wall that is the second layer of defense. The next layer behind the coastal road is a commercial center with some mixed-use buildings around a central train station. Followed by residential neighborhoods, hospital, and schools all built on plateaus surrounding the town (Figure 12.7). The zoning strategy and urban master plan moves people away from vulnerable areas and restricts activity such that when another disturbance occurs, the associate scale of risk to life is substantially reduced.

## *Surgery Continues*

The Onagawa example has many layers of resilient measures built in, such as engineered base planes that mitigate earthquake vibrations for the entire town, water management and power supply upgrades, and the transportation infrastructure upgrades already mentioned. Additionally, the Japanese pay close attention to social resilience and planning around community-based resilience. The displacement and sheltering plans are well communicated throughout one's life in the community. Familiar facilities are places of shelter and overtly communicated as such. Cities in Japan have pre-designated sites for temporary housing siting that is pre-staged with infrastructure connections to respond rapidly. These processes make Japan one of the leaders in disaster preparedness and provide strong examples of urban resilience.

Urban resilience for New York must address rezoning and managed retreat quite soon. The 400,000 citizens in zones of known risk are in neighborhoods that will have to adapt rapidly to daily nuisance flooding in the short-term, living with water in the near-term, and loss of neighborhood in the long-term. These LOW communities, LOW lying, LOW rise, LOW-income areas are high risk and exposed. Options for relocation as these realities of climate change force relocation means potential loss of wealth to those who can least afford to lose multigenerational assets. In rezoning LOW communities, the value of property drops substantially. Cities and states cannot afford market rate buyouts, and as insurance rates rise for those in these areas, forcing relocation occurs—which is already taking place.

## *Mission Critical Functions, Band-Aids, and Time Horizons*

As illustrated in Figure 12.8, resilient strategies surround our communities with multiple resources that are needed to survive shocks and stresses: redundant energy sources, communication technologies, potable water reserves, transit, health care, and jobs. All these elements combine to compose a resilient city. Avoiding single supply chains and developing autonomous horizontal systems embedded

# 4D! RESILIENT DESIGN IN FOUR DIMENSIONS

## RESILIENCY

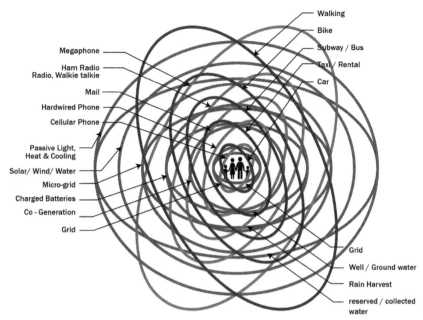

Figure 12.8 Achieving resilience through layers of redundancy. Illustrating that single chains can easily breakdown, whereas layers of redundant systems create a web that can fail with grace allowing for the continuation of operation or livability with some diminished capacity. Image Credit: +LAB Architect.

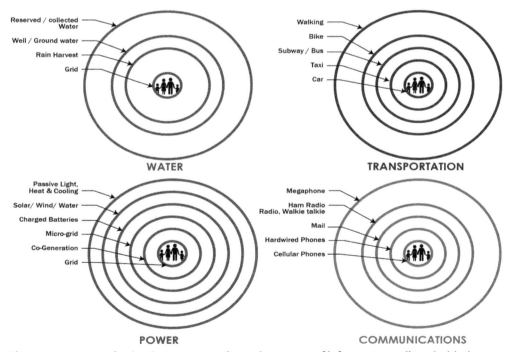

Figure 12.9 Layers of redundant measures for each category of infrastructure aligned with the most sustainable on the outermost layer or first layer of resilience. Image Credit: +LAB Architect.

within cities create local supply chains and resources tied to local, circular economies. Major disturbances (Super Storm Sandy) to minor incidents (nuisance flooding or severe thunderstorms) reveal time and time again that single source, single path materials, supplies, and infrastructure are inherently fragile. The key to resilience is to recognize intersections of infrastructure and components in the built environment that offer redundancies without increased cost or intensity.

### *Networking Elements, Hard and Soft, Offer a Far More Resilient Outcome*

Well-considered, responsible design at all scales delivers sustainability and resilience. These are no longer optional add-ons; rather they are the bare minimum response to building better and smarter in all aspects of operation and continued use, as well as preparing for and forecasting how to deal with expected disturbances. By combining elements of sustainability and resilience in every design, from the individual to all aspects of the built environment, we not only lighten our environmental impacts, we also increase survivability (Figure 12.9).

### *Challenges We Face*

Challenge 1

New York City has several challenges illustrated by the following series of maps (Figures 12.10 and 12.11). Over the next 80 years the changes to the hydrological-cycle and rising sea levels eat away at the current urban footprint. Within those areas of known risk, the current numbers illustrate that major surgery is needed to our living patterns. Over 400,000 residents live in LOW zones, not to mention the 80 schools, 74 daycare centers, 18 hospitals, 9 senior centers, and 4 waste treatment plants (NYCEOM, 2014).

These numbers are static referencing what exists in those zones today and do not incorporate the numbers and development that will occur over the course of the next 80 years. From that perspective, some of what we are seeing in the Japanese models is quite relevant for cities looking to perform major urban surgery.

The manner in which the US approaches large-scale resilience is challenged by our expectation that private investment will make up the difference when federal dollars are spent for mitigation of climate impacts. That scenario has not played out in the eight years since Hurricane Sandy as the city is still waiting on major planned infrastructure to break ground. Finance models are changing due to climate change, and so too must the built environment's approach for coastal cities to thrive in the next century.

Along the way, there are elements that are working. The Band-Aids do buy us time and effectively push back the critical time horizons. The aforementioned Green Streets programs and phase one of the Special

Figure 12.10 Known population and facilities at risk to daily flooding and permanently underwater due to sea level rise projections. Sources SIRR report NYC, New York City Panel on Climate Change. Image Credit: +LAB Architect.

Initiative for Rebuilding and Resiliency (SIRR) report are complete in NYC, which harden and address many a vulnerable areas. This buys us time to sort out the larger issues of infrastructure, UpZoning, and managed retreat. City planning has initiated a Resilient Neighborhood Initiative (Figure 12.11) that recognized LOW zone neighborhoods. Zoning text amendments limiting new construction is a start for preparing the city for potential surgery. The question of equity remains to be answered, yet a positive start to rethinking our urban footprint.

## Challenge 2

The danger here is complacency, thinking the Band-Aids will save the city, while in the long run we ignore larger problems. Land values at the coast across the country are being devalued. This is a huge, predicted, and known problem, with no real answers to come forward. The loss of wealth to those LOW zone communities and owners will be devastating and profoundly impact the economy,

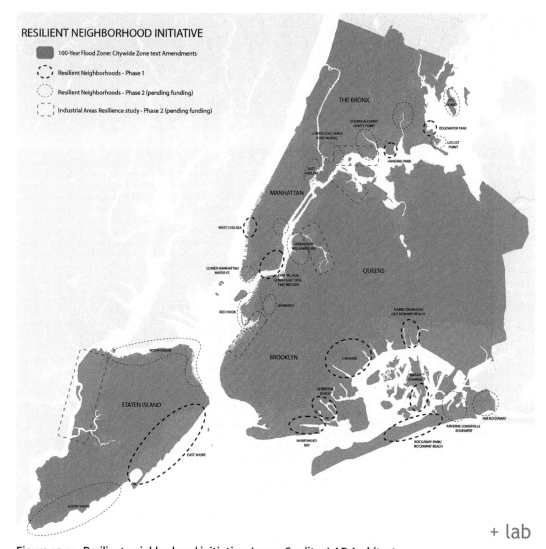

Figure 12.11 Resilient neighborhood initiative. Image Credit: +LAB Architect.

similar to that of post-Katrina losses to the long-vested communities (Figure 12.12).

*Challenge 3*

Ultimately, we can see the tip of the iceberg with large problems yet to come. The other danger is constant debate around the issues being perceived as progress rather than action and implementation. When one reads headlines that debate mitigation and action, then complacency seeps in and nothing of substance is realized. Of late, the debate of giant walls and floodgates for New York Harbor has again entered the debate circles, even though science bears this measure out as ineffective in the long run. A piece of infrastructure is one-dimensional in its protection and does nothing for major areas of Queens, Brooklyn, and

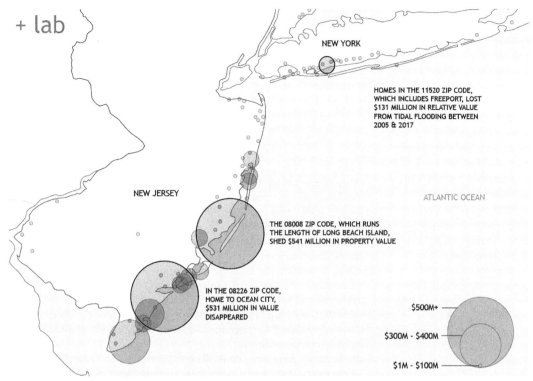

Figure 12.12 Loss of property values based on zip code. Image Credit: +LAB Architect.

Staten Island. A wall fails to meet the need. It is archaic as it would spend money and resources preparing for the last storm rather than on comprehensive resilience capacity building. A harbor barrier does nothing for extreme heat, drought, high wind events, hurricanes with a different profile, along with a slew of other known hazards that the city faces.

We are already in retreat. Eroding LOW zone neighborhoods as mentioned above are in a state of uncontrolled retreat from rising waters. Communities in Alaska, such as Shaktoolik, and those in Louisiana, such as the Isle de Jean Charles tribe, are in retreat. These like so many others being taken by climate change and sea level rise will only grow. Indonesia is moving the entire city of Jakarta in the greatest example of major surgery to date; something that we all need to recognize and learn from. Moving entire cities will not be uncommon strategies as we rethink our urban footprint in the future. It is how we plan and adapt to these changes, that is the issue. The social and economic disasters that will inevitably take place without proactive four-dimensional planning will be catastrophic to many.

In conclusion, rethinking our urban footprint in four dimensions is a proactive forward-thinking process that cannot ignore equity of people and communities in high-risk LOW zones. We cannot wait for market forces to take up the slack, and time is not on our side when planning for these major changes. Looking well into the future when planning and incorporating an all-hazard approach to our solutions is needed to avoid one-dimensional, expensive measures. Those three, coupled with policy changes in zoning that thankfully are underway, give us the fourth dimension coastal cities need to adapt to the needs of the 21st century.

## References

Blaszczak, L.N.D. "The Changing Shoreline of New York City" New York Public Library NYC Space/Time Directory. Retrieved on 12/12/2020 from http://spacetime.nypl.org/the-changing-shoreline-of-nyc/.

Bowery Boys. 2013. "The Corona Ash Dump: Brooklyn's Burden on Queens, a Vivid Literary Inspiration and Bleak, Rat-Filled Landscape." May 9, 2013. https://www.boweryboyshistory.com/2013/05/the-corona-ash-dumps-brooklyns-burden.html.

Brown, O. 2008. "Migration and Climate Change." International Organization of Migration. Geneva, SUI.

C40. 2020. "C40: Programmes." Retrieved on 12/12/2020 from https://www.c40.org/programmes.

Gerstein, A. and Gilbride, C. 2013. "Pioneering Blue and Green Roof Improves the Health of the East River, Creates Jobs for Formerly Incarcerated." NYC Department of Environmental Protection Public Affairs, September 4, 2013.

Horsley Witten Group. 2006. "CNMI and Guam Stormwater Management Manual." Prepared for Commonwealth of the Northern Mariana Islands and the Territory of Guam.

Hyde, S. 2019. "Recovery and Resilience: Tsunamis and Seawalls." *Building Safety Journal*, February 9, 2019. International Code Council, Washington, DC.

McMurray, J. 2014. "Tsunami-Proof 'Great Wall of Japan' Divides Villagers." *The Guardian*, June 29, 2014.

Next City. 2020. "Next City: About Us." Retrieved on 12/12/2020 from https://nextcity.org/about.

NYCEOM New York City Office of Emergency Management. 2014. "NYC's Risk Landscape: A Guide to Hazard Mitigation." November 2014, New York.

Podesta, J. 2019. "The Climate Crisis, Migration, and Refugees." Brookings Blum Roundtable on Global Poverty. The Brookings Institution, Washington, DC, July 27, 2019.

SOPAC, South Pacific Geosciences Commission. 2004. "Harvesting the Heavens: Guidelines for Rainwater Harvesting in Pacific Island Countries." Report for the United Nations Environment Programme, Suva, Fiji Islands.

Strassler, E. and Strellec, K. 1999. "Preliminary Data Summary of Urban Storm Water Best Management Practices." Report for the US Environmental Protection Agency, Washington, DC.

Gunther, B. and Jackewycz, A. 2010. "Best Practice: Greenstreets: Green Roadways." Report for The New York City Global Partners, March 24, 2010.

The Rockefeller Foundation. 2019. "100 Resilient Cities." Retrieved on 12/12/2020 from https://www.rockefellerfoundation.org/100-resilient-cities/.

UN DESA Department of Economic and Social Affairs. 2018. "68% of the World Population Projected to Live in Urban Areas by 2050, Says UN." May 16, 2018. https://www.un.org/development/desa/en/news/population/-2018-revision-of-world-urbanization-prospects.html.

Wrathall, D.J., Van Den Hoek, J., Walters, A., Devenish, A. 2018. "Water Stress and Human Migration: A Global, Georeferenced Review of Empirical Research." Food and Agriculture Organization of the United Nations, New York.

# 13
# UNDERSTANDING SUSTAINABILITY AND RESILIENCE AS APPLIED

## Tracking the Discourse in City Policy

*Martha Bohm*

### Introduction

Both sustainability and resilience are important terms for framing and orienting the planning and design of the built environment, but both terms are freighted with a long history of usage, and consequently have a range of meanings reflecting an evolution over time. This condition allows for a plurality of uses and a discursive inclusivity, where meanings are clustered around idea centers, rather than boundaries. This can be advantageous, as the terms become "tools of inter subjectivity" allowing many parties to converse when they may, in fact, be talking about different things, or even disagree (Hajer and Versteeg 2005).

Further, the territories defined by sustainability and resilience overlap substantially: at a basic level, both sustainability and resilience describe an attitude toward long-term planning. Both are "traveling concepts," meaning they facilitate conversations, but are not fixed. They travel—between disciplines, scholars, historical periods, and geographic areas—and flexibly take on new meaning and operational value in each (Bal 2002, 2009). Like physical boundary objects, they allow for communication without demanding consensus.

Thus, people mean different things when they use the terms sustainability or resilience; this is both helpful and problematic. The problematic condition is intensified when the two similar, and similarly fuzzy, concepts share discursive space, and pragmatic things like resource streams. Concepts of sustainability and resilience are different enough that they could in fact be at odds with each other. The many meanings of these concepts require an openness to uncertainty and difference within the terms (Berardi 2013). For example, resilient cities or buildings are those which, on some level, persist through change. On its surface, this sounds like sustainability. However, the means to ensure persistence is frequently resource intensive, which is the *opposite* of sustainability. How can we resolve this conundrum? This chapter will discuss the historical origins of sustainability and resilience,

DOI: 10.4324/9781003030720-13

and then specifically address how these are deployed in policy, using an example in New York City to illustrate ways of framing the issue.

## Pre-Modern Sustainability

Early, pre-modern notions of "sustainability" came from the necessity of living within the means at hand. On an annual basis, one could not consume more than one grew. The husbanding of tangible resources prompted behaviors to secure one's well-being against scarcity—it required one to look into the future and plan accordingly for survival. One of the earliest explicit references to sustainability is from Hans Carl von Carlowitz, an 18th-century (1714) German accountant who formulated an approach to sustainable forest management where resources could be extracted for ongoing use (Bosselmann 2008; Knauf 2014). In 1804 Georg Ludwig Hartig, a forestry lecturer, explained the term *Nachhaltigkeit* (meaning "lastingness" or "persistence," but now translated as "sustainability") in terms of providing for future usage. Reynolds et al. (2007) quoted him as writing, "Every wise forest director has to have evaluated the forest stands to utilize them to the greatest possible extent, but still in a way that future generations will have at least as much benefit as the living generation." Stewart Brand has illustrated similar ideas by discussing renovation of the medieval dining hall at New College, Oxford. The oak beams supporting the ceiling, built in the 14th century, had become infested with beetles, and needed replacing. The College Council was aghast, wondering where they could find new oak timbers 2' square and 45' long. They called in the College Forester, who had been waiting for just such an inquiry. The oaks planted shortly after the college's founding had by then grown large and were ready for harvest (Brand 1994). The College Forester predecessor had, centuries before, planned for this day. By this definition, modern industrialized societies cannot be considered "sustainable" without fundamental change to economic systems (modern capitalism) and/or social behavior (consumerism). The modern system presupposes continued, consumption-based growth; at a fundamental level this conflicts with the core meaning of sustainability (Garcia and Vale 2017). Is it therefore possible to be sustainable in the contemporary age? Excepting the Ecological Footprint method (Wackernagel 1996) we lack the assessment tools to say whether a given region is, in aggregate, sustainable.

## Weak and Strong Sustainability

A recognition of the modern conflict between our socioeconomic structure and the fundamental principle of sustainability has led to the contemporary notions of sustainability. A widely agreed upon definition of sustainability uses the Brundtland report of 1987. This states that the "needs of the current generation should not compromise the satisfaction of those in future generations" (World Commission on Environment and Development 1987). This echoes Carlowitz and Hartig's 18th-century approach to forestry. Brundtland does not

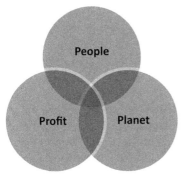

Figure 13.1 Weak and strong sustainability models. The "weak sustainability" model (left) says that sustainability occurs when society, economy, and the environment (people, planet, and profit) are given equal importance where they overlap. The "strong sustainability" model (right) says that economic and social systems must be constrained by planetary limits.

define "needs," and thereby leaves much open to interpretation, but endeavors to balance current and future. It embraces development which values limits of future use at the same time as growth.

Contemporary sustainability takes two forms. "Weak sustainability," the overlapping model shown in the left of Figure 13.1, says that sustainability only occurs when society, economy, and the environment (people, planet, profit) are given equal importance. This "three legged stool" suggests that all three aspects must be present for balance. Some constructs based on the overlapping model (specifically sustainability rating systems like LEED) broaden sustainability to include practices which are simply more conserving than typical, such that the overarching notion of limits is lost (Knauf 2014). In fact, efficient resource use does not necessarily lead to sustainability, but usually exacerbates resource consumption. As William Jevons argued in the 19th century, "with fixed real energy process, energy-efficiency gains will increase energy consumption above what it would be without those gains" (Sorrell 2009). An example of this occurs when a building owner upgrades to a more efficient heating system, and then takes advantage of cheaper operating costs to run it at a higher temperature for longer. This phenomenon, known as Jevons' paradox, is well known in the literature exploring "rebound," where potential energy savings from energy efficiency improvements are not realized. Jevons' paradox-driven rebound is a consequence of "weak sustainability."

Another interpretation of Brundtland provides a hierarchical interpretation of economic and ecological systems. "Strong sustainability" argues that everything must be contained within the ecological/ environmental (planet), as shown in the right of Figure 13.1. This frame explicitly sets limits to economic (profit) and social (people) systems, though the limiting mechanism is not clearly established. The contrast between weak and strong sustainability underscores that sustaining economic growth is not the same as creating economics for a sustainable society. In fact, while it is likely not possible for the majority of the world's population to sustain their present circumstances and societal arrangements (Marcuse 1998), the term "sustainable" frequently is attached to the term "development"; core to this idea is that *economic* development is essential to achieve *sustainable* development (Haughton 1999) or even environmental improvement (Davoudi 2000). This thus sets up a discourse constructed by imperatives of competition, growth, and globalization, despite these being the causes of exploitation and degradation of people and environments (Barry and Paterson 2004; Byrne and Glover 2002; Doyle 1998; Rees 2003). Gunder (2006) argues that the sustainable development frame, as an international orthodoxy for government-led planning, leads to policy responses which are, at best, marginal reforms to problems demanding fundamental change.

### Engineering and Ecological Resilience

The term resilience traces its early uses to two different fields. In engineering, resilience initially referred to mechanical properties of elasticity, specifically describing the ability of a material to rebound or recoil. The first written use in English was by the 19th-century English engineer Thomas Tredgold, writing about the property of timber to deflect and support loads without collapse (Garcia and Vale 2017). Later, the modulus of resilience came to describe a material's ability to deform without catastrophic failure. Now, engineering resilience describes the time it takes a system to return to its stable state—the faster a system recovers, the more resilient it is (Gunderson 2000; Pimm 1984).

In the 1970s the Canadian ecologist C. S. Holling (1973) wrote a seminal paper describing ecosystems as entities which are inherently dynamic and constantly changing. Ecosystems do not exist in one stable condition, but instead have "conditions for persistence" of species within. Resilience is therein defined by Holling (1973) as something that "determines the persistence of relationships within a system, and is a measure of the ability of these systems to absorb changes … and still exist." This is illustrated by the lifecycle of the spruce budworm in the boreal evergreen forests of eastern Canada (Garcia and Vale 2017). There have been six outbreaks of the pest since the early 1700s, and between these events, the budworm is almost nonexistent. When an outbreak occurs, pests decimate the balsam firs, and other trees (spruce and birch) survive and regenerate in intense, crowded stands. The crowding stresses these fir competitors, and as the forest evolves, the fir comes to predominate again, setting the stage for the next infestation. Mature stands of fir after a dry spell are ripe for the budworm population to explode beyond predator control mechanisms. The destruction of so many trees forces a budworm population collapse and the reinstatement of a new equilibrium. Between outbreaks, fir outcompetes other trees; during outbreaks, spruce and birch have the edge. The interplay maintains persistence of species otherwise excluded by competition. Note that these fluctuations are highly unstable. Stability, to Holling, is the ability to return to a given equilibrium state after a disturbance, akin to the *original* engineering definition of resilience. Resilience is the persistence of *systems*, and their ability to absorb disturbance and maintain relationships, repeatedly finding *new* equilibriums. Ecological resilience suggests that complex systems, such as the boreal forest, with the capacity to adapt to disturbances may come to new equilibria without losing identity, organization, and structure (Walker and Meyers 2004).

## Adaptive Cycle

Holling illustrated how systems persist by finding new equilibria with the "adaptive cycle." Change happens in a cyclic manner, or adaptive cycle as shown in Figure 13.2 (Gunderson and Holling 2002). The first step of this is exploitation, which is a period of rapid development. This is not very stable, but highly resilient. This would correspond to a phase of rapid tree growth following a catastrophe like a bushfire or pest outbreak, or city reconstructing after a major disaster. The second step is conservation, which is an accumulation of "capital," such as forest tree biomass or building square footage. More trees attract more species of insects and birds, and more predator-prey relationships exist between them. More buildings create more economic and interpersonal relationship. The conservation stage of "typical growth" is more stable, but more rigid and hence fragile. The third step is release, which is when important connectivity and potentials are lost rapidly, as in a forest fire or major urban storm event. The fourth step is reorganization where either a new cycle of exploitation (rapid growth) begins, or the entire system moves to a different stability state (for example, a forest gives way to a desert, or a storm-ravaged city center is redesigned).

As local stability increases, the system overall becomes more rigid, unstable, and unpredictable (Holling 2004). This is the resilience problem with our built environment. Things are most resilient when they

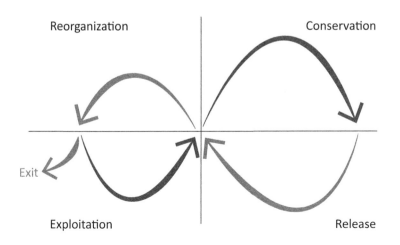

Figure 13.2 Adaptive cycle diagram. This diagram of the adaptive cycle shows in a dark color (exploitation and conservation) the growth phase of accumulations of physical capital (trees, or buildings and infrastructure). In a light color (release and reorganization) is the crisis and the "opportunities" in its aftermath. After Gunderson and Holling (2002).

are just starting, or are under construction, but people don't want to live in a perpetual construction site. Hence, a city, like an ecosystem, becomes more complex and rigid until it either adjusts or collapses. Collapse need not be physical, but is any rapid and significant loss of sociopolitical complexity. The Roman Empire's "collapse" didn't mean the end of language, people, or religion, but of the complex systems supporting global dominance. Collapse occurs when the difference between the cost of growth (becoming more complex) and the cost of maintenance reaches a tipping point.

## Panarchy

The adaptive cycle helps us think about interactions at various scales; this ecological thinking is helpful in its application to the built environment. As shown in Figure 13.3, adaptive cycles occur across scales, referred to as a panarchy, with emergent, meta-influences pushing from bottom and top. "Revolts" are the relatively rare bottom-up processes, which have impact at larger scales. A built environment example of this is the restructuring of villages and open spaces in Britain after populations were decimated by the plague in the 14th century (Herlihy 1997). "Remember" forces are those that try to keep the system stable. A built environment example of this is zoning and land use codes which cement historical organizations or vernacular traditions, based on memories, experiences, or stories that provide it with meaning. Too many "revolts" create insufficient stability for development and too few result in stagnation, rigidity, and fragility. Thinking panarchically about resilience across scales shifts awareness beyond the level at which we are most keenly interested. After all, what good is a resilient building without a resilient neighborhood, or a resilient neighborhood without a resilient city?

## Method of Investigation

In this chapter I ask the question, to what extent are the constructs of strong sustainability, weak sustainability, engineering resilience, and ecological resilience evidenced in how we describe sustainability and resilience actions? To shed some light on this question I analyze in detail one exemplar of sustainability and resilience implementation planning: *One New York: The Plan for a Strong and Just City*, produced by the New York City Mayor's office to shape sustainability and resilience activities in the New York City area (2015). Rather than a critique or assessment of the quality of the plan, what follows is a close examination of its linguistic structure to delineate the frames of sustainability and resilience embodied in its language. Planners and others consult *One New York* to understand the city's strategic direction. How does its language shape the views of reality around sustainability and resilience?

I looked at each action described in the plan, and interpreted the dominant subject, objects, and mechanisms of each one. I analyzed

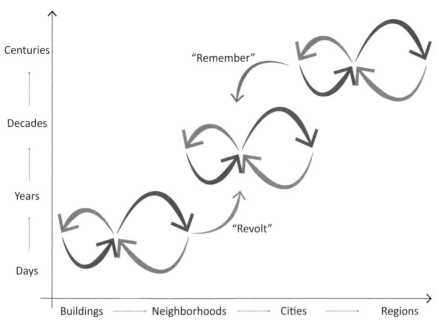

Figure 13.3 Panarchy diagram showing interactions of adaptive cycles at various scales of space and time.

the plan's discourse based on an idea that language shapes views of reality and serves to define appropriate policy responses (Hajer and Versteeg 2005). In so doing I followed a methodological approach after Tozer, who analyzed how climate change was framed in 15 municipal sustainability plans in Canada, and Hilding-Rydevik, who analyzed four documents framing the discourse around the Swedish Strategic Environment Assessment Directive (Hilding-Rydevik and Åkerskog 2011; Tozer 2018). This framework for examining the logics and practices of governance delineated the actors/entities involved, the subjects/spheres worked on or through, the objects/materials worked on or through, and the mechanisms employed.

The section below describes four dimensions of each action described in the plan: Actor/Entity, Subject, Object, and Mechanism. I used questions to articulate these dimensions. First, for actor/entity, which agent initiates and is responsible for the action? Here the actor is the city, taken to include all of the New York City government's constituent agencies. Second, for subject, which stakeholder group does this action work on? Third, for object, what material does this action work on? What problem(s) is the action intending to solve relative to sustainability or resilience? Fourth, for mechanism, how does the action work? What solutions are identified?

## Results and Discussion

The six tables in this section delineate the dimensions of subject (Tables 13.1 and 13.4), object (Tables 13.2 and 13.5), and mechanism

**Table 13.1** Subjects of Sustainability Actions.

| | |
|---|---|
| Other governmental entities | e.g. "Work with the State to ensure these and future funds are used to support renewable and energy efficiency programs;" "work with the MTA to explore creating new system transfers;" "work with the City Council to reduce the overall impact of these products on our local environment" |
| Private businesses/ property owners | e.g. "Work with commercial building owners and tenants to raise awareness of tenants' energy use and encourage investments in energy-efficient retrofits;" "create a Zero Waste Challenge program for large commercial waste generators;" "initiate a grant program of up to $1M per year through 2020 to encourage on-site water reuse on private properties;" "assist building owners through loans and incentives to comply with LL88 lighting upgrades and install modern lighting and controls" |
| Public school students | e.g. "Develop an educational module on sustainability and health for outreach in public schools;" "Teaching the City's 1.1 million students about proper recycling practices" |
| NYCHA residents | e.g. "Work with NYCHA to train residents, community leaders, and staff on recycling and waste reduction practices" |
| Neighborhoods/ CBOs/NGOs | e.g. "For… these neighborhoods, we will assist community brownfield planning by preparing an existing conditions study;" "work with communities and other partners to convert underused streets into pedestrian plazas;" "work with local non-profit organizations and private-sector partners to develop additional capacity for sorting and processing organic waste" |
| Individuals | e.g. "Promote an existing phone app that allows residents and visitors to find water fountains and stations around the city;" "implement data-driven GreeNYC public education campaigns to foster energy-consumption reduction for residents" |

Source: One New York: The Plan for a Strong and Just City (The City of New York Mayor's Office 2015).

**Table 13.2** Objects of Sustainability Actions.

| | |
|---|---|
| Infrastructural assets | e.g. "Provide incentives for newer, cleaner generators;" "achieve further reductions in energy consumption across all of the wastewater treatment plants;" "relieve congestion on major subway corridors;" "improve and expand bus transit throughout the city;" "leverage the commuter rail system to better serve NYC communities;" "expand the ferry network;" "continue to expand the City's bike-lane network;" "encourage water and rail freight to the NY region;" "rehabilitate and reconstruct the 21 interconnected bridge structures that carry the Brooklyn Queens Expressway" |
| City-owned buildings and properties | e.g. "Install 100mW of renewable energy on City-owned buildings by 2025;" "NYCHA will implement a series of Energy Performance Contracts projected to total over $100M;" "constructing new recycling centers at all NYCHA developments;" "institutionalize stormwater management into the design of public property, including streets, parks, schoolyards, and public housing;" "invest in new street trees and other plantings, benches, way-finding signs, and other amenities" |
| Privately owned buildings | e.g. "Facilitate solar PV adoption on private sector buildings;" "encourage more private property stormwater retrofits |
| Carbon | e.g. "Reduce emissions by 30 percent or more in 10 years" |
| Solid waste | e.g. "Ban on all expanded polystyrene foam food-service containers and packing peanuts;" "require all food-service establishments and related businesses to separate their organic waste for composting" |
| Air pollution | e.g. "Replace or retrofit 90% of its diesel on-road vehicles to meet 2007 emissions standards;" "rebates to trucks servicing the Hunts Point market for voluntary upgrades to cleaner vehicles or fuels" |
| Brownfields | e.g. "Brownfield Incentive Grants provide numerous financial incentives to promote brownfield cleanup and redevelopment" |

Source: One New York: The Plan for a Strong and Just City (The City of New York Mayor's Office 2015).

# TRACKING THE DISCOURSE IN CITY POLICY

**Table 13.3** Mechanisms of Sustainability Actions.

| | |
|---|---|
| Financial and fiscal tools (incentives, tax credits, investment) | e.g. "implement a series of Energy Performance Contracts projected to total over $100M;" "leverage direct capital investment, power purchase agreements, and emergent solar deployment models;" "protect and invest in deep-water marine terminals" |
| Market support | e.g. "work with other market participants, NYISO, and State and Federal regulators to eliminate the barriers to entry that now exist;" "work with key stakeholders to enhance the viability of large-scale wind projects by increasing demand, lowering costs to meet market electricity prices, and advocating for financial assistance;" "launch the Energy and Water Retrofit Accelerator, which will offer technical assistance and education programs;" "expanded the NYC Solar Partnership to facilitate solar PV adoption on private sector buildings;" "working with trade associations, industry groups, waste management companies, and some of the world's largest consumer goods manufacturers and retailers to identify barriers to increasing recycled content of new products;" "work with the NY Independent System Operator, regulators, and suppliers to change the market rules to value these benefits" |
| Regulatory | e.g. "Initiate commercial recycling regulation and enforcement system reforms;" "work with the City Council to pass a version of this bill that reduces energy-wasting light pollution from large buildings;" "launch EPIC environment, a web application that automates and streamlines cleanup-project navigation" |
| Promotion, collection of information | e.g. "Use LiDAR technology – land cover mapping based on aerial remote imaging;" "initiating a study of bike access to the 15 Harlem River bridges;" "expanding educational opportunities to improve building operations and maintenance" |
| Voluntary programs | e.g. "A voluntary carbon reduction program among universities, hospitals, commercial offices, and multi-family buildings to reduce emissions by 30% of more in 10 years;" "develop a voluntary audit program to track commercial waste generation trends;" "create a Zero Waste Challenge program for large commercial waste generators" |

Source: One New York: The Plan for a Strong and Just City (The City of New York Mayor's Office 2015).

**Table 13.4** Subjects of Resilience Actions.

| | |
|---|---|
| Neighborhoods/- community-based organizations (CBOs) | e.g. "Strengthening community-based organizations' services, information capacity and ability to conduct community-level emergency and resiliency planning;" "connect organizations and programs in need of support with available volunteers" |
| City staff | e.g. "Expanding the exiting Corporate Emergency Access System ... into an emergency access credential for City Agency staff;" "increasing staffing of dispatchers and supervisors;" "reestablish and expand the Waterfront Management Advisory Board;" "include front-line staff in emergency planning, training on public communications, and table-top exercises" |
| Private businesses | e.g. "Provide tailored resources and technical assistance in preparing and planning for future disruptive events to businesses citywide;" "leverages innovative resiliency technologies in energy infrastructure, telecommunications, and building systems for small businesses" |
| Individuals | e.g. "Ensure all investments that strengthen the city's resiliency will create job opportunities for residents and low-income applicants;" "developing further public education campaign materials for city residents living in and near the floodplain" |
| Other government entities | e.g. "Call on the State to ensure cooling access during extreme heat;" "propose that the NYC Board of Health amend the health code;" "coordinating these efforts across government stakeholders;" "working with FEMA to institute reforms;" "aim to have all NYC agencies adopt standardized resiliency design guidelines" |
| Infrastructure systems | e.g. "Coordinates closely with its partners in the energy telecommunications, and transportation sectors across the region to facilitate planning for and investment in the resiliency of their assets" |

Source: One New York: The Plan for a Strong and Just City (The City of New York Mayor's Office 2015).

**Table 13.5** Objects of Resilience Actions.

| | |
|---|---|
| Social infrastructure | e.g. "Working to expand civic engagement and volunteerism;" "bolster neighborhood resiliency and civic participation" |
| Buildings | e.g. "Continue to repair and upgrade City-owned buildings;" "execute a comprehensive resiliency program across 33 public housing developments;" "demonstrate how best to prepare homes and neighborhoods for the future;" "exploring other protective strategies to improve single-family homes and upgrade multi-family homes;" "securing physical assets for emergency response such as power generators, light towers, and others;" "invest in emergency shelter sites" |
| Policy | e.g. "Continue to align zoning and building code updates with reforms to the National Flood Insurance Program and expected changes to the Flood Insurance Rate maps;" "develop and adopt consistent resilient design guidelines for buildings;" "evaluate and establish a framework for adaptive land use planning;" "pursue a comprehensive set of activities to promote investments in physical risk reduction and better policies;" "developing and implementing a set of design guidelines for resiliency;" "explore new governance models to support the completion and long-term operations of integrated coastal resiliency measures" |
| Infrastructure systems | e.g. "Invest in the resiliency of its transportation network;" "work to ensure the resiliency of our freight network;" "planning exercises to identify vulnerabilities to the freight network;" "planning for green infrastructure installations;" "commit to ensuring our dams safely pass the full probable maximum flood;" "populating its backup data center with replication and backup of critical applications;" "develop strategies to promote and enforce resiliency for telecommunications providers;" "work with wireless carriers to ensure cell sites and networks are hardened and resilient;" "proceed with the retrofit of critical buildings;" "call on regional infrastructure providers and operators... to make critical resiliency investments in their systems;" "a $3.7B program of infrastructure investments, natural area restorations, and design and governance upgrades;" "invest $30M toward commercial corridor enhancements in Coney Island and the Rockaways, including stormwater management, streetscape and place-making projects to enhance the connectivity of these places, and improvement of local infrastructure that provides basic services to businesses" |

Source: One New York: The Plan for a Strong and Just City (The City of New York Mayor's Office 2015).

(Tables 13.3 and 13.6) of both sustainability and resilience actions in New York City's *One New York* plan. I then briefly describe the frictions and overlaps among these dimensions, and conclude this section by highlighting needs for further research.

### Sustainability as Applied

In the New York City plan, subjects are frequently in the public and non-profit sector, though many are in the private sector. While individuals are included, they are not the focus of the majority of activities. Business are the subjects of actions in some cases, but not the majority. The majority of the programs facing businesses use market levers (e.g. PV facilitation, energy/water innovator, retrofit accelerator program for fuel oil boilers, truck upgrade rebates, water reuse grant program) rather than regulatory levers (e.g. commercial recycling regulation, enforcement, audits, enforcement of control technology requirements for mobile air polluters). There are signals in the plan that the city is seeking new regulatory control over plastic bag usage (an outright ban) and lighting of non-residential spaces. Other governmental organizations are frequently the subject of sustainability actions, wherein the city endeavors to persuade other entities

Table 13.6 Mechanisms of Resilience Actions.

| | |
|---|---|
| Contractual tools | e.g. "modify standardized contracts to require service providers to participate in the City's emergency protocols;" "develop a system of standardized on-call contracts, with agreed upon payment and risk management terms;" "adopt standardized language for all procurement documents and contracts for resiliency-related work, and require contractors and consultants to report on efforts and outcomes related to local hiring and training" |
| Market support | e.g. "Pursue a comprehensive set of activities to promote investments in physical risk reduction and better policies, including those that promote NFIP affordability;" "develop strategies to promote and enforce resiliency for telecommunications providers through the franchise renewal process" |
| Promotion/collection of information | e.g. "Explore options to provide additional support where the need is greatest;" "developing strategies to evaluate the best available science on the urban heat island effect in order to invest in better data collection;" "explore incentives to balance the costs of improvements;" "feasibility studies of several investment opportunities;" "explore new governance models to support the completion and long-term operation of integrated coastal resiliency measures;" "develop a comprehensive, interactive web-based platform to map both small and larger community organizations and activities;" "an enhanced NYC Service platform will connect organizations and programs in need of support with available volunteers" |
| Policy + planning | e.g. "Integrate its Hazard Mitigation Plan with climate resiliency plans;" "develop and adopt consistent resilient design guidelines for buildings;" "evaluate and establish a framework for adaptive land use planning;" "identify vulnerabilities to the freight network, improve redundancy, and provide resiliency strategies;" "establish a Hurricane Sandy Task Force to make recommendations;" "coordinating through a new Urban Heat Island Working Group;" "coordinated through the Climate Change Adaptation Task Force;" "reestablish and expand the Waterfront Management Advisory Board;" "explore, with our State and academic partners, the preparation of a Regional Resiliency Assessment Program;" "conduct an analysis and develop recommendations to enhance the resiliency of the city's food supply chain;" "provide tailored resources and technical assistance in preparing and planning for future disruptive events" |
| Fiscal tools | e.g. "Invest in emergency shelter sites;" "building out a fully redundant, second 911 answering center;" "invest $30M toward commercial corridor enhancements;" "repair and upgrade City-owned buildings;" "invest in the resiliency of its transportation infrastructure;" "green infrastructure installations across the five boroughs;" "proceed with the retrofit of critical buildings;" "strengthen its coastal defenses by completing many vital projects in all five boroughs;" "call on regional infrastructure providers and operators... to make critical resiliency investments in their systems" |
| Regulatory | e.g. "Continue to align zoning and building code updates with reforms to the National Flood Insurance Program and expected changes to the Flood Insurance Rate Maps" |

Source: One New York: The Plan for a Strong and Just City (The City of New York Mayor's Office 2015).

of its objective. New York City Housing Authority (NYCHA) residents were singled out separately from general city residents for some actions (recycling education, recycling facilities, energy performance contracts). Table 13.1 lists the subjects of sustainability actions.

Objects are frequently infrastructure or other assets in the public or private domain, but generally speaking (with a few notable exceptions) resources and pollutants (e.g. energy, water, greenhouse gases

(GHGs), solid waste) are the governable object in the discourse. While the ultimate goal within the energy space is 80% reduction of GHGs by 2050, the actual program targets are described by the fuel mix of the city's power supply; the number of MW of renewable energy generation; the efficiency of wastewater treatment technology; the safety, sustainability, and accessibility of the transportation system. Table 13.2 lists the objects of sustainability actions.

The plan includes a range of different mechanisms: direct fiscal tools, market support, information collection or dissemination, regulatory and voluntary. Generally, these actions suggest a shaping rather than a transformation of the economic activity of the area. They look for efficiencies in existing systems (performance contracts), reduce barriers to entry of better technologies (accelerator, solar partnership), or induce voluntary improvement. Many actions use various examples of language of enabling ("facilitating," "encouraging," "promoting") rather than regulatory governance ("requiring," "banning"). Most frequent was "work with," and somewhat less frequent was "invest in." Mechanisms often cite a partnership or the attempt to create the conditions for an action to take place instead of directly requiring an action. The most transformative actions surround solid waste reductions, especially composting, and a plastic bag ban. Table 13.3 lists the mechanisms of sustainability actions.

## Resilience as Applied

The subjects of resilience actions are frequently vague, perhaps because they are implied through the development of a policy or plan. For example, "demonstrate how best to prepare homes and neighborhoods for the future." Businesses and public or private organizations are frequently the subject of resilience actions. An exception to this is the identification of "workers" as a group singled out by several resilience actions. Table 13.4 lists the subjects of resilience actions.

The objects of resilience actions are quite varied, and include physical buildings, infrastructure, and landforms (the coast) as well as significant policy and planning. Table 13.5 lists the objects of resilience actions.

The mechanisms deployed span a range of approaches, from contractual tools to planning studies to significant outright investment. Several of the goals focus on the plan itself as a subject. Some mechanisms are unclear in their path, such as "coordinate closely with… partners in the energy, telecommunications and transportation sectors across the region to facilitate planning for an investment in the resilience of their assets." This puts the City in a passive role in the improvements of some private infrastructures. Some mechanisms require nested layers of research, for example, "developing strategies to evaluate the best available science on the urban heat island effect in order to invest in better data collection," which appears to be studying how to study what to study. There is a lot of investment

($3.7B) and frequent study/task force creations. The plan authors may be aware that this investment may suggest leaping before looking, and proposes several mechanisms to steer some of this spending to help the local workforce. Some mechanisms try to span potentially conflicting sides: "the City's coastal communities continue to be threatened by escalating flood risk and rising NFIP premiums." If building continues to occur in coastal areas where risk is high, insurance premiums will rise and displace those with less economic power. The city therefore is attempting to educate consumers about flood risk, insurance purchase requirements, and to encourage insurance purchasing. Fiscal structures in general are not as varied as the ones for sustainability planning, which attempt to shape the market. Policy appears to be both an object and a mechanism. Table 13.6 lists the mechanisms of resilience actions.

## Friction and Overlap

The subjects of sustainability actions are frequently in the public/non-profit sector (though many private subjects exist). Individuals are included, but are not the focus of most of actions. Rather than inspiring changes in attitudes, the actions are about creating conditions for market-based mechanisms to move toward sustainability. The objects are frequently infrastructural assets. Pollutants and resources (energy, water, GHGs, and solid waste) are also governable objects. Sustainability mechanisms vary considerably in scale and type.

At the same time, the subjects of resilience actions are often vaguely defined, but are frequently businesses and organizations. Individuals are frequently constructed as "workers." The objects are predominantly infrastructural systems and buildings. Policy is frequently an object in itself. Flooding and overheating are not themselves governable objects. Resilience mechanisms are predominantly direct fiscal investment and policy development, but a range of approaches exists. While some goals are potentially transformative, many are incremental changes or reversions to status quo.

## Research Needs

Research can shed light on sustainability and resilience discourse, and the extent to which it facilitates or constrains actual change when applied. First, if an adaptive cycle of collapse and reconstruction is acknowledged, what opportunities does this provide for overhaul and transformation? The ecological notion of resilience suggests that complex systems, by their nature, face cycles of collapse and reconstruction. As cities adapt to increase their resilience, there is a more conservative approach—what must be saved, and what can be lost. Active adaptation describes what can be gained or transformed when inevitable changes occur (Pelling 2011). What can be gained or transformed from active, forward-thinking adaptation, rather than simply saved or lost in more conservative adaptation?

Second, a related question to policy makers, then, is how these cyclic catastrophes themselves can be harnessed to shift the overall complex system of the city toward organizations that are themselves less extractive and exploitative of human and ecological systems. How can the intense resource consumption required to move a complex system toward resilience take place within an economic system bounded by ecological limits? Does the intense resource consumption required to move a complex system toward resilience flout ideas of sustainability? Will policies direct the city to rebound and assume its same original shape, no matter the demands this places on human (including economic) and ecological systems?

Third and last, at least in the case of New York City, there is considerable research and information development ongoing to improve sustainability and resilience policy. Despite a proliferation of indicators and frameworks in recent years, we need better tools to measure our actions, not just in the local scale, but also in a larger-scale synthesis of sustainability and resilience. Are we making places that can endure through change? How have others done so historically? This is important especially for smaller cities and towns that do not have anything like the economic resources of New York City to plan for, fund, and assess actions. Which policy and fiscal levers work in weaker markets without the kind of public awareness grown from a catastrophic event like 2012's Super Storm Sandy in New York City? Research mapping the complexity of the urban system to understand its historical changes at multiple scales of the complex urban system is needed. Knowing the quantity and diversity of elements at different scales (like an ecological field analysis) would allow one to examine the city, more directly, as a complex adaptive (eco)system using tools from ecology. We can answer how much and what kind of diversity is needed for true resilience.

## Conclusions

The very language we use influences how the present and future built environment is analyzed, made, and remade. The nature of "who" is sustained or made resilient is unclear or vague, and potentially in conflict. Sustainability actions are slightly more bottom-up than resilience actions, which are more top-down. Resilience planning around businesses and infrastructures suggests that these are the elements that are intended to endure, not individuals, families, or homes.

Objects of actions vary, but the range of object types in sustainability actions is greater than in resilience actions, which focus on infrastructure and policy. The "governable objects" in resilience actions generally do not include floodwater or air temperature in the same way that sustainability actions govern water use or air pollution.

The nature of the goals of many sustainability mechanisms suggests that the challenge is numeric (insufficiency or surfeit of something) rather than systemic. While some goals are potentially transformative, many are incremental updates to the status quo. Many set out to reshape, not overhaul, problematic systems and structures. They attempt to nudge the market toward less resource consumption, rather than setting limits to it, and tend toward market supporting mechanisms rather than regulatory ones.

The logics of sustainability and resilience both exist in the planning document examined here, and seem to be sharing space in shaping the rationalities of city planners. While each action on its face is laudable, this muddies the waters about the overall trajectory. While ecological resilience is in evidence, an engineering notion of resilience predominates. Resilience goals suggest that existing systems must be strengthened and hardened.

Goal framing is an opportunity for a city to construct a narrative of itself, and establish the parameters for change. Sustainability actions appear to aim to reshape (weak sustainability). Resilience actions appear to aim for stability (engineering resilience). However, the high resource consumption for engineering resilience is at odds with notions of limited resource consumption of sustainability, weak or strong. Resilient systems are unstable. Trying to increase stability will reduce resilience; things persist because they change.

## References

Bal, Mieke. 2002. *Travelling Concepts in the Humanities: A Rough Guide*. University of Toronto. http://www.miekebal.org/publications/books/travelling-concepts/.

Bal, Mieke. 2009. "Working with Concepts." *European Journal of English Studies* 13 (1): 13–23. https://doi.org/10.1080/13825570802708121.

Barry, John, and Matthew Paterson. 2004. "Globalisation, Ecological Modernisation and New Labour." *Political Studies* 52 (4): 767–784. https://doi.org/10.1111/j.1467-9248.2004.00507.x.

Berardi, Umberto. 2013. "Clarifying the New Interpretations of the Concept of Sustainable Building." *Sustainable Cities and Society* 8: 72–78. https://doi.org/https://doi.org/10.1016/j.scs.2013.01.008.

Bosselmann, Klaus. 2008. *The Principle of Sustainability: Transforming Law and Governance*. Aldershot: Ashgate.

Brand, Stewart. 1994. *How Buildings Learn: What Happens after They're Built*. New York: Viking.

Byrne, John, and Leigh Glover. 2002. "A Common Future or towards a Future Commons: Globalization and Sustainable Development since UNCED." *International Review for Environmental Strategies* 3 (1): 5–25.

Davoudi, Simin. 2000. "Sustainability: A New Vision for the British Planning System." *Planning Perspectives* 15 (2): 123–137. https://doi.org/10.1080/026654300364056.

Doyle, Timothy. 1998. "Sustainable Development and Agenda 21: The Secular Bible of Global Free Markets and Pluralist Democracy." *Third World Quarterly* 19 (4): 771–786.

Garcia, Emilio Jose, and Brenda Vale. 2017. *Unravelling Sustainability and Resilience in the Built Environment*. New York, NY: Routledge.

Gunder, Michael. 2006. "Sustainability: Planning's Saving Grace or Road to Perdition?" *Journal of Planning Education and Research* 26 (2): 208–221. https://doi.org/10.1177/0739456X06289359.

Gunderson, Lance H. 2000. "Ecological Resilience--In Theory and Application." *Annual Review of Ecology and Systematics* 31: 425–439.

Gunderson, Lance H., and C. S. Holling, eds. 2002. *Panarchy: Understanding Transformations in Human and Natural Systems*. Washington, DC: Island Press.

Hajer, Maarten, and Wytske Versteeg. 2005. "A Decade of Discourse Analysis of Environmental Politics: Achievements, Challenges, Perspectives." *Journal of Environmental Policy & Planning* 7 (3): 175–184. https://doi.org/10.1080/15239080500339646.

Haughton, Graham. 1999. "Environmental Justice and the Sustainable City." *Journal of Planning Education and Research* 18 (3): 233–243. https://doi.org/10.1177/0739456X9901800305.

Herlihy, David. 1997. *The Black Death and the Transformation of the West*. Edited by Samuel Kline Cohn. Cambridge, MA: Harvard University Press.

Hilding-Rydevik, Tuija, and Ann Åkerskog. 2011. "A Clear Case of 'Doublespeak': The Swedish Governmental SEA Implementation Discourse." *Journal of Environmental Planning and Management* 54 (4): 495–515. https://doi.org/10.1080/09640568.2010.517989.

Holling, C. S. 1973. "Resilience and Stability of Ecological Systems." *Annual Review of Ecology and Systematics* 4: 1–23.

Holling, C. S. 2004. "From Complex Regions to Complex Worlds." *Ecology and Society* 9 (1): 11. https://doi.org/10.5751/ES-00612-090111.

Knauf, Marcus. 2014. "Is the Sustainability Revolution Devouring Its Own Children? Understanding Sustainability as a Travelling Concept and the Role Played by Two German Discourses on Sustainability." *Forests* 5 (11). https://doi.org/10.3390/f5112647.

Marcuse, Peter. 1998. "Sustainability is Not Enough." *Environment and Urbanization* 10 (2): 103–112. https://doi.org/10.1177/095624789801000201.

Pelling, Mark. 2011. *Adaptation to Climate Change: From Resilience to Transformation*. London: Routledge.

Pimm, Stuart L. 1984. "The Complexity and Stability of Ecosystems." *Nature* 307 (5949): 321–326. https://doi.org/10.1038/307321a0.

Rees, William E. 2003. "Economic Development and Environmental Protection: An Ecological Economics Perspective." *Environmental Monitoring and Assessment* 86 (1): 29–45. https://doi.org/10.1023/A:1024098417023.

Reynolds, K., A. Thomson, M. Shannon, M. A. Shannon, Duncan Ray, and Keith Rennolls. 2007. *Sustainable Forestry: From Monitoring and Modelling to Knowledge Management and Policy Science*. Wallingford, CT: CABI.

Sorrell, Steve. 2009. "Jevons' Paradox Revisited: The Evidence for Backfire from Improved Energy Efficiency." *Energy Policy* 37: 1456–1469.

The City of New York Mayor's Office. 2015. *One New York: The Plan for a Strong and Just City*.

Tozer, Laura. 2018. "Urban Climate Change and Sustainability Planning: An Analysis of Sustainability and Climate Change Discourses in Local Government Plans in Canada." *Journal of Environmental Planning and Management* 61 (1): 176–194. https://doi.org/10.1080/09640568.2017.1297699.

Wackernagel, Mathis. 1996. *Our Ecological Footprint: Reducing Human Impact on the Earth*. Edited by William E. Rees. New Catalyst Bioregional Series. Gabriola Island: New Society Publishers.

Walker, Brian, and Jacqueline A. Meyers. 2004. "Thresholds in Ecological and Social–Ecological Systems: A Developing Database." *Ecology and Society* 9 (2): 3. https://doi.org/10.5751/ES-00664-090203.

World Commission on Environment and Development. 1987. *Our Common Future*. Oxford: Oxford University Press.

# 14

# PERSPECTIVES FROM PRACTICE

*Jason Swift, Braden Kay, Terry Schwarz, Dana Kochnower, Kevin Bush, Jodi Smits Anderson, Allison Anderson, Matthew Elley, Erin Hatcher, Janice Barnes, and Rachel Minnery*

## Perspectives from Practice

In this chapter, practicing architects, planners, policymakers, developers, and staff of non-profit organizations share their own perspective on climate adaptation and resilience in the built environment. These short interviews were conducted by phone in early 2020, audio recorded, transcribed, and then edited for length. This preserved each person's voice and their individual approach to climate change.

The interviewees live in locations that span from Alaska to Arizona, Washington D.C., to Washington State. However, the interviews are not organized in this chapter by profession or geographic location, but instead by their theme. For example, the topic discussed at the end of one interview may be picked up by the next interviewee even though the interviews were held at different times, and there were no conversations among the interviewees related to this book.

Themes of equity, collaboration, and working in cross-disciplinary teams transcend professional and geographical boundaries in these interviews. This shows that practitioners are dealing with many of the same issues across North America and that we may have lessons to learn from each other even though our professions or climate zones may be different.

Finally, many of the individuals shared how they became involved in adaptation and resilience in their interviews. These histories are informative for students and those new to the various fields represented here, perhaps trying to determine how they might engage their communities or organizations in addressing the climate crisis. With that being said, it is important to note that these are individual perspectives on practice and not official policy statements or representative of the organizations where the interviewees currently or formerly worked.

DOI: 10.4324/9781003030720-14

### Jason Swift, Alaska

**Q: Can you talk a little bit about what kind of work Environmental Concerns, Incorporated (ECI) does, and about some of the work you've been doing in Alaska in general?**

So, we've been around since the early 1980s. It was the main Anchorage library that really kind of set the stage for the firm from its inception until now—that we really focus on people places. So, we do a lot of community spaces, schools, higher education, research, healthcare, pretty much everything besides single family residential or multifamily. But we're even starting to venture into that. But in general, Alaska is an isolated market in a lot of ways. And so, there's not a lot of specialist firms up here—we have to serve essentially the whole spectrum.

It's pretty rare that we would go down to the Lower 48 and do a project. Sometimes we'll get pulled into projects through collaboration—sometimes it's of a technical nature, because we do tend to focus on our envelopes up here. If you have a failure in your envelope, it's usually not just a light failure, it's usually a drastic failure. And so, we do spend a lot of time on that.

**Q: Envelope detailing is especially important in Alaska, right? Because the temperature difference between inside and outside is pretty extreme in some places?**

We get extreme temperature differentials, but even if we design a really high-performance envelope, you have these high rates of ventilation required as part of current ASHRAE (American Society of Heating, Refrigerating and Air-Conditioning Engineers) standards. And that's a really costly thing to do, even with a mechanical system. And so, when I say "envelopes," it's really how the whole building reacts to its surroundings.

The logistical costs of construction and development in Alaska are really high. So, whenever you do something, you want to make sure you do it well, because you're not going to have a chance to do it again. There's just not the fiscal environment to support that. We go back and visit buildings that are 60 years old, that no one probably ever thought would still be used, but they are. And it's just because they aren't going to be replaced and so communities keep using them.

And so, because of that, when we do build something new, we spend a lot of time making sure that our envelopes are very well designed and coordinated—that we've taken in to account thermal bridging and vapor drive and things like that.

**Q: Interesting. What you're doing in Alaska, how has that started to change in the face of climate change? Has it started to change how people are thinking about and approaching some of these problems?**

It has. It's had a growing effect to how we operate, how we work with our clients and with communities, and the types of conversations we have. A lot of it is cultural. For a lot of communities up in Alaska and the whole Northern region, they're actually dealing with a cultural shift. It's a way of life change and that affects architecture significantly.

You have all these isolated communities that are often not linked by road systems. So, looking at each one—it's a community, it's people's homes, their schools, their ways of life—but when you start to overlay climate change on top, it drastically affects the conversation.

Well, you start asking questions like, "Is it feasible to still be in this location? Where is our community going? What is the context around this school going to be in 50 years?" A lot of the conversations become this long-term cultural conversation.

I mean, if you look at it from a pure architectural response to the cultural conversations, you start looking at, well, is your program resilient? Is it a program that can be responsive to a community that might drastically change how it operates, the number of people that live there, the general makeup of the population?

And then you can step into even more technical pieces. Geotechnical is a good example. At least across Alaska, it varies pretty significantly. I mean, you'll have areas of extremely stable soil, but then you start getting into areas of permafrost or semi-frozen soil, or coastal communities and near waterways, where they're starting to see large-scale, rapid land erosion.

A lot of rural projects, especially in tundra areas, are built on a pile system. They might've dug down 5–15 feet and laid a wood cribbing system on ice and then built up from there. Well, now 30–60 years later, we go back and we look at those buildings and we find that the permafrost is now below the pile system. It's receded to a point where the piles are really just there by friction alone. What does that mean for this building or this project?

Is it appropriate, fiscally, to reinvest in this facility without addressing the foundation system? Do we have to re-freeze the ground with a re-freeze system? Can we drive the piles so deep that they'll work no matter what? Because we have to assume that the permafrost in this region will eventually go away and the building will then just be supported as-is. Most of the physical parameters, I feel, are fairly solvable. It really just becomes a matter of asking yourself, "do you have enough resources to solve it?"

**Q: It sounds like you're almost grappling with how do you make decisions about what that building should be 50 years from now? Are you looking at other things like how temperatures or precipitation or other things might really change?**

In general, I think what we're seeing is the extremes are just getting larger. Overall it's getting warmer, but we're getting colder cold snaps. We're getting warmer warm snaps. And I think across the world, people are kind of grappling with, "Well, our envelopes have to be more responsive to those fluctuations."

And I think the other piece is, what resources are you using to operate the building? And that is one opportunity, I think, that we have up here—the cost of our resources, either from transportation or just fuel and energy, is really high. And so, that does allow us to have some really wonderful conversations with clients about envelopes and how buildings operate, and often it does result in really high-performance buildings because they need to control that long-term cost.

**Q: A lot of Alaska's economy is from oil and mineral extraction, right? Do you see a shift or change in the political discussions around these issues?**

I do. That's a really good observation. How does one respond to climate change? It requires resources, usually financial resources. But our extraction of oil, and essentially the income coming in from oil, has been on a decline. It used to be one of the primary parts of our economy. Now it's not.

And unlike the Lower 48, Alaska has actually been hovering near recession since about 2008. Our fiscal environment is not balanced right now. That has a really big impact on projects because, all of a sudden, fewer schools are being funded, and for the ones that are, the funding is less. And so, you have to do more with less. You have to be very strategic about what you do.

The state is also going through this political conversation about how best to utilize the resources we have, the general fund, the dividend fund, to best benefit the people of Alaska. It is happening at all levels. And I don't know if it's only happening in response to climate change, but it will affect all levels from government to transportation and everything.

**Q: Based on your experience, what advice might you give someone in the Northern parts of the Lower 48, about how to start thinking about preparing for climate change? About that process or the conversations they need to have?**

I think the best advice that I can give is to make sure that everyone's actually talking to each other—make sure that you're communicating. That you're having these broad-scale regional and open conversations. That the design community is talking to each other. That the governing agencies are talking to each other.

That information is shared as freely as possible, because there's no one "aha" solution. It varies so drastically by region that you can put these kinds of umbrella goals over large areas, but ultimately, how each region responds to those goals is going to be a little bit different. And I think there needs to be a lot of flexibility in this conversation with response to climate change.

There's this legacy of imprints you're leaving with every project, but I'd argue that climate change is not dealt with on a building-by-building perspective, it's really built on a community and a regional perspective.

## Braden Kay, Arizona

**Q: What are you currently working on in the realm of climate change and climate adaptation?**

So it's basically been four and a half years of helping set up an office around sustainability and resilience for the City of Tempe. We're part of the Urban Sustainability Directors Network. And our office is set up to be sort of a holistic, cross-departmental office that supports long-term visions and strategic plans. Right now, we have focus areas around transportation, waste, land use, water, and social sustainability.

We passed the first climate action plan that the City of Tempe's ever done. Ninety-nine percent of our non-consumption-based emissions, our scope one and scope two emissions, are energy and transportation. So we've been working on that. And then in terms of resilience work, we really felt the need to focus on extreme heat.

And now we're sort of getting to the next phase of this work. We're doing a climate action plan update, which uses 2020 emissions data to understand where we've gotten in the last five years, and to create a more sophisticated trajectory around the city's climate action work.

And we've set some guiding principles for that work. So there's fiscal responsibility, equity, and enterprise, which is really the role of business and social enterprise in climate action, and the role of evidence—so the work that we've been doing with the team at Arizona State University (ASU)—how we use weather and climate data for infrastructure and program decision-making in cities. And then the fifth one is engagement.

And what we realized in the beginning of our resilience work is that people can't really touch and feel some of the concepts that we're talking about, especially in terms of some of the solutions, like green infrastructure and green buildings. And so we're trying to push ourselves to figure out how to do that resilience work in a way that people will really understand how we're going to be affected by climate change in the future, and the role that neighborhoods and residents can play in that change.

**Q: You mentioned earlier that one of the major things that Arizona's facing is extreme heat. Could you talk a little bit more about how the city is trying to address that topic?**

So the four main actions we have in our first climate action plan around extreme heat are passing green infrastructure standards, adopting the International Green Construction Code, growing and further investing in our urban forestry master plan, and establishing an emergency management program.

Then, we're building this research program with ASU around how we use both weather projections and weather data, and then seed that into city decision-making. We spent last summer collecting microclimate data around four types of infrastructure in the city: so, play areas/playgrounds; multi-use paths, which are basically bike and pedestrian paths; parking lots; and arterial walls, which separate residential areas from streets. We took that data and worked with city staff to get a set of design guidelines and recommendations on how to design that infrastructure for thermal comfort, and to reduce the negative impact that infrastructure is having on the human experience.

Also, another critical piece of this work is figuring out how to build the business case for investments in urban cooling and green infrastructure to the private development community. So we're trying to work on some partnerships with Urban Land Institute and other private development organizations to figure out how we advance that business case argument.

And even though we've had this uptick in deaths due to extreme heat, a lot of people still view that as something that's happening to old people and poor people, and not necessarily something that should be guiding our development pattern.

We recently received funding from the Robert Wood Johnson Foundation to fund the *Cool Kids, Cool Places, Cool Futures* project that aims to center youth and people of color in our place-based resilience to extreme heat work. Youth have the urgency and desire for action that is needed to change behavior and building patterns that have not changed in our region despite the increasing threat of extreme heat.

**Q: Do you find that working with the university helps to make some of those cases based in science?**

Yeah, we certainly want to continue to make the argument to have universities deeply invested in this work. One of those reasons is because data and evidence are important. Another is because you need institutions that can outlast political cycles. And then the other is that students are invigorating to elected and city staff, and they want to have students engaged and involved. I'm working on trying to create the interdisciplinary team on the university side that can do this holistic work.

We're in a very early state in our understanding about how to manage urban heat and what the effects of urban heat are. We're just starting to understand how to measure, what types of weather measurements matter. We're just understanding which key conditions affect people the most and how they affect people. And so that's been another reason to have the university involved.

**Q: You have a lot of "snowbirds" who come to get away from the cold and people like homeless populations that are more vulnerable. Do you find that these different populations are challenging to work with?**

From a public health perspective, we have a lot of challenges. Especially in Tempe, we have a huge student population that changes out every four years. We have a large snowbird population that's on six months, off six months, or on four months, off eight months. The fact that there's a lot of shifting populations here does mean that figuring out how to communicate about threats and how to have that kind of consistent dialog is really hard.

I've been really sobered by some recent conversations I've been having with the sustainability manager in Sedona. At least a third of the homes in Sedona are now rentals, and a lot of the people that work in Sedona live an hour away now. In a lot of places in Arizona, we have such transient populations and we have populations that live very far from where they work because of growing inequalities. And so, figuring out how you deliver messages and how you get people to have ownership is definitely a challenge in a lot of Arizona cities. We need regional and statewide collaboration and solution building.

Looking at the Buffalos and Clevelands and Detroits of the world—I lived in St. Louis—you had people that just couldn't handle the economic hardships and the cultural shifts and left. I think the ownership challenge is figuring out how you get people to change their behavior instead of just saying, "No, we're going to do things in a status quo way and move when it doesn't work anymore."

And I think that that's one of the challenges we have as a country. That kind of ping pong to our population dynamics is not the best way to have a sustainable and resilient country, let alone the stresses that put on specific cities. Phoenix could continue to import people fleeing crises in California, or it could export people to the Midwest that are in search of heat relief and water.

**Q: Is there any other take away that you would like to stress about climate change adaption or climate change resilience?**

So, we understand more and more that we need to address racial equity, we need to address the affordable housing crisis, and figure out how we're building in a way that doesn't exclude people of color in frontline communities.

And so now, I think you're starting to see some really interesting work develop that's doing deep listening in frontline communities, and trying to figure out how to shift power, and center people of color, and deconstruct institutional and structural racism.

But I think we're still in the very early stages of understanding how that actually gets embedded into decision-making, and how elected officials are going to respond to that, especially when residents who have traditionally had power fight against the necessary shift of power and resources to people of color and frontline communities. Targeted universalism is not yet universally accepted.

And then we're telling developers and cities, you also need to be doing a better job of incorporating quantitative data of climate projections and the impacts of infrastructure on people, as well as people's experiences, and more human-centered design. It's a lot to hold up, and a lot to figure out how to do in a consistent way.

In most American cities this sort of deeply mindful way of doing urban development does not yet seem to be catching on. In communities that are really being hit hard by climate impacts, like Australia, and some in northern California, you're starting to see this understanding that we need to do things fundamentally differently. Northern California is now understanding we have to tackle our affordable housing crisis and our homeless crisis. We have to do this energy transition in a way that isn't harming young people and the elderly.

But what's interesting to me is that people here in Arizona don't feel like they have the amount of threats that California has. And so many residents just want to believe that they can do things in a simpler, old school way that doesn't do this kind of progressive jiu-jitsu that they see happening on the West Coast. And I could see it going both ways. I could see Arizona being a more affordable, more resilient, and more inclusive place than California for decades to come, or I could see the Sun Belt becoming the Rust Belt of the 21st century.

### Terry Schwarz, Ohio

**Q: To start off, would you talk a little bit about the Cleveland Urban Design Collaborative (CUDC) and how that work relates to climate change?**

The CUDC is the outreach division for the College of Architecture at Kent State University. We simultaneously run a non-profit urban design practice and also have a research agenda. The climate resilience work has fallen at that overlap spot between the two. We've worked on a variety of research projects related to population loss and urban vacancy, around infrastructure networks and reconfiguring them in response to demographic changes.

Primarily, the climate resilience work is linked to vacant land and the reconfiguration of cities that have lost a lot of population. There's tremendous flexibility for cities to reinvent themselves along new patterns of development, based on the surplus real estate within municipal boundaries, especially, when that real estate is in a land bank and therefore publicly controlled.

We specifically worked on a project around climate resilience in four Cleveland neighborhoods, looking at a variety of issues related to disaster preparedness and community capacity. If we have more than 30,000 vacant lots within the City of Cleveland, are there ways that we can use that real estate to buffer people from the adverse impacts of climate variability and change?

**Q: How do you see the reuse of vacant land happening at multiple scales, to begin to build resilience in places like Cleveland?**

Yeah, well, quite frankly, it's been a pretty big challenge here because what we know about vacant land, whether we're looking at an outcome of traditional development or food production or storm water capture or urban forestry, is that bigger sites are more useful than scattered sites. But vacant land doesn't emerge in nice big chunks, it's scattered all over. So, there's the most potential for action at the partial scale.

And so the Re-imagining a More Sustainable Cleveland vision has always been a decision-making framework, to help guide choices about where to build in a traditional sense, where to do infill development and new construction, and where land should remain as various kinds of green space—whether that's reforestation, or wetlands, or other rainwater-absorbing landscapes. What are all the ways that vacant land can increase the resiliency of the city? And how do you do that as not just one big initiative but as dozens, hundreds, maybe even thousands of actions unfolding over a period of years?

I think it's not a one and done deal. Originally, in the Re-imagining pilot projects, people were given $10,000–$20,000 to create a green space project. And that generated excitement and attention until people realized that having a vacant land greening project is like having a child.

You may have the resources at the beginning, but the care and tending of that space over time is a lot to ask of communities. It represents this huge shift of the responsibility for public space maintenance and management from the municipality to the residents.

And the idea that you could make one investment and expect it to last in perpetuity is, I think, misguided. I think that maybe what could have happened, and maybe what still could happen, would be that the city would recognize that it's an investment that you have to make on an on-going basis.

Maybe it's both the scale of the intervention and releasing resources at regularly scheduled intervals. That way, when things start to become less useful—when the community garden is overgrown, when the urban farm is abandoned by a farmer who's moved out of town—there's a mechanism for additional resources and additional partners to step in and help.

**Q: Each of our disciplines brings a slightly different perspective to the table, each offers a piece of the solution. But how do we get people to work together, to have these larger conversations across disciplines, and how do we sustain those working relationships in the long-term?**

It's a challenge. From the sewer district's perspective, for instance, when they're thinking about their response to climate resilience, they need to build a pipe big enough so that if it rains a lot, these pipes can prevent flooding. They're focused on hazard mitigation, but that does nothing for social cohesion or energy reduction. It takes energy to move water through big pipes, as opposed to allowing gravity to infiltrate on vacant lots, but they're not calculating that kind of energy reduction.

It's recognizing that each of these agencies or each of these disciplines not only has a specialization, but also, particularly for public agencies, they must answer to their constituency. People are already paying a lot of money for the sewer district to do the one thing that they're supposed to be doing: keeping sewage out of Lake Erie. Whenever the sewer district tries to do other things to promote environmental education or create community amenities, they get all kinds of pushback—why are you spending taxpayers' money on these things that are not your job to do?

**Q: It seems like a lot of the climate resilience work in Cleveland has been, in some ways, a replacement for what city planning may have been in the past. How do you think planning for these issues changes when it's funded by a foundation as opposed to funded from tax dollars?**

I've never really thought about that. I think maybe from the perspective of outcomes, foundations like to fund projects that become models that can be replicated. But then they very rarely provide resources to actually replicate those models because they like to fund the innovation rather than the replication.

At the municipal level for projects delivering on a civic good, if you can demonstrate that there's a return on the investment, cities could continue to invest on an on-going basis, as opposed to sporadic philanthropic investment.

**Q: Oftentimes I hear people saying that climate change is not going to be that bad for cities on the Great Lakes, so maybe we don't need to do as much about it. Even from an economic development perspective, people talk about how cities like Cleveland and Buffalo are going to be a climate refuge. How do you feel about that?**

Conflicted. I think part of it is people being in denial, or just not really understanding that the changes are not only on the horizon, but are already happening. I just heard on the news this morning that Geneva on the Lake, a community just east of Cleveland, has lost 35 feet of land in a matter of weeks through lakefront erosion.

To pretend that nothing's happening here is not right. Also, the idea that the salvation of Great Lakes cities is going to come because of apocalypse elsewhere around the country and the world is not the best way to look to the future. If we're not careful with our Great Lakes resources, they could disappear at any time.

## Dana Kochnower, New York

### Q: How did you get into resilience as a topic?

After working as a broadcast journalist for several years, I went back to grad school and studied marine conservation at Scripps Institution of Oceanography. While I was there, I was really interested in coastal resiliency.

During my master's program some of my research was on the use of nature-based features for coastal hazards. In addition, I had actually done some research on the National Flood Insurance Program. Those two areas together, when I was looking for a job, the New York City Mayor's Office of Resiliency was actually looking for somebody to help communicate about the new flood maps that the city was getting at that time. And so, my skill sets and my areas of interest came together in that.

And since I've been here, so it's five years now, I've really worked on the National Flood Insurance Program. That portfolio covers flood risk awareness, flood insurance, outreach, education, and policy. It also covers mitigation at the building scale. And when I say mitigation in terms of flood, I'm talking about what kinds of work and changes people can do to their homes and buildings to make them more flood resilient.

### Q: How are buildings in New York City impacted by climate change?

One of the most important things to know about buildings in New York is how many we have. We have roughly a million buildings in the city. We are a very, very densely built environment here, and we also have a lot of old buildings that are still standing and are projected to still be standing well into the future.

To think about climate hazards, and the building stock in New York City, is largely a retrofit challenge. So, when I'm talking about climate vulnerability, I'm really talking about the existing building stock that's standing. So, there's a mix of buildings, a very diverse mix of buildings from bungalows that are out in the outer boroughs, a single story wood frame home, to multifamily buildings in Manhattan with hundreds of units.

When increasing resiliency of existing structures, there are a lot of challenges, primarily due to the density of the built environment. There are multifamily buildings, for instance, that are nearly impossible to elevate physically. But there is the economic constraints of losing usable space, which because space is at a premium here, it's hard to think about giving up any living space in order to elevate a home or lose a garden-level space that would be below the base flood elevation.

If you look at the history, a lot of our waterfront neighborhoods were at one point industrial and less desirable areas. And so, that's where this naturally occurring affordable housing was developed, why we have lower-income neighborhoods that are in the floodplain.

And then in other areas like the Rockaways, Staten Island, around Jamaica Bay, you have what were once vacation communities with summer homes. Over time, they were winterized and people stayed full time.

At the time of Hurricane Sandy the city's flood insurance rate maps (FIRMs) were being updated by the Federal Emergency Management Agency (FEMA). Right after the storm, FEMA issued preliminary FIRMs. The City of New York proactively adopted those preliminary maps for the building code. So, anything that was rebuilt after Sandy should be built to the base flood elevation plus 1–2 feet of freeboard above that, what is called the design flood elevation.

In addition, the City issued climate resilience design guidelines which are currently voluntary, but apply to all city-owned and city-funded projects. They incorporate the projections from the New York City Panel on Climate Change and create a methodology for designers to use based on projected asset life and potential risk.

**Q: Given its size, it seems that New York City is its own unique animal. It seems like other parts of New York State are always looking to the City to learn what needs to be done.**

We are always learning from how other cities and other places are doing things. So, I don't think that we think we have all the answers, nor do I think that we have all the capacity that we need.

We still are grappling with the same challenges, which is understanding what the future landscape holds across multiple climate hazards, understanding how all of those are going to interact with the existing infrastructure, and built environment that we have here, plus our population.

Sea level rise isn't happening by itself, sea level rise is happening in conjunction with increased precipitation and more varied precipitation, and sea level rise is happening with aging infrastructure as well. We need a lot of outside insight and help because this is new for everybody.

The issue that we're discussing is this building's retrofit question; we've been struggling with this, because it's really big. I think, in some ways, New York as an older, fully built out city is not necessarily in any sort of a better situation than someplace that's newly developing and growing. Because they can plan with the future in mind in a different way than we can, knowing that what we have is still going to be here decades into the future.

And not that there's no room for change, but all of those changes have different consequences in a place that's already built out, and there are already people living in those areas.

Q: What about extreme heat as an issue?

For extreme heat, there's both the design of the inside and the outside of buildings, but it ultimately comes down to people.

The City took a number of social factors and created a heat vulnerability index. It actually looks at different neighborhoods across the city, where different demographic and social factors lead to a higher incidence of heat-related mortality.

It also comes into play with access to air conditioning, and places where there is, again, a limitation in a way, due to economic factors, and the age of the buildings, along those lines.

And so, the City of New York has a program called Cool Neighborhoods, which has a number of different approaches to try and mitigate the impacts of extreme heat. It includes everything from tree plantings, to coating the roof of buildings in white paint, to increasing access to cooling centers, and finally to increasing access to air conditioning.

Q: Do vulnerabilities between flooding and heat overlap?

So, with heat and flooding, there actually are very few areas where they overlap because the areas that are susceptible to coastal flooding have more sea breezes, and the highest heat areas are more inland. But when you start to bring in increased precipitation and inland flooding, then you do see more overlap.

For our coastal flooding neighborhoods, we do see a lot of overlap in vulnerability as lower-income areas. Also, there is public housing that's built in some of our coastal areas. And then on top of that, there's also senior housing. And so, we're definitely aware of all of those vulnerabilities.

Q: Is there any kind of takeaway you would really want to emphasize to someone who might be reading this interview in the future?

We've had such a focus on Sandy and the risk from big storm surges, but what we're learning more about is actually much more frequent, tidal flooding, which we're actually starting to hear about, is a shift from viewing the hazards as a future condition to a current condition.

We're really working to bring in some of the local knowledge of people living in these communities, to track what's happening there and help to validate some of the models. But we're also trying to do some qualitative data gathering, and understand what the lived experience is like.

That's what's going to help us not only plan for these particular communities, but almost looking at these locations as the canary in a coal mine, the communities that are going to experience this kind of flooding because this is related to sea level rise and low lying areas.

The other piece that we are constantly working on is how to do all of this work equitably. Really thinking about, what are the social factors and potential ramifications of any policy going forward. And the final piece is funding, which is just a challenge for everyone.

It's really, really hard, especially with resiliency. In the best case scenario, things continue to work. It's really hard to make an argument for resilience; it's like the argument for insurance, right? In the best case scenario, you're paying into insurance and you never use it.

### Kevin Bush, District of Columbia

**Q: How did you come to the issue of resilience? Can you share a little bit of your superhero origin story?**

Well, I was bitten by a radioactive bug. No. I was working for the U.S. Department of Housing and Urban Development (HUD) and was briefly detailed over to the White House Council on Environmental Quality to work with all the departments and agencies to develop their first climate adaptation plans. That is, everybody from the Department of Defense (DOD) to the Environmental Protection Agency (EPA) to the Department of Health and Human Services (HHS), you name it.

Around that same time, Hurricane Sandy hit and President Obama got reelected. And he gave an interview where he said that climate change was one of his top three priorities. He actually hadn't really said that before. Suddenly, we were writing all sorts of memos, including one to create a Hurricane Sandy Rebuilding Task Force, to focus on some of the longer-term things, and to provide some executive level coordination for the recovery, because it was such a large scale.

When the President issued the executive order, I was asked to go over to the Sandy task force, where I had a great DC job title of "special projects lead." Within that capacity, I worked with Henk Ovink to create Rebuild By Design, and with the National Security Council to get the first ever federal flood risk reduction standard.

When the task force ended, I went back and formed HUD's first team devoted to climate policy, infrastructure finance, and community policy, more broadly. When DC was accepted to the 100 Resilient Cities Network, I ended up moving to DC government to be the chief resilience officer (CRO).

**Q: So, how did the 100 Resilient Cities Network come about and what is that working on?**

The Rockefeller Foundation launched this initiative in response to three big changes that were going on, as they saw it. One, the world's becoming rapidly urbanized. Two, the world is becoming more globalized and more interdependent than ever before. And three, climate change is acting as a kind of threat multiplier and poses existential threats to many cities around the world. The effort focused, initially, on 100 cities, to fund the creation of a CRO position, and to support the city in developing their first resilience strategies.

**Q: What does a CRO do? What is your day-to-day like, and how do you guide a city towards becoming more climate resilient?**

Well, the first two years were really focused on figuring out what resilience meant to DC and coming up with a plan. A metaphor that I often use to describe resilience is kind of the immune system of a city. So, a lot of that was stakeholder engagement, working across disciplines. We went around and met with a whole bunch of civic leaders, and we asked very open-ended questions, just trying to figure out where our immune system was weak and where it was strong.

We used the results of that conversation to come up with these five, big, almost unanswerable questions, and then we organized interdisciplinary groups around those questions. Those groups spent an entire summer doing best practice surveys, literature reviews. We even had a group that biked up and down the Anacostia River and mapped public access points.

We brought all those groups back together at the end of the process and said, "What did you learn and where do you think there's an opportunity to build resilience?" All of that information went into a kind of briefing document that we put in front of the Mayor's Resilience Cabinet and the Commission on Climate Change and Resiliency.

We focused on being resilient to three main drivers of change: climate change, economic and population growth, and technological change, and that's ultimately how we structured the strategy. Each initiative, in theory, addresses multiple shocks: flooding, economic downturn, a stressed housing market, stressed transportation systems, those sorts of things. There's an alluvial diagram in the front that attempts to illustrate the complexity.

When we released the resilience strategy, it was right around the same time that the Rockefeller Foundation decided to end the 100 Resilient Cities Program, and I lost a lot of the day-to-day support that I had. We made a decision to take a kind of high-level approach to implementation. My boss controlled the budgets and the performance management systems for the entire district. He issued a memo to all of the deputy mayors and said,

Thou shalt implement this strategy through your agencies. And if you don't have money to do something that you're assigned, then ask for it. And make sure that when you're reporting on your agency's performance, you are including the activities that are outlined for you in the strategy.

And that actually worked better than I would have thought. It kind of grew legs of its own, in a way. And now, we're formulating the budget for the next fiscal year, and saying, "This budget request that this agency made will allow us to implement this initiative." We're not losing sight of the strategy.

**Q: DC is sort of a unique animal in a lot of ways, because it's not a city and it's not really a state, and there's a huge federal presence. What are some of the major challenges that you see?**

I think one of the biggest resilience challenges for the district is that we're on a delta. Both of the rivers in DC are tidally influenced, and are experiencing some of the fastest rates of sea level rise along the East Coast. That's just riverine and coastal flooding, but then we've also got interior rainfall type flooding.

On the growth side, we're currently 700,000 people in 68 square miles, with a pretty severe height restriction. Our official state population projection is a million people by 2045. And if you look at population growth mapped next to housing start projections, there's a large gap now, and that gap will get even wider in the future.

If you take the pressure of growth and the pressure of rising sea levels, those two things are directly in conflict. That's why, right in the front of the strategy, we've got a focus area, which is kind of like a mega initiative, on the idea of creating resilient riverfront communities.

Most of the important cultural assets in DC are federal, so we would never have the authority to move the National Monument, for instance. But a lot of the stuff downtown in the federal triangle area is actually protected by a flood wall—if you look at the national mall, it is actually partially a levee. We have an enclosure that's operated by the National Park service. If there's going to be really bad flooding, they will block up 17th street and that completes the levee. That predates me, but it was a project between the city and the federal government.

**Q: If you were giving advice to other cities or other states, how would you encourage them to move on some of these issues?**

I think it depends on the size of the city. Not every city has the resources of New York or DC. Even before the 100 Resilient Cities support, we used local money to downscale climate projections and develop a climate adaptation plan, Climate Ready DC. New York City's got the New York City panel on climate change.

For smaller cities, I think you do have a challenge of resources and almost a need to partner up and work together. Because a lot of the solutions can be fairly replicable, particularly if the cities are in the same state.

One of the best resources is the Georgetown Climate Center—State and Local Adaptation Plans. I like it because it's very practical. Here are some model ordinances, some best practices and examples for projects, actual legal arrangements, and that sort of thing.

For a small city that has one planner on staff, I would not advise wasting money on climate projections. I think that a consulting contract could be useful, though, for outlining 20 things that the city could do to tweak their building codes, their development review process, and their design guidelines for road construction projects. Those sorts of things add a climate kind of overlay to the day-to-day.

**Q: How do you get all of these individual strategies to work together across scales, in a way that's really powerful for the city?**

I would say there has been a tendency to pigeonhole climate change into one department or another. It's like, "Oh, climate, that's a thing that environmentalist care about, so I'm going to put it in my department of energy and environment." I think governments, at all scales, should resist that.

Climate change is a threat multiplier. It affects other things that we're already concerned about. The Health Department is already concerned about childhood asthma. The Department of Public Works is already concerned about flooding. The Department of Human Services is already concerned about heat-related deaths and exposure.

I think the offices of sustainability, offices of resilience, and offices of climate change should ultimately, at some point, be a thing of the past. If they do exist, it should only be an initial task force to figure out what to do.

I think it's a matter of how do you create the executive level, multi-agency effort to get everybody on the right track with respect to incorporating climate into their mission, into their programs, and into their operations. Once you've done that, then it should just be part of the way we do things.

## Jodi Smits Anderson, New York

**Q: How do you incorporate issues of sustainability and resilience into your work at the Dormitory Authority of the State of New York (DASNY)?**

A big change that was made really early is we set a sustainability policy for construction. Every project that could use the Leadership in Energy and Environmental Design (LEED) rating system, for example, a new building or a significant renovation, used that system to inform the project's development. If it was a small project like a reroofing or a bathroom renovation, you still had to define specific sustainable goals.

But setting a policy does not change everybody; you can't flip a switch. So it's been reminders, education. We have a lot of opportunities to get all of our staff to understand not only how sustainability affects our projects—how the people we serve need us to pay attention to the sustainability and resilience of those projects—but also how their own personal carbon footprint relates to that, as well.

**Q: How has the definition of sustainability or the approach changed to also include things like resilience?**

Yeah, that's actually a great question. Really. I mean, sustainability is the world's most overused word right now. And actually, there is no really good word to use. You can't say "sustainability." People misinterpret it left, right, and center. You can't use "green" because it sounds too cute. You can't use "resilience" because then everyone immediately thinks walls to keep the sea back, which isn't exactly what resilience is either.

So we get stuck in all of this terminology. And I think one of the challenges has been to help people remember that sustainability is not limited to one meaning—it has so many different parts and pieces that need to tie in.

It's been evidenced most effectively in the building community, recently, because of the attention on health in the building space. Talking about the comfort, productivity, and well-being of the people in the space, that's changed the relationship to sustainability, we can broaden the discussion and bring more people into these conversations.

We're also getting much more involved in embodied carbon and biogenic carbon. If we start to tabulate the embodied carbon loss because of climate situations, whether they're purely climate change related or whether they're exacerbated by climate change, we should be able to assess some understanding of order of magnitude, and where that carbon loss also has an impact on our climate.

So resilience is not just about defending against climate change, but also making sure that we're not throwing away carbon and increasing the problems.

**Q: Was Hurricane Sandy a big driver in New York State to shift the conversation about sustainability?**

I think it was a big driver in New York State. We've been working with the Governor's Office of Storm Recovery for a couple of years. I think we're now seeing that our project types in the future will be more related to civil engineering, including green infrastructure and nature-based systems along the edge for protection.

And I don't think that we've embraced that thoroughly enough at this point. When you build a green infrastructure installation, it doesn't just affect the geopolitical boundary of that community. It actually affects the rainwater catchment for the aquifer.

So we need to start talking about how we're affecting nature-based systems in addition to community-based boundaries.

**Q: How has resilience shifted the discussion from a focus on heating, ventilation, and air conditioning (HVAC) systems and the energy systems in buildings, to thinking about the role of the structure, building envelope, and so forth?**

One of the problems with just swapping out existing systems for more efficient systems, without tightening the building envelope or improving its thermal performance, is that you're sizing something bigger than it needs to be. If you have invested in that building envelope, the part of the building that's going to be there for 50–100 years, you've invested in the longest lived system.

If you're investing in mechanical and electrical systems, you're investing money in something that you're going to have to replace in a 30-year timeframe. The envelope is really where the money has the greatest impact for the longest time—that's a big shift in our understanding. It's also the most difficult thing to do, especially with the wonderful, old building stock that we have.

Then the other thing we haven't done, we haven't even come close, is to understand how people affect the carbon emissions and energy efficiency of a building. We honestly think that people are just going to use the building the way we expect, that they're always going to use it the same way, and that they're never going to override systems or screw anything up.

**Q: There's a great article, by Kathryn B. Janda, called "Buildings Don't Use Energy, People Do." It talks about how people's habits and societal expectations are a big part of the functionality and operation of a building, yet, these are often overlooked when planning for energy efficiency.**

Yeah. Another thing that I instigated very early on during my time at DASNY was to change the set points, because we were at 73 degrees all the time—summer, winter. We work in a 180,000 square foot, 6 story office building that was built in 1997—it's a great building and we've tightened it up over the years.

Anyways, that was it. The set point was 73. So we said, "Yeah, mother nature doesn't work like that, and people don't work like that either. Maybe the building needs to be able to ebb and flow a little bit." And so we changed the set point to float between 78 degrees in summer and 68 degrees in winter.

And, very important, at the same time we changed our dress code. In the summer, people could wear summer dresses, business casual short sleeves, and didn't have to wear three piece suits and ties. And then in the winter you could wear the sweater that your grandmother knitted for you. That gave people responsibility for their own comfort, within the parameters of the building comfort set point. And it really made our building much more efficient.

Although, just to make the story even a little more illustrative of how people think. We changed all the set points and had that change for two weeks. We didn't announce anything. No complaints at all. No issues. And then we announced the change and announced the dress code change, and for the next month we were dealing with complaints.

**Q: Obviously you're working at the state level and you're working with a large state agency, but for architects or designers who might not have that same control when they're working with a client, what advice would you give?**

Actually, right now at DASNY, we're realizing that not only do we know how important zero net energy and resilience are, but we know some of the skills and tools and guidance documents that we need to be employing. And we deal with many consultants and many contractors. So wouldn't it be wonderful if DASNY said,

> We see that these things are going to become important over the next couple of years, and if you have these skills, you should be telling us you have these skills, and if you don't have these skills, you should be developing these skills.

And in fact, we're working on a position paper with the American Institute of Architects (AIA) and with the American Council of Engineering Companies (or ACEC) to do just that. To list the five to eight things that we know are going to be important to the industry, now and for the next decade.

But it's more than just telling people that we know these things are important. If we have the skillset, we need to develop the training to teach firms how to do post-occupancy evaluations or do building envelope commissioning. How to have conversations with them in a way that we can inform, not only this project, but the next one.

**Q: Are there any other thoughts or topics that we haven't touched on yet that you think are really important takeaways from this conversation?**

What I've been thinking about a lot lately is how much nature knows that we have been totally ignorant of. And I think the building industry has picked up on a lot of it.

Biomimicry is about using the principles of nature and developing new products and new services based on what nature already knows, such as Velcro learning from burrs, wind turbine blades learning from whales' tales, and all that other good stuff. Then biophilia is recognizing our connection to nature and how it heals us. Nature knows about diversity and redundancy and resilience. And nature knows about the value of beauty and team building and systems thinking.

If we can reconnect to nature and how nature serves us, while we're serving it, and if we can learn from nature, I think sustainability and resilience will end up being core principles by accident.

## Allison Anderson, Mississippi

**Q: From watching your presentations, I know that you have a great superhero origin story. Would you be willing to share that?**

Yeah, sure. When I was in undergraduate school at the University of Southern California, our education was really built around designing with climate.

We had, at that time, some amazing instructors. We had Pierre Koenig, who was one of the original Case Study House designers, and he was working in the wind tunnel in the basement. No one ever saw him.

We had Ralph Knowles, who dealt with solar envelopes, who had a studio that was really concerned with the equity of solar access for everybody in dense urban environments.

And we had Marc Schiller, who was a fantastic early adopter of environmental design principles. He taught our mechanical and electrical systems classes, but he taught us much more than that as well. So we had an early inculcation in environmental design principles.

John (Anderson) is my partner in life and work, and we both were in school together, and we both understood the importance of sustainability. We both went off and worked for four years, and then went back to grad school at the University of Texas in Austin.

At Texas, we were in the Charles Moore program, which was very, very different: playful aesthetics and philosophical tenets. But we were really looking at the why: why we build things the way we do. And so, matching those two was a great introduction into sustainability.

Around 2000, we both started looking at the U.S. Green Building Council LEED principles, studying them, and adopting them. And John and I both took the LEED exam in 2002, which was pretty early on. It ended up that I was the first LEED-accredited professional in Mississippi, and he was the first in Louisiana, because we were working in different states at that time. And that was really important as a differentiator, for us to be a vanguard of sustainability.

And around that time, we built our house. It was finished in July of 2005. And five weeks later, Hurricane Katrina came along.

Every other house was demolished, erased, down to the slab, and our house was still standing. And so of course, it brought a lot of attention. "Why is the architect's house still standing?"

And there were really three reasons. First, we built it to code. Second, we had built it with some additional interior shear walls that went from the ground floor up to the roof. And then the third reason was we had a grass roof, and that grass roof obviously required some pretty stout structure underneath it. And that whole thing acted as an anchor for the rest of the house.

And then there was actually a fourth reason, and it's the weirdest thing. But the fourth reason was we had this chain-link fence on the water side of the house, and there were some spindly little trees, trash trees, little things, maybe 3–4-inch diameter trunks, and those things stopped an entire house from crashing into our home. And so we understood that we did the right things as architects, but we also had the advantage of these little landscaping elements that basically stopped the whole house from getting submarined.

So that was our watershed moment. We understood that sustainability had a relationship to resilience.

Now we had another project that had just been completed; the same code, the same kind of attention to detail, the same attention to sustainability, but much closer to the water. It was completely erased.

We really started to think that we can't call ourselves sustainable if our building only lasted five weeks. That's not sustainable. We really started looking at what are the principles of resilience and how can we make buildings that last much longer. We started looking at how service life and materials play a role, and that was the start of our interest in resilience.

**Q: And you built off of that work, doing a lot of storm shelters after Katrina?**

We did, yes. Those were some of our first projects. And again, nobody had done a really good community shelter, and so we had to do a lot of research to figure out how we would direct wind over and around the buildings. All of the shelters were located well outside the 500-year floodplain, and also well outside of the Katrina surge limits, which basically covered the bottom third of our county. So we looked at different opportunities and different wall assemblies and ended up building nine different shelters, using four different wall types. One is masonry, one is precast, one is tilt-up, and one is cast-in-place concrete.

**Q: And so you used your own personal experience of what happened with your house to really begin to inform your practice?**

Absolutely, there were just a lot of crazy ideas that happened after Hurricane Katrina. A lot of people said, "Well, we can only build round houses because only round houses can survive the storms." There was this sort of crazy thinking. And, "we can only build houses that are 20 feet off the ground because those are the only ones that survived the storm." But really, I think there's no hard and fast rule, you have to really study the vulnerability of a specific site and find the best solution. There's no magic design that works everywhere.

**Q: Absolutely. So now that we're more than 15 years after Hurricane Katrina, there's been a lot of work on these issues in Mississippi and Louisiana. How do you see things changing to respond to climate change?**

Well, it's very interesting. It's all over the map, quite honestly. You see some people who raced to rebuild exactly what they had before, so that they could get it in before the FEMA and FIRM changed. And those people are now in danger of paying a much higher premium for their insurance.

Then you have the people on the other end who are like, "Well, I'm going to have to fortify this building so that it never fails, and I'm going to build a concrete house." Between that is a whole spectrum of individuals, many of whom did the smart thing and built back smaller footprints and built back with greater elevation to manage the unknown FIRM changes and sea level rise.

Later, after Hurricane Sandy, when we were on Staten Island, I will never forget this man standing on his porch. He was gutting the house, and he just looked at us with tears in his eyes. He was like,

> What am I going to do? I own this lot. I own this house. I've got enough here that I don't want to lift it up because that's going to cost me money. But if I lift it up, I'm not going to have room on the lot to build a long enough stair to get upstairs. And if I don't, what are my insurance costs going to be in the future?

And we just don't have good answers for that.

**Q: What kind of information do you currently use in your design process to support the work that you do?**

One of the things we always do is map the hazards. That's our first step. The FIRM map is the first stop, but it's not always the last stop. We look at the National Oceanic and Atmospheric Administration's (or NOAA) Sea Level Rise Viewer, and we try to guide our clients to an informed science-based decision. "Hey, this is what they're saying right now. It's 36 inches by 2050. It's four to five to six feet by 2100." You can look at the American Society of Civil Engineers (ASCE) 7 Hazard Tool. That's another one we look at. And of course the International Building Code (IBC) has wind regions in it. Those are our first four that we look at on every project.

**Q: And do you see your peers really taking this on as an issue or do you still feel you're out in front and the vanguard on some of these issues?**

Unfortunately, I still feel like we're a bit unconventional in our attention to this matter. Anybody on the coast has to look at the FIRM maps. I think everybody looks at the IBC wind regions.

But I think that most of the decisions about resilience are still very much client-informed, client-led decisions. They're not architect-led decisions. And I feel like we need to be leading these discussions. Obviously, we don't make the decision about service life, about features that might improve performance, but there are places where we can certainly, and need to, lead the discussion.

### Matthew Elley and Erin Hatcher, Washington and Illinois

**Q: So can you just tell me a little bit about each of your own backgrounds and how you came to work with AMLI Residential, or how you became interested in sustainability and resilience as a topic?**

MATT: Sure. My undergrad was in construction management, and then I went back to school for real estate development and finance. I read *Collapse* by Jared Diamond—that got me turned on to the topic—and then I got LEED accredited. And now I'm on AMLI's Sustainability Committee.

ERIN: I actually studied interior design and decided to pursue a LEED AP. After working in consulting for a while, I joined AMLI and focused mostly on new construction and building certifications. My position has grown, as AMLI's needs have grown, to reflect the evolving topics within sustainability and resilience.

**Q: Let's talk about AMLI Residential and how the company began engaging on issues of resilience and climate change in buildings.**

MATT: AMLI Residential is an apartment owner, developer, and operator. We have 20,000 plus units across the country in nine different markets. We primarily develop mid-rise and some high-rise projects in the core areas of the cities that we invest in.

ERIN: We have officially been working on incorporating sustainability into our new developments and the management of our buildings since 2006. Initially, we just started with a focus on building certifications for new construction. We formally adopted LEED for new construction, and we also maintain our buildings to those same standards for the ownership period, which is typically 10–12 years.

We've now moved into a more data-driven focus on sustainability. We're collecting utility bills to understand and report on building performance, specifically around energy, water, waste and greenhouse gas emissions.

In the past three years, we've begun to focus on resilience. Thinking ahead to the future, what should we be doing to prepare for some of the knowns and unknowns that exist across our portfolio, and specific to each of those markets?

As VP of Sustainability, I also work on the investor reporting piece of this, which has significantly grown in the past four years.

**Q: How has your company started to take into account some of the investor reporting, or things like that related to risk and resilience?**

*ERIN*: I think the first initiative was investing in an ESG (environmental, social, and governance) reporting platform that tracks all of this data that we collect about our properties. In some cases, we can't get the whole building's data because the utilities might be directly contracted with our residents. So, if there's not a cooperative effort, we do have gaps in the data. But we probably get, I'd guess, around 70% of our energy data, and almost all of our water and waste data. All of that information that we gather funnels through AMLI, and then eventually through our investor reporting.

**Q: You mentioned some of the different risks or perhaps threats to some of your buildings. Could you outline what some of those might be, especially as they relate to climate change?**

*ERIN*: We're thinking ahead about transitional risks, possible resource strain or carbon taxes, even the price of utilities going up.

And then, of course, there's the actual physical risks associated with some of our assets that may be in climates that are experiencing more flooding or more storms. Temperature is also something that we're thinking about. Are the systems in our buildings going to be able to accommodate more 90 degree days in places where maybe we didn't initially anticipate that?

So we are working with our investors to figure out what are the right tools to be able to understand that.

**Q: You said that AMLI primarily holds buildings for between 10 and 12 years, right? So, how does that time horizon affect how you look at something like climate-related risk?**

*MATT*: I mean, we're a long-term holder. Ten to twelve years has been our typical hold, but we have even identified assets, now, that we have no plans to sell—"forever assets," we would call them. It's a similar kind of mindset to REIT, a real estate investment trust. And because we have this long-term hold, making the right decisions matters a lot more to us.

*ERIN*: I think the direction we'll probably move with this is to think about it from a portfolio level. Depending on how long we intend to keep an asset and depending on the location of our existing assets, we may be willing to take on a little bit more risk to pursue certain opportunities, knowing that we're not going to have an entire portfolio that is at risk. I think that is probably something that's going to continue to weigh into decision-making in the future.

**Q: Do you find that apathy or even hostility to talking about climate change is a common attitude in the development community?**

*MATT*: Well, Seattle is a progressive city, so I would say, most people here do not have that attitude. But there are people within the community that are deniers, and I think attempting to bridge the gap between perspectives is important. I try to use the framework of ecological overshoot which encompasses the climate change issue.

*ERIN*: And I think there is hesitation on moving ahead and doing something different from what's been done in the past, because it could be viewed as a poor investment if it doesn't get utilized. On the other hand, if you have this catastrophic event, you may have missed an opportunity to save lives, or save the building a lot of money, or whatever the case is. And I think long-term investors are looking at this very differently than short-term merchant builders, who are only planning to hold properties for three to five years.

**Q: What kind of tools would really help to move that conversation forward? Would having better climate models or better information help, or is this more of a political discussion in some ways?**

*ERIN*: We have used quite a bit of information from the NOAA. I think as we're learning more, we're finding more and more resources out there, and also trying to leverage predictive analytics.

But I think that a lot of the information that we need is taking time to collect. From a risk management standpoint, we're tracking the change in insurance costs, which can change very quickly.

For cities that need new or improved infrastructure to handle more frequent hurricanes or flooding, what are the costs? How do these things get funded? Does it become a real estate tax? That could help inform decisions.

But we need more time. Right now, we're building a lot faster than this information can be produced. And I think it's also taking some time for the climate modeling projections to be absorbed and accepted.

*MATT*: When I think about trying to convince a climate denier it does become political, and I think to be effective it requires reframing the discussion at some level. Instead of just discussing the climate I also include energy conservation and utility cost savings as the reasons to care as that should resonate with everyone. Hydrocarbons are a non-renewable and finite resource, and we have a long way to go to before we can run our society completely on the alternatives that exist.

**Q: Some people that we've talked to have started working with companies that are forecasting climate change and some of these risks to portfolios. Is that something that's common in your field, or is that something that's still emerging?**

ERIN: This is a maturing industry with interest, demand, and emerging leaders. Science-backed predictive analytics is extremely important for making informed decisions related to climate change risks.

We have lot of internal discussions about sustainability benchmarking and sustainability reporting, and also resilience. Investors certainly take this seriously and put pressure on us to figure out how to do sustainability in a way that still makes sense—both short-term and long-term.

**Q: Are there other things that someone reading this book should understand about the multifamily sector or investments related to climate change?**

ERIN: When we're talking about sustainability and multifamily, there are things that we directly associate with climate change. Like I mentioned, we're tracking our utility usage, trying to reduce it, trying to build smarter.

But looking beyond that, we can also start to figure out strategies that incorporate best practices for public health, for the health and wellness of our residents. And working in multifamily, we're building people's homes—it's very personal. It's a great opportunity to engage with our residents on these topics.

We certainly invest a lot more time than some of our direct competitors in understanding basics with sustainability. We teach our staff about the green features in our properties. We take the time to step them through why we're doing this, why it's important, and then how to talk to residents about it.

We educate a lot of people, and even if they move on to other organizations, we're hopeful that they're transferring some of that information and spreading the word. Because it's not typically something that's well-supported by industry groups, at least not yet.

You can build a really great building, but it can all quickly be undone if there's not good information share and education.

## Janice Barnes, New York

**Q: You have a lot of experience with organizational leadership. How has that influenced your work on resilience?**

My PhD work (at the University of Michigan) was in organizational behavior through the School of Business, and also Environment and Behavior through the College of Architecture. And that gave me a way of looking at how organizational structures—behaviors of leaders and team members—and strategy need to come together.

There's a whole design problem linking the way organizational strategy meets design strategy. How do you get whatever the organization is to be self-reflective and aware of its decision-making compared to its strategy? And how do those relate to what you're trying to get the physical environment to achieve?

Anyway, that work and that practice, that way of thinking, were very directly transferable to the question around climate adaptation planning. It helped in my work at Perkins and Will, when I was leading the firm-wide strategy group, and when I moved from that role to leading a resilience effort.

We recognize that the firm (Perkins and Will) holds a particularly important role in the industry, helping to model doing the right thing, to try to get others in the industry to follow and do the right thing.

So, we set up the resilience lab to make sure that the projects that Perkins and Will was touching had climate adaptation, climate awareness, and vulnerability awareness integrated into them.

**Q: One of the major challenges with climate change is that it's so politicized and divisive. It has become difficult to have any kind of reasonable discussion about it.**

Oh, that's absolutely true. I grew up in rural Appalachia, where in the 1980s, Al Gore came, I guess as a senator, and he made a commitment in the community that I'm from. That commitment tied to a paper company that was dumping dioxin into a river. Many of the families who live along that river have lost family members to cancer because of dioxin-contaminated well water from a shared aquifer.

The ask was to get this paper company to stop doing that, and he was supposed to talk to the community, talk to the leader of the paper company, and make this happen. Made the commitment to do that.

So apparently, something changed, and instead of meeting with the community, he bailed and he went to meet with the paper company. Never met with the community and then eased off the restrictions.

So I was talking to a local farmer, who believes in climate change and, in his jovial way, is trying to convince other farmers to pay attention to this, to think more broadly in this small community.

And I asked him, "What do you think it's going to take to get more folks here to listen or to be active in this?" And he said, "We need a Republican to say that," and started telling me the story of Al Gore and that river contamination. He said people are still angry from the 1980s.

So if you have that kind of situation, where you've got multigenerational anger—and that river is still contaminated, by the way, you still cannot fish in it and you still have to worry about your water, nearly 40 years later—we have a problem. We have a problem because we have a name attached to it, and we also have a violation of trust. It's not a need for more data. It's a need to acknowledge this other challenge.

**Q: What are some of the different tools or strategies that you've seen people applying in projects to begin to adapt to climate change?**

The tools or strategies? I think that certainly what the National Environmental Modeling and Analysis Center (NEMAC) put out, the U.S. Climate Resilience toolkit is a great touchstone resource. I think that the downscaled climate models that some municipalities have invested in are helpful.

Katharine Hayhoe did the downscaling for the work we did with Climate Ready DC. Having the downscaled work is almost like a psychological support. A security that says, "This is mine. This is my climate," as opposed to a more generalized tool like the U.S. Climate Toolkit.

I think that the modeling that we're seeing coming out of NASA is helpful—the Landsat imagery that shows what the heat currently is, and then the modeling that suggests, given the impervious surface and the projected heat in the future—what that could become. Christian Braneon at NASA Goddard has been an excellent collaborator on that.

I think that modeling, in general, is so complex; it is way out of the wheelhouse of any of the architects I know. So having the right friend, the right "boundary buddy" to help you interpret it, is a key tool.

And if you stand on that data as guidance, it's a touchstone that the district leadership can point back to and say, "This is based on these data." And as the data are updated, you know what the ripple effect could be, because you've tied your system together that way.

I think from an architect's perspective, one of the things that's been incredibly helpful has been visualizing what these things mean, in terms of the human experience. That kind of visualization takes data that comes in a completely different format and makes it accessible to a broad audience. And I think breaking down that technical barrier is a key tool, as well.

The Collider. That's actually another tool. It's a business incubator (in Asheville, NC) that focuses on climate change and the technical capacities that are necessary, and then puts those together by leveraging some seed money, so that those businesses can grow and get their work done.

**Q: Could you talk a little bit about the work you've done with the Science to Action Community and how that's related?**

We have this gap between scientists and architects, and there needs to be more of a commitment in the design professional industries—planning, engineering, architectural design, urban design—to say, how do we stay on top of the latest in climate science? How do we strengthen relationships so that we can collaborate? And so that our design decision-making is standing on the best available science?

We've spent the last year and a half now, trying to get a commitment across the industries and the professional organizations, to request that their members make this kind of commitment to design principles for climate science integration. To say, "We're going to do this regardless of federal, state, county, city, or private sector policies, because it is the right thing to do."

In 2020, with the Resilience Building Coalition, a network of over 50 organizations focused on the built environment, we presented a webinar for members with an emphasis on integrating the best available climate science in investment decisions. To say,

Here's the big picture, if you don't know it. Here are the tools, if you haven't seen them. And if you need more tailored help, here's a whole range of climate scientists, the Science for Climate Action Network (or SCAN) team, who could work with you. If you want to do something specific to a region where you're working, here's how that might happen. And if you don't need customized help, here are the national resources that you can draw from, that have been vetted by those same scientists.

This was a pivotal effort to link those making investments with those who offer guidance on our climate future and to available resources that simply need to be part of their decision-making.

And while we originally started with, "Would you be willing to sign on to these principles and make this commitment publicly?" it may not be a formal adoption. Maybe there's a way to integrate the intent because the ownership is not relevant. The intent is what's relevant.

**Q: Since you've gone through a couple of different programs and have this diverse experience in the field, how do you think we should be training or thinking about educating the next generation?**

Yeah, I think that we all are seeing that what we went through and what we now need to go through don't really align. There are programs, like the one at the University of Pennsylvania, where they're training specifically on resilience building, but I don't see the National Architectural Accrediting Board (NAAB) having a requirement for that. If you were to look across all of the accrediting bodies for design, engineering, architecture, landscape architecture, where is climate change in the accreditation requirements?

And then when you look at architecture, where are the incentive programs? Are awards programs requiring a climate-ready solution? We need to line up the incentive programs to do the right thing, and then make sure that we grow our capacity.

Understanding policy adjustments is important, as well as understanding findings and funding. The National Parks Conservation Association came to me and said, "All this stuff that architects are doing is great, but you keep putting stuff out in New York City that has no ability to be executed because it conflicts with policy." And part of that is also trying to figure out how to get financing and funding savvy to the architecture population. To that end, we're collaborating with innovative finance experts so that design and financing are part of a co-production approach for any program. We're also encouraging institutions such as the AIA to deepen their members' understanding of benefit/cost analysis as well as funding and financing mechanisms. They're also trying to raise up important policy issues so that members better understand the implications.

## Rachel Minnery, Washington

**Q: How did you become interested in the issue of resilience and disasters? And why do you feel that this is such an important issue for our profession?**

I, like many college students, back in the day, was really idealistic about being able to help make a positive difference in the world. I was studying in Miami, just a few years after Hurricane Andrew had decimated the southeast portion of the state. That hurricane had a very strong influence on building codes. I think it also helped us realize that the disasters that impact highly populated areas can be life changing in many, many ways.

One of my mentors at Florida International University showed me that very simple design choices can have an incredibly positive impact, in terms of how these buildings are resilient to storm surge or winds or flooding.

And I was hooked, because I knew this wasn't something that was prescribed, it was something that required design innovation. It required awareness of problems that weren't part of our everyday consciousness.

After graduation, I worked as an architect for 15 years in Seattle, Washington. I focused on nonprofit design, and helped to launch Architects Without Borders Seattle, as well as taking a leadership role in the AIA Seattle Disaster Preparedness and Response Committee. I think we feel an obligation to these issues once we know the impact that we can have as design professionals.

**Q: Can you talk a little bit about what prompted your move to the AIA in DC and some of the work you've been doing for them for these last couple years?**

Well, it was a couple of things. So after Hurricane Katrina, AIA created a national committee because of the incredible outpouring of support and interest by architects. They drew architects from all over the country, so different geographic regions, different hazards, and I was on that first committee. We helped to create what is now the AIA's Disaster Assistance Program.

After Hurricane Sandy hit in New York, I was asked to come out to the New York region to help with Architecture for Humanity's Disaster Response Program. And I did that thinking it was going to be a sabbatical from my day job, but I found the work very fulfilling. Shortly after, the AIA job in DC opened up, which shifted my work from disaster assistance programs to creating a new strategy around resilience.

Right around that same time, the Rockefeller Foundation and the 100 Resilient Cities started taking off. Up to this time, most cities were doing their best to hide their crime statistics and not give way to panic about hazards.

But this new era brought about by the Rockefeller Foundation allowed us to say, "You know what? Instead of doing that, why don't we start talking about these issues, looking at them together as a community, and trading best practices and lessons learned, from city to city." And I really feel like that was a culture shift in the way that we collectively approach things like hazards, and crime, and civil unrest, and that sort of thing.

**Q: Why do you feel like architecture, or are architects particularly suited to some of these tasks?**

I really think it's taking the foundations of our role as architects and applying that to a new problem set. I think in school there's a strong focus on building-by-building design. But once you're in practice, you start to realize all of the connections that your building has to the natural environment, society, and the bigger goals of the city.

Architects often lead complex, multidisciplinary design teams—they coordinate with the public agencies and with the client and the user groups. And that kind of coordination of information, and the decision-making going toward prioritizing issues, that is an opportunity and a responsibility that I think architects are uniquely suited for.

And one of the reasons resilience is so appealing is that it really calls on you to do more coordination. To recognize that if you make any change to any component of a system, it will have a ripple effect on the rest of the system.

And architects, I think, intuitively have to make connections on their projects where they aren't readily apparent. And for that reason, I think they're very valuable translators, in a sense, in community discussions. Some of what I've learned being on staff at AIA is that our members really care deeply about their communities, and how they can best serve those communities.

But we need people at all different scales to help us see what isn't readily apparent. When we're talking about resilience and climate, there's a lot of policy work to be done. And these multidisciplinary groups of professionals need to work together on unified goals in order to overcome the status quo.

**Q: How is AIA seeking to address some of these issues related to resilience, or make those connections with different disciplines, or train architects?**

The hazards we're experiencing today are not our grandparents' hazard events. They are increasing in severity, scope, and frequency, and we need to do something different in order to make sure that people don't suffer in the future. So our program goal has been to cast a wide net, while establishing awareness of what these issues are.

AIA coauthored the 2014 building industry statement on resilience. And we are currently working with a coalition of 50 other building industry organizations, including ASHRAE (American Society of Heating, Refrigerating and Air-Conditioning Engineers), ULI (Urban Land Initiative), NAHB (National Association of Home Builders), and NIBS (National Institute of Building Sciences), to educate our members and get the word out. Our Resilience Certificate Series launched just over a year ago. So we're very eager to get folks to start taking the series and then applying it to their projects.

Something I've learned is that the number one preference of our members is to learn by example or through case studies. So we really look to higher education and research folks to help us do that.

Another piece is, right now, there are very few comprehensive building vulnerability and risk modeling tools that allow architects and their design teams to choose mitigation strategies. So part of our focus is to develop better tools that will provide complimentary guidance on not just the primary hazards, but also secondary hazards that are associated with common hazard events.

**Q: You said you were a very idealistic young college student. How can we encourage the current cohorts of idealistic college students to take up these issues?**

I think, as they say, people are either motivated by fear or hope. I feel like at least once a day I see something about a new disaster or the risks associated with climate change. If we're not paying attention to those things, I think that we risk being slightly irrelevant in the future, or having projects that are short lived. Liability issues are certainly something that's on the horizon.

And I think there's also a lot of innovation opportunity, particularly for the tech savvy architects, to find ways to better model some of these performance characteristics, or develop good case studies.

**Q: Are there other things we haven't talked about that you think we should be touching on as part of our discussion?**

There are a couple of things. First, especially when working with students, is to be very cautious when using data because it may be outdated and incomplete, and generally only reflects historic hazard information. So that's something we try to be really careful about, and why we're trying to get more design professionals involved.

And second, I really believe that we all need to advocate to value risk accurately. Right now flood risk is heavily subsidized. And I think if we pull the string on federal disaster recovery funding, we're going to see the house of cards collapse. So many of our financial and insurance institutions are relying on the federal government's ability to pay out disaster funds after each disaster. When the funding, financing, and insurance profile changes for buildings, it will certainly have an impact on design and construction. We want architects to be prepared for that change.

Lastly, I briefly touched on climate migrants or disaster refugees where people have been or will be displaced by disaster or climate relocations. There is a strong pull to keep what is familiar the same, but when risk outweighs reward change can be a path of hope. Architects can help people visualize a different future for their home, business, or community—one they get to choose rather than waiting for the next event to dictate the terms.

And, I totally agree, we don't want to make it sound opportunistic. But I recognize that a lot of these communities, particularly coastal communities, are living with a lot of fear. And if we don't give them something positive to look forward to, it's going to make that change a lot more difficult. That's where I see the opportunity for building design professionals to help.

# Index

Note: **Bold** page numbers refer to tables and *italic* page numbers refer to figures.

action: mechanisms of resilience **217**; mechanisms of sustainability **215**; mitigation 182–184; objects of resilience **216**; objects of sustainability **214**; shifting power to communities through 89–108; strategies for adaptation 184–185; subjects of resilience **215**; subjects of sustainability **214**
adaptation: climate change and environmental justice 112–113; climate change and equity 112–113; climate change and health 112–113; co-designed climate 54–56, *55*; cultivating culture of sustained adaptation in areas of risk 177–178; elevating 184; inland floodplain housing to changing climate 172–187; role of planning 185; strategies for 184–185
adaptive capacity: building through inclusive design 131–133; built environment 131–133; education and communication 133–137; inclusive design and resilience 129–131; policy 135–137
adaptive cycle 211–212
Adger, W. Neil 69
affordable housing 115; activists 115; multi-family 112
African American 126
Agarwal, Minu 41
Age Friendly Communities 136
agency, access to 73–76
air quality 129
American Institute of Architects (AIA) 69, 242, 253–255

American Public Health Association (APHA) 110
American Society of Heating, Refrigeration, and Air-conditioning Engineers (ASHRAE) 6, 8, 16, 28, 224, 255
Americans with Disabilities Act (ADA) 104, 106
Andersen, Marilyne 41
Anderson, Allison 243–246
Anderson, Jodi Smits 239–243
architects 1, 6, 56, 69, 71, 101–102, 144, 223

*Baby It's Cold Inside* report 144–145
Bartosh, Amber 57
beach nourishment and dune restoration case studies 165–166
Binghamton, New York 175–176
Black Indigenous and People of Color (BIPOC) 2, 90, 91, 95, 107
Bloomberg, Michael 143–144
Bloomberg Philanthropies program 65
Bosher, Lee 70
Boyle Heights Arts Conservatory (BHAC), Los Angeles 100
Brand, Stewart 208
British Standards Institute (BSI) 6
Brundtland report of 1987 208
Building Simulation and Optimization (BSO) (England) 9
building: codes and standards 6, 72; energy resilience 10–14; faith-based 92; multi-hazard resilient 76; naturally ventilated 6; resilient building and landscaping 101–102
*Building Research & Information* 144

building sector: and climate resilience 113–115; holistic approach linking climate resilience and 118–120; and improved health and equity 113–115
built environment 131–133
Burroughs, Steven 7
Bush, Kevin 236–239

C40 190
Carlowitz, Hans Carl von 208
case studies: health and equity and enhancing climate resilience 116–117; placing equity at the center of our work 119–120; Tohoku Regional Recovery, Focus Onagawa Town, Japan 193–198
Center for Disease Control and Prevention (CDC) 70
Chartered Institute of Building Service Engineers (CIBSE) 6, 40
Chicago heatwave of 1995 100
Chronic Obstructive Pulmonary Disease (COPD) 126
city policy 207–221; adaptive cycle 211–212; engineering and ecological resilience 210–211; friction and overlap 219; method of investigation 212–213; overview 207–208; panarchy 212; pre-modern sustainability 208; research needs 219–220; resilience as applied 218–219; results and discussion 213–216; sample of 81–82; sustainability as applied 216–218; as a watershed 191; weak and strong sustainability 208–210
climate: adapting inland floodplain housing to changing 172–187; sample of 81–82
climate adaptation planning: challenges of access to knowledge and agency 73–76; existing residential fabric 71–73; limits of 71–76; mandates or incentives 71–73; vulnerable populations 73–76
climate change: changing risk due to 179–180; data for building simulation 39–40; facing and addressing systemic issues 115–118; and health 110–122; holistic approach linking climate resilience and building sector 118–120; key adaptation research 121; key existing research 121; as a matter of health in New York State 110–111; research gaps/needs 121; strategies to reduce climate-health vulnerabilities 121
climate data visualization: community energy empowerment 50–51; role of 50–51
climate disasters 68, 73; Hurricane Katia 175; Hurricane Katrina 115, 141, 151, 243, 254; Hurricane Sandy 103; 165, 240, 254
climate-health vulnerabilities: and exposures to extreme weather events 111–112; increasing 111–112; strategies to reduce 121
climate resilience 107; advancing 113–115; building sector and 113–115; holistic approach linking building sector and 118–120
Climate Resilience Consulting 106
climate resilient simulation 9–10
climate stressors: impacting Northeast 128–129; and social isolation 127
climatic data for simulating dynamic systems 38–39
coastal flood hazards 153
co-designed climate adaptation 54–56, 60–63
communication: and education 133–137; resilient 100–101
communities: marginalized 91–92; shifting power through action 89–108
community energy empowerment: co-designed climate adaptation strategies 60–63; designing interactive user experience 59–60; discussion and future directions 63–65; energy feedback technologies 51–52; interactive energy visualization platform 56–63; interactive experience with energy data 57–58; role of climate data visualization 50–51; sociotechnical energy feedback 52–54; software workflow and spatiotemporal data visualizations 58–59; Syracuse,

New York 56–57; tools for 50–65; toward co-designed climate adaptation 54–56
community input and alternate plans 198–199
Complete Streets 136
Cool Cities 53
coral reef case studies 162–165
COVID-19 pandemic 1, 5, 91, 96, 105
Covington, Lorne 57
Crawley, Drury B. 40
critical user questions and interface 84

Dainty, Andrew 70
data model 82–83
Dean, Robert G. 165
dense and urban coastal development 161–162
Department of Housing and Urban Development (HUD) 106, 115, 182, 236
design: disturbance as a driver for 185–186; risk as a driver for 186; uncertainty as a driver for 186–187
designing: interactive user experience 59–60; resilient coastal communities with living shorelines 153–168
Design Reference Year (DRY) 7
Design Summer Year (DSY) 7–8
Disaster Mitigation Act of 2000 185
disturbance as a driver for design 185–186

ecological resilience 210–211
economic development 210
education and communication 133–137
Elley, Matthew 246–253
emergency management 107
emergency shelters, Resilience Hubs not as 93–94
energy data: exploring 58; interactive experience with 57–58
Energy Democracy Working Group 117
energy feedback technologies 51–52
Energy Foundation 116
EnergyPlus software 6, 41
Energy Savings Index (ESI) 13
engineering resilience 210–211
engineers 6, 69, 101, 144
Enterprise Green Communities 7, 74
environmental justice 112–113

eQuest (DOE2) 6
equity: adapting to climate change 112–113; building sector improving 113–115; inland floodplain housing 180–181; protecting and promoting 112–113; resilient social safety net reinforcing 118–120
extreme temperatures and Northeast 128
extreme weather events: and climate-health vulnerabilities 111–112; exposures to 111–112

Federal Emergency Management Agency (FEMA) 80, 106, 129, 173, 175–178, 182–183, 184, 234, 245
Federal Insurance Administration (FIA) 172
Flood Disaster Protection Act (1973) 172
Floodplains by Design 183
Future Energy Jobs Act (FEJA) 120

geographic information systems (GIS) software 50; of natural hazards 80–81; of social/ infrastructural hazards 80–81
GHG mitigation 107
Gillibrand, Kirsten 176
Global Assimilation of Information for Action (GAIA) project 50
Global Circulation Model (GCM) 8, 38
Global Research Network (GRN) 77
Global Resilience Institute (GRI) 77
Goals of Universal Design 130, 134
Great Midwest Floods 173
green building 130, 146, 150
Green Business Certification, Inc. (GBCI) 146
Guan, Lisa 39
Gunder, Michael 210

habitability zone, defining 146–147
Hansen, James 110
Hartig, Georg Ludwig 208
Hatcher, Erin 246–253
hazards: flood-related 3; natural 80–81; sample of 81–82; social/ infrastructural 80–81
health: adapting to climate change 112–113; building sector improving 113–115; climate change and 110–122; protecting and promoting 112–113

Health and Human Services (HHS) 106
Hilding-Rydevik, Tuija 213
Holling, C. S. 210–211
human health 89, 92, 102, 107, 110–113, 151
Hurricane Katrina 141, 199
Hurricane (Superstorm) Sandy 103, 132, 144, 167, 183, 220
Hybrid Resilience Systems (HyRS) 103

Integrated Environmental Solutions, Ltd. (IES) 6, 19
inclusive design: building adaptive capacity through 131–133; increasing adaptive capacity of vulnerable populations through 125–137; and resilience 129–131
inclusive resilient strategies: increasing accessible permeable pavement 132; increasing vegetation and tree cover 132; install windows with shading devices 132
indoor comfort and overheating resilience 14–19
infectious disease 129
inland floodplain housing 172–187; Binghamton, New York 175–176; changing risk due to climate change 179–180; cultivating culture of sustained adaptation in areas of risk 177–178; disturbance as driver for design 185–186; elevating 184; equity 180–181; levees/infrastructure 183–184; mitigation 182–184; Owego, New York 176; risk as a driver for design 186; role of planning 185; strategies for adaptation 184–185; studying geography, communities, and flood history 174–175; taking action 181–185; uncertainty as a driver for design 186–187; undeveloping (buyouts) 182–183
Insurance Institute for Business and Home Safety (IBHS) 80
Integrated Pest Management (IPM) 133
Interactive Design and Visualization Lab (IDVL) 56
interactive energy visualization platform 56–63

interactive user experience, designing 59–60
Intergovernmental Panel on Climate Change (IPCC) 39
International Council for Local Environmental Initiatives (ICLEI) 75
International Union for Conservation of Nature (IUCN) World Conservation Congress 159
invasive species 129

Jevons, William 209
Jevons' paradox 209
justice, environmental 112–113

Kay, Braden 227–230
Keenan, Jesse M. 69
key adaptation research 121
Klinenberg, Eric 100
knowledge, access to 73–76
Kochnower, Dana 233–236
Kresge Foundation 116
Krietemeyer, Bess 57

The Lancet Commission 112
landscape architects 101–102
Latin United Community Housing Association (LUCHA) 119
Lawrie, Linda K. 40
LEED pilot credits on Resilient Design 145–146
levees/infrastructure (in relation to housing) 183–184
living shorelines: background on 153–156; design and plan for 157; designing resilient coastal communities with 153–168; elements of design as flood mitigation strategies 155; legend for elements of living shoreline design **156**; site characteristics and applicability of living shoreline techniques **158**; strategies for Waikiki 164
long-term disruptions 90, 96
LOW zones 191

machine-learning algorithm 82–83
Maisel, Jordana 130
mandates/incentives 71–73
marginalized communities 91–92, 107
MATLAB model 10, 12–13

# INDEX

Merson, Joanna 167
metrics of passive survivability 143–144, 146–147
Metropolitan Mayors Coalition of Greater Boston 78
microclimates 15, 38, 64
Millar, Kevin 180
Milton J. Rubenstein Museum of Science and Technology (MoST) 57
Minnery, Rachel 253–256
mission critical functions 200–202
mitigation: defined 182; inland floodplain housing 182–184
morphing 40
motivation for RHOnDA 76–80
Multihazard Mitigation Council of the National Institutes of Building Sciences 80

*Nachhaltigkeit* 208
NASA's Goddard Institute for Space Studies 110
National Flood Insurance Act 172
National Flood Insurance Program (NFIP) 4, 172
National Flood Insurance Reform Act 173
National Institute of Building Science (NIBS) 73–74
National Science Foundation 76
Nature Conservancy Coastal Resilience website 157
neighborhood: levee acts as a gate to a floodplain 173; LOW zone 199, 205; residential 200; Resilience Hubs 89, 107; resilient neighborhood initiative 204
networks of Resilience Hubs 104–105
*The New Orleans Principles* 141, **142**
New York City 41; Building Resiliency Task Force, 2012–2013 144; marginalized people of 190; New York City Green Streets Program 192
New York City Green Codes Task Force 143
New York City Greening the Codes Task Force, 2008–2010 143
New York City Housing Authority (NYCHA) 217
New York State 110–111; Binghamton 175–176; Owego 176
Next City 190

NOAA 80; Conceptual Framework for Considering Living Shorelines 156; Guidance on Living Shorelines 157
Non-Governmental Organizations (NGOs) 74, 79
Northeast: air quality 129; climate stressors impacting 128–129; coastal flooding/sea level rise/increased precipitation 129; extreme temperatures 128; infectious disease/invasive species/pests 129
Northern Manhattan Climate Action Plan (NMCA) 116–117
nuisance flooding 153

older adults 3, 112, 125–127, 133–137
Owego, New York 176

panarchy 212
pandemic and Resilience Hubs 105
Passive House Institute U.S. (PHIUS) 149–150
passive survivability 141–152; addressing metrics of 143–144; *Baby It's Cold Inside* report 144–145; compliance paths 147–150; defined 141; defining "habitability zone" and metrics of 146–147; initiatives to address 143–146; LEED pilot credits on Resilient Design 145–146; methodologies for assessing 147–150; New York City Greening the Codes Task Force, 2008–2010 143; New York City's Building Resiliency Task Force, 2012–2013 144; Passive House certification 149–150; psychrometric analysis 147–148; RELi rating system 146; research and standards 151–152; setting agenda for 151–152; standard effective temperature 148–149
Passivhaus Institute (PHI) 149
pests 129
Petersen, John 52, 54
planner 1, 4, 36, 45, 50, 133, 141, 156, 168, 180, 212, 223; city 50, 56, 221; local and regional 72–73; municipal 71; urban 56
planning for a changing climate: proposed solution 41; simulations

with diverse inputs 41–45; without accurate predictions 35–46
PlaNYC initiative 143
policy and adaptive capacity 135–137
power and communities 89–108
power outages and thermal habitability of buildings 141–152
Pralle, Sarah 178, 180
predictions: planning for changing climate without accurate 35–46
pre-modern sustainability 208
The President's Hurricane Sandy Rebuilding Task Force 167
PROMETHEUS dataset 18
ProQuest Science 9
public health 3, 71, 110–111

Quinn, Christine 143–144

Rastogi, Parag 41
Regional Climate Model (RCM) 8, 38
RELi rating system 146
Representative Concentration Pathway (RCP) scenarios 8
research: gaps/needs 121; needs 219–220; setting agenda for passive survivability 151–152; and standards 151–152
residential building typologies 82
resilience: as applied 207–221, 218–219; ecological 210–211; engineering 210–211; inclusive design and 129–131; synergies between sustainability and 150–151
Resilience Hubs 89–108; communities actively working to establish 107; Community Emergency Hubs 94; described 92; developed as concept 93–94; five foundational areas 97–98, **98**; Hub funding puzzle 105–106; location of hubs 94–95; networks of 104–105; not emergency shelters 93–94; overview 89–90; in a pandemic 105; prioritizing marginalized communities 91–92; reframing resilience for 90–91; resilient building and landscaping 101–102; resilient communications 100–101; resilient operations 104; resilient power systems 102–104; resilient services and programming 98–101; three modes for **95**, 95–97
resilient building and landscaping 101–102
resilient coastal communities: assess risk and vulnerability 157; background on living shorelines 153–156; beach nourishment and dune restoration case studies 165–166; coastal flood hazards 153; coral reef case studies 162–165; deliberate alternatives with stakeholders 157, 159; design and plan for living shorelines 157; designing, with living shorelines 153–168; determining study areas 156–157; overall approach 156; Sunset Beach, O'ahu, HI 159–161; supporting case studies 162–166; supporting case studies and research 157; vegetation case studies 165; visual communication and stakeholders 166; visualize future flooding 157; Waikiki Beach, O'ahu, HI 161–162
resilient communications 100–101
resilient communities 107
resilient design in four dimensions 189–206; band-aids 200–202; challenges faced 202–206; community input and alternate plans 198–199; consequences and paralysis 199–200; long-term change through positive adaption 189–193; LOW zones 191; major surgery 193–206; managed retreat and urban footprint 192–193; mission critical functions 200–202; networking elements and resilient outcome 202; rethinking urban footprint 189–193; social adaptive models ready for retreat 199; surgery candidates 190–191; surgery continues 200; time horizons 200–202; Tohoku Regional Recovery, Focus Onagawa Town, Japan 193–198; treating city as a watershed 191; wisdom from everywhere 192
Resilient Design Institute (RDI) 143–144, 146
resilient design modeling 6–30; analysis and discussion 19–30;

# INDEX

building energy resilience 10–14; climate resilient simulation 9–10; indoor comfort and overheating resilience 14–19; methodology 9; objective 8–9; overview 6–8
Resilient Homes Online Design Aid (RHOnDA) 2, 68–85, 71; climate adaptation planning 71–76; critical user questions and interface 84; data model 82–83; developing and testing 80–85; foundational research for 76–80; geographic-based database of hazards 80–81; identified residential building typologies 82; machine-learning algorithm 82–83; motivation and foundational research for 76–80; overview 68–71; recommendations 83–84; research and applications on multi-hazard resilient buildings 76; sample of cities, climates, and hazards 81–82; shifting research priorities 76–78; stakeholders' motivations and concerns 78–80; stakeholder testing 84–85
resilient operations 104
resilient power systems 102–104
resilient services and programming 98–101
resilient social safety net: reinforcing equity 118–120; reinforcing improved health outcomes 118–120
Reynolds, Keith 208
risk: assessing 157; changing, due to climate change 179–180; cultivating culture of sustained adaptation in areas of 177–178; as a driver for design 186; visualize future flooding 157
Robustness Index (RI) 13
Rockefeller Foundation's 100 Resilient Cities program 78
Royal Dutch Meteorological Institute 10, 17

sample: of cities 81–82; of climates 81–82; of hazards 81–82
Schumer, Chuck 176, 178
Schwarz, Terry 230–233
ScienceDirect 9
Scopus 9
short-term disruptions 90, 96

SimBuild (USA) 9
simulations: climate resilient 9–10; with a diverse sample of inputs 41–45
'Snowvember' 128
social adaptive models 199
social/infrastructural hazards: geographic-based database of 80–81
social isolation 127
Social Vulnerability Index 70
sociotechnical energy feedback 52–54
software workflow and spatiotemporal data visualizations 58–59
Solar One 117
Solar Uptown Now (SUN) 117
Southeast Sustainability Directors Network (SSDN) 103
spatiotemporal data visualizations 58–59
special flood hazard areas (SFHAs) 173
Special Report on Emissions Scenarios (SRES) 8
stakeholders: deliberate alternatives with 157, 159; motivations and concerns 78–80; visual communication to deliberate alternatives with 166
stakeholder testing 84–85
Steinfeld, Edward 130
strong sustainability 208–210
Summer Climate Severity Index 12
Sunset Beach 159–161
SurgingSeas 80
sustainability: as applied 207–221, 216–218; pre-modern 208; synergies between resilience and 150–151; weak and strong 208–210
Sustainable CUNY (SCUNY) 116–117
sustainable development 210
Swedish Strategic Environment Assessment Directive 213
Swift, Jason 224–227
Symposium on Simulation for Architecture and Urban Design (SimAUD) conferences 9
Syracuse, New York 56–57
Syracuse Center of Excellence for Environmental and Energy Systems (SyracuseCoE) 56

Systems Approach to Geomorphic Engineering (SAGE) Shoreline Stabilization brochure 157

Test Reference Year (TRY) 7
thermal autonomy (TA) 15
thermal habitability: achieving multiple benefits 150–151; of buildings during power outages 141–152; defining "habitability zone" 146–147; initiatives to address passive survivability 143–146; methodologies for assessing passive survivability 147–150; metrics of passive survivability 146–147; overview 141–143; setting agenda for passive survivability 151–152; synergies between resilience and sustainability 150–151; understanding and quantifying 141–152
time horizons 200–202
Tohoku earthquake and tsunami 191, 193
tools for community energy empowerment 50–65
Tozer, Laura 213
Trane TRACE 6
Tredgold, Thomas 210
TRNSYS 6, 19
Typical Meteorological Years (TMY) 7

UKCP09 project 7, 17
uncertainty, as driver for design 186–187
undeveloping (buyouts) 182–183
United States Green Building Council (USGBC) 75, 141, 146
urban footprint: long-term change through positive adaption 189–193; managed retreat is essential in rethinking 192–193

Urban Green Council 143–144; *Baby It's Cold Inside* report 144–145
Urban Homesteaders Assistance Board (UHAB) 117
Urban Resilience Hubs 94–95
Urban Sustainability Directors Network (USDN) 94, 103–104, 106
U.S. Army Corps of Engineers (USACE) 155, 179, 183–184
U.S. Climate Resilience Toolkit Climate Explorer (NOAA) 50
U.S. Climate Resilience Toolkit Steps to Resilience 157
U.S. Department of Housing and Urban Development 115

vegetation case studies 165
vernacular architecture 141
visual communication 166
vulnerability: additional factors contributing to 126–128; assessing 157; visualize future flooding 157
vulnerable populations: access to knowledge and agency 73–76; increasing adaptive capacity of 125–137

Wagner, Melissa 167
Waikiki Beach, O'ahu, HI 161–162
Waikiki Beach Special Improvement District Association (WBSIDA) 162
watershed, city as 191
WE ACT for Environmental Justice 116–117
weak sustainability 208–210
Wentz, Elizabeth 167
World Bank 75
World Climate Research Programme's CMIP3 model 14
World Health Organization (WHO) 105

9780367467333